THE ESSENTIAL HISTORY OF RUGBY UNION

# SCOTLAND

FOREWORD BY ANDY IRVINE

NICK OSWALD AND JOHN GRIFFITHS

WH S

First published in 2003
by Headline Book Publishing
for WHSmith, Greenbridge Road, Swindon SN3 3LD

10 9 8 7 6 5 4 3 2 1



ISBN 0 7553 1272 4

Design by designsection, Frome, Somerset
Editor Julian Flanders
Designers Rhiannon Sully and Kathie Wilson
Photographs supplied by Ancient Art and Architecture Collection Ltd page 7; Colorsport pages 4, 129, 134, 135, 137, 146, 149, 151, 155, 161, 165r, 174r & 184; Corbis page 8; EMPICS pages 41, 57, 60, 61, 70, 72, 74, 84, 85, 86. 87, 92, 95, 97, 98, 100, 102, 104, 109, 112, 117, 119, 122, 123, 128, 131, 136, 140, 144, 147, 148, 157, 164, 165l, 166, 167, 170, 171, 174l, 175, 176, 179, 180, 182, 183, 185, 186, 187, 188, 191, 193, 199, 217, 273, 276, 291, 298, 301, 313, 318 & 320; Mary Evans Picture Library page 11; John Griffiths pages 17, 206, 207, 214, 223 & 243; Getty Images, Hulton Collection pages 13 & 192; the Scottish Rugby Union pages 12, 16, 20, 25, 29, 30, 32, 33, 40, 42, 46, 48, 51, 53, 54, 69, 75, 77, 79, 82, 94, 96, 107, 111, 113, 118, 121, 124, 125 & 133; Twickenham Museum and Library page 21

The authors would like to thank all concerned in making this book happen, in particular Julian Flanders, Andy Irvine, Bill McMurtrie and the Scottish Rugby Union. Special thanks to Fiona White in the SRU library for dealing so effectively with frequent requests for help and guidance. The reference works of John Davidson, Terry Godwin, R.J. Phillips and Sandy Thorburn proved invaluable in the compilation of the book.

Printed and bound in Great Britain by Clays Ltd, St Ives PLC, Bungay, Suffolk

HEADLINE BOOK PUBLISHING
A division of Hodder Headline
338 Euston Road
London NW1 3BH

www.headline.co.uk
www.hodderheadline.com

# Contents

# Foreword
## By Andy Irvine

I have been asked many times why New Zealand is so good at rugby with a population of only 3.5 million, while in Scotland we have 5 million people and yet have never beaten the All Blacks. Well, the answer is quite simple. In New Zealand virtually the whole nation follows the game with a fervour that we can't match in Scotland in any sport. We tend to think of Glasgow as a soccer-mad city because of Celtic and Rangers, but if you multiply that intensity ten times over, then you approach the level of interest rugby generates in New Zealand. From a much smaller population base New Zealand can boast ten times more rugby players than Scotland.

In fact, on the world stage, taking into account playing numbers, Scotland has competed remarkably well since the days of that first international between Scotland and England, held at Raeburn Place in 1871. Scotland has also contributed significantly to the game in the British Isles, producing a total of 125 British Lions, including seven captains.

We have produced many world-class players, administrators and referees, yet possibly the one individual who has helped promote the game more than anyone else is Bill McLaren. Born and bred in Hawick, Bill has helped to popularise the game worldwide through his radio and television commentaries and is held in the highest esteem from lay followers through to the top internationalists.

During an international career spanning 12 seasons, I had the good fortune to savour some magical moments, countered, however, by severe lows. The thrill of running out at Murrayfield for my first cap against the All Blacks in 1972 will always remain with me. Over 60,000 screaming fans were there, yet I was oblivious to any noise and the game flashed by in a blur.

One of my most enjoyable experiences was the 1975 match at Murrayfield against Wales. In those days, Wales was the big one. Almost their entire team had represented the Lions and their hordes of support from the Valleys were legendary. That Saturday in March 1975 the official attendance was 104,000 but some estimates put the figure nearer 120,000 as the game was not all-ticket and many fans did not gain entry into the ground until half an hour after kick-off. I well remember walking on to the pitch over an hour before the game to inspect the surface and the stadium already looked full to capacity! Scotland won a bruising encounter 12-10, but my memory of the match is of the atmosphere rather than the victory.

Another highlight was to captain the only Scottish team to win a major international in the southern hemisphere when we secured a well-deserved win over Australia at Ballymore, Brisbane, in June 1982.

There were, of course, some real low points, none more than the two Triple Crown deciders against England in 1973 and 1975, both played at Twickenham. There could be no complaints about the loss in 1973 when England ran out worthy winners, but in 1975 we lost 7-6 to a more than dubious try. Had the video camera been in operation I suspect the result would have gone Scotland's way.

For a Scotsman, it was always especially enjoyable to savour a victory over the old enemy. Not just in rugby, but in virtually every sporting contest between the two countries, an English scalp tends to mean a great deal to the Scots. From my point of view, it must be said that the intense rivalry was not especially directed at the individual players. Indeed, in my time, many of the English lads I played against I also toured with on Lions and Barbarian tours and they were great company and have remained life-long friends.

Since rugby turned professional in 1995 the game has changed enormously and, of course, for the top players it is now a career rather than a pastime. Top players now put in more hours of training in one day than internationalists of the 1970s and 1980s did in a full week. Compared to when I started my career in 1972 the average international player is now two stone heavier and the levels of fitness are in a different league. To me the biggest change is in the forwards, where not only is their sheer athleticism of a much higher standard, but also their skill level. Of course, all the players now have individual training programmes, special diets and some of them even have their own sports physiologists. In the early 1980s, the Scottish Rugby Union did try to experiment with dietary recommendations for the team and indeed there was one occasion when, on the Friday evening prior to a game against Wales, our dinner was restricted to a meagre portion of fish and a few potatoes. While most of the players reluctantly accepted the situation, Ian Milne (known as the Bear for obvious reasons) was caught by one of the committee members sneaking three fish suppers into his room at midnight. He claimed they were for sharing but no one really believed him!

Nick Oswald has done a remarkable job in tracing the game back to its very origins and deserves great praise for the accuracy and thoroughness of his research. I am indebted to him for rekindling some of my own memories, both bad and good, and for recounting the history of Scottish rugby with a pride and fondness that I suspect is shared by every Scottish rugby fan.

I'm sure you'll enjoy the story as much as I did.

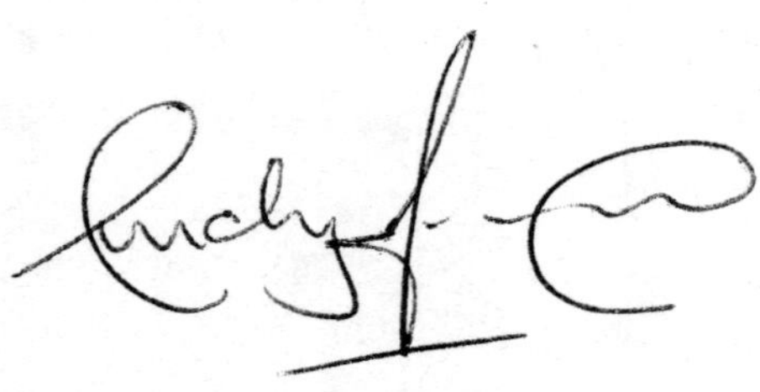

Andy Irvine

# Chapter One: 2500 BC-1870
# Early Ball Games

On the eve of the fifth Rugby World Cup, to be played in Australia in October and November 2003, when 20 nations will compete for the William Webb Ellis trophy – or 'Bill' as it is known in the host nation – the sport of rugby has changed beyond all recognition since it evolved into a codified game through the public schools and universities of England and Scotland in the middle part of the 19th century. Now into its third century the sport has truly global appeal, is played in 111 countries worldwide and the aforementioned Rugby World Cup tournament is rated third only in size and popularity to the Olympic Games and the soccer World Cup. Action will be broadcast to 189 countries with a projected global audience of 4 billion and it is estimated that the staging of the tournament will generate $Aus 1 billion (£0.42 billion) to the Australian economy.

## Rugby's Ancient Roots

Rugby is clearly big business at the start of the third millennium but its exact origins, like any sport, are lost in the mists of time. Hands are held up to claim rugby as 'ours' from all four corners of the globe, but there is no conclusive proof that rugby emanates from one particular source. There is documented evidence in ancient China, around 2500 BC, that a game was played involving the kicking of animal skins between tall poles, probably by soldiers as part of their military training.

More contemporary records from around AD 50 confirm that a game called 'tsu chu' was played in China incorporating a round ball and a square goal. Five hundred years later there are stories of a game in Mexico played on a specially designed court requiring a ball to be forced through a hole in the court's wall. Other nations and cultures with supporters include ancient Egypt, France and the Roman Empire.

*A ring on the wall of the Mexican ball court at Chichen-Itza, Mexico.*

*A Jedburgh Ba' Game in the 1930s.*

There is a strong case to be put for the Roman game of harpastum being the ancestor of the Ba' games so popular in many towns and communities in the Scottish Borders over the years and an annual match is still played in Jedburgh. Harpastum was a team game played with a small hard ball by Roman soldiers on a delineated rectangular court with a centre line. The object was to drive the ball over the opponents' line and the skills so familiar to rugby followers in the 21st century of running, passing, throwing and tackling were all used.

The Romans had a presence in Britain for 350 years early in the first millennium. They advanced beyond Hadrian's Wall into Scotland and set up camps, fortlets and forts along what became known as Dere Street which ran north from Corbridge through the Cheviots, over Carter Bar and through the middle of the Borders, past Jedburgh, Ancrum and Newstead and on to Inveresk near Edinburgh. The largest garrison fort and administrative centre was set up at Trimontium (Newstead) near Melrose and was a thriving centre until around AD 196. Sandy Thorburn, author of *The History of Scottish Rugby*, is one eminent rugby historian who linked the Roman presence in the Borders to the eventual establishment of the Scottish Ba' games. In addition to Jedburgh there are records of matches being played in Hawick, Hobskirk, Lilliesleaf, Denholm, Ancrum, Selkirk, Galashiels, St Boswells, Melrose, Kelso, Duns, Yetholm and Morebattle. Although ball games are recorded in other parts of Scotland it is nevertheless surprising how many of these towns lie close to Dere Street and the other main Roman thoroughfare through Scotland further to the west.

The Ba' game was played by two teams. In Jedburgh the teams were divided according to where they lived in the town, hence the Uppies v the Doonies. The game was played with a small, hard ball covered in leather and the aim was to hail the ba' to a target beyond the opposition area. The town itself was the venue and it became quickly congested because of the numbers involved with play which included a lot of pushing, shoving and wrestling for long periods without either side making any significant ground. As society evolved the importance of recreation increased as an important release from the harsh, grim realities of day-to-day existence. Initially, games were played on holidays and the two Ba' games in Jedburgh were played on Candlemas in early February and Fastern's E'en which was usually Shrove Tuesday.

The earliest written reference to football is found in a Latin work by William Fitzstephen, a monk from Canterbury who, in a history of London, describes how Shrove Tuesday was celebrated in 1175. 'The morning was spent in cock-fighting and other boyish pastimes. Then, after dinner, all the youth of the city proceeded to a level piece of ground just outside the town for the famous game of ball. The students of every different branch of study had their own ball as did various tradesmen. The older men, the fathers and the men of property, arrived on horseback to watch the contests and, in their own way, shared the sport of the young men. These elders were filled with excitement at seeing so much vigorous exercise and participated, vicariously, in the pleasures of unrestrained youth.'

## The Ball Game Develops

Clearly the sport was developing and in this part of London at least had moved away from the streets to a designated playing area. The game of ball drew a crowd of all ages and backgrounds and would indicate that it had the tacit approval of society. However, over the next few centuries the law makers of many countries in northern Europe became increasingly agitated at the amount of time the lower orders were devoting to fun and enjoyment at the expense of practising their military skills, such as archery, in preparation for the more or less constant threat of war. In England starting with 'Proud' Edward II in 1314, shortly before he headed north for a date with destiny at Bannockburn, attempts were made to ban play. In France just five years later all ball games were banned.

Closer to home following a meeting at Scone Palace in 1424, James I issued an Act declaring, 'It is statut and the king forbiddis that na man play at the fute ball under the payne of xl.s.' This act, along with those passed in

England and France, would appear to have cut little ice with the public at large as regular follow-ups were issued over the following years. In Scotland James II aimed to spoil the fun for a broader range of his citizens when he added golf to the banned list in 1458. James III and James IV issued similar edicts in 1471 and 1491. But in 1497 after over 70 years of public antipathy to Stewart wishes, James IV eventually appears to have adopted the approach, 'If you can't beat em, join em', as the Lord Treasurer, who looked after the royal purse, paid two shillings to buy footballs for the king.

Football's popularity refused to wane despite John Knox's efforts as he and his ilk tried their best to frighten their parishioners from the pulpit, warning them of the evils of enjoyment at the expense of godliness. Concerned that the citizens would stop going to church if the law makers continued to legislate against the pursuit of games, while Knox and others continued to breathe fire and brimstone, King James in 1618 had a declaration issued from every pulpit in Scotland and England which gave official sanction to the playing of games on Sundays and on holy days after they had worshipped in the kirk.

### Schools Embrace the Sport

Educational establishments too supported the notion of constructive physical activity and in addition to holidays and the Sabbath, Scottish universities encouraged students to take outdoor exercise. In Glasgow students were given access to the Green and in Edinburgh in 1591 the town council allocated the college pitch on the Burgh Muir where students exercised under supervision on official play days. Schools also started to encourage pupils to take exercise and play to refresh themselves. By 1696, for example, the High School in Edinburgh allocated a free afternoon per week for this very purpose.

Society was changing rapidly and Edinburgh's working population increased dramatically in the second half of the 18th century as the 'Athens of the North' became established as a literary, medical and legal centre in Britain. The city boundaries began to expand and to the north of Princes Street the New Town proved popular with the upper classes. The High School could not cope with the sudden influx of the sons of the professionals attracted to Edinburgh and consequently a new private school, Edinburgh Academy, was opened on the north side of the city in 1824 to meet this new demand. Other new private and boarding schools sprang up in response to these opportunities, including Loretto (1827), Merchiston Castle (1833) and Fettes College (1870), and they all played an important part in the establishment and development of rugby.

Although Edinburgh was at the hub of this new educational system and the handling code, other schools appeared such as Dollar Institution (1819),

*A 19th century engraving showing mob- or folk-football in England.*

Glasgow Academy (1845) and Trinity College Glenalmond (1847) which would play their part in the development of ball sports in Scotland.

A combination of schoolboys who had been educated in public schools in England and school masters who had taught in these schools arriving at the Scottish equivalents during the 1850s brought with them 'Rugby' rules which were eagerly adopted. The rugby code takes its name from Rugby School where William Webb Ellis, as the legend goes, 'With a fine disregard for the rules of football as played in his time first took the ball and ran with it, thus originating the distinctive feature of the rugby game in AD1823.'

The brothers Alex and Francis Crombie who had been pupils at Durham Grammar School arrived in Edinburgh bringing with them the Rugby rules. Francis became the first captain of football at Edinburgh Academy in 1854 and Alex studied law at Edinburgh University and was elected as the first captain of Edinburgh Academicals in 1858.

Three schoolmasters were to play a major role in developing rugby in Edinburgh's public schools. Thomas Harvey, Hely-Hutchison Almond and John Rogerson all taught at public schools in England – Harvey and Almond attended Balliol College, Oxford – and all three taught together at Merchiston from 1858 to 1862 when Harvey was headmaster. Harvey went on to become rector at the Edinburgh Academy from 1869 to 1888, Almond was headmaster at Loretto from 1862 to 1902 and Rogerson headmaster at Merchiston 1863 to 1898 where his reign 'was remembered as the days of unbeaten rugby sides'.

All three were great believers in the merits of training the minds and bodies of their pupils in spartan regimes and Almond was known as 'the great apostle of muscular Christianity in Scotland'. The schools turned out a stream of well-rounded pupils who benefited from an education which placed as much value on playing games as it did on formal learning and moral guidance. Masters often took part in the sports played. Almond, in particular, was very enthusiastic and was still playing rugby when he was 45. Pupils tended to stay on at school to the age of 18 or 19 and, with their fitness and skills developed through regular practice, were often more than a match for the former pupil sides which were beginning to emerge.

## Former Pupils' Clubs

The first clubs in Scotland sprang from the public schools as like-minded individuals wished to continue their involvement in the game after they left school: Edinburgh Academicals (1858), Merchistonians (1860), West of Scotland (1865) and Glasgow Academical (1866). And it was from these clubs that the first formalised laws of the game were produced. Individual schools had been playing their own variations of the game and in February 1868 following a number of meetings G.T. Chiene, Secretary of Edinburgh Academicals, sent a proof of the rules to Almond at Loretto for approval. This proof was adopted within the *Green Book* and it is almost certain that they were the laws used for the first international played in 1871 between Scotland and England at Raeburn Place, Edinburgh. No copies of these laws have survived but they pre-date the laws produced by the Rugby Football Union in London which was formed three years later.

The sport was becoming increasingly popular and by the end of the 1860s was even attracting newspaper coverage. Rugby was played in at least eight schools and clubs had formed in Edinburgh and Glasgow as well as Blairgowrie, Kilmarnock, Ayr, Dollar, Alloa and Perth. By comparison, the round ball code's development at this stage was somewhat arrested. There were only four clubs in Scotland at this time and all were based in the Glasgow area playing under the Football Association's rules. They were Queen's Park (formed in 1867), Thistle (1868), Hamilton (1869) and Airdrie (1870).

*H.H. Almond.*

# Chapter Two: 1870-71
# The First Ever International

It was the Football Association, based in London, who made the first attempts to play international matches and in March 1870 they organised a series of four games to be played between England and Scotland at the Kennington Oval in London which was to host official rugby and football internationals before the cricket Tests for which it is now most famous. These matches are not recognised officially as there had been no invitation issued to the Scottish clubs to provide players and consequently all the participants lived in England, and were selected by the FA. Some of those selected to play for 'Scotland' had the loosest possible Caledonian connections with one owning an estate in Scotland, one apparently enjoying a fondness for the 'cratur' and one visiting Scotland annually to shoot grouse.

Regardless of the absence of an official Scottish team the series was deemed a success and C.W. Alcock, secretary of the FA, decided to have another match. However, mindful of Scottish unhappiness over the selection of the 'Scottish' side, on this occasion he wrote to several Scottish newspapers asking for clubs to nominate players to take part in the match to be played in London in November 1870. An extract from the letter lays down the challenge, 'In Scotland, once essentially the land of football, there should still be a spark left of the old fire, and I confidently appeal to Scotsmen to aid to their utmost the efforts of the committee to confer success on what London hopes to found, an annual trial of skill between the champions of England and Scotland.'

*C.W. Alcock, secretary of the FA.*

Regrettably the challenge did not stir the patriotic spirit of any players but with few clubs playing the game at the time it is perhaps not surprising, however disappointing. Nevertheless, his letter did spark correspondence in the Scottish papers. One suggestion was for ten members of the rugby clubs of Scotland to combine with ten exiles for a 20-a-side match. Alcock's response was dismissive: 'More than 11 we do not care to play as with greater numbers it is our opinion that the game becomes less scientific and more a trial of charging and brute force.'

Almond, by then headmaster of Loretto, entered the increasingly passionate public debate by writing to *The Scotsman* with his firm views on the two codes: 'Mr Alcock is a very leading supporter of what is called the "association game" which is to Rugby football, or whatever its detractors may please to call it, as moonlight unto sunlight and as water unto wine.'

## The Challenge is Issued

Alcock's initiative may not have captured the imagination of Scottish football clubs but it had stimulated their rugby counterparts into action. A meeting was held after a match between Merchistonians and Edinburgh Academicals and it was agreed that a challenge should be issued through the press. The following letter, signed by the captains of the five leading rugby clubs in Scotland, appeared in *The Scotsman* and *Bell's Life in London* on 8 December 1870:

> *There is a pretty general feeling among Scotch football players that the football power of the old country was not properly represented in the late so-called International Football Match. Not that we think the play of the gentlemen who represented Scotland otherwise than very good – for that was so amply proved by the stout resistance they offered to their opponents and the fact that they were beaten by only one goal – but that we consider that Association rules, in accordance with which the late game was played, not such as to bring together the best team Scotland could turn out. Almost all the leading clubs play the Rugby code, and have no opportunity of practising the Association game even if willing to do so. We therefore feel that a match played in accordance with any rules other than those in general use in Scotland, as was the case in the last match, is not one that would meet with support generally from her players. For our satisfaction therefore, and with a view of really testing what Scotland can do against the English we, as representing the football interests of Scotland, hereby challenge any team selected from the whole of England, to play us a match, twenty-a-side, Rugby rules, either in Edinburgh or Glasgow, on any day during the present season that might be found suitable to the English players. Let this count as the return to the match played in London on 19th November or, if preferred, let it be a separate match. If it be entered into we can promise England a hearty welcome and a first-rate match. Any communication addressed to any one of us will be attended to.*

*We are etc.*
*A.H. Robertson, West of Scotland FC*
*F. Moncreiff, Edinburgh Academicals FC*
*B. Hall Blyth, Merchistonian FC*
*J.W. Arthur, Glasgow Academical FC*
*J.H. Oats, St Salvator FC, St Andrews*

Alcock did not respond to the challenge but it was noticed by rugby-playing clubs in the London area. B.H. Burns, the Scots-born secretary of Blackheath, the oldest rugby club in England, accepted the challenge and both nations set up committees to make the arrangements. In Edinburgh the committee comprised six prominent officials from the leading clubs and one school. They were H.H. Almond (Loretto), J.W. Arthur (Glasgow Academical), B.H. Blyth (Merchistonians), A. Buchanan (Royal High School FP), Dr J. Chiene and F. Moncreiff (Edinburgh Academicals).

The date for the match was fixed as Monday 27 March 1871 and negotiations opened with Edinburgh Academicals Cricket Club who controlled Raeburn Place for the use of the ground for the first international match in any sport to be played anywhere in the world. The cricket club committee after discussion 'resolved by a majority that the ground be granted'.

Scotland held two trial matches, one in Glasgow on 11 March and one in Edinburgh on 20 March before selecting the final team. England, on the other hand, did not have trials, choosing instead 12 players from the London area while Liverpool and Manchester, the two leading clubs in the North, were asked to nominate four players each.

The lack of a standardised set of laws led to a number of wrangles before the match and, as it turned out, more protracted and heated arguments during the match. The original challenge specified that the match would be 20-a-side but at the end of February England wanted to reduce the numbers to 15-a-side. Just 12 days before the match was due to be played, England relented, agreeing to play 20-a-side. The two other issues related to the laws of the game were eventually resolved.

## The Teams are Selected

Thirteen of Scotland's 20 players lived in Edinburgh and the average age of the team from the records available was fractionally over 21, reflecting the relative newness of the sport and, being an amateur sport for the middle classes, the difficulties experienced in balancing a commitment to sport and the pursuit of a profession.

## Great Matches

**INTERNATIONAL MATCH** **Raeburn Place, Edinburgh, 27 March 1871**

**Attendance: 4,000**

**Scotland 1 goal, 1 try England 1 try**

On a perfect early spring day a crowd estimated at around 4,000 paid 1/- (5p) each to watch Scotland play England in the first international sporting fixture in the world. The win for Scotland was thoroughly deserved but England's travel arrangements did not help them. Travelling from London in third-class carriages overnight on the Saturday, the England party had only wooden benches to sit on. Arriving in Edinburgh at dawn baths were drawn for them in order to take the stiffness out of their bones. Furthermore, the players had to pay all of their own expenses.

The players of both teams warmed up on the pitch with a five-minute punt about before the match, played in two periods of 50 minutes each, began. Moncreiff, the Scotland captain, kicked off with the wind at his back shortly after 3 o'clock. Scotland enjoyed the better of the opening exchanges and for the first 10 minutes play was concentrated around the England 25-yard line. The most exciting moment of the half came as Finlay made a powerful surge for the line and seemed certain to score when Osborne, folding his arms across his chest, ran full tilt at him. As both were big, heavy men there ensued a shuddering collision which sent both men crashing to the ground. The crowd went silent for a few seconds but cheered when both got to their feet none the worse for wear. The half ended scoreless.

In the second half Scotland were soon on the offensive and Ritchie was driven over the line with half a dozen men on top of him and claimed a try. An Englishman also claimed to have control of the ball and as no agreement could be reached the umpires awarded Scotland a hack-off at 5 yards. The Scots' forwards drove as one over the line and Buchanan grounded the ball for the first try in international rugby. The award was hotly disputed but as the umpires could not make out the nature of the complaint as so many Englishmen were arguing, the score was ruled valid.

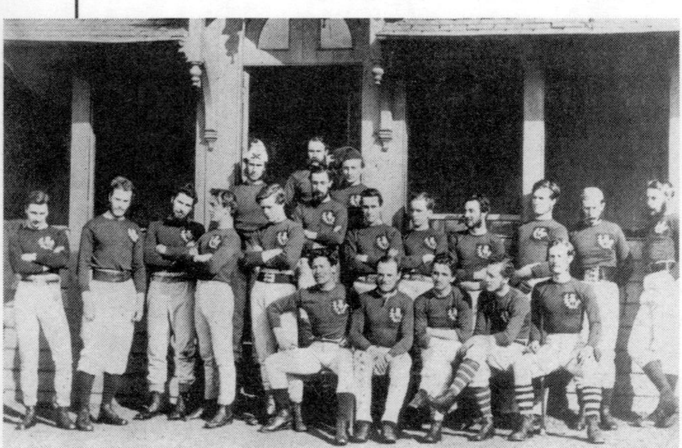

*The Scotland team.*

*The England team.*

The try at goal (conversion) was not easy. The ball was placed by Arthur and kicked between the uprights by Cross to a huge roar from the crowd. This score was crucial because, under the laws of the time, it was goals that counted, not tries. A try was a way of being able to 'try at goal'.

England pressed hard for a score and Green, who had caused the Scottish defence many problems, had three magnificent runs in quick succession. On his third run he was stopped in his tracks by the tough-tackling Chalmers and he was so badly injured that he had to leave the pitch and never played rugby again. Despite being reduced to 19 men it was England who scored next when Birkett scored a try near the corner. Stokes missed the try at goal, so Scotland led by virtue of a goal.

As the match drew to its climax the England forwards were visibly tiring. The Scotland forwards were on top and Mein, Arthur, Buchanan, Thomson, Colville and Finlay combined to drive towards the England line only to see the ball go into touch. A Scot threw it in and Arthur knocked it forward attempting to catch it but Cross was alert enough to pick it up and score Scotland's second try. Another dispute followed but knock-ons were not illegal provided they were unintentional and the umpires ruled in Scotland's favour. Cross missed the try at goal and 90 seconds later the match was over.

**Scotland:** W.D. Brown (Glasgow Academical), T. Chalmers (Glasgow Academical), A. Clunies-Ross (St Andrews University); T.R. Marshall (Edinburgh Academicals), J.W. Arthur (Glasgow Academical), W. Cross (Glasgow Academical), A. Buchanan (Royal HSFP), A.G. Colville (Merchistonians), D. Drew (Glasgow Academical), J.F. Finlay (Edinburgh Academicals), J. Forsyth (Edinburgh University), R.W. Irvine (Edinburgh Academicals), W.J.C. Lyall (Edinburgh Academicals), J.L.H. Macfarlane (Edinburgh University), J.A.W. Mein (Edinburgh Academicals), F.J. Moncreiff (Edinburgh Academicals, captain), R. Munro (St Andrews University), G. Ritchie (Merchistonians), A.H. Robertson (West of Scotland), J.S. Thomson (Glasgow Academical)
**Scorers: Tries** Buchanan, Cross **Conversion** Cross

**England:** A. Lyon (Liverpool), A.G. Guillemard (West Kent), R.R. Osborne (Manchester); W. MacLaren (Manchester); F. Tobin (Liverpool), J.E. Bentley (Gipsies), J.F. Green (West Kent). R.H. Birkett (Clapham Rovers), B.H. Burns (Blackheath), J.H. Clayton (Liverpool), C.A. Crompton (Blackheath), A. Davenport (Ravenscourt Park), J.M. Dugdale (Ravenscroft Park), A.S. Gibson (Manchester), A. St. G Hamersley (Marlborough Nomads), J.H. Luscombe (Gipsies), C.W. Sherrard (Blackheath), F. Stokes (Blackheath, captain), D. P. Turner (Richmond), H.J.C. Turner (Manchester)
**Scorer: Try** Birkett

**Umpires:** H.H. Almond (Scotland), A. Ward (England)

Scotland selected a side with six backs and 14 forwards compared to England's selection of seven backs and 13 forwards. The backs were listed as three full-backs and three half-backs and the forwards listed alphabetically have no designated position.

The England team was slightly older on average than their Scottish counterparts, but the average was still an extremely youthful 22. With the possible exception of Munro, the oldest player on the pitch was Arthur Gibson who was 26 years 227 days and although Robert Irvine was the youngest at 17 years 343 days there were six other teenagers on the pitch including England skipper Fred Stokes who was 19 years 269 days.

It is recorded in *The Edinburgh Academical FC Centenary History* that James Carmichael, a master at the Academy, was heard to shout at the end of the match 'Flodden is at last revenged' and threw his tall hat in the air in his excitement. This is the first example of national pride being avenged in the sporting arena. Although as the disastrous Battle of Flodden Field, in which King James IV perished, was fought in 1513 Scotland had had to wait the small matter of 358 years for revenge.

# Chapter Three: 1872-79
# From 20- to 15-a-Side

The euphoria following the win over England buoyed up the players, clubs and supporters of rugby in Scotland who all looked forward with relish to future clashes with the 'Auld Enemy'. England may not have won the on-pitch battle but they had stolen an administrative march on the Scots by having formed the Rugby Football Union (RFU), their own governing body, just two months before the first international.

The Scottish clubs had, since 1868, been using the *Green Book* as its guiding light but this had not prevented some serious disputes from arising. The most extreme example was an argument over a try in a match between Glasgow Academical and West of Scotland in February 1870. When agreement could not be reached, even after having consulted the *Green Book* and the clubs' respective lawyers, the matter was settled by arbitration referring the matter to the editor of *Bell's Life in London* for a binding decision.

## Scottish Clubs Join RFU

Clearly the game would not survive for long if disputes could not be resolved quickly so the Scottish clubs – recognising that the RFU's new set of laws were more up-to-date, comprehensive and agreed – took the pragmatic, but nevertheless admirable, decision to join the Rugby Football Union. Glasgow Academical, West of Scotland and Edinburgh University joined immediately in 1871 and Edinburgh Academicals, Edinburgh University and Royal High School FP signed up the following year.

The Scottish clubs had therefore accepted the RFU as the rule-maker for the burgeoning game and it was a decision which was to result in even more wrangles a short time into the future and arguably one which still affects the game today.

The more pressing matter in late 1871 was the invitation issued in November from the RFU to the Scottish clubs for a return international match. The invitation was accepted with some alacrity and it was settled that the match would be played on 5 February 1872 at Kennington Oval in London. It was also proposed and accepted that the fixture become an annual event played on a home and away basis in alternate years.

## England Get their Revenge

The Scottish selectors with a committee in place and more time to choose a fully representative team set about their task with great enthusiasm. Two trial matches were arranged but, unfortunately, a combination of poor weather and, inexplicably, the non-appearance of many of the nominated players saw the abandonment of the trials resulting in a less rigorous selectorial process than had been planned.

Captained once again by Moncreiff, Scotland awarded nine new caps for the return match and included four exiles. Colville (Blackheath) survived from the first match and three new players with military backgrounds were awarded caps: Reginald Maitland (Royal Artillery), F.T. Maxwell (Royal Engineers) and Henry Renny-Tailyour (Royal Engineers). Indeed Renny-Tailyour was the first player, and the only Scot, to play rugby and football at international level for Scotland.

*Francis Moncreiff was Scotland's first captain.*

The Scotland team contained another multi-talented sportsman who was Scotland's answer to the legendary C.B. Fry. Capped as Leslie Balfour (he later changed his surname to Balfour-Melville) he had been chosen to play in the first international while a pupil at Edinburgh Academy. A bite from an unfriendly dog caused him to withdraw but he made his debut at the Oval one month shy of his 18th birthday. It was an appropriate place to play as he was a brilliant cricketer, making his debut for Edinburgh against an England XI at the age of 15, and top-scored at the start of a long and illustrious career as a brilliant free-flowing batsman and an exceptionally good wicketkeeper. But it is as a golfer that he is probably best known. In the British Amateur championship between 1888 and 1897 he reached two finals and six semi-finals; he won the title in 1895, beating John Ball by one hole. It was an impressive scalp as Ball was the reigning champion at the time, four-time winner of the event and the first man to hold the Open and Amateur titles simultaneously.

England, by contrast, went for wholesale changes with just six players surviving from the original match. Like Moncreiff, Stokes was again appointed captain but this time England opted for a much heavier and, as it transpired, fitter pack. Their painstaking selectorial procedures paid off and the combination of the heavy forwards and the swift running backs was too much for the lightweight Scots.

Despite the loss, an anonymous Scottish player caused the biggest laugh when he had his breeks ripped right off. To cover his embarrassment he was immediately surrounded by colleagues until, in the words of the day, 'he was handed a macintosh in which he encased himself and amid considerable amusement repaired to the pavilion to obtain another garment'.

## Formation of the Union

Rugby in Scotland was quickly increasing in popularity and, mindful of the successful creation of the RFU, the Scottish Committee realised that a similar organisation needed to be formed north of the border. Affiliation to the RFU had only been a temporary solution and a meeting was held over a convivial dinner in the University Club in Edinburgh in late 1872 to discuss the formation of a Scottish Union. The meeting was attended by Dr. John Chiene, James Wallace, R. Craigie Bell and Harry Cheyne (Edinburgh Academicals), B. Hall-Blyth (Merchistonians) and Albert Harvey (Glasgow Academical). This group of professional businessmen

*An artist's impression of the second international, England v Scotland, the Oval, 1872.*

was still young enough to be playing the game and they were to put in place the template which was followed for the running of the union well into the 20th century.

A notice appeared in the *Glasgow Herald* on the day of the third Scotland v England international at Hamilton Crescent on Monday 3 March 1873. The notice called a meeting to be held that day in the old Glasgow Academy in Elmbank Street at 4.30pm (immediately after the international match) to consider 'the propriety of forming a Football Union in Scotland on a similar basis to the Rugby (Football) Union in England'.

The meeting took place with Dr Chiene in the chair and it was agreed that the union should be formed with the proposed objectives of:

i) Providing funds for a cup;

ii) Bringing into closer connection the clubs then playing;

iii) The formation of a committee by whom the Scotch International team might in future be chosen.

A provisional committee to draw up the bye-laws of the union was appointed, made up of the captain and one other member from Edinburgh Academicals, Glasgow Academical, Merchistonians, Royal High School FP, West of Scotland and the three universities, Edinburgh, Glasgow and St Andrews.

The first AGM of the Scottish Football Union (it was renamed the Scottish Rugby Union in 1925) was held on Thursday 9 October 1873 in Keith & Co's Rooms, 65A George Street, Edinburgh at 4.30pm. Mr H. Cheyne was in the chair and the first task was to approve and pass the bye-laws as drafted by the provisional committee.

With reference to the cup withdrawn the revised objectives were proposed and agreed as:

i) The encouragement of football in Scotland;

ii) Co-operation with the Rugby Football Union;

iii) The selection of the International Team.

The make-up of the new committee of the SFU was President, Vice President, Honorary Secretary and Treasurer plus the captains of the member clubs. The joining fee to the SFU was set at one guinea (£1.05) and the annual subscription was 5 shillings (25p).

### The Local Cobblers

The third meeting between Scotland and England was held in Glasgow and a crowd estimated as being up to 6,000 turned out to watch the match. Unfortunately, it was not much of a spectacle as on a bitterly cold day the pitch and overhead conditions were horrendous.

The English side decided to try and improve their chances by sending 20 pairs of boots to a local cobblers to have leather bars fixed to the soles in a bid to increase their grip in the slippery conditions. Whether the cobbler could not cope with the demand or whether there was some patriotic gamesmanship afoot not all of the boots could be found when they were collected. This caused understandable consternation in the English camp and the players arrived late for the kick-off. Eventually a few players, including C.W. Boyle, one of their most dangerous backs, had to play wearing one boot and one dress shoe.

The match itself was a no-score draw featuring little action of note. Indeed the main talking point in the crowd was the great plumes of steam rising from the players' sweaty bodies in the many mauls which punctuated the match.

Dinner in the evening after the match was a splendid affair. Mr Arthur Budd commenting later gave full credit to the Scottish hospitality although he does acknowledge that one of the English forwards appeared to have over-indulged during the evening. He was discovered by some team-mates around midnight driving one of Her Majesty's mail carts around town. How he may have acquired the vehicle is not revealed but he may have been one of the first and most certainly not the last rugby player to get up to high jinks in letting off steam in the aftermath of an international. Indeed, in R.J. Phillips' own words in *The Story of Scottish Rugby*, 'When gentlemen assembled of an evening around the social board the best gentleman of the party was the one who was last to fall beneath the table.' Clearly rugby's drinking traditions were established early.

## Key Decisions

The game was becoming much better organised in Scotland with the formation of the union and the necessary sub-committees who were devolved work to carry out on a number of issues. The RFU made alterations to the laws of the game every year, often to the consternation of the SFU, but because of their agreed close co-operation with the so-called 'mother' union they had little choice but to follow suit.

Although eligibility to play international rugby remains a thorny issue today there are at least guidelines in place to determine suitability. Scotland has long been accused of interpreting the rules to the maximum but the problems of the 1870s have resonances in the early 21st century. Traditionally, Scots have left their homeland to seek work and have made an impact all round the world. In the early years of international rugby, England wanted the sole criterion to be residency. With so many Scots either leaving school to go to English universities or, once they had finished their further education at home heading south to pursue their careers, this would have severely handicapped Scotland's chances of fielding the strongest available 20. The Scottish proposal was for players to be selected on birth or parentage and this was adopted.

In the formative years of rugby, matches were decided on the number of goals kicked and the value of a try was nil. Indeed, as we saw in the first international, scoring a try was really only a mechanism for taking a kick at goal. This scoring system had the potential to throw up some distinctly peculiar results and one match between Royal High School FP and Edinburgh University in 1872 underlines the nonsensical methods in force at the time. The match was declared a draw with RHSFP scoring one goal and seven tries against one goal and one try. By modern scoring methods Edinburgh University would have been hammered 37-7, but if RHSFP had not converted their seventh and final try they would have lost the match as the University were at that stage winning by a goal to nil.

With results like this the SFU successfully lobbied the RFU who discussed a points scoring system at their AGM in October 1875. The system proposed – 10 points for any goal, 5 points for a try and 1 point for a touch down or touch in goal – was rejected but at a subsequent meeting the following month Rule Seven was altered to read: 'A match shall be decided by a majority of goals, but if the number of goals be equal, or no goal be kicked, by a majority of tries; if no goal be kicked or try obtained, the match shall be drawn.'

This was a significant step forward and the SFU at a meeting in December adopted the ruling and implemented the new scoring system for the start of season 1876-77.

Another issue that preoccupies the SRU to this day is the number of active players in Scotland. Scotland has always had a low playing base and has managed to punch above its weight for much of its history. But the playing of 20-a-side matches was probably a bigger problem domestically than it was on the international front.

The senior clubs were often short of numbers and either had to borrow opposition players or frequently played 15s to ensure a game. And although the original challenge to England was at 20-a-side it was not long before the SFU suggested to the RFU that the numbers be reduced to 15. Their first approach in December 1875 was rejected as it was felt to be too close to the next scheduled international match, just a few months away. However, a second approach in October 1876 was favourably received and it was agreed to play 15-a-side thereafter. Scotland's first match at 15s was against Ireland on 19 February 1877.

*John Macfarlane: inventor of the passing game.*

## The Last of the 20-a-side Matches

Scotland put in some creditable performances in the remaining three matches at 20-a-side but the best result was a home draw in 1876. The 1874 match at Kennington Oval was the first where passing was in evidence with Scotland scoring the only try to a drop goal. Edinburgh University had developed what was known then as 'chucking' the ball. This was a practice developed by John Macfarlane – at the time of the match critically ill and tragically soon to die following an illness triggered by the dislocation of his knee playing rugby – and A.K. Stewart.

Macfarlane encouraged his players to 'chuck' the ball before and not after they were held. This was quite revolutionary thinking as up until this stage it was rare for players to pass in any circumstances. Players tended to carry the ball as far as they could either dying with the ball or starting a maul.

In the international the chucking of Stewart, Grant and Hamilton was commented on in the match reports as 'a striking novelty in the play'. The Scottish backs were clearly superior to their English counterparts but the sodden pitch made it difficult to exploit this advantage. Hamersley, the English captain, admitted afterwards that the weather and ground conditions had helped his team greatly. With Scotland attacking in the first half Finlay scored in the corner and Chalmers just missed the conversion. Then came the crucial point of the match. Scotland were pressing again and 'scored' through Stewart, but his try was disallowed. The decision cost Scotland the match as Freeman dropped a colossal goal to win the match for England.

A footnote to this match underlines the difficulties Scotland has faced over the years against England in terms of numbers playing the game. Even at this early stage it was recorded that as captain of the England team, Hamersley had over 200 candidates to choose from. In Scotland at the time there were barely more than 200 adults playing the game let alone being of sufficient quality to perform at the top level. A further illustration of why the Scots were so keen to play 15 and not 20-a-side.

**50 Greatest Players**

**ROBERT IRVINE Forward**

**Club:** Edinburgh Academicals

**Debut:** v England, 27 March 1871

**No. of Caps:** 13 **No. of Points:** 1 try (before scoring by points was introduced)

First capped as a 17-year-old in the inaugural international, Irvine became the first truly great name in Scottish rugby. Remarkably, his international career spanned 10 seasons and he was the only man to play in Scotland's first 13 internationals. Known as 'Bulldog', he was exceptionally strong and athletic as befits a champion hammer-thrower, and was famed for his devastating tackling, skilful dribbling and clever line-out work, and his leadership skills were acknowledged when he was appointed Scotland captain at the age of 22. He led his country eight times, experiencing just two losses during his spell in charge. In 1879 he had the honour of captaining Scotland in the first Calcutta Cup match at Raeburn Place, which ended in a draw. His final match was against England in 1880 and was his tenth successive match against the Auld Enemy, a staggering achievement. No Scotsman has played in more Calcutta Cup matches and only Scott Hastings, with 11 appearances, has played more times against England.

The 1875 match, the fifth in the series, was also the second 0-0 draw in the series. Despite the lack of points it was described as a thrilling encounter played in front of a record crowd of 7,000. It was perhaps most notable for the number of brothers who played in the match. James Finlay, playing in his fourth and final match for Scotland, was joined by his younger brothers Arthur and Ninian, who were making their debuts on their home ground at Raeburn Place. For England, the versatile Reginald Birkett, whose son John won a record 21 caps from 1906-12, was joined by his brother Louis on his debut.

The match itself was a battle of styles with Scotland trying to force the ball over the line at any opportunity and England by contrast letting fly with drop kicks from all angles. Scotland were fortunate that a number of efforts shaved the posts and it was a rare effort by Ninian Finlay which flew between the uprights, only to be disallowed for claims of offside.

The final 20-a-side match was back at Kennington Oval and was won by England.

## The Irish Connection

Scotland played their first match against Ireland in 1877 although Ireland and England had commenced fixtures two years earlier. Two unions had been formed in Ireland, the Irish Football Union in Dublin in November 1874 and the Northern Football Union of Ireland in Belfast two months later. The two unions did not see eye-to-eye, and even in those days cross-border co-operation seemingly was not without its difficulties.

Although Scotland played Ireland in Belfast in 1877, the return fixture planned for Glasgow the following season was declined because of internal wrangling between the two Irish unions. Eventually, their differences were settled and a single Irish Union was formed in 1879.

In their six encounters to date with England, Scotland had scored a collective total of three tries, one goal and one drop goal. The reduction from 20 to 15-a-side helped Scotland and allowed them more space, which they fully exploited against an inexperienced Irish team, scoring six tries, four of which were converted, and two drop goals. Robert MacKenzie (Glasgow Academical) enjoyed a splendid debut appearance, scoring the first international hat-trick of tries and dropping two goals, another first in an international match. Almost 50 years later, as Sir Robert, he was President of the SRU during the first Grand Slam season in 1925.

Led by Irvine, the great man was impressed with the rich, albeit very raw, potential the Irish had at their disposal. He considered however that, 'Much

## 50 Greatest Players

**NINIAN FINLAY Half-back**

**Club:** Edinburgh Academicals

**Debut:** v England, 8 March 1875

**No. of Caps:** 9 **No. of Points:** 3 drop goals (before scoring by points was introduced)

Finlay is the youngest man ever to play international rugby, capped from school at the age of 17 years and 36 days. By an amazing coincidence Charles Reid was capped for Scotland at the exact same age, but Finlay is accorded 'youngest ever' status by virtue of having lived through four leap years as opposed to Reid's five! One of seven brothers, five of whom played together in at least one match for Edinburgh Accies, Finlay made his international debut alongside two of them – James and Arthur; the first time that three brothers played together in an international. Finlay was an awesome player. Although a back, he combined the power and physique of a forward with natural speed and agility and he was judged to be the finest exponent of his era in the art of drop-kicking. His finest moment came in the 1879 Calcutta Cup match when he tied the match by dropping a goal 'with a couple of Englishmen hanging on to him'.

good Hibernian breath was expended shouting which would have done more good to the distressed country if spent shoving.' And he also reveals hearing a despairing but classic shout from an Irishman in the crowd: 'Oireland, Oireland get behind yourselves.' We think we know what he meant. He was trying to encourage his boys to get back to defend their line against the rampant Scots.

Two weeks later, Scotland built on this confidence-boosting performance and faced England for the first time at 15-a-side. In a hard-fought match played at a fast and furious pace Scotland just had the edge and won by a late drop goal to nil. Scotland defended well into the wind in the first half and had the territorial advantage in the second half. With five minutes left J.H.S. Graham grabbed the ball and chucked it to Malcolm Cross near half way who, quick as a flash, dropped a great goal to sneak a first win against England since the opening match in the series.

The extra space afforded by each team losing five players was dramatic and the match was improved greatly as a spectacle. The home supporters in particular enjoyed the result with its exciting climax and all agreed that there was to be no going back to 20s; 15s were here to stay.

In 1878, with Ireland still sorting themselves out, Scotland and England locked horns again for the final time at Kennington Oval. They competed well and this was probably their best performance on English soil to date with the forwards once again excelling; but the backs too played their part in full. Finlay was the match of Lennard Stokes, the outstanding English three-quarter, and in Bill Maclagan Scotland had unearthed another truly great player. Renowned for his fierce tackling, Irvine was fulsome in praise of his defensive qualities: 'I would rather fall into the hands of any back in the three kingdoms than into those of W.E. Maclagan when roused.'

In good conditions Scotland enjoyed the better of the first half with Cross going closest with a drop at goal. In the second half England had the better of the play and Stokes went close with a drop at goal and almost scored a try. The match finished 0-0.

## The Calcutta Cup is Born

In 1879 a special trophy had been put up by the Rugby Football Union to be awarded to the winner of the annual battle between the two countries. The trophy is, of course, the Calcutta Cup and it is the oldest cup contested annually at international level in any sport in the world.

The cup's origins are, as the name suggests, in India. In 1872, a group of ex-patriot Old Rugbeians organised a match in Calcutta which was played on Christmas Day. Despite playing the energy-sapping game in the ferocious heat it was deemed a great success and led to the formation of the Calcutta Football Club. The club joined the RFU in 1874 but the lack of other clubs to play against made fixtures difficult to obtain. The presence of a number of army regiments provided some opposition but when the 3rd Buffs departed India in 1876 the club was left with no opponents.

The club reluctantly decided to disband but wanted to use their remaining funds constructively. It was agreed to commission a trophy locally and present it to the RFU to help keep alive the memory of the club. The club closed their bank account, withdrawing the balance of £60 in rupees. The rupees were melted down and they engaged the finest Indian craftsmen to create a slightly tapering cup, about 18 inches in height, with three snake handles and a cover of a modelled elephant, which could be removed.

Later a massive wooden base was purchased and on this base can be found the dates of every match with the name of the winning country and the name of the two captains. It has been an enduring, and unique feature of Scotland v England encounters over the years and the Calcutta Cup clash is still one of the most eagerly awaited sporting contests in the international calendar.

*The Calcutta Cup trophy.*

After having comfortably disposed of a more competitive Irish side at Hamilton Crescent Scotland looked forward with confidence to the England encounter. The rather dull weather did not prevent a record crowd of 10,000 spectators turning up at Raeburn Place. Scotland, playing into the wind, spent most of the first half defending for their lives as the English backs ran well with ball in hand and Stokes had many drop kicks at goal. Maclagan's ferocious tackling halted several

*The Scotland team to face England in 1879. The legendary Robert 'Bulldog' Irvine is seated second from the left in the middle row.*

English attacks but unfortunately for Scotland a weak clearance by Cross was fielded by Burton who ran in for an easy score and Stokes kicked the conversion.

Scotland's tactics with the elements in the second half were to try and drive the ball over the England line. Despite considerable pressure they could not manage this. Late on in the match Scotland equalised through a brilliant piece of play by Finlay. Receiving the ball from Gordon Petrie he made a run for the line but was blocked. Then with a couple of Englishmen hanging on to him he dropped a goal and one report of the match states that the crowd did not stop cheering for a full five minutes afterwards, such was their excitement. The match finished honours even and the first Calcutta Cup was shared.

# Chapter Four: 1880-89
# A Decade of Scottish Glory

The first decade of international rugby was inevitably a time of enormous change as the game's players and administrators began to get to grips with the sport. By now the game was expanding not only domestically with more clubs and therefore players appearing throughout Scotland, but also slowly throughout the world.

Rugby was played throughout the British Empire by this stage as former public schoolboys and university graduates accepted foreign postings and took with them games such as rugby, football, tennis and golf. The game was spreading rapidly but there were still many issues to resolve particularly relating to the laws and the administration of the game. This was the decade when the International Board (now the International Rugby Board) was formed, in 1886. But the 1880s was also eventful on the pitch for Scotland and turned out to be one of the national team's most successful eras.

## Saturday Matches

The first home match against Ireland was at Hamilton Crescent, Glasgow in 1880 and is notable for being the first international Scotland had played on a Saturday; all the others had been played on Mondays. This was still at a time when most people worked all day on a Saturday, but half-day working was becoming more frequent. The fine weather suited the Scottish backs and the Irish forwards were considerably more competitive than they had been in the first fixture two years earlier. However, it was still a comfortable win for the home side with the forwards in splendid form combining well with their dribbling.

The Calcutta Cup match was played at Whalley Range in Manchester, the first time it had been played outside London and the first to be played on a Saturday. Scotland arrived in confident mood knowing that in contrast to their good form against Ireland, England had struggled to win in Dublin. However, despite another excellent display from the forwards the backs leaked a record five tries and it was on a flat note that Irvine ended his marvellous international career. Indeed, when he looked back on this match he unleashed an uncharacteristically withering verdict on his backs' play that day. 'Once an English back was past the Scotch forwards the backs seemed

## 50 Greatest Players

**BILL MACLAGAN Full-back/Wing**

**Teams:** Edinburgh Academicals, London Scottish

**Debut:** v England, 4 March 1878

**No. of Caps:** 26 **No. of Points:** 3 tries, 4 conversions (before scoring by points was introduced)

Maclagan enjoyed a long and illustrious career in the blue jersey stretching over 13 seasons and three decades. He retired as Scotland's record cap-holder and his career span was unbroken for 60 years. Maclagan was a very aggressive and demanding player who led by example. He was only the second Scot to play as a single full-back and was later capped as a wing.

A determined rather than elusive runner it was for his ferocious tackling that he was particularly famed. His performance in the 1879 Calcutta Cup match was truly heroic as it was his full-blooded defence at full-back that limited England's scoring to just one try. In his final season for Scotland he led the team to wins over Wales and Ireland before narrowly missing out on a Triple Crown against England. Having retired from the international scene he led the first British Isles tour to South Africa in 1891, winning all 19 matches, including three Tests, scoring 224 points for and only 1 against.

suddenly seized with a paralysis, pawed him like old women, as if to encourage his onward career.'

### Reid and Wright in Opposition

In 1881 the season started badly for Scotland as they suffered a shock defeat against Ireland. Consequently five new caps were introduced to the side for the England match with quarter-back Andrew Don Wauchope being the most significant introduction. Although he endured a torrid debut at the hands of his opposite number Rowley, he was to become a mainstay of the back division for most of the decade. Another newcomer, the remarkable Charles Reid, who had made his debut as a schoolboy aged 17 years 36 days against Ireland, had a storming match in the forwards and went on to play a record 20 times for Scotland. But perhaps the most remarkable feature of a quite exceptional match was that Reid, a pupil at Edinburgh Academy, found himself in direct opposition that day to a fellow classmate, Frank Wright, a Manchester lad who boarded at the Academy.

Wright had been called into the England team as Henry Taylor had missed the train north and England had no reserve players in their party. Both boys acquitted themselves well with Reid forcing himself over the English line only to lose control of the ball and Wright pulling off a number of important tackles. Harry Stevenson, a classmate of the aptly named scholars Reid and Wright, who was to become one of Scotland's most famous players, wrote about their return to school after playing in the match and the ecstatic greeting the pair received: 'Tommy Harvey was rector. "Hippo" (Reid) and Frank came in with their class just as Tommy did to say prayers. There were no prayers on that day! We cheered and cheered and cheered – and Tommy gave it up.'

The match was a fast and open affair played in excellent conditions with a temporary stand erected to help accommodate the 12,000-strong crowd.

Halfway through the second half the brilliant Len Stokes, who along with the equally magnificent Ninian Finlay was making his last appearance in an international, landed a quite breathtaking drop goal from all of 80 yards. But right on full time Finlay made one last long run and dropped at goal. Although it missed, Brown, backing up, scored a try which, although disputed, was awarded. Begbie held his nerve to kick the conversion to secure the draw and almost as the ball cleared the bar the crowd invaded the pitch in their excitement.

*The Scotland team in 1882. Charles 'Hippo' Reid, standing third from the right, with Bill Maclagan on his right, was blessed with a formidable physique.*

**Great Matches**

**INTERNATIONAL MATCH** **Whalley Range, Manchester, 4 March 1882**
**Attendance: 8,000**

**England Nil** **Scotland 2 tries**

Scotland's win was the first recorded away from home by either nation in the Scotland v England series and owed much to the magnificence of the Scottish pack. Charles Reid, referring to their dominance, later stated, 'Give me a forward team like we had at Manchester in 1882 and I do not care how many three-quarter backs you have; we could go through them.'

On a heavy, greasy pitch the Scots managed to knock England out of their rhythm particularly in the loose. In fact the large crowd surrounding the pitch gave Scotland as many problems as their opponents did. A combination of their enthusiasm and ineffective stewarding brought play to a standstill on several occasions as they spilled on to the pitch. It got so bad that serious consideration was given to abandoning the match. Bob Ainslie, who had a wonderful match, took a pass from Don Wauchope in the first half and had to thread his way through a crowd of spectators to score the opening try. But Payne of England was not so fortunate, narrowly missing a try in part due to the presence of spectators on the pitch.

Ainslie's second try sealed an historic win for Scotland but it would have been more emphatic still if Maclagan's goal from a mark had not been disallowed as he had not properly made his mark when claiming the free kick.

**England:** A.N. Hornby (captain); W.N. Bolton, E. Beswick; J.H. Payne, H.H. Taylor; C.H. Coates, W.M. Tatham, C. Gurdon, P.A. Newton, H. Vassall, H.G. Fuller, J.T. Hunt, G.T. Thomson, E.T. Gurdon, H.C.Rowley

**Scotland:** J.P. Veitch; W.E. Maclagan, A. Philp; A.R. Don Wauchope, W.S. Brown; A. Walker, R. Ainslie, C. Reid, D.Y. Cassels (captain), W.A. Walls, D. McCowan, R. Maitland, T. Ainslie, J.G. Walker, J.B. Brown
**Scorer: Tries** R. Ainslie 2

**Referee:** Mr H.L. Robinson (Ireland)

The dispute over the try was further fuelled when the President of the RFU made some provocative comments at the RFU's AGM later that year: 'They (England) certainly did not win the Scotch match but that was no fault of theirs, for they sent a team that was fairly strong, but the Scotch team was strong also, their strength being in umpiring. Since that match, however, they had made such representation to the Scotch authorities that they hoped in future to have unbiased referees who understood their duties.' The increasingly fraught relationship with the RFU was stretched even further by these remarks, reigniting simmering resentment which was to come to a head in 1884. However, neutral referees were appointed for the first time for the England v Scotland match the following season.

Ireland continued to endure selectorial problems and awarded 18 new caps for the three internationals they played in 1882. Despite the disruption Scotland had to work hard for their win, eventually overcoming a stuffy Irish display by two tries to one. For the first time in the Scotland v England series an away win was recorded with Scotland triumphing by two tries to nil and there is no evidence of any complaints from either team about the handling of the match.

## The First International Championship

With hindsight, 1883 was a most significant year in the development of rugby as an international game as Scotland, England, Ireland and Wales all played in a series of matches over an 11-week period from December 1882 to March 1883. Scotland and England played three matches each but Ireland and Wales only two each as they did not play a fixture against each other.

Research carried out by Terry Godwin for his book *The International Championship 1883-1983* reveals the earliest documented evidence referring to a championship dates back to 1894, fully 11 years after the inaugural round of matches. In *The Field* it is stated that Ireland 'stands in the proud position of being champion of the nations'. The *South Wales Daily News* on 18 March 1895 refers to the 'championship' and the 'wooden spoon' and in March 1896 *The Times*, previewing the Ireland v Wales match at Lansdowne Road, predicted, 'Ireland have only to win to become the international champions of the season.'

Two days later *The Times* published a 'championship' table:

| | W | D | L |
|---|---|---|---|
| **Ireland** | 2 | 1 | 0 |
| **Scotland** | 1 | 1 | 1 |
| **England** | 1 | 0 | 2 |
| **Wales** | 1 | 0 | 2 |

Back in 1883, meanwhile, Scotland played a series of three international matches for the first time, adding Wales to their list of opponents. The match was played on 8 January 1883 on a frozen pitch at Raeburn Place and this time of year, as many will know, has never been the ideal time to schedule matches of any description in Scotland.

Nevertheless, 4,000 hardy souls turned out to watch Scotland play against the new boys on a cold, crisp Monday afternoon. Scotland won quite

**50 Greatest Players**

**CHARLES REID Forward**

**Club:** Edinburgh Academicals

**Debut:** v Ireland, 19 February 1881

**No. of Caps:** 21 **No. of Points:** 4 tries (before scoring by points was introduced)

An enormous man, he was reckoned to stand 6 foot 3 inches tall and weigh between 15 and 16 stones, and team photos from the time confirm that he was literally a giant amongst men. First capped as a schoolboy, he was known from his school days as 'Hippo', not because of his physique but apparently because of his failure one day in the Greek class to give the meaning of the word for a horse! Considered by the experts of his day to be the greatest ever Scottish forward, the supporting evidence cited is impressive: extraordinarily brave, a destructive tackler, excellent in the line-out, highly mobile and with a great pair of hands. And he was considered to gain more ground than any other when dribbling the ball. Reid was the key player in a side which lost just four times in his 21 internationals and he led Scotland to their first championship win in 1887. He retired as Scotland's record cap holder having played eight seasons of international rugby but still at the ludicrously early age of 24.

comfortably by three goals to one and the mesmeric running of the dynamic Don Wauchope produced two tries.

A second win was recorded in Belfast in the most appalling weather conditions. Rain had fallen for days on the NIFC pitch at Ormeau and a veritable sea of mud greeted the players.

The Calcutta Cup again was a contrast in styles. The Scotland team, fielding five backs and ten forwards, relied on the swift, dribbling rushes from their mobile forwards to gain territory. Ironically the English backs, superbly marshalled by Alan Rotherham, employed the 'Oxford' style passing game, which suited their strong runners. It is ironic because the 'Oxford' style had its roots in the form of rugby first popularised in the Scottish public schools. Scotland lost by two tries to one and despite Maclagan's brave tackling even he could do nothing to prevent Wilfred Bolton's brilliant solo effort for the winning try.

## The Year of the 'Dispute'

The following year, 1884, was another momentous one in the annals of international rugby. It started brightly for the Scots. Comfortable wins were enjoyed against Wales at Rodney Parade in Newport and Ireland at Raeburn

Place for the first time. England too had beaten Wales and Ireland and so the Calcutta Cup match at Blackheath became a Triple Crown decider.

Encouragingly, Scotland led by a Jamieson try at half-time and, playing well, they were confident of winning. But then came a moment that was to have massive implications for the running and governance of the game. England were awarded a try which was converted and ultimately won the game. The bare facts, which are indisputable, are that R.S. Kindersley gained possession of the ball and set off on a run to 'score' a try. However, the legitimacy of the score was the subject of an immediate protest by Scotland and a protracted and heated debate ensued which stopped the match for fully ten minutes. Unable to resolve their differences on the pitch the Scots allowed the conversion to be taken but the ramifications of what became known as the 'Dispute' rumbled on for several seasons.

There are, as in all arguments, two sides to the story. To help illustrate the opposing views it is worth considering the following extracts from two men who were intimately involved in the case. G. Rowland Hill, secretary of the RFU, recorded that, 'In the course of play the ball was knocked back by a Scotsman [C.W. Berry], one of the English team secured it and a try was obtained. The Scots claimed that "knocking back" was illegal; the English held that it was not an illegal act and even though it had been, the act was done by a Scotsman and as no Englishman claimed for it, the Scotsmen could not claim for or profit by their own infringement.'

The Scottish view is provided by Andrew Don Wauchope who played in the match. 'In those days there were two umpires who carried sticks, not flags, and a referee without a whistle. The ball was thrown out of touch, an appeal was made. The umpire on the touchline [J.H.S. Graham] held up a stick, all the players with the exception of four Englishmen and two Scotsmen stopped playing and England scored a try. The only question of fact decided by the referee was that a Scotsman knocked the ball back. This, according to the Scottish view of the reading of the rule, was illegal and the whole question turned on the interpretation. The point that no Englishman had appealed was never raised at the time and to judge by the fact that 11 of the English team ceased play, it would appear that their idea was that the game should stop.'

An exchange of correspondence between the SFU and the RFU ensued and although adamant that a try should not have been awarded, the SFU proposed that a neutral body settle the matter. However, the RFU would not go to arbitration citing that the referee's decision must stand. As a consequence of failing to reach agreement the Scotland v England match for 1885 was cancelled.

Ireland and Wales met to discuss a way of settling future disputes between rugby nations and proposed the formation of the International Board. This proposal was accepted by the Scots and initially by the English though they chose not to attend the inauguration of the International Board in early 1886.

The newly formed IB informed the RFU that they were now the law-makers of the game and that all international matches would be conducted under their rules. Furthermore, unless England became part of the process and joined the Board, no one would play against them at international level. The RFU refused to cede their power to a new organisation and as a consequence they did not play Scotland, Ireland or Wales in 1888 or 1889.

After a long standoff England reopened talks in late 1889 by proposing the matter be submitted to arbitration before two people, one nominated by the International Board and one by the RFU. Lord Kingsburgh, the Lord Justice Clerk, was the International Board's nominee and Major Marindin, President of the Football Association, was nominated by the RFU.

These appointments were enough to restart matches with England in 1890 and by April the two gave a judgement that was binding on all parties. The International Board became the administrative and regulatory body for all internationals, taking the role out of English hands for the first time, but they were handed the balance of power on the new 12-member board. England had six places and the Celtic nations just two each.

With England sidelined, Scotland played just two matches in 1885, against Wales and Ireland, although, oddly, two matches were played against the Irish because foul weather conditions caused the abandonment of the first match. The match against Wales was played at Hamilton Crescent and finished as a 0-0 draw, one of only three draws in the series between the two nations.

The Irish match was to prove more controversial. Once again conditions at Ormeau were truly appalling although as day broke on the morning of the match the weather was clear. However, an almighty storm blew in from the west, flooding the pitch and wrecking the match as a contest. The Irish played into the teeth of the storm and Scotland took an early lead through a try by John Jamieson (West of Scotland). After about 20 minutes Morrow, the Irish full-back, had to retire hurt, and at this stage the pragmatic decision was taken to call off the the match, the only occasion that a championship match has been abandoned. Afterwards, Scotland insisted they would claim the match unless Ireland agreed to replay it in Edinburgh. The Irish readily agreed to the ultimatum and two weeks later the rescheduled match went ahead at Raeburn Place with Scotland running in three tries to nil.

## Scotland Start Winning

In 1886, wins over Wales and Ireland and a draw with England, who had been welcomed back into the fold, saw Scotland win the championship for the first time. Indeed, the late 1880s was a period of some considerable success for the Scots who lost just once in 12 matches between 1885 and 1889.

One of that season's innovations was the introduction of a whistle for the match referee, who continued to be supported by umpires who waved sticks when they spotted an infringement.

Scotland arrived for the match in Cardiff to be greeted with the news that Wales were experimenting with the radical new idea of playing with four players in their three-quarter line instead of the standard three. To achieve this they had to withdraw a forward from the pack but such was the dominance of the Scottish forwards over the Welsh octet that they reverted to a three-man three-quarter line during the match. Another comfortable win followed against Ireland with Don Wauchope in fine form in both matches, scoring three tries and creating other chances with his trademark dodging, 'deer-like' runs.

It was England's turn to travel north and both teams arrived at Raeburn Place having won their matches over Wales and Ireland, for the championship decider. Scotland's greater scoring power appeared to give them an advantage as they had run in eight tries to nil in their two matches as opposed to England's three tries to one. The match, played on a bitterly cold day in Edinburgh, is captured in a splendid painting by W.H. Overend and L.P. Smythe, a copy of which hangs in the Edinburgh Academicals clubhouse at Raeburn Place. It is a fascinating snapshot of rugby as it was played then, set against the magnificent backdrop of late Victorian Edinburgh. It is recorded that 36 officers were in attendance at the match for the first time, including mounted policemen who are depicted in the background of the painting. The detail extends to the cold breath exhaled by the players, confirming just how bitter the weather was in mid March-that year.

The match itself was a hard-fought 0-0 draw, with England at a disadvantage early on when a knee injury to F. Bonsor severely limited his contribution to the match from quarter-back. Although Scotland enjoyed most of the territorial advantage, with Asher, Don Wauchope and Reid prominent, they could not score.

*A painting by W.H. Overend and L.P. Smythe of Scotland v England at Raeburn Place in 1886. Reproduced courtesy of Edinburgh Academicals FC.*

The following year Scotland won the championship for the second successive season. They played some scintillating stuff to outscore the other nations by 16 tries to one, but once again they stumbled to a draw in the final match against the 'Auld Enemy'. Three tries were scored against Ireland and then Wales were despatched in imperious style with the Scots running in a record 12 tries at Raeburn Place. In current day terms this would equate to a 68-0 win but it appears in the record books rather blandly as a win by four goals and eight tries to nil. George Lindsay of London Scottish, on his first appearance of the season, had a day of days and ran in five tries, setting a championship record which remains unbettered to this day.

The Calcutta Cup match ended in stalemate for the seventh time in 17 matches with both sides scoring one try apiece.

## Professionalism Raises its Head

In 1888 England's non-participation devalued the series of matches as the three Celtic nations won and lost one match each. Scotland's loss came at the hands of Wales for the first time, but the win over Ireland was more encouraging. Reid, playing in his final international, signed off in style. He was at his rampaging best throughout the match and, much to the delight and hilarity of the crowd, had one characteristic long run 'with the bulk of

## 50 Greatest Players

**ANDREW DON WAUCHOPE Quarter-back**

**Clubs:** Fettesian-Lorettonians, Cambridge University

**Debut:** v England, 19 March 1881

**No. of Caps:** 12 **No. of Points:** 6 tries (before scoring by points was introduced)

One of the great attacking players of his era from his position at quarter-back, Don Wauchope made full use of the copious quantities of possession won by his forwards. A useful link between forwards and backs he was at his most dangerous with ball in hand where his blinding pace and elusive running wreaked havoc in opposition defences. Built close to the ground, his low centre of gravity made it difficult for tacklers to knock him down and he had the rare gift of being able to feint and sidestep at top speed. Although he played with his younger brother Patrick, it was in tandem with A.G.G. Asher that Scotland played some of their best rugby of the 1880s, the pair losing only once in six matches together.

the Irish forwards hanging on to him'. The season was also notable for the introduction of Harry Stevenson, a controversial character, who was to become one of Scotland's greatest backs.

In 1888 a British side toured abroad for the first time and the matter fairly vexed the SFU. The tour was organised by Alfred Shaw and Arthur Shrewsbury, a pair of cricketing entrepreneurs, who had been involved in a number of Test tours to Australia. They notified the RFU of their intention to arrange a rugby tour to Australia and New Zealand and although they would not officially sanction the tour they raised no objection to it provided that the strict amateur rules were not broken.

The players were recruited primarily from the north of England and the Scottish Borders and a party of 21 players set sail from Britain on 8 March 1888 on a tour which would last fully eight months. Five players from Scottish clubs (three from Hawick and two from Edinburgh University) went on the 35-match tour and the SFU Committee closely examined the expenses of the three Hawick players (the brothers Burnet and A.J. Laing) to ensure that they had upheld the strict principles of amateurism. Although no action was taken against the players, the minutes of the SFU suggest that there were still question marks in the minds of these upholders of the strict amateur codes: 'Their assurances being satisfactory, the matter was dropped until such time as direct evidence might be adduced in support of any alleged professionalism.'

Though Scotland won both their matches in 1889, against Wales in Edinburgh and against Ireland in Dublin, the annual spice of the England encounter was badly missed and it was a relief all round later in the year when England agreed to the arbitration which led to their re-entry to the international fold and their joining the International Board.

*Scotland v Wales, 1889. The match was reduced to 30 minutes each way because of the foul weather conditions apparent in this team photo.*

# Chapter Five: 1890-99
# Keeping it in the Family

Scotland enjoyed a further decade of success in the 1890s and won their first two Triple Crowns in 1891 and 1895. The championship and Triple Crown honours were fairly evenly distributed during those years, bringing first Triple Crowns for Ireland and Wales while England also continued to add to their honours list. The 1890s saw further acrimony with the 'Broken Time' payment problems in the north of England which came to a head in 1893, leading to the formation of the Northern Union and ultimately the creation of a new code, rugby league. Players at clubs in the working-class towns of Yorkshire and Lancashire could not afford to take time off work to play rugby and, although not seeking payment to play, were looking for fiscal compensation for time away.

At the RFU's AGM in 1893, Yorkshire and Lancashire put forward a motion 'That players be allowed compensation for bona fide loss of time'. It was defeated 282-136 and as a consequence 22 clubs in Yorkshire and Lancashire resigned from the RFU, breaking away to form the Northern Union. This move was to severely hamper England as a rugby-playing force for over a decade as many clubs left rugby union for the lure of rugby league. The effect was most marked in their rapidly declining membership. In 1893, 481 clubs were members of the RFU. By 1896, it was down to 383 clubs and by 1903, ten years after the split, they had been reduced to 244 clubs. It was not until 1924 that club numbers exceeded the 1893 total.

The SFU was fully supportive of the RFU's position and threatened Scottish clubs with expulsion if they played any clubs who were members of the Northern Union. The first Scot to turn professional was Alex Laidlaw, a Hawick player capped in 1897. A stonemason by trade, he joined Bradford in 1899 and, as was the custom of the time, was banned sine die from rugby union and not allowed membership of any club in Scotland. This practice continued for over 100 years and it was not until rugby union went professional in 1995 that the rules were relaxed. Alan Tait was the first Scottish player who had gone to league who managed to resurrect his union career. His form with Newcastle earned him a call-up to the Scotland A team who played Wales A in 1997 and he forced his way into the Scotland side against Ireland as he made a successful late run for a place on the 1997 Lions tour to South Africa.

But rugby faced other problems too, often about money. Wales were forced into resigning from the International Board over the A.J. Gould testimonial fund. A.J. 'Monkey' Gould was a brilliant centre and regarded as the leading Welsh player of his generation. The first 'superstar' of Welsh rugby, he played a record 27 times for his country from 1885 to 1897. His admirers set up a testimonial fund for him with the blessing of the WRU with the aim of raising enough money to buy him a house in recognition of his achievements. When the SFU received a request from the WRU for a contribution to the fund, it immediately raised the hackles of the organisation's devoutly amateur members and they hastily passed the matter over to the International Board. The International Board asked for the WRU to sort the matter out either by disbanding the fund or not selecting Gould and when they refused they were forced to resign from the International Board. Gould eventually provided the solution by retiring from international rugby but this did not satisfy the SFU and Scotland refused to play against Wales for two seasons.

## The Laws Continue to Change

As is customary in rugby even to this day, there were several law changes implemented during the 1890s. Probably the most far-reaching was the introduction of a scoring system in the late 1880s with the first one valuing a try as 1 point, a conversion 2 points and a drop goal 3 points. There were still discrepancies even at international level, however. The two tries scored by England against Scotland in 1890 were worth two points each according to the SFU scoring system and therefore the result was recorded as 4-0. Two weeks later at Blackheath, England scored three unconverted tries and according to the RFU's points valuation system this gave England a 3-0 win.

The following season the International Board introduced the first points scoring system which was adopted by all four home unions as follows: Try – 1 point; Conversion – 2 points; Drop goal – 3 points; Penalty goal – 2 points; Goal mark – 3 points. A further change the next season was made to increase the value of the try and in 1893-94 another change was made to further adjust the values: Try – 3 points; Conversion – 2 points; Drop goal – 4 points; Penalty goal – 3 points; Goal mark – 4 points. And with only a slight adjustment – the value of a goal mark was reduced from 4 to 3 points early in the new century – these scoring values remained intact until 1948.

Touring increased in popularity during the decade and three British representative sides visited the southern hemisphere to help spread the game throughout the Empire. Unlike the 1888 tour, these all had the blessing of

**50 Greatest Players**

**MATTHEW McEWAN Forward**
**Club:** Edinburgh Academicals
**Debut:** v England, 13 March 1886
**No. of Caps:** 15 **No. of Points:** 3 tries, 2 conversions, 1 drop goal (before scoring by points was introduced)

Another Academicals forward very much in the Reid mould, McEwan possessed all of the great man's attributes: hard, fast and aggressive he was another renowned dribbler of the ball. He too had a splendid nickname, being known as 'Saxon' on account of his fair hair and impressive build. But where he surpassed Reid was in becoming the first Scot to captain his country to a Triple Crown, in 1891. The mythical Crown was won in some style as Scotland scored 14 tries in three matches, accumulating a total of 38 points and beating England in a head-to-head decider. McEwan's younger brother Bill won 16 caps for Scotland and featured in the 1895 Triple Crown side before emigrating to South Africa where he won two caps for his adopted nation.

the authorities and the few Scots selected were not hauled up in front of the SFU to undergo a grilling about the legitimacy of their expenses. Maclagan was selected to captain the 1891 side, which enjoyed a successful tour of South Africa. Three other Scottish caps were included in the tour party of 21, which won all 19 of their matches. They were Paul Clauss (Oxford University), Willie Wotherspoon (Cambridge University) and 'Judy' MacMillan, the rumbustious London Scottish forward. Rugby was in its infancy at the time in South Africa and the tourists had a great time. On the pitch they scored 224 points and conceded just one, winning all three Tests. Off the pitch, although most of their travelling was done in horse-drawn carriages, Clauss cheerfully described the tour as 'all champagne and travel'.

The 1896 tour to South Africa did not include any Scottish caps but the 1899 tour to Australia, although not a full-strength representative side, did for the first time include capped players from all four unions. Alfred Bucher (Edinburgh Academicals) and Alec Timms (Edinburgh University) were the Scotland caps who toured, with both enjoying successful tours, playing and scoring tries in the Test series which was won 3-1.

## A Home of their Own

Ever since the first match at Raeburn Place in 1871 there had been a strained relationship between the SFU and Edinburgh Academicals regarding the use of the cricket field for international rugby. The Accies Cricket Club committee had only granted use of the field for the first international by voting on it, although the treasurer's report later that year noted 'the large sum of £13 was obtained from the football fund, being the balance of gate money on the day of the first international match after deducting expenses'.

The Edinburgh Academy School also used the cricket field and the school was unhappy about its use for international rugby, especially when it switched to a Saturday on a regular basis, as pupils were constantly using it. The club was concerned about the wear and tear on the pitch caused by the matches and the erection of temporary stands. In turn the school upset the union as they had problems preparing the field and ground for the match when in use by the pupils. From 1889 there were protracted meetings between the school, the club and the SFU over the rental and conditions and it was clear that the SFU needed to look for a permanent solution to the problem. They managed to continue to use Raeburn Place until 1895 when the Academical club confirmed with the greatest reluctance that they would not lease the ground again to the SFU. Home matches were then switched to Old Hampden Park and Powderhall as preparations for a new ground continued.

In 1890, James Aikman Smith was appointed honorary secretary and treasurer to the SFU; this marked the start of more than 40 years' unswerving service to the union. A chartered accountant, Aikman Smith ruled the SFU with a rod of iron, possessing a steel fist in a steel glove. He was bitterly opposed to any hint of professionalism and strove to keep Scotland's standing at the forefront of a game for the dedicated amateur. He identified and started negotiating for a field at Inverleith as early as 1891 but it took time to resolve a number of planning issues and it was not until 1897 that it was finally agreed to purchase the field for £3,800. A very astute man, Aikman Smith came up with the innovative idea of funding the project primarily by the issue of debentures, demonstrating how far ahead of his time he was on business matters. The SFU therefore became the first union to own and run its own ground, which was opened in February 1899.

*James Aikman Smith served the SFU for over 40 years.*

## Triple Crown Glory

The decade opened promisingly with the team led by Maclagan, playing in his last international

## 50 Greatest Players

**HARRY STEVENSON Centre/Full-back**

**Club:** Edinburgh Academicals

**Debut:** v Wales, 4 February 1888

**No. of Caps:** 15 **No. of Points:** 2 drop goals (before scoring by points was introduced)

*The Scotsman* once described Stevenson as 'the greatest footballer in the world'. A daring centre or full-back, he possessed a rebellious, uncompromising streak which brought him into conflict with the national selectors. In 1891 they wanted the centre to pass the ball wide to his wings but Stevenson refused, believing this style to be wrong. Instead of dropping him he was switched to full-back where his aggressive defence and belligerent attacking brought a new dimension to the back line and helped Scotland to a Triple Crown. An outstanding cricketer, he was an underarm bowler of some renown. He would throw innocuous looking lobs to the batsman, rush up the wicket after them and take astonishing off-the-bat catches. One bemused victim commented he had never faced a silly-mid-on, silly-mid-off and silly bowler at the same time. The man loved to live dangerously.

campaign, beating both Wales and Ireland. The selection of Adam Dalgleish, who played against Wales and England, was a major milestone for Borders and Scottish rugby. A member of Gala, Dalgleish is regarded as the first genuine Borderer to play for Scotland and it was the first acknowledgement of the playing strength outside the established heartland of the Edinburgh and Glasgow schools and universities. Dalgleish was the first of eight Borderers to play for Scotland during the decade and late on in the 1890s it was not unusual for three or four Borderers to be selected for international duty as the balance of playing strength began a slow but significant shift.

Having beaten their fellow Celtic nations, Scotland hosted England at Raeburn Place in 1890 as fixtures were finally resumed after a two-year gap, but for the fifth time in seven seasons England spoiled the party and denied them a Triple Crown. Maclagan was coerced into playing as he was suffering from sciatica but he bravely led his team out to face the 'Auld Enemy'. The English pack had a hard core of Yorkshiremen who supplied plentiful ball for their quick wingers who caused the Scotland defence many problems and ran out worthy winners by one goal and one try to nil.

However, better was to follow in 1891 as the heart of an increasingly experienced team remained. The balance of the team was improved by switching the fiery Stevenson from centre-back to full-back. Stevenson did not approve of the wide passing game that was becoming fashionable and refused to play in this style. He was too good a player to leave out so he was switched to full-back and proved to be a revelation, bringing to the position his bold and aggressive running skills, and can be regarded as one of the first running full-backs. This allowed a half-back line of Paul Clauss, Gregor MacGregor and Willie Neilson to be played, a combination which worked wonderfully well being fed plentiful ball by the quarter-backs Charles Orr and Darsie Anderson. Neilson, a 17-year-old schoolboy at Merchiston, made his debut alongside older brother George against Wales, and this record has only been equalled once since, when the Hastings brothers, Gavin and Scott, made their debut together against France in 1986. The fulcrum of the back line was MacGregor who was a marvellous passer of the ball and who brought to his rugby some of the outstanding natural ball skills which enabled him to play eight cricket Tests for England as a wicketkeeper from 1890 to 1893. Disparaged in a number of quarters for his poor defence, MacGregor was nonetheless a key member in this team and it is no coincidence that Scotland scored 14 tries during the season including nine by the backs.

Wales were taken apart by seven tries to nil and Clauss was given plenty of ball to demonstrate his fast and determined running abilities. In addition to the Neilsons, Scotland also fielded the Orr brothers, Charles and John, who enjoyed successful careers in the Scotland shirt and all four played for West of Scotland. Three of the brothers scored against Wales with a try each

*Scotland's first Triple Crown-winning side of 1891 which included George (back row, far left) and Willie (front row, far right) Neilson who made their debuts against Wales.*

for the Orrs and a debut drop goal from Willie Neilson. Against Ireland, the backs scored all five tries, and Willie Wotherspoon at quarter-back became the second Scot to mark his debut with a hat-trick of tries. 'Saxon' McEwan, another of the great forwards produced by Edinburgh Academy, led the side throughout the season and was outstanding in an impressive pack, which included the likes of John Boswell, Herbert Leggatt and William Gibson.

The Triple Crown decider at Richmond was played in front of a huge 20,000 crowd who braved some appalling weather to watch the match. And at last, after a period of nine years, Scotland beat England to win the Triple Crown and the championship and take the Calcutta Cup back home.

## Great Matches

**INTERNATIONAL CHAMPIONSHIP** — **Richmond, 7 March 1891**

**England 3 Scotland 9** — **Attendance 20,000**

This match was a Triple Crown decider as England had beaten both Wales and Ireland away from home. They had drawn much praise for these wins but in front of an expectant crowd their pack of forwards was overwhelmed and their back line was positively anaemic.

The conditions were far from ideal as it was a stormy day but it did not deter the crowd nor a fired-up Scotland team. Within just eight minutes the Scots led as Charles Orr and MacGregor linked and MacGregor's clever switch pass to Clauss gave the winger the time and space to drop a neat goal with his left foot. Although there was no more scoring in the first half, the Scots dominated every facet of the match.

Scotland started the second half in fine style with MacGregor's passing once again instrumental. It was his exquisitely weighted pass which put John Orr into space and the burly forward showed an impressive turn of speed to outflank the defence and score by the posts to give MacGregor an easy conversion. 6-0. Then, with holes appearing in a dishevelled English defence, Willie Neilson, supporting MacGregor's fine break, took his well-timed pass to score and the conversion stretched the lead to 9-0. Despite a consolation score by Lockwood, Scotland had won their first Triple Crown in the most emphatic way possible.

**England:** W.G. Mitchell; P. Christopherson, F.H.R. Alderson (captain), R.E. Lockwood; W.R.M. Leake, J Berry; E.G.H. North, T. Kent, S.M.J. Woods, E. Bonham-Carter, J.H. Rogers, D. Jowett, R.T.D. Budworth, J. Richards, R.P. Wilson
**Scorer: Try** Lockwood **Conversion** Alderson

**Scotland:** H.J. Stevenson; P.R. Clauss, G. MacGregor, W. Neilson; C.E. Orr, D.G. Anderson; F.W.J. Goodhue, J.D. Boswell, H.T.O Leggatt, G.T. Neilson, J.E. Orr, W.R. Gibson, M.C. McEwan (captain), I. MacIntyre, R.G. MacMillan
**Scorers: Tries** J.E. Orr, W. Neilson **Conversions** MacGregor 2 **Drop Goal** Clauss

**Referee:** Mr J. Chambers (Ireland)

## Brothers in Arms

Although the 1892 championship campaign was not ultimately as successful as the previous year, the season once again went down to the wire with another Triple Crown showdown against England. This time, unfortunately, the English got their revenge in a very tousy match at Raeburn Place and went through the season without conceding a point. Prior to this Scotland had seen off the Welsh and Irish challenges but not with the same conviction as in 1891.

Scotland countered the Welsh four-man three-quarter line by pulling John Orr out of the pack at times to stop their chucking of the ball. But once again it was Scotland's strength up front that counted with Boswell inspiring the win at Swansea by scoring a try and kicking a conversion in the 7-2 victory. Boswell was a highly gifted forward who was particularly renowned for his penchant for attempting dropped goals from all points of the compass. His ability was in direct contrast to his distinctly unathletic appearance as he was described as 'florid and stout almost to rotundity'.

After beating Ireland, Scotland once again prepared for the visit of England who had stiffened their side, which included eight Yorkshiremen, for the trip north and had evidently planned for a battle royal up front. The play is described as having been very rough on both sides but the home crowd grew increasingly annoyed with the constant offside tactic of the English which the referee, Mr Warren of Ireland, failed to penalise. The pounding meted out to Orr and Anderson affected the quality of ball provided and the referee managed to upset the crowd further when he disallowed two Scotland tries.

Just two wins were recorded out of six matches over the next two seasons as great stalwarts such as Stevenson, the Orr brothers, Leggatt and Boswell began to bow out. The one bright spot each season was the win over England with Boswell prominent in both, dropping one of the two goals in the 8-0 win in 1893 and scoring two tries in his final match in 1894 having captained the side all season.

During the 1894 season two younger brothers of prominent Scotland caps Bill McEwan and Gordon Neilson were capped as schoolboys from Edinburgh Academy and Merchiston respectively. McEwan was the brother of the legendary 'Saxon' and, although not quite able to live up to his brother's exploits, he became a fine player himself, winning 16 caps before emigrating to South Africa. Curiously Neilson's cap, won in extraordinary circumstances, was to be his only one for Scotland, although it is certain that he subscribed to the view: better to have loved once than not at all. The Scotland team played a warm-up match against Merchiston two days prior to the England international. Gordon had such an outstanding match against them that Boswell and a number of his senior players pressed for his nomination as first reserve for the England match. He became the third of the four Neilson brothers to be capped; ironically after his older brother George had to withdraw through injury, Gordon replaced him in the pack, joining brother Willie in the team.

## Penalties Win Triple Crowns

The winter of 1895 was a most severe one, which is underlined by just how badly the weather affected the Wales and Ireland matches in Edinburgh. The Welsh match should not have gone ahead as the pitch was barely playable and the teams struggled to keep their footing in the dangerous conditions. A try by James Gowans, converted by Harry Smith, gave Scotland a 5-0 lead at the break. Despite a brave Welsh fightback and a breathtaking drop goal from near halfway by legendary Welsh full-back Billy Bancroft, Scotland sneaked home by a point.

The Irish match was twice postponed because of the severe January frost and by the time it was played in March both teams suffered a number of call-offs because of a rampaging flu epidemic. After an even first half, tries by George Campbell and Robin Welsh were enough to set Scotland up for another crack at the Triple Crown and championship against England.

*The Scotland team v England at Richmond, 1895, was captained by Robert 'Judy' MacMillan of London Scottish (middle row, second from left).*

Scotland played a tight, controlled match keeping the ball largely amongst the forwards. Only one try was scored but the match is significant in that Fred Byrne kicked England's first ever penalty and George Neilson slotted a fine kick from the touchline to equalise with Scotland's first penalty goal. It is incredible to discover that Neilson's penalty was the last by a Scotsman in a Calcutta Cup match until 1925. Neilson added a second half try to win the match 6-3 and a second Triple Crown for Scotland.

Six new caps were selected against Wales for the first match in 1896, including 18-year-old Mark Morrison who was to establish himself as one of the leading forwards of his generation in Britain. Morrison played 23 times for Scotland from 1896 to 1904, captained his country a record 15 times and led the 1903 British Isles team to South Africa. In a side led by George Neilson, Morrison's debut was a losing one on a sea of mud at Cardiff Arms Park and the side only did slightly better at Lansdowne Road, eking out a scoreless draw in what was actually a fast and exciting match.

They were to fare much better against England, however, recording a fourth successive win in front of a 16,000 crowd at Old Hampden Park, home of Queen's Park FC, as Scotland sought temporary refuge while negotiations for a new ground at Inverleith were underway. The 11-0 win, including tries for James Gowans, Henry Gedge and the 15-stone centre Charles Fleming, was well merited.

## Inverleith Opens

In 1897 and 1898 just two matches were played each season as the fallout from the A.J. Gould affair rumbled on and the Scots refused to play the Welsh. A win against Ireland was balanced by a loss to England in Manchester. Whether through over-confidence or an administrative oversight – it is not clear which – but the SFU did not bring the Calcutta Cup south with them and consequently this was one of the rare occasions when the famous cup has not been presented to the winning captain. McMillan bowed out after a distinguished career spanning 11 seasons, 1887 to 1897, and 21 caps. He was on the winning side no fewer than 14 times, won two Triple Crowns, the second as captain, and shared in four Calcutta Cup wins.

The 1898 season was another odd affair with just the two matches and Scotland achieved a win against Ireland and a 3-3 draw against England. The Irish match was a triumph for Tom Scott, both of them. The team contained T. Scott, a pacy winger, and T.M. Scott, a mobile forward, both members of Hawick, but first capped out of Langholm and Melrose

*Action from Scotland v Ireland at Powderhall Stadium, Edinburgh, 1897.*

respectively. In the second half the pace of Tom the winger helped him score two tries, the first of which was converted by Tom the goal-kicking forward. Powderhall, the old athletics and greyhound-racing stadium, was the venue for the Calcutta Cup match as the nomadic Scots waited patiently for Inverleith to be completed. A late McEwan try in the second half ensured a 3-3 draw.

James Aikman Smith's vision of a new home for the Scottish team became a reality as Inverleith was finally opened on 19 February 1899. The first match should have been against Wales, now back in the fold, but yet again severe cold caused the game to be postponed an incredible four times.

The unveiling of the magnificent new facility at the match against Ireland attracted a huge crowd but was a bit of an anti-climax as Ireland spoiled the party by winning 9-3. But the Welsh match brought better fortune as Scotland, led by the 21-year-old Morrison for the first time, overturned the form book and won 21-10 in a thrilling match which contained five tries. Wales had thrashed England 26-3 in their previous match and therefore arrived as justifiable favourites. They shaded the first half and led 10-3 at the break. But Scotland roared back into the match with tries from Douglas Monypenny and Smith, and a valuable eight points from a goal mark and a drop goal sent the crowd home in fine fettle.

## 50 Greatest Players

### MARK MORRISON Forward

**Club:** Royal High School FP

**Debut:** v Wales, 25 January 1896

**No. of Caps:** 23 **No. of Points:** 0

Morrison is the only Scot to have captained his country to two Triple Crowns (1901 and 1903) and he also led the British Isles tour to South Africa in 1903. He made the transition from schoolboy to senior level with ease and won his first cap as an 18-year-old at Cardiff. The teenager played splendidly, utilising his agricultural strength to great effect in the loose and wreaking havoc with his fearless destructive tackling. His quiet air of authority was rewarded in 1899 when he was installed as captain at the age of 21 and led his country to a comprehensive 21-10 win over Wales, the first of a record 15 matches as Scottish captain. Morrison was the first Scottish captain to win three matches against England and remains the only one to win three Calcutta Cups. His record of nine victories, two Triple Crowns and three championships over five seasons in a period of sustained success is mightily impressive and one which none of his successors have come close to matching.

Scotland finished the century in grand style, winning the Calcutta Cup clash 5-0 with late replacement John Gillespie scoring a debut try after being drafted into the team in place of Robert Neilson who had fractured his nose against Wales. Neilson's absence brought to an end a magnificent sequence for his family as it was the first time in 25 matches, since his brothers Willie and George made their debuts together against Wales way back in 1891, that at least one Neilson had not been in the starting line-up.

# Chapter Six: 1900-14
# Power Changes Hands

The period from the turn of the century up to the outbreak of the First World War saw profound changes in the game as the boundaries were pushed back, quite literally, particularly on the international scene. The closing years of the previous century had witnessed pioneering tours to the southern hemisphere which spread the rugby gospel. However, the tours to South Africa in 1903 and Australia and New Zealand in 1904 were sobering experiences for the colonial masters. Their pupils had learned their lessons well and the Test series in South Africa and New Zealand were close affairs but ultimately won by the host nations.

But worse was to follow for the four home nations when New Zealand toured the UK and France in 1905-06, with South Africa following the next season. New Zealand in particular, who were quickly dubbed the 'All Blacks' by the press on account of the colour of their kit, brought innovative new tactics which produced bold attacking play and they lost just once on their 35-match tour. South Africa were not as tactically astute as the New Zealanders and had problems adapting to the cold playing conditions in Europe but their party included massive, athletic forwards and strong-running, quick backs who set new benchmarks in terms of fitness standards. The tables had been turned in a very short period of time and it was now the southern hemisphere teams who were setting the agenda.

## Old-fashioned Values

By comparison rubgy in the British Isles had evolved slowly and particularly so in Scotland and England, where the game was run by administrators with public school backgrounds. The SFU especially was a very reactionary, autocratic body and the period was one peppered with conflict as the SFU, conservative to the core, seemingly fell out with everyone on the domestic and international fronts.

During the opening decade of the 20th century there were tours from Canada, New Zealand, South Africa and Australia as the game flourished in the nations of the British Empire, and France too made her first tentative steps into the international arena. Indeed a Scot, Cyril Rutherford, who had settled in France, was the prime mover in getting France international fixtures. A member of Racing Club de Paris, he was a good enough player to have captained France in an unofficial match against Canada in 1902 and he was also involved in making the arrangements for matches against the touring All Blacks and England in the 1905-06 season.

Rutherford had made contact with the SFU in 1907 about a match between Scotland and France but he was rebuffed as the SFU wanted to see how their other early matches went. Wales played against France in 1908 for the first time and Ireland had a match with them the following year but it was not until 1910 that Scotland played their first match against France in what was the first full Five Nations Championship season.

Having crossed swords with Wales over the A.J. Gould affair a few years earlier, in 1903 the SFU questioned the WRU's decision to allow international forward George Boots to play for his club Newport after he had signed forms for a Northern Union club. The SFU instructed their clubs not to play any team which included the aptly named Mr Boots and the WRU queried this diktat. The matter was referred to the International Board who agreed with the SFU's viewpoint, ruling that '... each union has full jurisdiction over its own clubs and it is in its power to prevent them playing against an individual player'. Although Boots played for Wales against England in January 1904, he did not appear against Scotland at St Helens a month later, but Wales had the last laugh as they won by a convincing 21-3 margin.

The following season the SFU turned the siege gun on their own players by passing a resolution forbidding any of them from profiting from writing articles on rugby for newspapers or periodicals. Shortly after that they even stopped clubs from handing out prizes at Sevens tournaments, allowing only medals or badges to be presented to the finalists to mark their achievements.

They then scrutinised the expenses of the All Blacks and Springbok touring parties. They passed the Springboks' expenses but, as they suspected, found daily expenses payments to the All Blacks players amounting to 3 shillings (15 pence) per day. When the SFU discovered that the RFU had agreed these expenses it affronted their amateur standpoint to such a degree that they threatened to cancel the next Calcutta Cup match. Once again the matter was passed to the IB who ruled:

i) Scotland was not entitled to cancel a fixture without reference to the IB;
ii) The question of those daily payments to players should not be pressed;
iii) In future no such allowances be made to any player.

In the best interests of the game the SFU went along with this verdict.

## 50 Greatest Players

**DAVID BEDELL-SIVRIGHT Wing forward**

**Clubs:** Cambridge University, Fettesian-Lorettonians, West of Scotland, Edinburgh University

**Debut:** v Wales, 27 January 1900

**No. of Caps:** 22 **No. of Points:** 6

Described by several sources as the hardest man ever to play for Scotland, Bedell-Sivright had a reputation for rough play which got him into trouble with referees and he also often riled his opponents and their supporters. Totally fearless and uncompromising as a pioneer of the wing forward role, he was far from one-dimensional, being a superb dribbler and a sure handler of the ball. He won just about every honour available; he is the only Scot to play in three Triple Crown-winning sides (1901, 1903 and 1907); the only player to tour with the 1903 and 1904 British Isles sides (he led the 1904 tour to Australasia at the age of 23); he captained his country, featured in two epic internationals against New Zealand and South Africa and captained Cambridge in two of his three Varsity matches. After retiring from international rugby he took up boxing and such was his skill and determination that he became Scottish amateur heavyweight champion in 1909.

### The International Championship Develops

The International Championship began to blossom during this period with the game becoming more tactical and an increasing number of tries being scored. Scotland enjoyed more success, landing three Triple Crowns and four championships between 1901 and 1907 and from 1900 to 1909 they beat England seven times and still held a narrow lead in the series by 1914. But if Scotland enjoyed a successful start to the century, it was Wales who dominated the domestic scene in an era often referred to as their Golden Age. From 1900 to 1911 they played 38 championship matches, winning 31 and losing just six. The Welsh won six championships, six Triple Crowns and three Grand Slams during this period and for 12 seasons were never out of the top two in the championship.

So Scotland's achievement in winning four titles in seven seasons is all the more remarkable as it came in the same era as one of the most successful sides of all time. Led by Morrison, the Scots continued to produce hard, skilful, mobile forwards well schooled in the arts of dribbling and purveyors of some of the most ferocious tackling witnessed at the time. Great players in this mould in this era include David Bedell-Sivright, Morty Dykes, Bill Scott, Bill Kyle, James McKenzie, James Greenlees, Charles Stuart and Podger Laing. Later in this era as the game became more open and forwards and backs linked more frequently, forwards such as John MacCallum, John Scott and Charles Usher came to the fore.

Behind the forwards, Scotland produced a stream of clever players throughout the back line. At half-back there were fine breaking players such as Gillespie, Ernest Simson, and Pat Munro. But it was not until the French match in 1912 that Scotland selected a recognised pair in the designated positions of scrum-half and stand-off with the Royal HSFP club partnership of John Hume and Alex Gunn who contributed positively to Scotland's fine 31-3 win.

In the centre there were such players as Phipps Turnbull, Alex Timms and later James Pearson and 'Gus' Angus, and a series of magnificent wingers in Willie Welsh, Hugh Martin, Wattie Sutherland, Willie Stewart, John Will, Alex Purves and Ken MacLeod. The team also had an abundance of reliable full backs in Harry Rottenburg, Archie Duncan, Douglas Schulze, Walter Dickson and Wattie Forrest.

## Stylish Triple Crown Success

Despite this abundance of talent, the century did not start too well for the Scots and they were winless in their three matches in 1900. Having won ten of their previous 15 encounters against Wales, they travelled to the Principality with a degree of confidence. Not only were they well beaten on the occasion but they were to record just three wins in the next 15 matches of the series. Remarkably, and uniquely in the history of the championship, Scotland completed the season with back-to-back 0-0 draws in Dublin and at home against England. That team captained by Morrison broke up at the end of the season as a number of very experienced players retired. These included the backs Scott, Campbell and Neilson and up front it was the end of the road for Scott and McEwan.

In 1901 the Scottish selectors responded boldly to the disappointments of the previous season by naming eight new caps, including seven from the outstanding Edinburgh University team, plus Beddell-Sivright, who had just the one cap. It was therefore a very inexperienced side, with a combined total of 43 caps, which trotted out to play Wales at Inverleith. Wales by comparison boasted three times as many caps and were packed full of experience. The match had been postponed from its original date due to the death of Queen Victoria and many of the crowd were dressed in black as a mark of respect. They were treated to a performance which lifted the spirits, the Scots overcoming some unsavoury tactics from the Welsh forwards to score four marvellous tries in their 18-8 win. Fell, Turnbull and Flett scored debut tries and Gillespie, who was to enjoy a record-breaking season, weighed in with a brace of tries and conversions.

Against Ireland, Scotland started in irrepressible fashion and scored all of their points in the opening 10 minutes of the match. The forwards dominated the Irish pack and the backs used the ball brilliantly. Fell and Dykes combined to put Gillespie in for the first try and then the centre pairing of Turnbull and Timms worked two openings in rapid succession for wingman Welsh to demonstrate his blistering pace and score two tries. Ireland fought back to score a try before half-time and, somewhat surprisingly, despite great enterprise shown by both teams in the rest of the match, there was no more scoring. Scotland won 9-3.

But the highlight of the season was the Calcutta Cup match. It was a remarkable triumph for this young, bold, attack-minded Scotland side who scored 11 tries in their three matches to clinch their first championship since 1895 and a third Triple Crown.

## From Heroes to Zero and Back

With the nucleus of the championship side still available it is a major surprise that Scotland managed to lose all three matches the following year, going from heroes to zero in one fell swoop. It was Scotland's first whitewash in a season where they still managed to play positive rugby but suffered some cruel injuries at key moments and, of course, were not permitted to bring on any replacements. Fell was injured early on in the 14-5 loss in Cardiff and Welsh, who had scored a brilliant try against Wales, was the victim of a heavy tackle against England and suffered a career-ending injury. Scotland had lost an outstanding finisher who ran in four tries in his eight internationals and at 22 surely had his best years in front of him. He later became a doctor and was president of the SRU immediately prior to the outbreak of the Second World War. Clearly the injury did not affect his longevity as he died in 1972, aged 93.

The selectors undertook another cull of players as they searched for the right combination for the 1903 season. And once again the introduction of fresh blood worked as six players made their debut in the first match of the season against Wales, with three further new caps selected later in the season. The result was a second Triple Crown and championship

## Great Matches

**INTERNATIONAL CHAMPIONSHIP** **Blackheath, 9 March 1901**

**England 3** **Scotland 18** **Attendance: 20,000**

Scotland produced a magnificent team performance with the forwards, spearheaded by Morrison and Bedell-Sivright, outgunning their counterparts up front, allowing the backs to shine and clinch the Triple Crown in marvellous fashion. England had endured a dismal season, losing to Wales (0-13) and Ireland (6-10), but after an early scare put Scotland under pressure in the opening 15 minutes. Having repelled England's best efforts Scotland effectively won the match in a thrilling 10-minute burst.

The pack's devastating dribbling rushes provided the platform for the first of three tries, scored by Gillespie who achieved the distinction of scoring the first try in each international during the season. Bell then found Welsh out wide with a long pass and the winger scorched over the line to score behind the posts. And then Fell and Turnbull, who had been at the heart of so many of Scotland's best efforts, combined once more for Timms to make the half-time score 15-0.

Perhaps inevitably Scotland could not sustain the frenetic pace they had set and the second period was not so spectacular with some poor tackling allowing England a consolation score. But it was the Triple Crown winners who had the last word as slick handling by the three-quarters from a scrum on the right put Fell over in the left corner to bring down the curtain as Scotland won the mythical prize for the third time in 11 seasons.

**England:** H.T. Gamlin; G.C. Robinson, W.L. Bunting (captain), N.S. Cox, E.W. Elliot; B. Oughtred, P.D. Kendall; A. O'Neill, G.R. Gibson, C. Hall, H.T.F. Weston, H. Alexander, N.C. Fletcher, C.S. Edgar, B.C. Hartley

**Scorer: Try** Robinson

**Scotland:** A.W. Duncan; W.H. Welsh, A.B. Timms, P. Turnbull, A.N. Fell; R.M. Neill, J.I. Gillespie; J. Ross, A.B. Flett, A. Frew, D.R. Bedell-Sivright, J.M. Dykes, M.C. Morrison (captain), R.S. Stronach, J.A. Bell

**Scorers: Tries** Gillespie, Welsh, Timms, Fell **Conversions** Gillespie 3

**Referee:** Mr R.W. Jeffares (Ireland)

*Gillespie (centre) opens the scoring for the third successive international.*

*Gillespie converts Scotland's second try, scored by Welsh, in the same match.*

in three seasons. But if the 1901 triumph owed much to the brilliance of the backs, this one was won through the good honest virtues of a tough, hard-grafting pack of forwards. Skipper Morrison and the increasingly influential Beddell-Sivright set the lead ably supported by Scott and Greenlees and youngsters such as Kyle, Cairns and West who quickly earned their spurs.

Scotland played Wales in foul conditions at Inverleith as a fierce gale blew in driving rain from the south-west. The waterlogged pitch was only declared playable after volunteers helped sweep the water away prior to kick-off. With the storm at their backs Scotland established a narrow 3-0 lead as Timms drop-kicked a penalty from halfway. Wales tried to play the ball through their backs in the first half to no avail and in the second half Scotland drove through their forwards to gradually gain the upper hand. Eventually Kyle was driven over for an excellent forward's try and a hard-fought 6-0 win.

An equally tough win over the Irish by one try to nil two weeks later was enough to send the Scots off in confident mood to Richmond to face a struggling England side. Despite being handicapped by the absence of Morrison and Bedell-Sivright, the pack did well in a scrappy encounter. England struck first but Timms countered with a magnificent drop goal, followed by a debut try by John Dallas to give them a deserved 7-3 half-time lead. In a seesaw match England scored next but Simson sealed the win with a superb weaving run to regain the Calcutta Cup and secure a fourth Triple Crown and championship.

## British Isles Tour to South Africa 1903

It is quite remarkable that the British Isles tour to South Africa went ahead as the Anglo-Boer War had just ended the previous year. And it says much for the passion for rugby that had developed in South Africa that they were prepared to host a tour from a nation against whom they had been in bitter conflict. The South Africans may have lost the war but they were to win the Test series. The days of missionary tours to the southern hemisphere were truly over. Mark Morrison headed a 21-man tour party which won 11 of its

22 matches and after drawing the first two Tests, lost the third and final match 8-0. As Scotland and Wales were the leading nations at the time, they provided the majority of the players. Scotland provided seven players for the tour: Morrison himself and fellow forwards Bedell-Sivright, Bill Scott and J.C. Hosack; and, in the backs, Gillespie, Louis Greig and Robert Neill.

Curiously, the first Test in Johannesburg was quite a reunion for a number of the participants. The British side included Morrison, Gillespie and Scott who had all played with Bill McEwan for Scotland in 1900. McEwan had emigrated to South Africa and was selected to play in the first Test for his new country, as was Alex Frew who had played in the 1901 Triple Crown-winning side with Gillespie, Morrison, Neill and Bedell-Sivright. To add further spice to the match, it was refereed by Bill Donaldson, who had played with Morrison (and McEwan) for Scotland back in 1896. Fittingly, after all these coincidences, the match finished as an honourable 10-10 draw.

For the first time Scotland retained the championship in 1904 in what was a fitting send-off for their legendary captain Morrison. Although there was to be no Triple Crown, Morrison did have the honour of lifting the Calcutta Cup for the third time. But the season started with a very heavy defeat at Swansea as they conceded four tries in the 21-3 defeat. However, Bedell-Sivright was at his belligerent best and he was spoken to by Mr Nicholls, the flamboyantly dressed referee, for 'roughing up' two of the Welsh backs, Bert Winfield and Dickie Owen. Mr Nicholls' attire for the afternoon – a close-fitting cap, a long overcoat and prominent white boots – would not be the choice of today's top officials although Steve Walsh of New Zealand took charge of the Wales v England match in 2003 wearing a fetching pair of bright red boots.

Four changes were made for the trip to Dublin and it seemed to do the trick as Scotland ran in five tries. Repelling early Irish pressure, Scotland fought back and Bedell-Sivright scored his first international try from a maul. Sound defence from the backs absorbed a ferocious onslaught from the Irish and Timms and Orr struck to give the Scots a 13-0 lead at half-time. In the second half, Gillespie was prominent in getting the back line moving and Simson, his fellow half-back, dummied his way over for an impressive individual try.

The final match of the season was at Inverleith where Scotland enjoyed a narrow 6-3 win over England. Left-wing John Crabbie scored the only try of the first half to make it a memorable season for the Crabbie family as his brother George had gained his only cap on the right wing against Wales. Scotland's winning try came from Simson's cleverly placed up-and-under which was misfielded and Macdonald followed up to collect the loose ball and score.

Morrison retired at the age of 26 to concentrate on farming. In Wales he would have been regarded as a national hero and perhaps rewarded with a testimonial fund. In Scotland his career and achievements are marked with a brief entry in the minutes of the SFU's AGM in 1904: 'The retiral of M.C. Morrison (Royal High School FP) was noted and appreciation expressed for his outstanding service and captaincy over the previous six years.'

Bedell-Sivright led the 1904 tour to Australia and New Zealand and was the only player selected who had toured South Africa the previous summer. All 14 matches in Australia were won, including the three Tests, but the tour hit the rocks in New Zealand where they won only two of five matches. Bedell-Sivright, plagued with injuries again, only featured in the first Test in Australia. He managed to make his mark in New Zealand, however, upsetting the hosts by making what were perceived to be patronising remarks. Bedell-Sivright was alleged to have implied afterwards that if New Zealand was to visit the 'Old Country' they may win matches against underdog teams but they would stand no chance in beating the four home nation sides. Magnificent player though he was, a soothsayer he was not, and his prediction was to be proved spectacularly wrong a little over a year later.

## Third Successive Calcutta Cup

In 1905, with Morrison newly retired and Bedell-Sivright taking an extended break 'jackerooing' around Australia after the British Isles tour to Australasia, the captaincy of the Scottish side passed appropriately to Bill Scott (West of Scotland). Scott, hewn from the same granite as his more illustrious team-mates, was vastly experienced, having played in two championship-winning sides and in all three Tests on the 1903 tour to South Africa. Four new caps were selected for the first match against Wales with half-back Pat Munro the one who was to make the biggest impact. A student at Oxford University, he was a very clever player with a keen eye for a break and went on to win 13 caps. Wales had not won at Inverleith but alas it was to prove third time lucky as they eked out a narrow 6-3 victory which set them on their way for a third Triple Crown in six seasons.

Ireland handed Scotland back-to-back defeats at Inverleith for the first time in recording only their second win in 12 away matches in the series. Their powerful centre Basil Maclear, who had been turned down by England for not being a good enough player, dominated the match. An eccentric character (he often wore white gloves – arguably the forerunners of today's 'grip mitts' – when playing), he was to be a thorn in Scotland's side for a number of seasons.

Despite competing well in the two opening matches of the campaign, Scotland travelled to London for the wooden spoon decider. England started and finished the match well but the Scots hung in and early in the second half created two vital scores. Simson, who had enjoyed an outstanding season, scored a sensational individual try. He lofted an up-and-under from the base of a scrum on the England 25 and using his pace followed up fast and caught the ball on the full to score in the corner. The second try was a triumph for teamwork with six players combining to put Robert Stronach in the clear, and the big forward just made it to the line in his last international.

Stronach is one of the unsung heroes of Scottish sport. A fine forward, he won five caps between 1901 and 1905, sharing in a Triple Crown and two Calcutta Cup wins, but he was an even more successful athlete. He excelled in the sprint hurdles and won the AAAs 120 yards title three years running, 1904 to 1906 in an era when they were regarded as the world championships.

## A Lesson from the All Blacks

Later that year, the All Blacks arrived for a tour of the British Isles and France. The early press comments were not favourable but they churned out win after win on the tour and quickly established a fearsome reputation. Tactically, they were miles ahead of the 'Old Country', adopting a seven-man scrummage formation with two in the front row, three in the middle row and

### 50 Greatest Players

**BILL KYLE Forward**

**Club:** Hawick

**Debut:** v Wales, 1 February 1902

**No. of Caps:** 21 **No. of Points:** 6

Kyle made his Scotland debut at the age of 20 in Cardiff in 1902 and although Scotland lost he played extremely well as one of the press reports emphasised, 'He alone of the team did not learn his football at a public school and he is a grand forward.' Indeed, Kyle was the first great forward from the Borders to emerge on to the international stage, cementing his place in the side as an outstanding all-round player and winning his first 16 caps in succession. A member of the 1903 Triple Crown side – his try ensured a 6-0 win over Wales – and the 1904 side that retained the championship, he was outstanding against the All Blacks in 1905. Such was his reputation in the line-out that the mighty Blacks deputed two men to sort him out! Kyle missed two seasons of international rugby but returned to share in successive Calcutta Cup wins in 1908 and 1909.

two in the back row. This formation allowed them to make a rapid heel and ensured quick ball. They also utilised three half-backs on their own put in. One put the ball in to the scrum and stood his ground in effect obstructing his opposite number. The second half-back could pick up the ball unhindered and feed the third half-back or 'rover' who was standing off. The result was a plentiful supply of quick, clean ball to feed a fast and athletic back line.

Well before the tour started the SFU made it clear that they would not pay New Zealand a requested guaranteed sum for the international match. They had a sizeable debenture debt and a bond on the new ground and would not undertake another guarantee. Instead they offered the net gate after deducting expenses for the two matches and that sum (£1,700) in actual fact turned out to be considerably more than the guarantee being sought.

There appears to have been a very cool relationship between the SFU and the New Zealand management. For their part, the New Zealanders claim not to have been met by the SFU on arrival at Waverley Station in Edinburgh and not to have been invited to a post-match dinner. This account does not quite square with a remark in the SFU AGM minutes of 1905-06 which reveals that the New Zealand management turned down the offer of theatre tickets provided by the SFU for evening entertainment. Regrettably, although the international was hard-fought and played in good spirit, the Scotland-New Zealand relationship was later to deteriorate further.

Led by Bedell-Sivright, Scotland fielded seven new caps for the international and included John Scoular and Ken MacLeod who had impressed the tourists in their 14-0 win over Cambridge University earlier on the tour. MacLeod, who was only 17, joined his brother Lewis in the centre and had a magnificent match, utilising his great pace and kicking skills to telling effect.

Having spoken with a number of players who had encountered the All Blacks earlier on the tour, the SFU imaginatively selected a seven-man pack to try and counter the New Zealand formation. Unfortunately, due to a lack of familiarity with the roles expected of them it resulted in confusion throughout the Scotland team. Nevertheless, on a frozen surface, which was not to the tourists' liking, the traditional Scottish dribbling, footrushes and fierce tackling knocked the tourists out of their stride. Scotland led 7-6 at the interval.

Significantly they lost the older MacLeod to injury early in the second half. His team-mates hung on bravely, but eventually the one-man advantage told and, as has become their trademark over the years, the All Blacks kept plugging away and scored two tries in the last five minutes.

## Domestic Disappointment

Following the encouraging performance against the All Blacks the championship season was a real disappointment, with a win over Ireland sandwiched between losses to Wales and England.

Indeed, Scotland started explosively in Cardiff and but for a bizarre incident early in the match they may well have come away with a win. Bedell-Sivright and Kyle put enormous pressure on the Welsh half-backs and the former, following up on a loose ball, touched it down for a try. Unfortunately, it was disallowed as the local chief constable was strutting about in the Welsh in goal area as Bedell-Sivright pursued the ball. The ball bounced off the policeman back into the Scotsman's hands but the referee ruled that the ball was dead and the score was disallowed. The outspoken Bedell-Sivright's thoughts on this incident have not been recorded but they are certain to have been uncomplimentary about high-ranking Welsh police officers.

Maurice Walter won his first cap in the 13-6 win over Ireland in Dublin having turned down an invitation to play for England against Ireland just two weeks earlier. He went on to win eight caps, playing in the 1907 Triple Crown-winning side.

England, having lost to both Ireland and Wales, and to Scotland for three successive seasons, were not expected to pose too much of a threat on their

### 50 Greatest Players

**WATTIE SUTHERLAND Wing/Centre**

**Club:** Hawick

**Debut:** v Wales, 5 February 1910

**No. of Caps**: 13 **No. of Points**: 12

Sutherland made his Hawick debut against Gala as a 17-year-old in 1908 and such was his progress that 16 months later he won his first Scotland cap on the right wing against Wales. He also played against England that year and impressed so much that he was invited to tour South Africa with the British Isles that summer. Unfortunately he had to decline as he could not afford the time away. He scored four international tries, the pick of them against England in 1912 when his searing pace took him clear of the cover to score in the corner. A double international (he also represented Scotland over 220 yards) he was not just a flying machine and drew huge praise for his defensive performance against England in 1913 when switched to centre because of injury.
One English paper commented, 'The fair-haired, anaemic-looking Scot, with the courage of a lion and the speed of a deer, was the heroic figure at Twickenham on Saturday.'

visit north. However, they turned the tables on their hosts, who were handicapped by early injuries to MacLeod and Bedell-Sivright, to win 9-3.

### Spectacular Score Sinks Springboks

The South Africans, led by Paul Roos, who coined the nickname 'Springboks' to prevent the British press inventing one of their own, may not have made the same impact as the All Blacks but after overcoming early difficulties in the scrum they lost just one Test match on the tour of 1906-07, against Scotland. They did not bring with them any real innovations but they impressed with their massive athletic forwards and strong-running backs. However, the popularity of rugby in South Africa was not in doubt as crowds of people flocked to Cape Town harbour to wave the tourists off, bringing the traffic in the city to a standstill.

Scotland were their first opponents in the Test series and, as the Scots had two other home matches, the international was awarded to Hampden Park. The Glasgow public responded magnificently to the occasion and a record crowd of 30,000 turned out to watch Scotland beat the tourists 6-0 on a rain-saturated pitch. The conditions were tailor-made for the fast-dribbling Scottish forwards and early in the second half came one of the most spectacular tries ever scored by a Scotsman. Munro, at half-back, broke to the left from a scrum and when confronted by defenders he aimed a high and clever cross-kick to the right wing. Ken MacLeod reacted the quickest and gave chase, his great pace enabling him to catch the sopping wet, heavy leather ball as he ran flat out. His momentum took him clear of the despairing defence as he sprinted along the touchline for a magnificent try at the corner. Sandy Thorburn later asked Tennent Sloan, who had played in the Scotland three-quarter line that day, about Munro's cross kick, 'I saw it all right and ran for it but couldn't get near it. It was only MacLeod's tremendous pace that allowed him to get under the ball and then he caught it safely at full pace.'

### More Domestic Glory

The win against South Africa was the catalyst for another successful season and the claiming of a fifth Triple Crown and a sixth championship in 1907. This Triple Crown made Scotland the most successful team up until this stage, placing them one ahead of Wales and two ahead of England in the success stakes. Four successive wins in the season was a new record as well for Scotland who had a wealth of experience at their disposal. They had a ferocious pack with Bedell-Sivright, Scott and MacCallum at its core, clever half-backs and a dashing three-quarter line full of verve and pace.

Wales persevered with seven forwards after the tactic worked effectively in their 22-0 hammering of England. But it foundered on a watertight defence and the opportunism of the Scottish backs who created excellent tries for flying wingers Alex Purves and Hugh Monteith to secure a narrow 6-3 win in the opening match.

The 15-3 win against Ireland took a while to come. During an even first half Maclear unleashed a devastating hand-off which knocked out Bedell-Sivright, rated as the hardest player ever to pull on the blue shirt, who needed time to recover on the touchline before resuming. But in the second half the Scottish backs got into their stride and began to carve great holes in the Irish defence which eventually conceded three tries.

Scotland arrived at Blackheath in search of a Triple Crown with England needing to win to avoid a whitewash. The Scots did all their scoring in the first half with the wind at their backs and MacLeod tried his best to exploit the conditions, launching at least six drop goal attempts at the English posts. But Scotland did their scoring with two excellent tries. The first from Simson, breaking from midfield, embarked on a weaving run for a wonderful individual effort, and then Purves got on the end of a forwards drive to score his fourth try in successive matches.

Bedell-Sivright is the only Scot to play in three Triple Crown-winning sides, which is a remarkable achievement, although Scott, who retired after this match, was first capped in 1900 but missed the 1901 season. The remarkable Simson, one of the great half-backs of his era, also retired after this match.

## Going Downhill

Scotland had enjoyed a marvellous start to the century, winning three Triple Crowns and four championships in seven seasons in one of the most successful eras that Scottish rugby has ever enjoyed. But, as they say, all good things must come to an end and during the period from 1908-14 Scotland's record was decidedly mixed. Fourteen of the 23 matches played had been won from 1901-07, but there were to be only nine wins in the next 27 matches in the seven seasons running up to the outbreak of the First World War. This included a real low in 1911 when Scotland were whitewashed, losing all four matches and becoming France's first championship scalp.

There were some occasional good results such as beating England to win the Calcutta Cup in 1908 and 1909, which meant that in the 17 matches played since 1893, England had won only three times. But by 1910, England had emerged from her slump in form following the defection of so many clubs to the Northern Union and they won the championship that year for

*The Scotland team v England, 1907. The plaster on Bedell-Sivright's nose (middle row, second left) was a reminder of the tackle made on him by Maclear in the Ireland match.*

the first time in 11 seasons. They had a new permanent home at Twickenham and Scotland's record there has been miserable. In 41 visits to Twickenham since 1911 Scotland have won just four times – in 1926, 1938, 1971 and 1983. Pre-Twickenham, when England played at a number of different grounds, Scotland recorded 10 wins in 18 cross-border raids and also earned a couple of creditable draws.

They lost the remaining seven pre-war matches to Wales and won just three of the remaining seven fixtures against Ireland. Even against France, who had little international experience, Scotland lost one of the three matches played though the SFU viewed the early matches against France as trial matches for later in the season.

The match they lost 16-15 Paris in 1911 was something of a farce as the Scottish team felt that the referee was very lenient with his interpretation of the laws in relation to the French but kept the Scots to the letter of the law. By the time he started to be more even-handed the damage had been done even though the result was still in Scottish hands so to speak. But when a late opening was worked and all an unnamed player had to do was hold on to the pass he knocked on with the line at his mercy. It was that sort of afternoon.

Finally, following disgraceful crowd behaviour at the France v Scotland match in 1913 which Scotland won 21-3, the SFU refused to play against

## 50 Greatest Players

### CHARLES USHER Forward

**Clubs:** London Scottish, United Services, Edinburgh Wanderers

**Debut:** v England, 16 March 1912

**No. of Caps:** 16 **No. of Points:** 6

Usher, a career soldier, was one of the great forwards of his era which spanned the First World War. First capped against England in 1912, he enjoyed a splendid debut scoring the second try which helped regain the Calcutta Cup. He won five more caps before the outbreak of war which included a spell as a prisoner of war but finished, with his promotion to captain, in the Gordon Highlanders. His leadership skills were much in demand as rugby resumed and he led Scotland to wins over Wales and Ireland in 1920. He also played in the win against France that season, coping admirably with the added distraction of having his new wife with him as part of their honeymoon! In Usher's final season he led the team throughout and in a deeply poignant and appreciated gesture piped the team out before the French match in Paris followed by his team-mates carrying a massive wreath in honour of the fallen players of both nations.

France the following season. The referee had incensed large sections of the crowd with some of his decisions and they were baying for his blood by the full-time whistle. Several spectators tried to assault him as he left the pitch and he had to be protected by players and the police. Scotland full-back Dickson, who was profoundly deaf, completely misinterpreted the crowd's hostile actions remarking to Usher as they left the pitch how sporting the spectators were, wanting to get so close to applaud the Scots off the pitch!

But the SFU, although not blaming the French organisation or the team for what happened, felt that an unacceptable situation had arisen where the referee's authority had been questioned and therefore they would not fulfil the next fixture with France even though it would have been in Edinburgh.

The period ended on a low note on and off the pitch as Scotland won just one of their six fixtures before the outbreak of the First World War. The Great War was to cost the lives of 111 international rugby players including 30 Scots, nine of whom played against France in 1913.

# Chapter Seven: 1920-29
# The Golden Age

After the horrors of the Great War it took Scottish club rugby a while to gather itself and begin the rebuilding process. Many brave young men from all four corners of the globe perished, including 30 Scottish international players.

The traumatic experience of London Scottish reflects that of many clubs at the time, having a large chunk of its playing membership wiped out during the hostilities. On the final weekend of the 1913-14 season, Scottish fielded four teams. Out of those 60 players 45 died during the war and in total over 100 members or former members of the club lost their lives during this tragic period with a further 52 wounded.

In common with a number of clubs it was considered nigh on impossible to field more than one team in the 1919-20 season. But as life returned to a semblance of normality so too did the desire for some camaraderie and fun and London Scottish eventually fielded three teams that season.

The SFU committee itself had lost members, with A.D. Flett, the honorary secretary-treasurer, lost in action. H.M. Simson (Watsonians) was appointed as his successor. As club rugby started to re-establish itself the committee was very sensitive to club needs and approved numerous grant applications to enable clubs to get back on their feet as quickly as possible. The grants helped them lease grounds or build new or enhance existing facilities.

### Renewed Enthusiasm

Once the club scene restarted it was soon apparent that there was a renewed enthusiasm for the game and large crowds were attracted to watch the big matches. For certain matches special trains were run between the cities and the capacity at Inverleith was frequently under pressure because of the demand to watch international rugby.

The international side enjoyed its most successful period ever in the 1920s and in the seven seasons from 1922-29 Scotland won a Grand Slam and Triple Crown, four Five Nations Championship titles and were runners-up twice with some magnificent players emerging. In the backs there were the likes of Dan Drysdale, the first in a long line of marvellous full-backs from George Heriot's FP; free-scoring wingers such as Ian Smith, A.C. 'Johnny' Wallace and a young chap called Eric Liddell; creative geniuses in the centre

*Left to right: Jimmy Nelson, Herbert Waddell, Jimmy Dykes and Max Simmers (all Glasgow Accies) all featured in the side during Scotland's golden age of the 1920s.*

led by 'Prince' Phil Macpherson and others such as Leslie Gracie, George Aitken, Jimmy Dykes and Max Simmers. And at half-back there was the telepathic Glasgow Academical club partnership of Herbert Waddell and Jimmy Nelson and Selkirk's Willie Bryce who would have won many more caps but for injury though somehow he managed to re-invent himself as an international hockey player. Up front there were many in the traditional Scottish mould: hard tackling, fast, mobile forwards with John Bannerman, John Buchanan, Doug Davies, David Kerr, and Jimmy Scott all making their mark at the very highest level.

The SFU Committee had lost none of its bite following the cessation of hostilities. Although international relations resumed with France which, but for the outbreak of war, would have re-started in 1915, the crusade against anything which smacked of professionalism continued.

Once again Wales' flirtation with the Northern Union caused the SFU to ask questions, this time querying the status of a number of their players selected to play an All Blacks XV in 1919. 'Jock' Wemyss, who was first capped in 1914, was quizzed about writing articles on rugby citing the bye-law introduced in 1903 prohibiting club members doing just that. Wemyss explained that he had retired from playing but caused consternation in the committee when he 'guested' for Leicester six months later against Heriot's at Inverleith. In similar vein, a journalist had a request for reinstatement as a player rejected; two Aberdeen players were suspended for providing match reports to newspapers; and six Borders players were suspended for playing in trial matches for Northern Union clubs.

Finally, they dealt with Scotland cap Neil Macpherson most severely after it emerged that his club Newport had given him a magnificent gold watch worth £21 as a reward for being a member of the unbeaten Newport team in 1923. The SFU wrote to Welsh-born Macpherson requesting that he return the watch to the club and when he courteously refused they suspended him sine die. Furthermore, they once again placed a ban on any Scottish club playing against Newport. The SRU then brought the matter to the attention of the IB which ruled that, with the exception of wedding presents, any mementoes given by a club to a player must not exceed £2 in value. The SRU, apparently satisfied with this ruling, lifted Macpherson's suspension but never again selected him to play for Scotland.

Two British Isles tours were planned during this period; however, the SFU declined to become involved in the organisation but accepted that if the IB considered it would benefit the game in the southern hemisphere they would not object. For the proposed 1930 tour to New Zealand they declined an invitation to have a place on the selection committee but did offer to answer any queries about players under consideration.

Although nine of the 29-strong tour party to South Africa were Scots, the SFU's lack of commitment to the selection process partly explained why only one Scot, Willie Welsh of Hawick, was selected for the 1930 tour.

Two major touring parties visited the British Isles in the 1920s, the All Blacks in 1924-25 and the NSW Waratahs (Australia) in 1927-28. Scotland declined to play the All Blacks, continuing the uneasy relationship between the two nations which was a great shame as the Scots won the Grand Slam later that season and it would have been a cracking match. The All Blacks, led by Govan-born Cliff Porter, won all 30 matches, became known as the 'Invincibles' and considered that their match against Oxford University to be the toughest on the tour. Three of Oxford's brilliant three-quarter line Macpherson, Wallace and Aitken, all starred for Scotland in the Grand Slam.

## Magnificent Murrayfield

A combination of a general upsurge in interest for rugby, particularly at international level, and the rapid deterioration in the state of Inverleith caused the SFU to start the search for a new international venue. During the war there had been little use made of Inverleith as a sporting venue and no maintenance work was carried out at all. As a result when it was examined a number of the wooden enclosure seats, which had been exposed to the elements for 20 years, had rotted and were replaced by metal seats. Essential painting work was required throughout the stadium and the facility had a distinctly shabby feel to it.

Though it would have been relatively easy to upgrade the facilities the old stadium was too small and demand for stand tickets in particular far

## 50 Greatest Players

**JOHN BANNERMAN Second row**

**Clubs:** Glasgow High School FP, Oxford University

**Debut:** v France, 22 January 1921

**No. of Caps:** 37 **No. of Points:** 6

In his first year out of school, Bannerman's rousing performance for Glasgow against Edinburgh brought his raw but richly promising abilities to the attention of the national selectors. Still only 19, he was drafted into Scotland's second row for the French match and he remained a permanent fixture for nine seasons during which he won 37 consecutive caps. At the time this was a world record and a Scottish record for almost 33 years. A great enthusiast and a powerful personality he made a huge impact on the world of rugby.

An exceptional line-out forward, solid scrummager and a veritable dervish in the loose, he was a master dribbler, a first-class exponent of the long forgotten but highly effective footrushes. A member of the great sides of the 1920s which won the championship in 1925, 1926, 1927 and 1929, he captained Scotland to a Calcutta Cup victory on his final appearance.

exceeded availability. One option was to build another stand on the east side of the ground and estimates were sought for this purpose but the costs in excess of £20,000 were deemed to be prohibitive. James Aikman Smith had again undertaken a thorough search of Edinburgh and in 1922 he reported to the committee that 19 acres of land in the Murrayfield area belonging to the Edinburgh Polo Club were available. Within three months the land had been purchased and plans were made to construct a new stadium.

Sir Robert McAlpine and Sons of Glasgow were appointed to construct the new facility and a design competition for a new stand was held and won by R.F. Shearer of Edinburgh. Once again the SFU successfully issued debentures to help finance the costs of the project and the initial issue was quickly over-subscribed. The new magnificent ground was opened on 21 March 1925 in the best possible circumstances for a match against England in which Scotland won their first Grand Slam plus the Triple Crown and the Five Nations Championship and, of course, the Calcutta Cup. A record crowd for any rugby international of 70,000 attended the match and justified the SRU's (as they were now known) bold decision to fund and build a second new stadium in 26 years.

## A Winning Side Takes Shape

Scotland and England were to be the two most prominent teams during the 1920s. The Scottish forwards might not have been quite as formidable a unit as some of their predecessors but they were fast, mobile and aggressive enough to supply plentiful good ball for an outstanding backline which featured the mercurial talents of Phil Macpherson at centre who struck up a deadly partnership with Ian Smith, the 'Flying Scotsman'. In those days it was commonplace for a centre and wing to work in partnership and there was no more potent combination than Macpherson and Smith. In 17 matches together – from Smith's debut against Wales in 1924 to Macpherson's final match against England in 1932 – Smith scored 21 of his record 24 tries. With such an incredible strike rate it is just a pity that circumstances and injury did not allow the pair to play more matches together.

## The International Championship Resumes

Scotland started well in the first championship after the war despite six of the team which lost to England in their previous match having perished during the conflict. Indeed, just three retained their places from that match, captain 'Gus' Angus and stalwart forwards Charles Usher and 'Podger' Laing. The Scots travelled to France for the first match at the Parc des Princes. Scotland fielded eight new caps as against France's 11 and the extra core of experience proved just about enough to secure them a narrow 5-0 win which included a debut try for wing George Crole. Usher, who was a career soldier, probably needed all his diplomatic skills when explaining to his new wife that their honeymoon in Paris would have to be interrupted for 80 minutes or so as he was playing in a rugby match. There is no record as to how successful the honeymoon was but Usher,

*The Scotland team that beat France on New Year's Day 1920 in the first international played after the First World War.*

**50 Greatest Players**

**PHIL MACPHERSON Centre/Stand-off**

**Clubs:** Oxford University, Edinburgh Academicals

**Debut:** v France, 2 January 1922

**No. of Caps:** 26 **No. of Points:** 12

Scotland's 1925 Grand Slam captain, rated as the most brilliant attacking centre of his era bar none, he had the full box of magician's tricks comprising pace, jinks, swerves, sidesteps and an eminently purchasable dummy. His defence was pinpointed as a weakness but he was convinced that a man on the ground was out of the game. Macpherson was a master shadow tackler often shepherding opponents out of play, but when required he could tackle with the best of them. But it was his legendary partnership with wing Ian Smith which posed the most potent threat. Between them the pair scored 25 of Scotland's 49 tries in their 17 matches together over eight seasons. Normally a right-wing partnership, they switched to the left for the 1925 season with electrifying results, yielding eight of Scotland's 15 tries in their three matches together.

who was prominent in the build up to the Scottish try, did well enough in the match to be appointed team captain for the rest of the season.

Having opened with a win the Scots hosted Wales at Inverleith. Wales were full of confidence having beaten Scotland in seven successive matches since 1908. But the Scots did well to stop the rot winning 9-5. Oddly, Scotland included two players who played for Welsh clubs, Neil Macpherson of Newport and Eric Fahmy of Abertillery. Perhaps their inside knowledge of the Welsh players helped. The match was hard fought in perfect conditions and Allen Sloan's try from a brilliant diagonal run that started in midfield and scored in the corner gave Scotland a lead they never lost.

Scotland were improving as the season progressed and they cruised to a 19-0 win over Ireland, recording their 13th win over the Irish in 16 matches. A Grand Slam and Triple Crown was at stake as the Scots travelled to Twickenham in good heart. But after losing their opener to Wales, England had won their next two matches and their big pack and fast backs were too much for a brave Scotland who went down 13-4, outscored by three tries to nil.

## The Glamour of International Rugby

The following year, 1921, was a frustrating one for Scotland after the bright start to the decade. Only one win was recorded, against Wales who were beaten at home for the first time in 29 years; but Scotland, too, lost at home – to France for the first time, albeit narrowly, and in Ireland by a single point before crashing heavily at home against England who won the Grand Slam. Bannerman was one of seven new caps that year and, if he was to be the most successful, Leslie Gracie in the centre was to make his mark in the next four seasons as an attacking centre.

The 3-0 loss to France was swiftly countered by a marvellous win in Wales at Swansea for the first time since 1893. Such was the interest in the match that a massive crowd of some 50,000 tried to cram in to the small ground at St Helens. Crowd congestion meant that spectators repeatedly spilled on to the pitch and at one stage the players retired to the changing rooms as mounted police tried to clear some space. The referee called the captains together to discuss whether they felt the match should be abandoned with the Scots tempted to vote with their feet at one stage.

However, it was agreed to continue and Scotland took full advantage of the wind at their backs to lead 11-0 at half-time. The Welsh tactics in the second half were to let fly with drop goal attempts at every opportunity and two successful goals reduced the Scots' lead to 11-8. However, close to full time Sloan broke away on the right and literally picked his way through a packed pile of spectators sitting in the goal area to find a place to touch down and seal the match. Due to the lengthy delays caused by crowd problems the match finished well behind schedule so the Scots dashed off the pitch, grabbed their clothes and rushed to their awaiting bus to make sure they caught the last train north. So much for the glamour of international rugby.

The rest of the season finished in disappointment, losing 9-8 at Lansdowne Road and, most embarrassingly, suffering an 18-0 home loss to England in a match which marked the 50th anniversary of the fixture.

*Six survivors of the first international pictured before the 50th anniversary match on 19 March 1921. Back row: A.S. Gibson (Manchester), Dr J. Forsyth (Edinburgh University), C.W. Sherrard (Blackheath) Front row: R.R. Osborne (Manchester), A. Buchanan (Royal High School FP), Sir J.H. Luscombe (Gipsies).*

## One Draw too Many

For the first time in the Five Nations Championship there were three draws during the season in 1922, a total equalled only once since, in 1962. Unfortunately, Scotland featured in two of them, which occurred in the first two matches against France and Wales.

Significant Scotland debutants this season included three outstanding backs in Macpherson, Dykes and the 19-year-old Eric Liddell. Liddell was not long out of school and had enrolled for a pure science degree at Edinburgh University the previous autumn. Pressed into service for the university as a centre or winger, his sensational club form earned him a Scottish trial and he was rapidly promoted to the international team.

Many sprinters are dismissed as being quick but lacking any real heart or determination on a rugby pitch. Liddell quickly earned the respect of his peers and opponents as a fearsomely determined runner who revelled in defensive chores. In his seven internationals he was only on the losing side once, against England in his last match, and scored three tries. It is impossible to argue with his decision to concentrate fully on athletics as he was to achieve immortality, winning the 1924 Olympic 400 metres title, but it will always be a case of what might have been on the rugby stage.

Liddell's debut against France on 2 January 1922 was, ironically, at the Stade Colombes, where just over two years later he would win his Olympic title. A record 37,000-strong crowd turned out to see the match played in dreadful conditions and each team scored a try apiece. Despite coming from behind and dominating the second half the Scots could not put the winning score on the board.

One month later the Scots achieved another draw, 9-9 against Wales, and just one of three draws in the series between the two nations. Agonisingly, having worked hard to hang on to a 9-5 lead, the Welsh equalised with an injury-time drop goal and it was a visibly stunned crowd which drifted out of the ground as the full-time whistle blew.

At last it was third time lucky as Scotland achieved a narrow 6-3 home win over Ireland despite trailing 3-0 at the interval. The Scottish pack grew in strength as the match progressed and tries by scrum-half Bryce and the winner by Liddell, his first for Scotland, earned them a thoroughly merited victory.

But, once again, the English scuppered Scotland's season as five changes were made for the Calcutta Cup match, four of which were in the back division. A converted try by Dykes gave Scotland the half-time lead and real hope of a first win at Twickenham but a splendid second-half performance by the legendary half-back pairing of Davies and Kershaw sparked England into action to win 11-5.

A third place finish was satisfactory for Scotland given the two draws but it was clear that the nucleus of a very good side was forming as the next few seasons would confirm.

## More Crowd Control Problems

In 1923 the Scots managed to get out of the drawing habit as they recorded three excellent wins at the start of the season. Significant additions to what was a fairly settled group included Dan Drysdale at full-back, Johnny Wallace on the wing and David Kerr, Drysdale's Heriot's FP clubmate, in the pack. Drysdale enjoyed a fine debut at Inverleith against France and Gracie's excellent all-round play brought out the best in his back line as Scotland won 16-3.

As was often the case the Welsh match was the one with most incident. The match was played at Cardiff and attracted a record crowd of 40,000 to the capital but it did not appear as if the WRU had learnt anything about crowd control. The police closed the gates before kick-off but it was too late and many of the crowd were forced to line the pitch during the match. Although Liddell equalised an early Welsh score the Scots trailed 8-3 with 15 minutes to go. A try by Ludovic Stuart narrowed the gap to two points, and with three minutes to go came a fantastic winning score by Gracie. From a wheeled scrum on the Welsh 25 Gracie took a long overhead pass from stand-off McQueen. Running diagonally left he aimed

*Captain Charlie Usher pipes out the Scotland team against France at Stade Colombes, 1922.*

to go between the two Welsh centres and as he did a gap opened as Johnson was worried by the threat of Liddell further out. Gracie swerved round Male, his opposite number, wrong footing him, and sprinted for the try line. He ran along the dead-ball line to score close to the posts but one of his boots caught a Welsh schoolboy, who was sitting on the line, full in the mouth and unfortunately removed his front teeth. That did not prevent a number of Welsh supporters from sportingly chairing him off the pitch at full time in recognition of his brilliant try.

Scotland won for a ninth time in 18 visits to Ireland and were therefore rightly confident for the Calcutta Cup match which proved to be a very tight affair with the result turning on a missed conversion by Scotland. Played in perfect conditions in front of the Duke of York there was nothing in it throughout the match. Level at 3-3 at half-time, Scotland nudged ahead with a fine try by skipper Gracie. Unfortunately, Drysdale missed the conversion and England's late try by Voyce was converted by Luddington to deny Scotland at least a share of the spoils.

## A Roller-coaster Ride

In 1924 Scotland finished as runners-up to England for the second consecutive season, but nonetheless would have been disappointed with what was a roller-coaster ride in terms of results and performances. The beginning and the end was hugely disappointing starting with a shock defeat by France and a heavy loss to the 'Auld Enemy', but sandwiched in between was marvellous win over Wales and solid victory over Ireland, both at home.

Once again poor weather conditions in Paris spoiled the match and French Secretary Cyril Rutherford worked something of a minor miracle by transferring the match from the flooded Stade Colombes to Stade Pershing. Despite the conditions, the Scots could not complain at the result as France outscored them by four tries to one.

Understandably, following the underachievement in Paris, changes were made for the Welsh match including the wholesale reshaping of the backline. Gracie was unavailable and this allowed the selectors to field the legendary Oxford three-quarter line for the first time. Only Wallace survived the French debacle. Macpherson replaced Gracie and new caps were awarded to Ian Smith and George Aitken. The result was nothing short of startling as the Scots ran in eight tries with Smith leading the way scoring a debut hat-trick, and Macpherson and Wallace chipping in with one apiece. The power, pace and imagination of the Scottish backs was too much for the dispirited Welsh who could only manage consolation scores after Scotland eased up after reaching 35-0.

An altogether tougher match against Ireland followed with Irish spoiling tactics almost paying off and Scotland were happy to score three tries, including a brace by Waddell, to win 13-8. But once again the season's finale was spoiled by the English who completed back-to-back Grand Slams for the first time, recording a seventh win in a row against the beleaguered Scots.

At the end of the season a British Isles tour party was selected to go to South Africa. Although nine Scots were selected in the party of 29, leading players such as Macpherson and Gracie declined invitations to tour. The Scots selected were: Dan Drysdale (George Heriot's FP), Roy Kinnear (George Heriot's FP), Ian Smith (Oxford University), Herbert Waddell (Glasgow Academical), Doug Davies (Hawick), Kelvin Hendrie (George Heriot's FP), Bob Howie (Kirkcaldy), Neil Macpherson (Newport) and Andrew Ross (Kilmarnock). All bar Ross played some part in the Test series with Drysdale, Kinnear, Macpherson, Howie and Davies appearing in all four Test matches. The tour was a very difficult one and the British team managed just nine wins in the 21-match schedule and lost the Test series 3-0 with one draw.

### The First Grand Slam Arrives

The following year, 1925, was momentous for Scottish rugby. Scotland won their first Grand Slam, the Scottish Football Union became the Scottish Rugby Union and the magnificent new stadium at Murrayfield was opened for the first match against England.

Not only was the season a great success but the Scots fulfilled their potential playing a marvellous brand of enterprising and entertaining rugby, scoring 15 tries as they swept all before them. Seven new caps were blooded during the season, the most notable being Jimmy Nelson, who joined club partner Waddell to form an outstanding half-back partnership. Nelson, who owed his place to Bryce's unfortunate career-ending knee injury, was to establish himself as one of Scotland's most outstanding scrum-halves and went on to win 25 caps over seven seasons.

The Scottish backs were in sensational form in their opening two matches and, quite remarkably, 12 of the 13 tries scored in these two games were shared between wingers Smith and Wallace. Wallace managed an impressive two tries in both, but Smith broke all records by scoring an unbelievable four times in each match. In just five matches at international level this remarkable young man, who had only started playing rugby when he went up to Oxford in 1922, had scored 11 tries, all of them in partnership with Macpherson.

For the last match to be played at Inverleith a crowd of some 20,000 turned out – some no doubt to witness a partial eclipse of the sun which reached its maximum during the first haf – but did not appear to affect the match. Macpherson, leading Scotland for the first time, was at his very best and had a hand in most of the scores, although it was not until the second half that the Scots got on top of the French. A devastating three-try burst from Smith, who, along with debutant Nelson, had an outstanding afternoon, killed them off and helped Scotland to a 25-4 win.

*Bob Howie wins a line-out for Scotland in the 1925 Grand Slam match against England.*

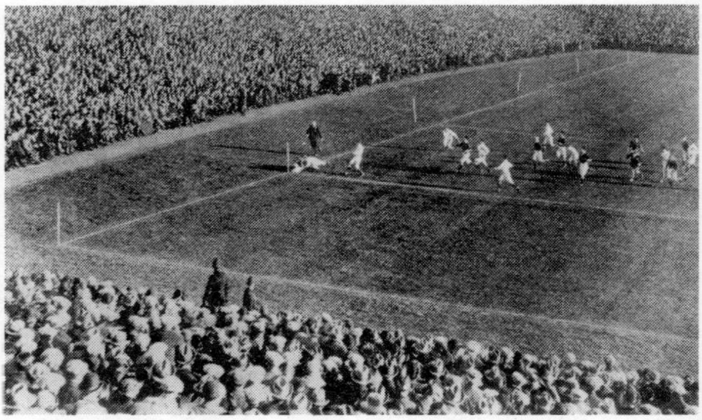

*Johnnie Wallace scores Scotland's second try in the same game.*

Smith started against Wales in the manner he had finished against France and opened proceedings with a hat-trick of tries to help Scotland to an 18-0 half-time lead. After the break, Scotland continued relentlessly and led 24-5 before Wales put in a strong finish to close the winning margin to 24-14.

Although the try-scoring feats slowed up against Ireland, determined defending restricting Scotland to just two tries, the pace and passing skills of the back line reached sensational heights at times. Macpherson was absent but Waddell returned at stand-off and ran the show, his dropped goal sealed the match and he sparked a fabulous move in which backs and forwards combined for MacMyn to score under the posts.

The magnificent new Murrayfield stadium opened its gates for the first time for the final match of the 1925 season – Scotland v England. A record crowd estimated at some 70,000 turned out on a beautiful day to watch a thrilling match during which Scotland came from behind three times and the result was in doubt right up to the final kick of the match.

## Great Matches

**FIVE NATIONS CHAMPIONSHIP** **Murrayfield, 21 March 1925**
**Scotland 14** **England 11** **Attendance: 70,000**

Such was the interest in the new Murrayfield stadium and the prospect of Scotland winning the Grand Slam, that several thousand disappointed spectators were turned away as the gates were closed early. This action drew vigorous protests from customers who demanded a refund or to be allowed admission. Eventually the protesters were allowed in through the players' entrance under the stand and accommodated around the touchline.

England drew first blood when Luddington kicked an early penalty. Just before half-time Scotland countered when skipper Macpherson cut through with a characteristic piece of magic, and found the supporting Waddell who fed Nelson. The scrum-half unleashed a ferocious hand-off to clear his path for a try by the posts. Drysdale's conversion made it 5-3. But just as it looked as if the home side would lead at the interval, Hamilton-Wickes scored and Luddington's conversion gave England the lead.

Worse was to follow as England struck first after the restart; this time Corbett's cross kick eluded the covering Waddell and England skipper Wakefield reacted quickest to score. Two conversion attempts were to have a dramatic outcome on the match. MacMyn charged Luddington and kicked away the ball before the conversion could be taken. Then, following Wallace's excellent try for which he sprinted 20 yards to score in the right corner to become the first Scot to score tries in all four championship matches in one season, Gillies landed a splendid touchline conversion. What could have been 8-13 was 10-11, thanks to the contrasting fortunes of the respective goal kickers.

For 20 minutes it was all Scotland but they could not find a way over England's line. Finally, with five minutes left, Nelson found Waddell with an enormous pass and from 25 yards out in front of the posts the stand-off coolly dropped a goal to regain the lead: 14-11. Now it was Scotland's turn to defend for their lives and they bravely tackled themselves quite literally to a standstill. Finding no way through the swarming blue shirts, Holliday unleashed a despairing long-range drop at goal which only narrowly missed. And Murrayfield erupted seconds later when the final whistle sounded as Scotland won a famous victory at their splendid new home.

**Scotland:** D. Drysdale; A.C Wallace, G.G. Aitken, G.P.S. Macpherson (captain), I.S. Smith; H. Waddell, J.B. Nelson; R.A. Howie, J.C.H. Ireland, D.S. Davies, J.M. Bannerman, D.J. MacMyn, J.R. Paterson, A.C. Gillies, J.W. Scott
**Scorers: Tries** Nelson, Wallace **Conversions** Drysdale, Gillies **Drop Goal** Waddell

**England:** T.E. Holliday; R.H. Hamilton-Wickes, H.M. Locke, L.J. Corbett, S.G.U. Considine; E. Myers, A.T. Young; R. Cove-Smith, J.S. Tucker, D.C. Cumming, R.R.F. MacLennan, W.G.E. Luddington, A.F. Blakiston, W.W. Wakefield (captain), A.T. Voyce
**Scorers: Tries** Hamilton-Wickes, Wakefield **Conversion** Luddington **Penalty Goal** Luddington

**Referee:** Mr A.E. Freethy (Wales)

## Success Continues

Scotland retained the Championship in 1926 recording excellent away wins at Stade Colombes and Twickenham for the first time, sneaking past Wales at home but inexplicably tripping up against Ireland to lose for the first time at Murrayfield. However, within this sequence of results, Scotland won six championship matches in a row to record their best ever run of results in the competition. Playing in his last match for Scotland, against France, Wallace scored a hat-trick and in total he scored 11 tries in nine internationals including one in each match of the Grand Slam season.

Scotland's win a fortnight later over Wales was a closer affair but it was their sixth consecutive victory over the Welsh. The Welsh had clearly done their homework on Smith as they had experienced the devastation he could wreak in the last two matches. Although the Welsh defence was good, the backs could do little with the ball and Waddell won the match cutting through for a fine solo try.

The first defeat at Murrayfield was hard to bear. The pitch cut up badly following persistent rain and the conditions became a great leveller. Scotland actually got over the Irish line a couple of times only to be called back for

### 50 Greatest Players

**DAN DRYSDALE Full-back**

**Club:** Heriot's FP, Oxford University, London Scottish

**Debut:** v France, 20 January 1923

**No. of Caps:** 26 **No. of Points:** 45

The first in the illustrious line of eight Herioters who have played full-back for Scotland, Drysdale set the standards for his successors to follow. Unquestionably the leading Scottish full-back between the wars, he was probably the best in his position of his generation in Britain. He carried out his defensive duties with aplomb and was greatly admired for his willingness to run the ball to link with his three-quarters. He toured South Africa in 1924 as the Lions' first choice full-back, playing in 13 matches and all four Tests. Back home, Drysdale was a heavy contributor to the 1925 Grand Slam and led Scotland the following season to a second championship, narrowly missing a second Slam. He finished with 45 points in internationals, a paltry total compared to the modern era, but 19 of his 21 kicks were conversions, indicative of the relative lack of importance accorded to penalty attempts in his day.

earlier offences but the balance shifted when Waddell was carried off with concussion with 10 minutes to go. It was still 0-0 and Scotland looked to have hung on for a hard earned draw when Gage scored in the corner deep into injury time to win the match 3-0 for Ireland.

Instead of going to Twickenham in search of a second consecutive Grand Slam, the Scots had instead to try and earn their first ever win in London. On a cold, dull day the teams were presented to King George V, a keen and knowledgeable rugby follower. There had been much speculation in the press about the SRU's firm insistence that their players' shirts should not be numbered. The King took the opportunity to innocently ask the redoubtable Aikman Smith why the SRU was so against the concept. To which he retorted, 'This is a rugby match and not a cattle sale.'

Clever kicking put the England full-back under pressure and his errors led to two of Scotland's three tries with Smith scoring a brace and Waddell the third. Although Scotland led 17-6 at one stage, England matched them for tries, but Waddell's two conversions and Dykes' drop goal were the difference between the two teams. The championship and the retention of the Calcutta Cup for the first time since 1909 were just reward for another excellent season.

## The Hat-trick

Scotland won the championship for the third time in a row in 1927 for the only time in their history. Macpherson had returned from Yale and led the side in the first three matches of the campaign once again striking up a profitable partnership with Smith. In fact the Scottish backs ran in nine tries including four of the five scored in a marvellous win over England at Murrayfield. This match was the first live radio broadcast at Murrayfield by the BBC and the following season the BBC was given permission to broadcast all the international matches played at Murrayfield.

*Left to right: Jimmie Ireland, Ludovic Stuart, John Bannerman and Hugh Mackintosh – more stars of Scotland's golden age.*

Rugby was once again spreading its wings, this time by embracing modern technology in allowing the sport to reach a wider audience.

France's first visit to Murrayfield resulted in a comfortable win for Scotland but with the forwards failing to gel they had to rely on the brilliance of their back division to win 23-6. Scotland started superbly, scoring all four tries, doubles for Waddell and Smith, before half-time to lead 20-3 at the break. But with little quality ball to work with in the second half the backs had to be at their best defensively to keep the French out.

Scotland faced Wales at Cardiff Arms Park on a sea of mud, but despite the difficult conditions the Scottish backs repeatedly found gaps in the Welsh defence and only desperate last-ditch tackling kept them out. However, from an up-and-under Davies managed to get a foot to the ball to push it into Kerr's path and he gathered to slither over in the corner. Gillies landed a superb conversion and Scotland had the edge for the rest of the match eventually winning 5-0.

If Scotland had the Indian sign over Wales, the same could be said for Ireland over Scotland. The Scots stumbled to a narrow loss for the second year in a row against Ireland which cost them a Grand Slam for a second time. This time the weather played its part as a storm of wind and rain blew straight down Lansdowne Road. Ireland took full advantage of the appalling arctic conditions and scored two tries in the first half. Conditions, if anything, were worse in the second half but the Scots could not score. Several players had to be treated for exposure but spare a thought for the

*The Scotland team v Wales, Cardiff, 1927.*

**50 Greatest Players**

**HERBERT WADDELL Stand-off**

**Club:** Glasgow Academical

**Debut:** v France, 1 January 1924

**No. of Caps:** 15 **No. of Points:** 45

Despite playing his debut international season at stand-off to the excellent Willie Bryce of Selkirk at scrum-half, Waddell's partnership with club-mate Jimmy Nelson, first established at Glasgow Academy, was a vital part of Scotland's success in the 1920s. Waddell toured South Africa with the 1924 Lions and played in three Tests but on his return illness caused him to miss the first two matches of the 1925 season. But he made a scoring return against Ireland, dropping an important goal, then landed the winning drop goal against England three weeks later to secure his place in history. Tactically astute, he was an important points-gatherer, landing five drop goals but impressively notching seven tries in 15 matches, a tremendous strike rate. Indeed, his try against Wales in 1926 demonstrated he could lace quality with quantity, producing a magnificent effort as he sliced clean through the defence with a great dummy to win the match.

poor spectators and reporters sitting in the newly opened stand which, unbelievably, had yet to have a roof installed. Exposed to the elements these poor souls were in a terrible state at full time but bore their lot stoically.

Thankfully, after two matches played in dreadful weather conditions, Scotland entertained England at Murrayfield in front of a 70,000 capacity crowd under blue skies which favoured the outstanding Scottish backs. Scotland won a thrilling encounter 21-13, outscoring England by four tries to two with Smith and Macpherson scoring three between them and Dykes producing the score of the afternoon with an excellent individual effort.

## One Last Hurrah

Scotland's excellent run came to an end in 1928 despite opening with wins over New South Wales Waratahs (captained by Johnnie Wallace) and then a comfortable 15-6 win in Paris. Since crushing Wales 35-10 at Inverleith in 1924 Scotland had won 14 out of 17 matches, a Grand Slam, three Five Nations titles and three Calcutta Cups in an era of unprecedented success. Although the Scots regained the championship in 1929 this was the

## 50 Greatest Players

### IAN SMITH Wing

**Clubs:** Oxford University, Edinburgh University, London Scottish

**Debut:** v Wales, 2 February 1924

**No. of Caps:** 32 **No. of Points:** 72

The 'Flying Scotsman' was holder of the world record for try-scoring in internationals, 24 in all, for over 50 years until David Campese broke it during the 1987 Rugby World Cup. And he is still joint-holder of the Scottish record, bracketed with Tony Stanger, although Smith's strike rate of 24 in 32 matches is considerably superior to Stanger's 24 in 52 matches. Remarkably, Smith did not play rugby until he went up to Oxford but took to the sport quickly and his considerable strength, exceptional pace and high knee action made him a difficult opponent to handle. He enjoyed a stunning debut season in 1924, marking his first cap with a hat-trick and touring South Africa with the Lions where injury limited his Test appearances to two. Eight tries in partnership with Phil Macpherson against France and Wales in 1925 was clear evidence that his first season had been no fluke and he finished his career in 1933 captaining Scotland to a Triple Crown.

beginning of the end for a marvellous side. In 1928 Scotland 'won' the wooden spoon for the first time since 1911 and could muster just six tries, five of them against France, in four matches.

One last hurrah at the end of the decade saw Scotland win the championship for the fourth time in five years and once again narrowly miss out on a Grand Slam, this time going down 14-7 to Wales in Cardiff.

A narrow home win over France by 6-3 was followed by the loss to Wales. Drysdale played the last of his 25 consecutive internationals for Scotland as captain against France before the captaincy passed to Bannerman for the rest of the season. For Bannerman too this was his last season at the top and he was one of four try scorers against Ireland. Once again the Smith/Macpherson partnership yielded two tries as the mercurial Macpherson weaved his magic spells to create space and chances for the hungry back division.

The final match of the decade was a wonderful affair, Scotland beating England 12-6 and with all the points being scored through tries. Either side of half-time, first Novis for England and then Nelson scored. Meikle countered for England to extend their lead to 6-3. But in a brilliant finish with the Scotland forwards clearly on top, the Scottish three-quarters repeatedly stretched their opposite numbers, and wingers Smith and Brown scored three tries to ensure a win in the most thrilling fashion.

# Chapter Eight: 1930-39
# The Curate's Egg

Following the spectacular highs of the 1920s, the 1930s can be viewed as a real curate's egg of an era for Scotland. Two Triple Crowns along with the championship were won in 1933 and 1938, but these successes have to be tempered against five bottom-place finishes, including three outright whitewashes in 1932, 1936 and 1939.

Though the mercurial Macpherson and Smith were entering their twilight years they still managed to conjure occasional mesmeric flashes of magic and there were other great players being produced. Ross Logan took over at scrum-half from the excellent Nelson and grew increasingly influential as the decade progressed and bright new stars such as Wilson Shaw, Charles Dick and Duncan Macrae emerged. Scotland's forwards found it tough going and often lost the set scrums by a ratio of as much as 4 to 1 and struggled too in the line-out. Nevertheless some very good players made their mark such as George Horsburgh, Jock Waters and Laurie Duff supplementing and, eventually, supplanting established players like Borderers John Allan, Jock Beattie and Willie Welsh.

The 1931-32 South African tour to the UK is blamed by some rugby historians for encouraging a more conservative brand of rugby than had hitherto been played. The tourists, who won all four Tests, played to their strengths with a well-drilled pack supplying half-backs Bennie Osler and Danie Craven with sufficient possession to ruthlessly control matches. Osler, at stand-off, was a brilliant tactical kicker and unceasingly kicked for position until reaching the opposition 25. Only then would he unleash his backs. To modern eyes it would probably appear boring, but the South Africans were the unofficial world champions of the time and drew huge crowds.

Statistics indicate that the average number of tries scored decreased quite dramatically in the 1930s, arguably supporting the new conservative approach, but this does not quite square with some quite breathtaking matches played and the appearance on the international stage of a number of brilliant attacking players.

Another probable reason for the decline in try scoring in the championship was the expulsion of France from the tournament in 1931. The home nations often rattled up a number of tries against the French who were still coming to grips with international rugby and were experiencing greater difficulties in satisfying the staunchly amateur home unions officials that their club rugby was run along strictly amateur lines.

## The First Wooden Spoon

Although the Scots went from top to bottom in one season they were a tad unfortunate to finish last with three points having beaten Wales and drawn with England at Twickenham.

Led for the season by Macpherson, they were outmuscled in Paris but a month later, with Waddell returning to the helm for one final match, they battled well against Wales at Murrayfield. Simmers added two tries to the one he grabbed against France and Waddell's late drop goal, a record fifth for Scotland, won the match 12-9. Incidentally, Ronald Warren (Glasgow HSFP) returned to the side at full-back against Wales, and retained his place for the season, a remarkable feat eight years after winning his last cap.

A rapid hat-trick of tries by Davy for Ireland before half-time at Murrayfield sank Scotland's chances and, forced into playing catch up, they could only close the gap to 14-11 by the full-time whistle.

Finally, the Scots played well in a fiercely competitive match at Twickenham but had to settle for a 0-0 draw; enough to win England the championship and the Scots an unwanted and unwarranted wooden spoon. The scoreless draw was the first in the series for 30 years, the sixth and final one between the two nations and the tenth draw in the first 52 matches. There have been a further seven since.

The Lions 28-match tour to Australasia that summer featured just one Scot, Willie Welsh of Hawick, who played in the fourth and final Test against New Zealand. This was no reflection on the abilities of the Scottish players but with the SRU having declined a place on the selection committee there was no voice to promote the merits of any Scots in contention.

In contrast to the previous season and confirming how unfortunate they had been to finish last, an additional point secured second place in the table for Scotland in 1931. John Allan, the goal-kicking Melrose forward was one of the stars of the season, kicking seven conversions, including five out of six, in the thrilling 28-19 win over England. Oddly enough, Allan's achievement remained in the record book for fully 53 years until Peter Dods (Gala) landed a 'full-house' converting eight out of eight tries scored in the 1984 Grand Slam-winning season.

The shift of power in the Scottish game continued apace with a greater spread of players selected for national honours than ever before. Harry Lind

**50 Greatest Players**

**HARRY LIND Stand-off/Centre**

**Club:** Dunfermline

**Debut:** v Ireland, 25 February 1928

**No. of Caps:** 16 **No. of Points:** 7

Lind won his first eight caps at stand-off and his second eight caps at centre over nine seasons as the national selectors seemed unable to decide where to make best use of his creative flair. Lind was one of five players from the Dunfermline club to play for Scotland between the wars. His own breakthrough came following an impressive display for the North against the touring Waratahs in 1927. Capped against Ireland a few months later, he had to wait another three years for his second chance, playing well in partnership with Jimmy Nelson and Ross Logan. Against South Africa he scored a wonderful solo try, his clever footwork piercing the defence and selling an outrageous dummy to wrongfoot the full-back. His most successful season was in 1933 when he was switched to centre and had the thrill of dropping the winning goal against Ireland to seal a seventh Triple Crown.

and Alf Wilson from the Dunfermline club were chosen together and for the first time not one player from an Edinburgh club was selected for the opener against France.

Scotland's win against France was their fifth in a row at home but they had to rely on two long-range efforts in the first half from Allan's trusty boot to squeeze home by 6-4 in a close, tense encounter.

Before the Welsh match in Cardiff a minute's silence was observed following the sudden death of James Aikman Smith who had devoted a huge part of his life to Scottish rugby and, somewhat appropriately, had died during the train journey south to the match. The game itself was a dour affair with Wales winning 13-8 although the Scots felt the final try, which was converted, came from a forward pass. The last time Wales and Scotland had met at Cardiff (in 1927) the Welsh had been numbered 1-16 (omitting the number 13) and lost. This time they appeared with letters on their shirts and won!

The match at Lansdowne Road was once again played in appalling weather conditions and Ireland squeezed home 8-5. The backs were blamed for the Irish defeat and five changes were made to the back line for the Calcutta Cup match with Macpherson returning as skipper to partner Smith while Lind teamed up with a new scrum half Ross Logan. The gamble paid off spectacularly and an epic encounter ensued with a record total of ten tries scored, six by Scotland, and bucket loads of attacking rugby by both teams. One report suggests that there was little serious tackling but the crowd went home with smiles on their faces having been royally entertained in a 47-point thriller.

During the season talks had been held with the FFR about rumoured professional practices in French club rugby. Furthermore, in January 1931, ten of the top French clubs formed their own union under the aegis of the FFR. The loss of control over the top clubs and the FFR's inability to stamp out professionalism was enough for the four home unions to break off relations with France and they were expelled from the championship until they restored the game to amateur status. Sadly this resulted in a 16-year absence for France from top-flight rugby.

## A Whitewash

Having played their part in consigning the French to the international wilderness the SRU did not let breaches of conduct go unpunished within their own borders. The ban on players writing press articles on rugby was extended to appearing on rugby radio broadcasts. And they showed their teeth by suspending two players from Aberdeen and two well-known international players who had allowed their thoughts on rugby to appear in the written press.

On the other hand the SRU was sufficiently enlightened to continue to permit radio coverage of Murrayfield internationals and allowed the North of Scotland v South Africa tour match to go ahead at the home of a professional football club, Aberdeen FC's Pittodrie. The international against South Africa drew a bumper 65,000 crowd, and ensured that Scotland still managed to play four matches in 1932, three of them at Murrayfield, which helped swell the SRU's coffers. Despite playing well in a cracking match against the Springboks, losing 6-3 to second half tries by Osler and Craven, and putting up the best display of any of the home unions in the Test series, the Scots were whitewashed in the championship.

A narrow defeat at the hands of the Welsh, wearing their lucky letters, was followed by heavy defeats to Ireland and England in which eight tries were

*Phil Macpherson introduces his team to the Duke of York at Twickenham, March 1932.*

conceded. It was a disappointingly low note for Macpherson to bow out on having contributed so much to the Scottish cause over the years but today he is rightly regarded as one of the best players ever to pull on a Scottish shirt.

## Scotland Bounce Back

In 1933 a Triple Crown followed the whitewash as the switchback ride of the 1930s continued rapidly rising from depressing dip to top of the heap in just 12 short months. This was Smith's last season and he was awarded the captaincy as the selectors carried out radical surgery for the first match against Wales, blooding eight new caps as just five players survived the sharp edge of the scalpel. As if the surgery was not radical enough, the SRU at last bit the bullet and the Scotland team ran out at Swansea with numbers on their backs for the first time.

Smith led from the front, running strongly to score the opening try and Scotland never looked back: 3-0 became 6-0, then 11-0, before Wales scored a late consolation try from schoolboy Wilf Wooller, whose 'club' was listed as Rydal School. Wooller later confirmed that early promise to become one of the greatest centres of his generation.

A narrow 3-0 win at Murrayfield over England followed, winger Ken Fyfe's try being the only score of the match, to set up a Triple Crown opportunity against Ireland. Scotland used just 16 players during the season and Fyfe, although selected, was injured in a car accident just prior to the match and sadly was forced to withdraw. The match, played on All Fools Day, had been postponed from late February as the Scotland party had been caught in a terrible storm sailing to the game. Their ship was forced to lie off Dublin Bay for 16 hours as the storm battered the Irish coast and in the morning most of the Scotland party were too unwell to play. This is the only time that rampant seasickness has been used as a reason to postpone a rugby international.

At the second time of asking the weather was kind enough to allow the Scots a safe journey to Dublin but they received a typically frenzied and full-blooded 'welcome' on the pitch. Ferocious tackling resulted in Smith hirpling early on and he was little more than a passenger for the rest of the match. Later, Lorraine was concussed and then debutant Gedge broke a bone in his hand, fending off an opponent. Nevertheless, Scotland led 4-3 at half-time thanks to Ken Jackson's drop goal, but Murray regained the lead for Ireland with a controversial try. With 10 minutes to go, and with only two fully fit backs on the pitch, Logan threw a long pass out to Lind who landed what proved to be the winning drop goal, clinching one of Scotland's hardest earned victories and a seventh Triple Crown.

*Ian Smith's Triple Crown-winning team against Ireland, 1933.*

The following season, 1934, was disappointing in terms of results as the Scots won one and lost two, but there was much to be proud of in the performances both individually and collectively. Wilson Shaw and Charles Dick were amongst the almost now traditional appearance of eight new caps to start the season against the Welsh. The duo worked brilliantly in tandem with Dick an established centre but Shaw a supremely gifted attacking back was capped at wing, centre and stand-off, his best position.

To be fair to the selectors, they picked five new boys for the season's opener but late call-offs by Beattie, Fyfe and Brown brought the total to eight. Wales were always on top and kept the scoreboard ticking over with flanker Fear giving Logan a torrid time often from a seemingly offside position. Trailing 10-0 with 20 minutes to go, Scotland at last got points on the board to close to 10-6. But a late Welsh score sealed their fate.

Despite a slow start against Ireland, Scotland recovered well to lead 11-3 at the break. Dick scored a marvellous try as the Scottish backs ran amok. Cotter made a fine break only to offload to Shaw who received man and ball. Lind reacted instinctively to his hurried transfer and, bending low, scooped the ball between his legs to Dick who sprinted past the startled full-back to score. The Scots grew in confidence as the match progressed and Crawford and Dick again scored to stretch the lead to 16-3. The Irish finished strongly to score two late tries to make the final score 16-9. The difference turned out to be Scotland's better goal kicking, landing three out of four attempts.

Scotland made the trek south to Twickenham with some confidence even though England were going for a Triple Crown. And the confidence was well founded as the Scots took the early lead in a terrific tussle with Shaw finishing off fine work by Dick and Lind in the corner. England's equaliser was a trifle fortunate as an attempted penalty goal deflected off a Scottish forward to allow Meikle to score. And despite having the better of the second period as the three-quarters found space time after time, fortune favoured England once again. In injury time, Lind made one final break but when the ball went loose it was gathered by Booth who sprinted almost the length of the pitch to score.

## Another Wooden Spoon

In 1935 Scotland beat England for the sixth successive time at Murrayfield to regain the Calcutta Cup, yet they were thoroughly outplayed by Ireland and lost narrowly to Wales to collect another wooden spoon. But there were flashes of outstanding rugby particularly from Lind, Dick and Shaw and the back row was very prominent against England.

Off the pitch the redevelopment of Murrayfield continued with major alterations to the stand approved. Two wing stands were added to provide seating for an additional 7,000 spectators and improvements were made to the changing rooms and committee room. And the secretary benefited from having a telephone installed at his home complete with ex-directory number.

If the SRU was prepared to bend a knee to embrace modern technology, it was clearly not willing to compromise on disciplinary matters. Four Gala players had been suspended sine die in 1896 and the club requested that the ban be lifted. Inviting comparisons to an elephant's memory the SRU Committee – almost 40 years after the punishment was meted – was in no mood to forgive, or forget, and turned down the not unreasonable request.

As with the visit of the Springboks in 1931-32, the Scots started exceptionally well against the touring All Blacks in 1935-36. Jack Manchester's All Blacks were a very popular bunch of tourists if not quite as

*Ross Logan (left) competes in the Scottish trials match, 1935.*

successful as their predecessors. Nevertheless they had to work hard to overcome a brave home side at Murrayfield and daylight between the two teams only appeared after Scotland went down to 14 men temporarily. The final score was 18-8 and if the hero was Pat Caughey who scored a hat-trick; full-back Mike Gilbert, returning to the land of his birth, was not far behind landing three out of four conversions.

Gilbert was born in Rothesay before his family emigrated to New Zealand

*Action from New Zealand's first visit to Murrayfield in 1935.*

when he was very young. He played in 27 of the 30 tour matches, including all four Tests, and was the leading scorer with a haul of 125 points. Gilbert switched to rugby league with Bradford Northern in 1937 enjoying a successful spell with the club before returning to New Zealand in 1940. Unfortunately, he ran into problems with the strict union regulations of the time and was banned from any contact with the code until he was reinstated in 1995 at the age of 84.

In the championship Scotland always struggled against Wales, trailing 8-0 at half-time. Although they struck back with a debut try by Murray, Wales ran out worthy winners 13-3. Three weeks later they played their third successive match at Murrayfield, against Ireland, but as in the Welsh match the contest was over by half-time, as they trailed 10-0.

The English match was, however, a far closer affair and although Fyfe did a great job in containing the dangerous Alexander Obolensky, the young Russian prince, who had sprung to fame scoring two wonder tries against New Zealand, England's three tries were just enough to squeeze home by the odd point in 17.

## 50 Greatest Players

**JOCK BEATTIE Second row**

**Club:** Hawick

**Debut:** v France, 19 January 1929

**No. of Caps:** 23 **No. of Points:** 0

First capped alongside John Bannerman in the second row, Beattie was a member of the 1929 championship-winning side. A real powerhouse in the scrum, he was a gifted two-handed catcher at the line-out, a terrier in the loose with sufficient skill to be part of the Barbarians team which won the Middlesex Sevens in 1934. Beattie was also a member of the 1933 Triple Crown-winning side and, although Scotland won only five other matches up until his retirement, he was very much the rock upon which the Scottish pack was built. A joiner by trade and a real character, he was known as 'Jock the Bleck' in Hawick as 'bleck' was the only word he used when swearing. In honour of his service to Scotland he was awarded the captaincy in his last match against England at Twickenham which was frustratingly lost by the narrowest of margins, 9-8.

### The Championship's 50th Anniversary

The 1936-37 season saw the championship's 50th birthday and the only way was up for Scotland who did indeed enjoy better fortune opening with a splendid win against Wales. In what surely be a unique occurrence in the history of international rugby both teams were led by Edinburgh Wanderers as Logan led Scotland and Idwal Rees, a fine utility back, led Wales. The Scottish pack was unchanged throughout the season playing well in the loose, as befits a unit containing four No. 8s, but struggling in the set-piece. In fact against Wales they lost the scrums by 31-16. Despite this handicap they won enough ball for their lively backs to wreak havoc in the Welsh defence and Dick and Shaw shared three tries. Duncan Macrae won his first cap in this match and the St Andrews University student made his mark in the three seasons before the war as one of a long line of clever, elusive midfield backs.

Another bruising and bloody encounter in appalling weather conditions followed in Dublin and although Scotland took an early lead, injuries to Shaw, Waters and Russell disrupted their rhythm and they crashed 11-4.

Finally against England the backs looked very dangerous with ball in hand; unfortunately they saw very little of it despite the best efforts of Shaw,

Macrae and Logan playing in his final international. Frustratingly, the Scots went down 6-3 and the win was enough to land England the Triple Crown.

Over the 50 years of championship rugby the English had enjoyed the most success, winning a total of 18 championships. But Scotland were not far behind and headed the Celtic challenge with 14 wins, followed by Wales (11) and Ireland (7). France had not had enough opportunities to build a sustained effort and had not won the championship at this stage. However, as we shall see shortly the balance of power would change considerably in the next five decades with a decline in Scottish and English fortunes and the rise of Wales and France as the dominant forces in the tournament.

## Triple Crown Try-scoring Bonanza

But the following season the Scots were to enjoy one final excellent campaign before the outbreak of the Second World War, squeezing past Wales but running in an extraordinary nine tries against Ireland and England including five in the Calcutta Cup clash in a marvellous match at Twickenham.

It was a breathtaking season for attacking rugby in general with a record 35 tries scored in the six matches played, eclipsing the previous best of 32 tries in 1904. Wilson Shaw was to enjoy a brilliant season as the Scottish selectors at last recognised they would get the best out of the tiny midfield maestro by playing him in his favoured stand-off position. He was also handed the captaincy for the full season for the first time. The midfield combination of Shaw, Dick and Macrae terrorised the opposition and the trio maximised to the full any ball that came their way.

Once again the selectors rang the changes for the Welsh match and eight new faces appeared at Murrayfield. Shaw and his opposite number Cliff Jones had a wonderful duel and it was the Welshman who enjoyed the better of the first-half exchanges helping them to a 6-0 lead. But Scotland, who had contained the dangerous Wooller, worked their way back into contention and the supporting Crawford crashed over for a try which he also converted. A nail-biting

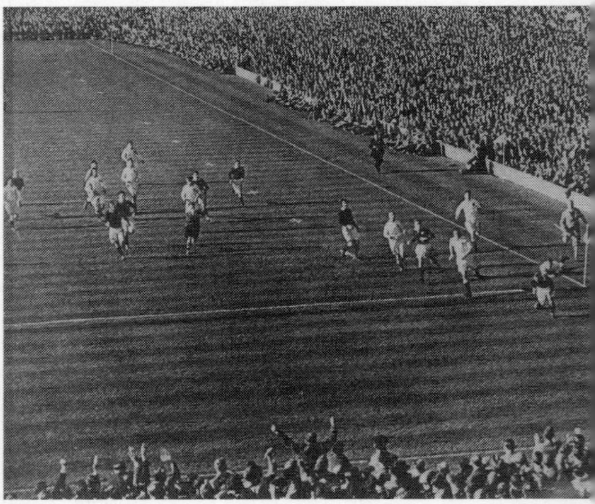

*Wilson Shaw touches down in the corner for the first of his two tries against England in 1938.*

## Great Matches

**FOUR NATIONS CHAMPIONSHIP** **Twickenham, 19 March 1938**

**England 16 Scotland 21** **Attendance: 70,000**

It was an explosive start. In what is now known as 'Shaw's Match', the great man was quickly into his stride, pouncing on a loose ball to set up winger Renwick for the first try. Parker responded with two penalties but the lead was short-lived as fine combination work by the forwards enabled the bullocking Crawford to create Renwick's second. Dynamic as they were in the loose, the forwards struggled in the set piece and their strength and weakness was illustrated in one captivating moment which led to Dick's try. Retreating at a rate of knots from their own put-in on the Scotland 25, the back-row of Duff, Young and Crawford recovered superbly to carry the ball up to halfway before an inside pass enabled Dick to stretch his legs and scorch over for a try which had swept fully 75 yards.

Unwin's try brought the scores level at 9-9, before Shaw scored a stunning solo effort. Receiving the ball in the middle of the pitch, Shaw's blinding pace took him clear of a bewildered defence. Confronted with full-back Parker, his brilliant footwork left the Englishman grasping at thin air as he cruised over the line for one of the greatest scores in a Calcutta Cup match. And with the crowd still buzzing with excitement, the referee blew his whistle for half-time.

England grabbed the lead back with Reynolds coolly slotting a drop goal only for Crawford to convert two long-range penalties for Scotland to edge ahead by 18-13 in this pulsating encounter. Back came England again and Parker landed a penalty to narrow the gap to just two points as the match boiled towards its climax. The Scots were hanging on by their fingertips when, with three minutes to go, Shaw eased the tension in the Caledonian ranks with the match-winning try. Winning a rare scrum in the middle of the pitch, Shaw broke left and once again his flaring pace carried him through the defence and his athletic dive took him over for a wonderful score to bring the curtain down on one of the epic matches in the championship's history.

**England:** G.W. Parker; E.J. Unwin, P. Cranmer, P.L. Candler, H.S. Sever; F.J. Reynolds, J.L. Giles; R.J. Longland, H.B. Toft (captain), H.F. Wheatley, R.M. Marshall, A. Wheatley, W.H. Weston, D.L.K. Milman, A.A. Brown
**Scorers: Try** Unwin **Penalty Goals** Parker 3 **Drop Goal** Reynolds

**Scotland:** G. Roberts; W.N. Renwick, R.C.S. Dick, D.J. Macrae, J.G.S. Forrest; R.W. Shaw (captain), T.F. Dorward; W.F. Blackadder, J.D.H. Hastie, W.M. Inglis, G.B. Horsburgh, A. Roy, W.B. Young, P.L. Duff, W.H. Crawford
**Scorers: Tries** Renwick 2, Dick, Shaw 2 **Penalty Goals** Crawford 2

**Referee:** Mr I. David (Wales)

## 50 Greatest Players

**ROSS LOGAN Scrum-half**

**Clubs:** Edinburgh University, Edinburgh Wanderers

**Debut:** v England, 21 March 1931

**No. of Caps:** 20 **No. of Points:** 6

A worthy successor to Jimmy Nelson at scrum-half, Logan and Nelson filled the No. 9 shirt from 1925 to 1937 in all but four internationals. Logan was a big man for a scrum- half and used his power to great effect. He was exceptionally strong, capable of making devastating breaks from the base of the scrum and possessed in his weaponry an outlandish dummy which he used cleverly. He settled quickly into the team and marked his debut against England in 1931 with a cracking try in the enthralling 28-19 victory.

By 1933 he was an experienced member of a largely inexperienced side, but the blend of youth and wisdom proved to be an effective combination. Indeed, it was Logan's mammoth pass to Harry Lind which gave the centre the time to drop a goal to win the Triple Crown.

finish ensued with wave after wave of blue shirts battering the red line, which held firm. However, at a maul Rees was penalised for lying on the ball and in the tensest of circumstances, Crawford kicked the goal to earn Scotland a tough but very well-deserved 8-6 win.

The Irish match was a more fluid affair with the midfield trio in irrepressible form cutting huge swathes in the Irish defence and left wing Forrest took advantage of these gaps to score two early tries. Scotland never let up and further tries for Macrae and Drummond and a Dorward drop goal extended the lead to 23-9 before a late Irish try narrowed the winning score to 23-14.

But the best was saved for last as England and Scotland locked horns at Twickenham. England had warmed up for the match with a 36-14 thrashing of Ireland and even the King and Queen were in attendance for what turned out to be a classic Calcutta Cup encounter.

The Lions toured again in 1938, this time to South Africa. There were just three Scots in the tour party, Duncan Macrae (St Andrews University), Laurie Duff (Glasgow Academical) and Jock Waters (Selkirk). Unfortunately players such as Shaw and Dick, who could have made a difference on the hard pitches, were unavailable. The tour was injury-riven but the tourists played positive attractive rugby and were adored by the large crowds who came to watch them. Only Duff played in the Test series, being selected for the third and fourth Tests. He scored a try in each and was the outstanding forward in the final Test.

## Gloom and War

After the high of 1938, the final season before the Second World War was a big comedown for the Scots as all three matches were lost for the third time in the decade. Once again the pack struggled to compete and even the best backs in the world need a certain amount of ball to make an impact. The championship was a strangely low-key, low-scoring affair with just ten tries posted all season. Perhaps the style of rugby was affected by the gloomy mood of the time.

In a mood of reconciliation and rugby friendship in these difficult times the Four Nations met with France and, having been assured that French rugby was now wholly amateur, agreed to re-admit them to the championship for the 1939-40 season. However, other matters were to ensure that the French did not play another championship match for a further seven years.

Scotland were well beaten in Cardiff in a match containing 12 debutants. Controversially, the Scottish selectors opted to choose William Brydon of Heriot's at scrum-half. Brydon was a fine Sevens player but could not win a place in Heriot's First XV. Unfortunately the bold experiment did not work and he was dropped and never played for Scotland again.

The now lethal concoction of foul weather and a fiery pack bowled the Scots over in Dublin and the Calcutta Cup match was a poor one-way affair as the English forwards had a field day. Thankfully, their backs were as poor as their forwards were good and squandered countless chances. One shaft of light from the season was the second Scottish try which was scored appropriately by skipper Shaw. It was a typically brilliant score as Shaw's initial burst of speed took him clear of the first line of defence whereupon his rugby brain took over, selling a delicious dummy to check the cover defence which bought just enough time and space to enable him to scurry over the line. The crowd rose as one to acclaim this final act of genius.

In response to the outbreak of war in September 1939 all international fixtures were cancelled and the club programme put on hold. However, the SRU did encourage clubs to fulfil fixtures whenever and wherever possible. For some clubs it was impossible to continue in any shape or form and they closed for the duration of the war. Some managed to continue either on their own or by amalgamating with near neighbours as with Edinburgh

## 50 Greatest Players

**WILSON SHAW Stand-off/Centre/Wing**

**Club:** Glasgow High School FP

**Debut:** v Wales, 3 February 1934

**No. of Caps:** 19 **No. of Points:** 26

Shaw was one of the most brilliant and imaginative backs ever to play for Scotland, featuring in an outstanding division which included such other talents as Harry Lind, Duncan Macrae, Charles Dick and Ross Logan. He was perhaps a victim of his own versatility, making his debut as a wing before moving infield to stand-off via centre. Shaw was a small, slightly built man whose greatest attribute was his searing acceleration off the mark, reputedly being able to hit top speed within a couple of strides. This priceless ability enabled him to scythe through even the tightest defences and his sustained speed and tricky footwork brought him many spectacular tries. Shaw's stunning performance at Twickenham in 1938 was his greatest moment: on starvation rations, he scored two tries and helped create three others in the 21-16 win which earned a marvellous Triple Crown.

Accies/Edinburgh Wanderers and West of Scotland/Kelvinside Accies, and others picked up fixtures with Forces sides stationed in their locale. However, the SRU would not permit an SRU XV to play against any Forces teams 'tainted' by the inclusion of rugby league players. The SRU altered its own bye-laws to allow the committee to continue to run the union's business on an interim basis and immediately made Murrayfield available for the war effort. The offer was swiftly taken up and the facility was taken over as a supply depot.

As the war developed a few service internationals were played against England each season from 1942 to 1945 including one played at Wembley, won 8-5 by Scotland. And at the end of the war six unofficial internationals were played, of which five were won, including a win over the New Zealand army. Two members of the New Zealand team, Fred Allen and Charlie Saxton, were driving forces in the post-war success of Kiwi rugby and the pair returned to Scotland over 20 years later as coach and manager respectively of the legendary 1967 All Blacks.

# Chapter Nine: 1946-59
# The Bleak Years

In the immediate aftermath of the Second World War the world was a pretty bleak and austere place and life took a long time to get back to some semblance of normality. There was a world food shortage and food was rationed in the UK with the Food Ministry thinking laterally at one stage by issuing a recipe for squirrel pie. A splendid gesture of support was received from Otago Rugby Football Union in New Zealand who kindly sent two lots of food parcels to the SRU. These were gratefully received and issued to players taking part in the Trial match and the England match in 1947. Further food parcels were later distributed among clubs.

League football restarted in Scotland and England in September 1946 and Scottish rugby emerged from its enforced hibernation to provide an outlet for the rugby community across the nation. In addition to food rationing there was also clothes rationing and the SRU did its best to help by making clothes coupons available to the district unions to help their clubs purchase rugby kit. For many the worst side-effect of the war for rugby clubs was the 50 per cent cut in beer production in early 1947!

The SRU was in a more benevolent mood post-war and was more open to approaches from organisations wanting to hire Murrayfield for non-rugby activity. With both Edinburgh sides getting to the semi-finals of the Scottish FA Cup in 1947, Murrayfield was made available in the event of a Hearts v Hibs Cup final. However, Hearts were knocked out by Aberdeen who then went on to beat Hibs 2-1 in the final at Hampden. The Lord Provost was given permission to hold the Highland Games at Murrayfield but the committee's new-found benevolence did not extend to allowing Scottish speedway to install a dirt track for a speedway meeting.

### Dull and Uninspiring

Despite being the best performers in the 1946 Victory Internationals, the immediate post-war period was a far from vintage period for Scottish rugby at international level and the Five Nations Championship in this period produced some pretty dull and uninspiring rugby. The championship reached its nadir in 1959 when a total of 93 points and 12 tries were scored in the ten-match series, with Scotland managing just 12 points in the entire season.

## 50 Greatest Players

**DOUGLAS ELLIOT Wing-forward**

**Clubs:** Edinburgh Academicals

**Debut:** v France, 1 January 1947

**No. of Caps:** 29 **No. of Points:** 6

The outstanding back-row forward of his generation and one of the best in the world, Elliot's 6 foot 3, 14-stone-plus frame would not look out of place among the giants of the modern game. An ever-present in the Victory International series of 1946 his name was one of the first to be pencilled in for his full debut against France on New Year's Day 1947. An abrasive, destructive tackler, he struck fear into the hearts of opposing half-backs and it was his ceaseless harrying which contributed to Wales' downfall at Murrayfield in 1951. But he was also a constructive player whose clever linking and sound hands made him the complete back-row forward. Selected for the 1950 Lions tour, he could not afford to be away for six months and offered to pay for his own flight. The generous offer was sadly declined and he missed out on a wonderful experience where his undoubted qualities would have been of enormous benefit to the Lions.

Although the Five Nations tournament appeared to have an inhibiting effect on the top rugby players of the era the exploits of the Lions tours of the 1950s confirmed that there was still a huge amount of natural talent in the game in Britain and Ireland. It was a pity for home supporters that the only time they could witness this at first hand was in Barbarians' matches or the traditional Easter tour to South Wales. The Lions toured in 1950 to Australasia, 1955 to South Africa and in 1959 to Australasia again. They did not manage to win a series, but the 1955 Lions led 2-1 going into the final Test only to lose 22-8. But they won many admirers with their commitment to open, expansive and entertaining rugby.

Between 1947-59 Scotland won 15 of the 56 matches they played. This included one awful spell of 17 consecutive losses from 1951 to 1955, including the 'Murrayfield Massacre' when they lost 44-0 to South Africa. As one wag put it, finding some solace in the sort of gallows humour which is often the only way to combat such results, on being asked what the final score was, '44-0 and we were bloody lucky to get nothing'.

Not surprisingly, the Scottish championship record was very poor during this painful period. In 13 seasons there were six wooden spoons, four

**50 Greatest Players**

**ANGUS CAMERON Centre/Stand-off/Full-back**

**Club:** Glasgow High School FP

**Debut:** v Wales, 7 February 1948

**No. of Caps:** 17 **No. of Points:** 18

A versatile footballer, Cameron was first capped at centre as a late replacement while on national service with the army. He was also capped at stand-off and full-back and led Scotland in nine internationals. Matches against South Africa were to provide him with the lowest and highest points of his international career. An astute kicker and tactician, he had the dubious distinction of captaining Scotland during the 'Murrayfield Massacre' in 1951 but experienced the ecstasy of sweet revenge on the 1955 Lions tour. The senior player and vice-captain, he played full-back in the first Test and kicked four out of five conversions as the Lions won a thriller 23-22 at Ellis Park. He played in the second Test too but, unfortunately, injury curtailed any further involvement in the tour.

whitewashes and no titles with a second place in 1950 being the best result. What is more, just 45 tries were scored in 52 matches with single tries registered in 1957 and 1959.

## Individual Excellence, Collective Failure

But it was not all doom and gloom as despite the lack of team success, Scotland continued to produce some outstanding individual players in this period. Douglas Elliot, the Edinburgh Academicals flanker, shone like a beacon in the immediate aftermath of the war, winning 29 caps from 1947 to 1954 and one of only two Scots selected to play for the Barbarians against the 1953-54 All Blacks. He was joined in the Scotland back row by the likes of Peter Kininmonth, who led Scotland to the famous 19-0 victory over Wales in 1951, Doug Keller and Chick Henderson, and later in the 1950s there were other outstanding back-row practitioners such as Adam Robson, Jim Greenwood, Ian MacGregor and Ken Smith. The tight five was probably Scotland's Achilles' heel at the time but there were some excellent individuals who came to the fore. Pride of place must go to Hawick's Hughie McLeod who won 40 consecutive caps on both sides of the scrum and toured twice with the Lions in 1955 and 1959. Other front-row forwards who made their mark include Tom Elliot, the goal kicking Gala prop, David Rollo and hooker Norman Bruce and in the second row, Ernie Michie and Hamish Kemp.

**50 Greatest Players**

**JIM GREENWOOD Flanker/No. 8**

**Clubs:** Dunfermline, Perthshire Academicals

**Debut:** v France, 12 January 1952

**No of Caps:** 20 **No. of Points:** 0

First capped as a flanker in 1952 against France in a strong back row alongside Douglas Elliot and Peter Kininmonth, he had to wait another three years for his second cap when he was recalled as No. 8 and captain. He then played in 19 of the next 20 internationals, nine as captain, establishing himself as a dynamic back-row forward. His excellent form won him a berth on the 1955 Lions tour where he was converted to flanker and played a key role in the Test series. A try scorer in the first and final Tests, he was regarded as the outstanding Lions forward in the series. He captained Scotland in the 1959 season and was a certainty for the Lions tour, and possibly its captaincy, when he dislocated a shoulder against Ireland, ending his international career. One of the great thinkers about the game, Greenwood went on to become an innovative coach with Loughborough Colleges, producing many excellent players over the years.

As with the Lions, if the forwards could have won just a wee bit more ball, then there were some outstanding individuals who would have maximised any additional possession to the full. Scrum-halves such as Dally Allardice, Gus Black, Arthur Dorward and Stan Coughtrie. Nobody really established themselves at stand-off until Gordon Waddell broke through in 1957. Angus Cameron, first capped at centre in 1948, suffered because of his versatility and also played at stand-off and full-back, his tour position with the 1955 Lions. Ranald MacDonald and George Stevenson were the pick of the centres and there were a number of strong-running wingers such as Tom Jackson, Doug Smith (a Lion and later manager of the 1971 Lions), Grant Weatherstone and Ian Swan, but unquestionably the most gifted was Arthur Smith, the 1962 Lions captain.

And the non pareil at full-back was Ken Scotland, another Lion who was way ahead of his time as a gifted attacking full-back and 'round-the-corner' goal-kicker in an age of toe bashers.

In the first season of international rugby after the war the Scots were whitewashed in the bleak winter of 1947. The United Kingdom had been in the grip of an Arctic winter since mid-January and as the Scottish party departed for London for the final match of the championship against England in mid-March there had been no club rugby at home for nine weeks.

## 50 Greatest Players

**HUGH McLEOD Prop**

**Club:** Hawick

**Debut:** v France, 9 January 1954

**No. of Caps:** 40 **No. of Points:** 0

For a man who did not play rugby until he was 16, McLeod achieved a huge amount in the next 13 years. Aged 19, he held his own for the South against the touring Springboks in 1952 and two years later he won his first cap against France. He went on to cement his place in the Scotland front row for nine seasons, playing alongside tough cookies such as Tom Elliot, Norman Bruce and David Rollo, winning 40 consecutive caps to set a new Scottish record eclipsing John Bannerman's total of 37. An excellent technician who could play either side of the scrum, he put in a lot of extra running sessions to attain extraordinary levels of fitness which undoubtedly helped his longevity at the top level. A double Lion (1955 and 1959), he played in all six Tests in 1959 and, demonstrating his versatility, he played in all three front-row positions on both tours and even kicked a couple of conversions against Eastern Canada.

On the Thursday before the match it took 20 hours for the party to complete the train journey as the weather continued to play havoc with travel arrangements, but worse was to follow for a couple of individuals.

Duncan McLean the Royal HSFP flanker was given permission to travel on the Friday and endured a 24-hour journey on a train with no restaurant or sleeping accommodation, arriving in London at 6.00am on Saturday morning, a matter of hours before kick off. Mickey Steele-Bodger, the England flanker, and great Barbarians stalwart for many years, was studying in Edinburgh at the time and, like McLean, travelled down late. His train had to be dug out of snowdrifts twice and he arrived in London just before McLean. After all this disruption it is little wonder that Scotland crashed to a heavy defeat and a first four-match whitewash since 1911.

### Eligibility Issues Cause Controversy

The 1947-48 Wallabies were the first post-war overseas touring party. They lost just six of their 35 tour matches and won three of the five-match Test series, opening with a comfortable win over Scotland at Murrayfield running in four tries to nil. Flanker Doug Keller, who had won his first cap at prop against New Zealand earlier in the season, burst from a line-out to set up Australia's third try and kill the match off as a contest.

At the end of the tour, Keller stayed on in London to continue his medical studies at Guy's Hospital and, with a strong Scottish bloodline, he joined London Scottish to play his club rugby. Although his medical commitments did not allow him to turn out for Scottish on a regular basis, when he did play his form quickly attracted the attention of the Scotland selectors. Controversially, just 14 months after he had played for Australia against Scotland, he played for Scotland against France and furthermore was appointed captain for the season. Keller's selection caused much comment and eventually led to a tightening of the eligibility criteria for international rugby. He was not the first player to be capped by another nation before playing for Scotland but the timing of his selection and being awarded the captaincy on his debut left a bitter taste in some mouths. As a short-term fix, however, it worked beautifully as Keller led Scotland to their first international away wins since 1938, beating France 8-0 at Stade Colombes and, three weeks later, squeezing past Wales 6-5 at Murrayfield.

Two South African-born players with Scottish qualifications, Kim Elgie and 'Chick' Henderson, were capped together in the 1953-54 season. Whereas there was no question about their eligibility and they had not been previously capped, both made a significant contribution in the Scotland shirt and went on to make an impact back home. Elgie, a powerful, goal-kicking centre who studied ophthalmology in London, was also an excellent cricketer and was capped for South Africa in three Tests during the South Africa v New Zealand series in 1961-62. A decent batsman, he was second top-scorer in the second Test in Johannesburg with 56. Henderson, who studied industrial engineering at Oxford University, played in the back row alongside Elliot, Robson and Kininmonth in his nine internationals. On his return to South Africa he worked in the media and was a well-regarded sports broadcaster, specialising in rugby and cricket.

But perhaps the man with the most tenuous of Scottish connections to be capped by Scotland – and the most unlikely Scottish name – was Frans ten Bos. Ten Bos, born in England to Dutch parents who had fled their native Netherlands during the war, was educated at Fettes College in Edinburgh. This is where he learned his rugby and his time in Scotland influenced him to do his national service with the Argylls. No questions were asked about his eligibility when he joined London Scottish and when his club form brought him to the attention of the national selectors, one unnamed selector,

## Great Matches

**FIVE NATIONS CHAMPIONSHIP** — **Murrayfield, 3 February 1951**

**Scotland 19 Wales 0** — **Attendance: 80,000**

A record crowd, including around 20,000 Welsh supporters, converged on Murrayfield to witness one of the most unexpected results in the championship's history. In the red corner, Wales, the confident, some might say cocky, reigning Grand Slam champions, fresh from thrashing England 23-5 and boasting 11 Lions from the 1950 tour to Australasia. In the blue corner, struggling Scotland, winners of just two of their previous seven internationals, one win only against Wales since 1938 and not given a prayer.

The early stages of the match did nothing to dent the critics' confidence as the Welsh took the game to the underdogs. However, there was a steely resolve about the Scots who matched Wales upfront and did not allow their dangerous backs to settle into a rhythm. Thomson, the 20-year-old Heriot's FP full-back making his debut, landed a penalty to give the Scots a narrow half-time lead.

*Robert Taylor on his debut shakes off the attentions of three Welsh tacklers.*

After the restart it was all Scotland as wave after wave of attack battered a brave Welsh defence almost to standstill. After being pounded for 20 minutes, Williams, the Welsh full-back, had to hurry his clearance which landed in Kininmonth's large hands. From out by the Welsh 25, the big No. 8 and Scotland skipper took one glance at the distant posts and unleashed the most sweetly struck of drop kicks which sailed between the uprights to deafening cheers. Welsh heads visibly dropped as Scotland raised the tempo of the match and the floodgates opened for Scotland to score three marvellous tries, two of them from the traditional forwards dribbling rushes which had the crowd screaming their famous cry of 'Feet Scotland. Feet'.

**Scotland:** I.H.M. Thomson; R.A. Gordon, D.A. Sloan, D.M. Scott, D.M. Rose; A. Cameron, I.A. Ross; J.C. Dawson, N.G.R. Mair, R.L. Wilson, H.M. Inglis, R. Gemmill, W.I.D. Elliot, P.W. Kininmonth (captain), R.C. Taylor

**Scorers: Tries** Gordon 2, Dawson **Conversions** Inglis, Thomson **Penalty Goal** Thomson **Drop Goal** Kininmonth

**Wales:** G. Williams; K.J. Jones, B.L. Jones, J. Matthews, M.C. Thomas; G. Davies, W.R. Willis; J.D. Robins, D.M. Davies, C. Davies, E.R. John, D.J. Hayward, A. Forward, J.A. Gwilliam (captain), R.T. Evans

**Referee:** Capt. M.J. Dowling (Ireland)

on being informed that Ten Bos had no Scottish blood in him, reportedly said, 'So long as a player feels Scottish, he doesn't have to be a Scotsman.' A few other players have been happy about that attitude over the years particularly, in recent times, David Hilton and Budge Pountney who, it has to be said, were great servants to the cause. Ten Bos, who weighed an impressive 17 stone, contributed much to his adopted nation and was capped 17 times between 1959-63, forming an enormous London Scottish international second row with the equally solid Mike Campbell-Lamerton.

## Live TV Coverage Arrives

The SRU continued its fight with the BBC over the televising of live international matches at Murrayfield and was worried when the RFU reported a loss in gate revenue after a match was broadcast live. Nowadays, of course, the revenue generated from the Six Nations Championship television contract is absolutely crucial to the funding of the game. There was a breakthrough in 1954 when the SRU agreed to allow the New Zealand match to be televised live and although the four home unions discussed the introduction of live television coverage, the SRU was the most nervous of the unions about its introduction. Eventually, in 1956, agreement was reached to permit matches to be screened live. Up until this time the SRU refused to accept any fee on principle – although it is difficult to understand exactly what principle they were adhering to – and it was agreed to accept the sum the BBC offered.

How times have changed. The Six Nations contract is now a matter of intense negotiation particularly when the BBC and Sky were both bidders for the contract which ran from 1998 to 2002. In the end the deal agreed for that five-season span was worth an estimated £70 million. However, as the BBC was the sole bidder for the current contract they held all the aces and although the Six Nations committee fought their corner tenaciously the BBC's final offer came with a take it or leave it tag. These monies are crucial to the funding of the game in all six countries and the negotiators need to squeeze as much as they can out of each commercial deal to help administer the sport as effectively as possible.

## Barren Spell

There is little point in dwelling for too long on the barren spell which lasted from 24 February 1951, when Scotland lost 6-5 at home to Ireland, until 5 February 1955 when Scotland produced an excellent performance to beat Wales 14-8. The real low point was the 44-0 home defeat at the hands of

South Africa in November 1951. The tourists won 30 out of 31 matches and all five Tests on tour, running in nine tries at Murrayfield.

In hindsight, it took Scotland at least four years to recover from this devastating defeat and it is probably the most painful and traumatic reverse the team ever suffered. Some heavy defeats followed but also some narrow ones, but when playing with a lack of confidence matches that could be won just seemed to slip away. A classic example of this was at the start of 1954 when Scotland lost 3-0 in successive matches at home. On McLeod's debut, France sneaked home by a single try to nil and against the touring All Blacks, with Elliot in outstanding form, the Scots put on a great show for the Murrayfield crowd, only to succumb to a Bob Scott penalty which crept over the bar from 30 yards out.

Scotland's barren spell finally ended four years after it had begun when they came up with an excellent 14-8 win over Wales with Smith's try the catalyst. Receiving the ball from Robson and hemmed in close to the right touchline, Smith raced 30 yards with ball in hand brushing off attempted tackles, before Edwards confronted him. Without breaking stride he chipped the full-back, ran around him and gathered the ball to score wide out in the corner for one of the most brilliant individual tries seen at Murrayfield.

Although this win did not herald the start of a successful era it gave the Scots self-respect and ensured they would not be taken lightly at international level. Wins were still devilishly difficult to come by though a second successive one followed against Ireland and six more plus two draws were to follow before the end of the decade.

And players like Angus Cameron, Arthur Smith, Tom Elliot, Jim Greenwood, Hugh McLeod, Ernie Michie, Ken Scotland, Stan Coughtrie, Ken Smith and Gordon Waddell were rewarded for good performances for Scotland with places on the 1955 and 1959 Lions tours where they proved they could perform at the highest level.

*Scrum-half J.A. Nichol, who made a try-scoring debut as Scotland ended their barren spell in 1955.*

## 50 Greatest Players

**ARTHUR SMITH Wing**

**Clubs:** Cambridge University, Gosforth, Ebbw Vale, Edinburgh Wanderers

**Debut:** v Wales, 5 February 1955

**No of Caps:** 33 **No. of Points:** 58

A magnificent athlete, Smith did not fully blossom as a rugby player until he went up to Cambridge in 1954 to research for a PhD. He was a beautifully balanced runner with a long elegant stride who perfected a devastating change of pace. An immensely skilful footballer, he was the master of the attacking kick as evidenced when scoring his sensational solo try on his debut against Wales.

A double Lion, he was injured early on the 1955 tour to South Africa but returned in 1962 as captain, playing in three of the four Tests. It says much for Smith's leadership skills that as a wing he led Scotland 15 times to equal the legendary Mark Morrison's record and in 1962 captained Scotland to their best championship campaign for 24 seasons, narrowly missing a Triple Crown by drawing with England.

A successful businessman, he was struck down by cancer and died at the tragically early age of 42.

In 1955, Cameron and Greenwood both made the Test side with only injury causing Cameron, the Lions vice-captain, to miss the final two Tests. He did well at full-back and was the most reliable goal-kicker on tour. Greenwood was one of the stars of the tour. Normally a No. 8, he was outstanding as a flanker, scoring tries in the first and final Tests in a classic series which went down to the final match. The first Test in Johannesburg was played in front of a world record 95,000 crowd and the Lions edged it 23-22 when Jack van der Schyff missed a conversion in front of the posts to win the match. Leading 2-1 going into the final Test South Africa won convincingly but Greenwood had another excellent match.

In 1959 it was Ken Scotland's turn to be one of the stars of the tour and such was the regard in which he was held that, unusually for a 'foreign' player, he was voted one of the five Players of the Year in New Zealand. McLeod played in all six Tests and Ken Smith had a great tour playing in four Tests but injured his groin and was never the same player again after that.

# Chapter Ten: 1960-69
# Resurgent Scotland

If the immediate post-war period had been a painful one in the heat of the international arena, the 1960s were to provide Scottish supporters with a bit of relief and restored Scotland's reputation on the world stage. Scotland twice missed out narrowly on a Triple Crown in 1961 and 1962, losing 6-0 to England at Twickenham in 1961 and drawing at home to the Auld Enemy the following year, and in 1964 Scotland recorded their best championship season since winning the Triple Crown in 1938 as they won three matches for the first time in 26 years. Furthermore, in three successive seasons they were, quite remarkably, the only home nation to remain unbeaten against southern hemisphere opposition creating a unique hat-trick by earning a creditable 0-0 draw against the All Blacks in 1964 and beating South Africa in 1965 and Australia in 1966.

*New Zealand's Colin Meads receiving a lecture from referee Mr R.C. Williams (Ireland), 1964. Three years later he was not so fortunate as he became the first player to be sent off in a Murrayfield international.*

So what brought about this dramatic improvement in their fortunes? There were a number of factors such as the emergence of some outstanding players particularly in the pack and at half-back; better consistency in selection allowing a degree of continuity and two pioneering short tours to South Africa in 1960 and Canada in 1964.

## Solid Foundations

Scotland's foundations were extremely solid in the early 1960s with the established front row of McLeod, Bruce and Rollo supplemented later by hardy denizens such as Brian Neill, Norman Suddon and Frank Laidlaw. In the second row, the colossal club combination of the double-barrelled Ten Bos and Campbell-Lamerton added significant physical and line-out presence to the front five and later Scotland unearthed the telescopic Peter Stagg who, at 6 foot 10 and 18 stone, was a worthy addition to the boiler house. If Wales has a fly-half factory somewhere in the Valleys, then Scotland has long been able to draw on a top-class bank of back-row forwards. Ken Smith, John Douglas and Kenny Ross, priceless incumbents early in the decade, soon made way for the talents of Ron Glasgow, Pringle Fisher, Jim Telfer and the brothers Grant – Oliver and Derrick.

A variety of combinations were tried at half-back: Waddell and Shillinglaw gave way to Laughland and Hastie before recalled scrum-half Coughtrie was given three different partners in seven internationals and then discarded himself. Finally, the selectors chose the outstanding Melrose pairing of Alex Hastie and David Chisholm together against Ireland in 1964 and they steadied the ship and cleverly used hard-earned possession to win matches. Further out Smith and Scotland wove their magic in the early years of the decade with Stewart Wilson a solid successor to Scotland at full-back. Ian Laughland was a versatile midfield back, Brian Henderson a belligerent, hard-edged centre and strong-running wingers like David Whyte and Sandy Hinshelwood made their mark.

Although still ostensibly a reactionary organisation in a largely conservative-minded sport, both the SRU and rugby began to change quite dramatically during the 1960s. Drug taking, wearing flares and listening to pop music may not quite have been the order of the day in the upper echelons of Murrayfield, but gradually and painfully the sport and its organisation began to move with the times. Although rugby was still staunchly amateur, other sports were beginning to embrace a commercial new world. Footballers were enjoying high-profile lifestyles and Manchester United's George Best became known as the fifth Beatle as much for his good looks, nightclub exploits and the string of beautiful blondes on his arm as for his footballing abilities. Cassius Clay, soon to become Muhammad Ali, brought showbusiness to the boxing ring with his brash predictions and celebrated poems describing how he would defeat his next opponent. And as television became a part of everyday life, it did not take long for bosses to realise that sport was relatively cheap to broadcast to a public with an increasing desire to watch such major events as Wimbledon, the Open, the FA Cup final, the World Cup and the Olympic Games.

Though Five Nations rugby was to form a key part of the BBC's sporting portfolio in the early 1960s the SRU still had its doubts. Indeed, it was not until 1967 that the BBC was able to provide full TV and radio coverage of the tournament. A portion of the SRU's television rights fees were distributed amongst the full member clubs in the form of grants. But at the same time the SRU was still very cautious in its commercial dealings. They permitted clubs to benefit from revenue generated by selling advertising space in their club programmes, but refused to allow the same clubs to display advertising boards at their grounds and, incredibly, objected to the Welsh Youth Rugby Union negotiating a £2,500 sponsorship deal. But these matters aside, in comparison to the ultra-conservative stance of their predecessors, the governing body was actually moving with the times, albeit at its own pace. A number of law changes during the decade, including a restriction on kickiing directly into touch and the introduction of replacements at international level, helped to transform the game into a more modern and exciting spectacle.

## A Fine Line

In the mini-league format of the Five Nations Championship, there can be a very fine line between success and failure. In Scotland's case, a win and a draw in 1959 could not prevent a wooden spoon, yet a year later one win out of four was enough to finish fourth. But these bare facts do not tell the whole story as the 1959 season saw Scotland muster just 12 points and one try but the 1960 season saw a big improvement on the scoreboard, yielding 29 points and four tries. Defeat at the hands of the French, who won the championship, was hard to bear, going down 13-11 at Murrayfield in a five-try thriller, albeit the Scots playing second-half catch up having trailed 13-0 at one stage.

Defeat in a dour encounter at Cardiff followed before a narrow win in Dublin gave Scotland a first win in the Fair City since Ian Smith's side clinched the Triple Crown there in 1933. A defeat at Twickenham was a low note on which to finish the season but, as in the French game, Scotland did not start playing until they were many points down, this time 16-0.

Six weeks later Scotland became the first home union to undertake a short tour in the southern hemisphere, playing three matches in South Africa. A 20-man tour party led by Gordon Waddell and managed by 1938 Triple Crown captain Wilson Shaw made their mark on the Springboks, going some way to avenging the 'Murrayfield Massacre' of 1951. They drew first blood in the Test as Norman Bruce scored a try in the opening minute and they finished the scoring with a Smith try and conversion. In between, their light, mobile pack caused the meaty Springbok octet many problems but the alertness of scrum-half Gericke created three tries to earn a hard-fought 18-10 win.

In a lovely gesture and as a gentle nod to the historic ties between the two nations, four survivors of the Scotland v South Africa match played at Hampden Park in 1906 were guests of honour at the match in Port Elizabeth and appeared in the official pre-match photo. Ken MacLeod, who scored a wonder try in the mud and the glaur at Hampden and who had emigrated to

South Africa many years before, represented Scotland, and H.W. Carolin, the Springbok captain in the match, W.S. Morkel and A.C. Stegmann welcomed their old friend from over 50 years before. Curiously, however, the Test was the opening match of the tour. With subsequent wins over Griqualand West (12-11) and Eastern Transvaal (30-16) it would have been interesting to see how the Scots would have done if the Test had been the final match.

In 1961, Scotland fielded just 20 players and despite losing their first two matches, to France and South Africa, the benefits gained from the tour to South Africa kicked in and they won two of the remaining three matches, travelling to Twickenham for the last match with eyes firmly fixed on a Triple Crown. An early injury to Kelso flanker Charlie Stewart scuppered Scotland's chances against France, but a gutsy performance against the formidable Springboks – Scotland were the only Test side to score a try against them – was the sign of better times ahead.

Ken Scotland was man of the match against Wales, giving a supreme display of his all-round skills in dreadful weather conditions. It was his perfectly timed arrival into the line which created the space for Smith to score the winning try and, on the back foot for much of the rest of the afternoon, he performed his defensive chores with aplomb, sinking the pacy Bebb without trace as the Welsh winger made 50 yards in search of the equaliser.

Ireland arrived at Murrayfield in February in confident mood with a pack that had played wonderfully well in their championship opener to defeat England 11-8. Scotland's hard-fought victory put them on course for a first Triple Crown since 1938. Unfortunately, the final act of the season did not live up to the hype as Scotland could not emulate their performance from the Ireland match. Campbell-Lamerton's late withdrawal did not help and the consequent reshuffling of the pack, with Douglas moving up to second row, made it look unbalanced and in a spluttering performance Scotland's season meekly expired as they lost 6-0 at Twickenham.

## The Old Stumbling Block

For the second season running the selectors tinkered with the team as little as possible and avoiding major injuries Scotland used just 17 players in 1962. The players rewarded the selectors faith, winning two and drawing one match they finished as championship runners-up and but for a draw against England would have won the Triple Crown. Led by Arthur Smith in his final season and with just the one new cap in Ron Glasgow, the 31-year-old Dunfermline flanker, who had had a Scottish trial back in 1955, the Scots got off to a most inauspicious start losing 11-3 to France at Murrayfield.

## Great Matches

**FIVE NATIONS CHAMPIONSHIP** **Murrayfield, 25 February 1961**

**Scotland 16 Ireland 8** **Attendance: 70,000**

On a damp but still afternoon an unchanged Scotland lined up against a confident Irish team and it was a battle royal up front in the opening exchanges as both sides were firmly committed to playing a fast open game, but it was the splendidly mobile and new back-row unit of Ross, Douglas and Smith who were to be the match winners.

The Irish scored first when flanker Kavanagh finished off good work by his forwards. Douglas countered for the Scots and Ken Scotland added the extra points and a penalty to earn a narrow 8-5 half-time lead.

*Norman Bruce escapes down the narrow side against Ireland.*

After the interval both sides threw everything at each other. But the Irish defence cracked first as Scotland escaped down the touchline to feed the supporting Ross for a terrific try and then converted it. Ireland refused to lie down and centre Hewitt finished off a move which swept from one side of the pitch to the other. Moffett's missed conversion meant Scotland were a score ahead but with 10 minutes to go Ross put matters beyond doubt when he popped up for his second and Scotland's third try of the afternoon and a well deserved victory.

**Scotland:** K.J.F. Scotland; A.R. Smith (captain), E. McKeating, G.D. Stevenson, R.H. Thomson; I.H.P. Laughland, A.J. Hastie; H.F. McLeod, N.S. Bruce, D.M.D. Rollo, F.H. ten Bos, M.J. Campbell-Lamerton, G.K. Smith, J. Douglas, K.I. Ross
**Scorers: Tries** Douglas, Ross 2 **Conversions** Scotland 2 **Penalty Goal** Scotland

**Ireland:** T.J. Kiernan; A.C. Pedlow, D. Hewitt, J.C. Walsh, N.H. Brophy; M.A.F. English, J.W. Moffett; S. Millar, A.R. Dawson (captain), B.G.M. Wood, W.A. Mulcahy, M.G. Culliton, N.A.A. Murphy, P.J.A. O'Sullivan, J.R. Kavanagh
**Scorers: Tries** Kavanagh, Hewitt **Conversion** Moffett

**Referee:** Mr M.H.R. King (England)

But there was no panic from the selectors and the only change they made for the next match against Wales was to bring back Coughtrie for Tremayne Rodd at scrum-half. This change made all the difference as Coughtrie mixed his game beautifully throughout the rest of the season. His long, swift service gave Waddell extra time and space to execute his decisions and Coughtrie's own kicking game asked many questions of the opposition. Against Wales the pack outmuscled their counterparts in dire weather conditions with Douglas and Ten Bos combining for Glasgow to score on his debut and from a Waddell up-and-under, Ten Bos grabbed the rebound and his 17-stone bulk was unstoppable from just a few yards out. Scotland contained Wales very effectively in the second half and celebrations continued long into the night as the 8-3 win was their first in Cardiff since 1927.

A fine 20-6 win at Lansdowne Road followed as Scotland recorded a hat-trick of victories to put a miserable series of results against the Irish well and truly behind them, Ireland having dominated the series since 1939. But England once again were the stumbling blocks and oddly it was the third 3-3 draw (all penalties) in five seasons between the oldest of rugby foes. All the scoring came in the first half and although the Scots had the edge in the balance of play they could not finish off their valiant opponents who very nearly stole the match from under their noses at the death.

## Salt in the French Wounds

Scotland were again very competitive in 1963 recording two wins, including a rare victory in Paris, and journeyed to London for the final match with a chance of winning the championship only to be undone by Richard Sharp's brilliant match-winning try. In Paris on a bone-hard pitch, the scores were tied at 6-6 when deep into injury time Campbell-Lamerton pilfered the ball at a line-out. Rollo fed Laughland whose drop goal attempt came up short of the left upright. An evil bounce evaded the covering winger's grasp and

*Ron Thomson takes full advantage of an outrageous bounce of the ball to score in injury time to earn a rare victory in Paris in 1963.*

## 50 Greatest Players

**KEN SCOTLAND Full-back/Stand-off**

**Clubs:** Heriot's FP, Cambridge University, Leicester, Aberdeenshire

**Debut:** v France, 12 January 1957

**No. of Caps:** 27 **No. of Points:** 71

A genuine world-class footballer who won most of his caps as a full-back but versatile enough to slot in comfortably anywhere in the back division. He burst on to the international scene as a 20-year-old, scoring all of Scotland's points in their 6-0 win over France at the Stade Colombes. He blossomed as an attacking full-back and was one of the stars of the 1959 Lions tour to Australasia, scoring 12 tries but, remarkably, is placed only 5th on the top try-scorers list. Scotland was a key factor in his country's resurgence in the early 1960s and his cleverly timed and angled intrusions into the line set up countless opportunities for his wingers. Indeed, Arthur Smith rated him as 'the best passer of the ball I played with'. He was also a competent goal-kicker, a pioneer of the round the corner goal-kicking style in an era of unsophisticated toe-bashers.

Thomson, Scotland's right wing, gathered the ball to score a marvellous opportunist try in the left corner. Scotland landed the conversion to rub salt into the French wounds.

The tactics employed by Clive Rowlands, the Welsh scrum-half and captain, at Murrayfield not only bored Scotland and the crowd to tears but led to a law change which revolutionised the way rugby was played. It was not uncommon to play nine- or ten-man rugby in this era but Rowlands took the tactical kicking game to new levels by kicking almost every bit of possession he received directly out of play as he stitched up the touchline. It was effective as Wales won 6-0, but it was later revealed that there had been 111 line-outs in 80 minutes of play.

A furious debate ensued and eventually in 1969 it led to the IB introducing a new touch law, Law 27, which permitted a player to kick directly into touch only from within his own 25-yard (now 22-metre) line. This has been a marvellous boon to the game and along with a number of other law changes particularly the increase in the value of the try, has led to a more positive, attack-minded approach to the game. Ireland were beaten by the narrowest of margins thanks to a Coughtrie penalty and

**50 Greatest Players**

**NORMAN BRUCE Hooker**

**Clubs:** Blackheath, the Army, London Scottish

**Debut:** v France, 11 January 1958

**No. of Caps:** 31 **No. of Points:** 9

A Borderer from Gala, Norman Bruce was ahead of his time as a mobile, dynamic hooker in an era when the hooker's primary function was to win the ball at the set scrummage. Ably supported in the front row by such solid pillars as Hughie McLeod, Tom Elliot and Dave Rollo, he won his share of scrummage ball, but it was in the loose that he excelled. Seemingly tireless he went in constant search of the ball and was the proud scorer of three international tries. In the opening minute of the Port Elizabeth Test on the pioneering tour to South Africa in 1960, he crashed over the line by the posts to open the scoring. And in his final international he scored the second of Scotland's three tries in the 15-6 demolition job on the Auld Enemy. A first pick for seven seasons he toured Canada in 1964 but unfortunately was then posted to the Far East with the army bringing to an end an illustrious international career.

despite leading 8-0 at one stage Scotland lost 10-8 at Twickenham which did away with any hope of the championship.

## Up Another Level

Scotland moved up to another level in in next few years and it started in 1964 when, for the first time since 1938, they won three matches in the season and shared the championship title with Wales, who won two and drew two.

A solid 10-0 opening win against France in horribly wet conditions was followed by one of Scotland's greatest ever results, a 0-0 draw against New Zealand. Wilson Whineray's fifth All Blacks were beaten just once on tour and Scotland were the only side not to lose to them in a Test match. Unfortunately, Scotland have never beaten the All Blacks but that day they had their chances to win in a marvellously disciplined performance. They adapted better to the poor conditions and, although giving second best in the scrum, their greater mobility in the loose and tenacious tackling badly rattled the Blacks who, unable to feed off any Scottish mistakes, were reduced to launching a series of speculative up-and-unders.

Frustratingly, after having contained the unofficial world champions, Scotland could not replicate their performance at Cardiff Arms Park and were comfortably despatched 11-3. The selectors crucially rang the changes as six players were axed in a bid to find the right blend for the trip to Dublin. And find it they did, pairing Hastie and Chisholm at half-back and restoring a better balance to the pack. With a 6-0 lead at the interval and provided with ample ball, the Melrose pair ran the show in the second half, revelling in the poor conditions, and snuffed out any chance the Irish had of winning in a tight finish.

*Norman Bruce scores Scotland's second try v England in 1964.*

With the season back on track the Scottish pack dominated the English in the match at Murrayfield as the back row of Fisher, Telfer and Glasgow rampaged around the pitch. Tries from Glasgow, Bruce and Telfer gave Scotland a 15-3 lead mid-way through the second half, killing off the contest, and the fans could relax and enjoy a famous Scotland victory over the Auld Enemy, the first at home since 1950.

On the face of it 1965 was a very poor season as Scotland finished bottom of the heap with one point in the championship, but there was an impressive 8-5 win over the Springboks to savour in a fine finale to the season. Yet, after being well beaten in Paris, the Scots were undone by a last-minute try at Murrayfield to lose 14-12 and seemingly having done all the hard work at Twickenham, leading 3-0 through a Chisholm drop goal as the stopwatch crept past the 80-minute mark, they were left reeling by Andy Hancock's length of the pitch effort to snatch an unlikely draw.

The South Africa match left a sweeter taste in Scottish mouths as a fine performance again from the Melrose halves kept the Springboks on the back foot. It was from Chisholm's garryowen that Shackleton scored and with the scores tied at 5-5 his crucial snap drop goal won the match in thrilling fashion.

Again a settled team the following year almost reaped the ultimate dividend as just 17 players represented Scotland during the season. Indeed, but for injury, it is likely that the same XV would have played throughout. The crucial blow was losing Chisholm for the Welsh match. But his attacking skills brought the only try of the match against France sparking a marvellous move in which backs and forwards combined for Hastie's long pass to put Whyte clear in the left corner. Unfortunately, the Scots could not convert their kicking chances and had to settle for a rare draw against France.

## 50 Greatest Players

**DAVID ROLLO Prop**

**Club:** Howe of Fife

**Debut:** v England, 21 March 1959

**No. of Caps:** 40 **No. of Points:** 0

A farmer from the unfashionable Howe of Fife club, Dave Rollo broke into the side in 1959 and quickly became a globetrotting prop, touring South Africa twice, in 1960 with Scotland and two years later with the Lions, and Canada with Scotland in 1964.

The first and only player, to date, from his club to play for Scotland, he was a hard man, playing most of his debut international with a broken nose, and eschewing the use of protection such as shin pads, he always played with his socks rolled down. In his last international against Ireland he equalled McLeod's record of 40 appearances for Scotland, although minor injuries prevented him matching McLeod's 40 successive caps.

In Dublin, the pack annihilated their Irish counterparts with the back row of Fisher, Telfer and Grant absolutely outstanding. Hastie enjoyed an armchair ride at scrum-half and was highly instrumental in Hinshelwood's two scores and his electric break set up Grant for the final try of the afternoon and a comfortable 11-3 win. Another fine all-round performance saw off England at Murrayfield with the Melrose pair running the show again, mixing sublime attacking skills with committed defence. And it was Hastie's huge pass that gave Chisholm enough space to feed Henderson who set Laughland away. Half checked, the centre off-loaded to the supporting Grant who provided the pass for Whyte to score the winning try in the corner.

### Victory against Australia, Defeat against New Zealand

The 1966-67 season started well for the Scots as they completed an unprecedented unbeaten hat-trick over southern hemisphere countries, beating Australia 11-5 at Murrayfield. As the Wallabies had just beaten Wales, they arrived in Edinburgh with a fair degree of confidence, and it took a fine performance to defeat them. Chisholm closed out an exciting first half, jinking through to score a clever try, and Boyle's solitary score in the second half secured the win.

## 50 Greatest Players

### JIM TELFER Flanker/No. 8

**Club:** Melrose

**Debut:** v France, 4 January 1964

**No. of Caps:** 25 **No. of Points:** 9

The man who has had the most profound influence on the development of Scottish rugby in the modern era has been committed to the cause for almost 40 years. Ostensibly a No. 8, Telfer was an abrasive and enthusiastic tackler, his bravery in search of winning or denying the opposition the ball knew no bounds as he selflessly put his body on the line. Twice a Lion and a devoted student of the game, he took the opportunity to learn about the game on tour. Appointed Scotland B coach in 1974 he now has a world-class coaching CV having twice coached Scotland to Grand Slam success and the 1997 Lions to a series win in South Africa in tandem with his rugby soul mate Ian McGeechan.

Scotland went into the championship with high hopes and opened impressively, winning narrowly in Paris. Against Wales, Chisholm's drop goal nudged the Scots ahead 6-5 and, hanging on by one point with minutes to go, Hastie broke through with a clever dummy and found Telfer on his shoulder who took the pass to bulldoze over the line. The season was shaping up nicely but, unfortunately, Chisholm missed the final two matches of the season as Scotland lost narrowly to Ireland and heavily to England at Twickenham for the season to peter out.

The revival came to a juddering halt in 1968 as the Scots suffered their first whitewash since 1954. And in that season they also lost to the All Blacks. Telfer was absent for the first four matches of the season with a cartilage injury and his influence was clearly missed. The All Blacks had to work hard to break down a brave home defence to win 14-3. They even coped with losing Colin Meads who was sent off for dangerous play, becoming the first player to be dismissed in a Murrayfield international. The selectors tinkered with the team throughout the season, but the search for a winning combination was fruitless. Narrow losses against France and Wales were followed by a 14-6 defeat by Ireland. Telfer returned as captain to inspire the pack to its best performance of the season during the Calcutta Cup match, but that also ended in defeat.

## 50 Greatest Players

**DAVID CHISHOLM Stand-off**
**Club:** Melrose
**Debut:** v Ireland, 22 February 1964
**No. of Caps:** 14 **No. of Points:** 15

Uncapped until the relatively advanced age of 27, David Chisholm, in tandem with club partner Alex Hastie, established himself as a stand-off of rare quality, confirming what many on the club scene knew but to which the national selectors appeared oblivious. A genuinely two-footed player he revelled in his defensive duties as much as seeking out and exploiting gaps to get his back line going. Chisholm and Hastie were astute tacticians and knew instinctively when to keep matches tight and when to play a more expansive game. In 13 matches together for Scotland they won 8, drew 2 and lost 3, and remarkably remained unbeaten in their first 10 matches together. This amazing sequence was achieved against the best teams in the world and included wins over South Africa and Australia, two Calcutta Cups, away victories in Dublin and Paris and a draw at Twickenham.

### The 'Telfer Try'

There was an immediate improvement in fortunes at the end of the decade as the first two matches were won, against Australia and France. But heavy home defeats followed at the hands of Wales and Ireland and although there was a good performance at Twickenham it was not enough to earn a victory.

The 1969 season saw the introduction of up to two replacements for injured players at international level only. This was a welcome change as international rugby was littered with cases of teams being severely handicapped by the loss of one or more injured players in a match. And in some extreme cases, players have bravely stayed on the pitch and aggravated their injury so badly that they never played again. Ian McCrae, the Gordonians scrum-half, became the first player in the Five Nations Championship to win a cap as a replacement when he took over from the injured Gordon Connell against France in Paris. And he made a remarkable impression on the match when, from a French scrum in their own 25, he robbed his opposite number of the ball and fed skipper Telfer who crashed over for the winning try. The 'Telfer Try' became part of rugby folklore as BBC Scotland delighted in replaying the grainy black and white images every two years as a part of their preview for the annual pilgrimage to Paris.

# Chapter Eleven: 1970-79
## The Tide Turns

A brutally savage tour of Argentina in the early part of the 1969-70 season gave the Scots a sharp reminder of how rugby was expanding and an indication that this was to be a decade of considerable change. At the time rugby was still little more than a hobby for most players, even those at the elite end of the sport. But the tide was turning and during the early years of the decade it became apparent that a more 'professional' and serious approach was required of players if they were to remain at the top with frequent national tours, the introduction of coaching and the unveiling of league rugby in Scotland in 1973-74.

Regular exposure to higher grade rugby both on tour and domestically, underpinned by the better organisation and innovative ideas adopted by coaches, helped improve Scotland's fortunes dramatically. The pushover days were over, particularly in the period 1971-75 when the famous front five provided a fearsome platform turning Murrayfield into a veritable fortress. In that four-year period, Scotland won 11 of the 12 internationals played at home, losing only to the All Blacks and that win was only sealed courtesy of an injury-time try.

*A typical line-out from the time, as the ball appears to go New Zealand's way in 1972.*

## Sobering Experiences

But the back-to-back tours to Argentina and Australia were sobering experiences for the Scots from which many lessons were learned. On arrival in Argentina the party, containing just 21 players, was greeted by a 24-hour strike and massive civil unrest during one of the country's least stable times. But 21 players quickly became 20 as Gala No. 8 Ken Oliver failed to shake off a calf injury and was sent home within four days of arrival.

A woefully small squad therefore had to play six matches and throughout the tour were, bluntly, confronted by dirty and dangerous play and what might be euphemistically described as inconsistent refereeing. All four provincial matches were won but the first 'non-cap' international was lost 20-6, before revenge was gained in the second 'Test' as Scotland ground out a gritty 6-3 win.

In his captain's speech after the final win Jim Telfer, never one to mince his words, launched into a 10-minute diatribe spelling out his views on the Argentinian style of rugby, telling them that if they continued with their cynical approach they would alienate themselves from the rest of the rugby world. As he sat down, the official interpreter translated Telfer's tirade into a brief, bland summary lasting all of ten seconds, telling the audience in Spanish what a wonderful country Argentina was. A classic case of the meaning not so much being lost but completely buried in the translation.

Just nine months later, following a season with an excellent start and finish in which South Africa were beaten 6-3 and England despatched 14-5, but a disappointing middle section, the Scots were on their travels again, this time to Australia. Although only three of six matches were won, many who had toured Argentina rated it the harder challenge. In many ways the Australia tour was fated from the start as tour manager Hector Munro, a Conservative MP, was called back to the UK when the Labour government called a snap general election. The organisational burden fell on assistant manager George Burrell's willing shoulders, but he was left with an impossible task. The tour party of 21 was quickly depleted with two injuries sustained in the first match and once again a weakened squad struggled to compete. By the Test match they were particularly under strength and unsurprisingly succumbed 23-3, as the Aussies ran in six tries to nil.

## The Vexing Question of Coaching

The subject of coaching had been on the SRU's agenda since the 1950s, a response to the disastrous run of international results in the early days of that decade which had caused a public outcry. However, the emphasis was clearly on the teaching of basic skills to schoolboys to bring through properly trained, new generations of players. Schoolteachers were targeted and a national coaching conference was held at Fettes College in 1955.

But it was to be some time before the SRU actively encouraged the development of club coaches. Following discussions over a number of years a coaching sub-committee was set up in 1968 and the first national course for club coaches was staged the following year. But if the SRU was being progressive at club level, they were very cautious at international level. They viewed with great suspicion and alarm the rise of international coaches in southern hemisphere nations and France, with the underlying connotation of professionals operating in an amateur sport, and were particularly dismayed when Wales appointed Clive Rowlands as their national coach in 1968. Their development tour to Argentina that year and regular get-togethers during the season gave Wales a clear edge in terms of fitness, organisation and team spirit and it is no surprise that they became the dominant force in European rugby in the late 1960s and 70s.

It was not until 1971 that Scotland finally relented. Bill Dickinson, the Jordanhill coach and senior lecturer in PE at Jordanhill College, had helped prepare the Blues team in the international trial but was not involved in Scotland's 13-8 defeat in Paris. However, Lex Govan, convenor of selectors, convinced his colleagues that the Scotland team needed help and Dickinson was appointed. Even then the SRU could not bring themselves to appoint him as coach, but instead he was given the handle 'adviser to the captain'. But he was coach in all but name.

Regardless of his moniker, Dickinson's appointment had a pretty dramatic effect on the team and performances. Previously the captain was in charge of team preparation as well as all the other off-pitch headaches. As coach, Dickinson could concentrate purely on match preparation and he brought a new level of organisation, concentrating in the early matches on improving the defensive roles.

## A Formidable Challenge

His first match in charge could not have been a more formidable challenge as Scotland, having lost four of their previous five championship matches, faced Wales who had lost just one of their previous eight and were fresh from hammering England 22-6. Behind a solid pack, the Welsh had a magical back division inspired by the peerless Gareth Edwards and Barry John, clever centres and the contrasting approaches in their back three: the twinkling toes of Gerald Davies and the physical menace of J.P.R. Williams and John Bevan.

## Great Matches

**FIVE NATIONS CHAMPIONSHIP** **Murrayfield, 6 February 1971**

**Scotland 18 Wales 19** **Attendance: 80,000**

In a pulsating match where the lead changed hands six times, Scotland were ahead on four occasions, there were never more than five points between the sides, with the result in doubt until the final kick. P.C. Brown and John traded early penalties and following a second Brown penalty, Taylor got over the line, finishing off with a flamboyant dive behind the posts. John's conversion made it 6-8 at half-time.

The second half was a try-scoring bonanza as the teams traded try for try. Edwards was first, only for Carmichael to bulldoze over from short range; then a Brown penalty nudged Scotland ahead 12-11. Then John ghosted through a gap only he could have spotted but was concussed in the process and missed the conversion: 12-14. Brown landed his fourth penalty and then Rea's aggressive running shrugged off a would-be tackler to score midway out on the left only for Brown to miss the kick: 18-14.

*Sandy Carmichael forces his way over the Wales line for Scotland's first try.*

With time running out Wales needed a converted try to win. And, from a line-out on the Scotland 25, Thomas won clean ball and it fizzed along the back line to the intruding Williams who created an overlap for Davies to score wide out on the right. Both sets of supporters held their breath as the left-footed Taylor lined up his conversion attempt. And it was the Welsh supporters who exhaled in joy as the ball went between the uprights for what has been described as 'the greatest conversion since St Paul'.

**Scotland:** I.S.G. Smith; W.C.C. Steele, J.N.M. Frame, C.W.W. Rea, A.G. Biggar; J.W.C. Turner, D.S. Paterson; J. McLauchlan, F.A.L. Laidlaw, A.B. Carmichael, A.F. McHarg, G.L. Brown, N.A. MacEwan, P.C. Brown (captain), R.J. Arneil
**Scorers: Tries** Carmichael, Rea **Penalty Goals** P.C. Brown 4

**Wales:** J.P.R. Williams; T.G.R. Davies, S.J. Dawes (captain), I. Hall, J.C. Bevan; B. John, G.O. Edwards; D. Williams, J. Young, D.B. Llewellyn, M.G. Roberts, W.D. Thomas, W.D. Morris, T.M. Davies, J. Taylor
**Scorers: Tries** Taylor, Edwards, John, T.G.R. Davies **Conversions** John, Taylor **Penalty Goal** John

**Referee:** Mr M.H. Titcomb (England)

But against all the odds, Scotland were involved in one of rugby's classic matches, only to lose at the very end.

If the 17-5 defeat at the hands of Ireland was a disappointing anti-climax to the high of the Wales performance, an historic back-to-back double against England more than made up for it. Scotland buried their Twickenham hoodoo to record a first win there since 1938 thanks to their own last-gasp match-winning conversion. In a tough, physical contest, Scotland outscored England by three tries to two with Chris Rea shooting over for the third try leaving Peter Brown to kick the goal. In his own inimitable style, he placed the ball on the ground, blew his nose, turned his back on the ball and retreated a few paces. Wheeling round, he had a quick sideways look at the ball, shuffled up to it, made a good contact and saw the ball follow its usual wobbly trajectory right between the posts for a fantastic 16-15 win.

*Peter Brown scores against England in the 16-15 win at Twickenham in 1971.*

Just seven days later, Scotland played England again, this time at Murrayfield in the Centenary International, exactly 100 years to the day since the first match at Raeburn Place. This time the Scots annihilated the Auld Enemy with John Frame scoring a try within 12 seconds of kick-off to set the tone for the afternoon. Scotland scored four more tries to run out 26-6 winners and wrap up a memorable week's work.

For seven fortunate players a Lions tour to New Zealand beckoned. Four of the famous 'Mean Machine' made the trip: Ian McLauchlan, Frank Laidlaw, Sandy Carmichael and Gordon Brown, as did three-quarters Alistair Biggar and Chris Rea, with flanker Rodger Arneil called up as a replacement for the injured Mick Hipwell of Ireland.

The Lions captivated New Zealand with their commitment to attacking rugby but unlike their predecessors they possessed a hardcore upfront who won enough ball to allow the brilliant backs to run the show. They won the Test series 2-1, with McLauchlan and Brown making outstanding contributions, the first time the Lions had ever won a series in New Zealand.

## Scotland Get the Mark Over England

The 1972 season was a curious one as only three championship matches were played. The SRU decided that it was too dangerous to travel to Dublin

## 50 Greatest Players

### IAN McLAUCHLAN Prop

**Club:** Jordanhill

**Debut:** v England, 15 March 1969

**No. of Caps:** 43 **No. of Points:** 0

Nicknamed 'Mighty Mouse' by 1971 Lions manager Doug Smith after his heroic, try-scoring performance in the first Test in Dunedin, McLauchlan's international career started somewhat belatedly in 1969 against England and finished almost 11 years later, at the age of 37, when he led his country for a record 19th time against the All Blacks.

A very hard, aggressive man who loved to compete, in conjunction with club coach Bill Dickinson he helped transform Scotland's fortunes in the 1970s, turning Murrayfield into something of a fortress with his ferocious brand of no-nonsense leadership. Under him, Scotland were unbeatable at home in the championship for four seasons. One of just five players to play in all eight Tests on the triumphant tours of 1971 and 1974 – the others being J.P.R. Williams, Gareth Edwards, Willie John McBride and Mervyn Davies – he deserves his position as a legendary Lion.

because of the political situation, so they pulled out of the fixture much to the disappointment of the players. Excellent home wins were achieved against France and England either side of a heavy defeat in Cardiff. Against France, the Scottish midfield were in particularly fine form, each scoring a try including Jim Renwick, who was making his international debut. Despite leading 12-10 early in the second half against Wales, a controversial try by Edwards following a line-out gave the Welsh a comfortable victory.

But Scotland bounced back with a satisfying 23-9 victory over England which gave P.C. Brown a hat-trick of wins as captain against them, equalling Mark Morrison's feat at the turn of the century. Furthermore, it was Scotland's fourth successive win over the men in white and nobody contributed more to these successes than Brown as he scored 34 of Scotland's 79 points, including three tries. Not bad for a No. 8.

The following season, 1973, was one of Scotland's most successful for some time and two backs of the highest quality made their bows in the international arena to add a new dimension to the team – Andy Irvine and Ian McGeechan. The duo made their debuts together against the All Blacks at the end of 1972, both making an immediate impact and becoming mainstays of the Scottish and Lions back divisions for the rest of the decade. If Irvine was the flamboyant, exciting cavalier then McGeechan

## 50 Greatest Players

**GORDON BROWN Second row**

**Club:** West of Scotland

**Debut:** v South Africa, 6 December 1969

**No. of Caps:** 30 **No. of Points:** 0

Known as 'Broon from Troon' or the 'baby-faced assassin', off the pitch Gordon Brown was the nicest guy you could wish to meet. But on it, and particularly in a Lions shirt, he was one of the world's most ruthless competitors. From a sporting family, elder brother Peter was an international colleague and father Jock an international goalkeeper. Brown was a fine athlete for such a big man. At 6 foot 5 inches and around 17 stone he shoved his weight in the scrum and was a marvellous line-out foil for the gifted Alistair McHarg. He established himself as one fifth of Scotland's 'Mean Machine' in the great side of the early 1970s but it was on Lions tours that he fully flourished. He forced his way into the 1971 Test side for the final two matches of the series and was a mainstay of the 1974 Lions pack when he was in the form of his life scoring a remarkable eight tries. Cancer claimed him at the tragically early age of 53.

was the quiet, effective balance creating the opportunities for Irvine's devastating running abilities.

Irvine was most assured against New Zealand, performing his defensive chores confidently and sparking counter attacks at any opportunity. His two penalties plus McGeechan's opportunist drop goal kept Scotland in touch and, heading into injury time, just a single point separated the sides. Sensing an historic victory, Scotland threw everything into one last attack. When the ubiquitous McHarg popped up in the back line he spotted an overlap and threw an ambitious overhead pass to the right wing. Unfortunately, Kiwi scrum-half Sid Going was alert to this and intercepted the pass to scamper 50 yards for the match-clinching score and a narrow 14-9 win.

There followed a narrow loss in Paris, a match in which English referee Ken Pattinson pulled up injured in the opening quarter and was replaced by French touch judge Francis Palmade. Today there are neutral touch judges to cover such an eventuality – as evidenced when Tony Spreadbury (England) replaced the injured Pablo Deluca (Argentina) at half-time during the Scotland v Wales match in 2003 – but Monsieur Palmade was scrupulously fair and the Scots had no complaints about his refereeing, losing out to an immaculate goal kicking display by Jean-Pierre Romeu.

## Bodies on the Line

Wales were next and once again arrived at Murrayfield brimming with confidence with nine Lions packed into their ranks, having just scored five tries in thrashing England 25-9. But Dickinson's influence was growing and the captaincy was handed to the abrasive McLauchlan, his club captain. Dickinson pummelled his forwards in practice and they spent one session pushing the scrummaging machine all over the back pitches at Murrayfield. Buoyed by the confidence this session instilled, the plan was to confront the Welsh pack from first to last. Edwards was singled out for special attention and opposite number Dougie Morgan, on his debut, and flankers Nairn McEwan and Jock Millican were charged with shackling the great man. And when the Welsh backs did get the ball they were to be immediately chopped down.

McLauchlan's inspirational pre-match talk called for his players to lay their bodies on the line and following his lead the Scots won a famous victory in a brutal encounter. Edwards was duly shackled and starved of possession, the Welsh lost the try count 2-0 with the Scots racing into an early ten-point lead thanks to tries by Colin Telfer and Billy Steele.

Another punishing match followed against Ireland and the narrow 19-15 win will always be remembered for a special piece of sportsmanship by Irish skipper Tom Kiernan. With time running out and leading 16-15, Morgan launched a drop at goal from near the left touchline. Mid-flight it appeared to run out of puff and as it came down it was unclear as to whether it had cleared the bar or not. Kiernan, playing in his final international, was perfectly positioned under the posts and sportingly signalled that the kick was good, a gesture deeply appreciated by the Scottish team and crowd. Today, 30 years later, in a high-pressure, money-driven game, it is difficult to imagine a modern day full-back in a similar situation being quite so generous.

The win was not without cost as McLauchlan cracked his fibula against Ireland and other forwards had taken heavy knocks. Remarkably, the cussedly determined McLauchlan made it on to the pitch at Twickenham just three weeks later with the aid of a painkilling injection and protective shin pads. The drama of his leg break, and the 'will he, won't he play' saga gave the newspapers a field day as Scotland were seeking a first Triple Crown in 35 years, even knocking from the back pages the usual blanket coverage accorded the Old Firm derby in the fevered build up to the match.

Alas, Scotland went down 20-13 and inevitably the post-match inquest pointed the finger of blame at the 'unfit' skipper. Conversely, if Scotland had won, McLauchlan would have been accorded legendary status. However, as at least three other members of the pack were carrying injuries any 'blame' has to be shared and unfortunately for Scotland the harsh reality was that a hard international season caught up with them.

*England's Chris Ralston just beats Alastair McHarg to the ball at Twickenham in 1973.*

## The First National League

The 1973-74 season was a very significant season for the development of Scottish rugby as Scotland became the first home nation to initiate a formal national league season. Since its inception in 1901-02 the Border League had led the way and undoubtedly managed to keep the standard of Borders rugby at a consistently high level over the years. So it was no surprise that two Border clubs, Hawick and Gala, dominated the First Division throughout the 1970s. Standards rose quite considerably in the early years with promotion and relegation each season concentrating the minds of clubs throughout the nation. Clubs such as Highland and Stirling County rose rapidly through the divisions to create new hotbeds of rugby in previously virgin territory. The advent of the leagues strengthened club rugby and consequently helped prepare the best players for the rigours of the international arena, maintaining Scotland's competitiveness in the closing years of the century.

Meanwhile, the 1974 championship season was also one of significant change. Since Scotland had first started playing France in 1910, the same rigid cycle of fixtures had been followed each season: France-Wales-Ireland-England. There had been a lot of hard talking over the years about breaking this cycle, particularly from England who felt they were at a considerable disadvantage as they often played France last in the early spring, when it is widely regarded that the French traditionally are at their best; with the Paris sunshine on their backs.

But Scotland's main desire was to keep the Scotland v England match in its traditional position on the third Saturday in March. However, they eventually

*Ian McGeechan played in all four Lions Tests in 1974.*

bowed to the inevitable and common sense decision to rotate the fixtures. So, Scotland's first opponents that year were Wales and in a fierce fight, the Welsh squeaked home by 6-0 thanks to another controversial try. This time Gerald Davies appeared to play the ball while on the ground in setting up the only try of the match for the supporting Terry Cobner.

The Calcutta Cup match provided magnificent entertainment value as both sides attacked at every opportunity and included a moment of pure theatre to bring down the curtain. Scotland were awarded a penalty in injury time about 40 yards from the English posts but wide out on the right. Up stepped Irvine to coolly slot the goal to win the match 16-14. He was promptly chaired off the field by his ecstatic team-mates. The remaining two matches resulted in a narrow loss in Dublin and a surprisingly comfortable 19-6 win over France who needed a victory to clinch the championship.

Three backs (Irvine, Steele and McGeechan) and three forwards (McLauchlan, Carmichael and Brown) were chosen to tour with the Lions to South Africa that summer and all contributed gloriously to the most successful Lions tour of all time. McLauchlan and McGeechan played in all four Tests and Steele and Irvine in two each as the Lions won the series 3-0 and all 18 provincial matches.

## So Close to Glory

The Scotland side had matured rapidly over three seasons and by 1975 was unbeatable at home and fiercely competitive on foreign soil. Although just two matches were won the losses were each by the slimmest possible margin, a single point. With a little luck certainly three and probably all four could have been won and with it Triple Crown or Grand Slam glory.

The front five selected itself and with two new back-row forwards, Mike Biggar and David Leslie, quickly establishing themselves, the pack remained formidable. With an astute pairing of Morgan and McGeechan at half-back they had plenty of exciting talent outside them to unleash, the pick of the bunch being Irvine, Renwick and Steele. Bill Dickinson had an extremely well balanced unit at his disposal.

Reigning champions Ireland had just beaten England and with a good record at Murrayfield were confident of further success. A drop goal by Morgan in the opening minute set the tone for the match, however, and tries by Renwick and Steele ensured Scotland led 14-6 at half-time. Two Irvine penalties steered the home side to a deserved 20-13 victory.

*Ian McLauchlan was an inspirational captain.*

In Paris a ferocious pitch battle erupted as Scotland went down by the cruellest of margins, 10-9. A real brawl broke out at the first line-out involving most of the forwards although the two players singled out for a warning, Carmichael and Bofelli, had been the least involved. Private skirmishes were the order of the day but the Scots refused to be intimidated. As coach Dickinson said afterwards, 'We won the battle, but lost the match'. Unfortunately, Irvine had a calamitous day with his boot and missed six penalties from nine attempts, including one from straight in front about 30 yards out with five minutes to go which would have snatched the match.

A second successive win over Wales at home was just the tonic to lift the team and their loyal support as somehow a world record crowd estimated at around 104,000 squeezed into Murrayfield. The capacity was 80,000 but matches were not all-ticket in those days and there were very often more present than there should have been. In a hard bruising encounter, Scotland looked to have done enough to win as they led 12-6 through the combined boots of Morgan and McGeechan heading into injury time. However, Gerald Davies' feet wove a typical piece of magic to create enough space for flanker Evans to squeeze in at the right corner. Four years on from Taylor, another forward, this time lock Allan Martin, had the chance to become a Welsh legend by landing a touchline conversion. Thankfully, lightning did not strike twice and Scotland had won the second leg of an elusive Triple Crown.

England once again lay in wait to ambush the Scots on their quest for glory. And really with the amount of good quality ball won by the pack that afternoon, the game would have been won but for poor finishing by the backs. Leading 6-3, Irvine and Morley contested hard for a bouncing ball in the Scotland goal area with both claiming they reached the ball first. TV evidence proved to be inconclusive and arguably, if the referee was in any

## 50 Greatest Players

**JIM RENWICK Centre**

**Club:** Hawick

**Debut:** v France, 15 January 1972

**No. of Caps:** 52 **No. of Points:** 67

Jim Renwick made his international debut as a 19-year-old in Scotland's convincing 20-9 win over France at Murrayfield in 1972, celebrating by scoring a debut try. A dazzling talent, he benefited from playing at inside centre, rather than the traditional left or right centre, being a good enough footballer to act as an auxiliary stand-off as required. But it was with ball in hand that he came into his element, cutting opposing defences to ribbons with a shimmy, a swerve and an injection of pace. Renwick was at the heart of many of Scotland's most cavalier attacking movements of the decade but his greatest individual moment probably came in Cardiff in 1982. He slashed through the Welsh cover and scorched home from fully 50 yards for a scintillating score. Mystifyingly overlooked for the 1977 Lions, he was belatedly honoured in 1980 and played in the first Test.

doubt, he should have ruled in favour of the defending team, but instead he awarded the try to make it 7-6 to England. That, unfortunately, proved to be the winning score as, despite having two very kickable penalties, the normally reliable Morgan missed both and as the match petered out, and with it all hope of the Triple Crown, a familiar gloom descended on the nation.

Scotland toured New Zealand in the summer and won four of the six provincial matches but it was the Test match – forever remembered as the 'Water Polo Test' – which was most notable. More than four inches of rain fell in less than 12 hours on Eden Park in Auckland and, but for the fact that the tour party was booked to fly home the following day, the match would have been postponed. It should have been as conditions were both farcical and downright dangerous with debutant hooker Colin Fisher trapped at the bottom of a ruck at one stage face down in the water convinced he was about to drown.

Scotland did extraordinarily well in the first half playing into the eye of the most ferocious storm and, despite losing Bruce Hay with a broken arm on his debut, they trailed just 6-0 at the interval. With the prospect of lashing rain and a gale-force wind at their backs things looked good for a

**50 Greatest Players**

**ANDY IRVINE Full-back/Wing**

**Club:** Heriot's FP

**Debut:** v New Zealand, 16 December 1972

**No. of Caps:** 51 **No. of Points:** 273

The Scottish superstar of his era, Irvine had pace and skill to burn and a furious desire to win by playing positive, attacking rugby at every conceivable opportunity. At club and international level he was as capable of losing matches as winning them, and his performance against France at Murrayfield in 1980 was typical of the emotions he could generate in the course of a match. Scotland were trailing 14-4 with 12 minutes to go and, unusually for a Murrayfield crowd, Irvine was being roundly booed for his nightmare performance. He had missed several kicks at goal including one from 15 yards slap-bang in front of the sticks. But in a wonderful finale this most charismatic of players scored two terrific tries and 16 of 18 points to turn the boos into cheers as Scotland won 22-14. A triple Lion, his 156 points in 1974 is a record, and he set New Zealand agog in 1977, the highlight being his five tries against King Country-Wanganui.

first win over the All Blacks. However, in the cruellest twist of fate, the elements swung right round through 180 degrees and they played the second 40 minutes into the teeth of the storm. Understandably the Kiwis ran out winners 24-0.

### The Good Times End

A first championship loss at home in four seasons to France in 1976 was countered by some excellent wins over Australia, Ireland and England. The victory at Lansdowne Road was particularly sweet as it was Scotland's first win away from home since 1971 and, astonishingly, the first away win for the likes of Irvine and McGeechan, both winning their 20th caps.

The following year Scotland were badly hit before the season started as they lost Leslie to injury and then Gordon Brown received a lengthy ban for retaliating to an unprovoked assault during an inter-district match. This suspension in effect finished Brown's international career although he did make it on to the plane to New Zealand for the Lions' tour at the end of

**50 Greatest Players**

**IAN McGEECHAN Stand-off/Centre**

**Club**: Headingly

**Debut:** v New Zealand, 16 December 1972

**No. of Caps**: 32 **No. of Points:** 21

A neat, tidy footballer sounds a rather patronising description but it is meant as a compliment. McGeechan was not a flashy player but he knew his role and played it to perfection whether at stand-off or centre for club, country and the Lions. He was an excellent all-round player, solid in defence, clever in attack and always aware; a master tactician who kept his cool in the white-hot arena of Test rugby. His trademark was the snap drop goal which often kept the scoreboard ticking over for Scotland, and in the second Test in Pretoria in 1974 his perfectly timed second half drop goal extended the Lions lead to 21-9 to kill off the Springboks' chances of winning the series. But he will probably be best remembered as one of the world's best coaches with two Grand Slams and a World Cup semi-final with Scotland to his credit and two Test series wins against Australia and South Africa in his three tours as Lions coach in 1989, 1993 and 1997.

the season and played in three of the four Tests. Brown was joined on the tour by Irvine, Hay, McGeechan and Morgan with only Hay not playing any part in the series, which was lost 3-1.

In the championship a narrow win over Ireland was the highlight but in the debit column heavy losses were sustained in London and Paris, and Wales won a Triple Crown in style at Murrayfield.

Scottish rugby owes a great debt of gratitude to Bill Dickinson who was relieved of his position as 'adviser to the captain' at the end of the 1977 season. He helped raise standards enormously over a period of six years, transforming Scotland into a genuinely competitive outfit. His successor, somewhat surprisingly, was Nairn McEwan, a flanker in Dickinson's side who was appointed as player-coach for the 1977 tour to the Far East. McEwan's 14-match reign over three seasons was not successful as Scotland were whitewashed in 1978, drew two matches in 1979 before beating France 22-14 in 1980 for his only win in charge. An innovative coach and a disciple of 15-man rugby he was not helped by the selection system. As national coach he was a member of the selection committee but had no final say in team selection and accordingly did not get an opportunity to mould the team in his own image.

# Chapter Twelve: 1980-89
# Scotland Supreme

The considerable value of frequent overseas tours during the most successful period in Scottish rugby since the 1920s cannot be underplayed as it paved the way to the first Grand Slam in 59 years, a second one six years later and a Rugby World Cup semi-final. In successive years starting in 1980 Scotland squads toured France, New Zealand, Australia, Romania, Canada and the USA, France and Spain, Zimbabwe and Japan. Indeed there were just two seasons in the 1980s when they did not tour: in 1983 when eight Scots plus coach Jim Telfer toured New Zealand with the Lions and in 1987, the year of the inaugural Rugby World Cup.

Furthermore, it is widely acknowledged by the players and coaches involved in this era that it was on the tour to France in 1980 when the foundations were laid for the successes that followed later in the decade. Telfer was appointed coach and he and Ian MacGregor, convenor of selectors, advocated the need to test Scotland's best players against the best in the world on a regular basis in order to improve.

That first tour may have been very short, just three matches, and it may not have been very successful in terms of results. There were losses to the French Barbarians (26-22 in Agen), a French XV (20-6 in Bordeaux) and a draw against another French XV (6-6 in Brive), but it gave Telfer an opportunity to closely examine the raw material at his disposal. He had previously worked with a number of the tourists as Scotland B coach and it was many of these players such as Jim Calder, Colin Deans, Peter Dods, David Johnston, Roy Laidlaw, David Leslie, Steve Munro, Keith Robertson and John Rutherford who were to form the basis of the 1984 Grand Slam side.

## Slow Motion Try

Led by Andy Irvine the Scots enjoyed a good season in 1981 when they played positive, attacking rugby with the emergence of John Rutherford and Roy Laidlaw at half-back as a world-class pairing. Jim Renwick and Keith Robertson formed an unconventional yet highly effective partnership in the centre and a solid front five, with a highly mobile Colin Deans at hooker, provided a platform for an excellent back row combination of Jim Calder, David Leslie and John Beattie.

*John Rutherford, a class act in tandem with partner Roy Laidlaw on a record 35 occasions for Scotland.*

Telfer's first international in charge was one of the toughest imaginable: France at the Parc des Princes. It was an inauspicious start as Scotland lost 16-9 although Rutherford scored a brilliant individual try; when probing the blind side, the defence parted like the Red Sea for him to ghost in. The match was also a personal milestone for skipper Irvine as his penalty set a new world record of 213 points in Test rugby eclipsing Phil Bennett's previous best of 210 points.

The Welsh match was one of contrasting fortunes for two of the world's finest full-backs – Irvine and J.P.R. Williams. J.P.R. had retired from international rugby in 1979 but was persuaded to help Wales out that season. Sadly, he was a pale shadow of his former self and Rutherford's brilliant tactical kicking tormented him all afternoon. Williams was never selected for Wales again. Irvine, on the other hand, wrote himself into the record books once more when, in hot pursuit of a loose ball over the Welsh try-line, a blatant piece of shirt-tugging by Gareth Davies was spotted by the referee and the first penalty try in the International Championship was awarded.

A thrilling match at Twickenham resulted in the teams sharing six tries but Scotland went down 23-17 before squeezing narrowly past Ireland by 10-9 largely courtesy of a try from fully 60 yards by wing Bruce Hay. Now Bruce was never the quickest player in the Scotland back division and his effort drew a classic remark from that sharpest of wits, Jim Renwick, who said: 'That's the first try I've ever seen live and in slow motion at the same time.'

## The Land of the Long White Cloud

The ultimate test of Scotland's early progress under Telfer followed on the eight-match summer tour to New Zealand. It was no mean feat to win five of the six provincial matches and the Scots' dynamic rucking game drew warm praise from knowledgeable Kiwis. Both Tests were lost but the Scots gave the All Blacks a real fright in the first Test at Carisbrook, Dunedin, going down all guns blazing by 11-4.

The tour opened with a comfortable 39-13 win over King Country as Telfer outwitted opposite number and All Black legend Colin Meads. Captain Irvine pitched in with 24 points to equal Dougie Morgan's record match total set against Wellington in 1975. The performance of the tour came just before the first Test when Scotland beat Canterbury 23-12 and had Telfer positively purring as he considered it the best performance he had seen by a Scottish team abroad. Significantly, the side was led by Jim Aitken and contained two-thirds of the first-choice Grand Slam side, namely the entire pack aided and abetted by Rutherford and Laidlaw.

Tight-head prop Iain Milne, who had missed the Five Nations through injury, was becoming an increasingly influential member of the squad and his massive presence in the front row had a mighty effect on the Scots scrummaging on the tour and for several seasons thereafter. Milne for Norrie Rowan and Iain Paxton (winning his first cap) for John Beattie, who was cruelly injured in a pre-tour training session, were the only changes from the championship team. In a hard Test the All Blacks led by 11 points going into the last quarter. Deans hit back with a try as Rutherford started to cut loose, nearly scoring himself and creating chances for Renwick and Munro but the Blacks line could not be breached.

Part of the pre-match marketing for the second Test at Eden Park underlined Irvine's iconic status in New Zealand. In the head-to-head promotion using images of the opposing captains, Irvine and Mourie, the strapline under Andy's name read, 'This is possibly your last chance to see this legend.' Quite a tribute in a land which has produced more than its share of home-grown legends. In the match itself, Scotland trailed just 10-6 at half-time and there looked to be an upset on the cards. However, luck was not on the Scots side as in quick succession flu victim Munro did not have the strength to score from an interception and then flanker Calder scored a try only for the referee to disallow it. The heads dropped after this double whammy and the All Blacks ran amok in the last quarter to win 40-15.

## Arduous Season

The disappointment of losing a Test series in New Zealand could be tempered by the marked improvements made on tour both individually and collectively and the preparatory groundwork was to bear some juicy pickings over the next three seasons. The 1982 season was arduous with eight internationals squeezed into the next ten months. But Scotland measured up well to the challenge winning five and drawing one, taking the prized scalps of Australia twice, which included a first win in the southern hemisphere, France and Wales in Cardiff for the first time since 1962.

The Scots looked to play open, attacking rugby, reflecting their captain's philosophy whenever possible, and although outscored by three tries to one by Australia at Murrayfield, Scotland actually created a number of try-scoring opportunities only to be denied by the Wallabies' willingness to cynically concede a rash of penalties rather than tries. Irvine's boot severely punished them for these indiscretions and he emerged with a record haul of 17 points in a 24-15 win.

A tedious Calcutta Cup match was drawn 9-9, with Scotland's blushes saved by Irvine's magnificent penalty from his own half and in Dublin, although Scotland won the try count 1-0, Ollie Campbell won the boot battle kicking all 21 points to wrap up Ireland's first Triple Crown since 1949.

But a strong performance from the pack against France and Rutherford's third try in successive matches against the Tricolours paved the way for a satisfying 16-7 win and the Scots travelled to Cardiff in confident mood. Scotland produced a classic performance as they wiped out 20 years of away day blues in Cardiff and ended Wales' remarkable run of 27 unbeaten championship home matches stretching back to 1968. They did not just beat Wales, they annihilated them. The win was sparked by a brilliant try when Roger Baird caught Gareth Davies' speculative chip into the Scottish 22. Fielding the ball with his back to the Welsh, the Kelso winger turned on a sixpence, wrongfooting the attackers, before hugging the left touchline and sprinting out of defence to launch a devastating counter attack. He offloaded to Paxton whose long raking strides took him deep into the Welsh 22. As he was tackled he fed the ball to the supporting Tomes who in turn linked with Calder to crash over for one of Scotland's greatest tries. Further tries followed from White, Johnston, Pollock and Renwick to complete a comprehensive and stylish 34-18 victory.

The season was rounded off by a second successive tough tour down under, this time to Australia, where Scotland won six of their nine matches. A fine 44-3 win over New South Wales preceded an historic win in the first Test, Scotland's first on the other side of the world, as they played heroically to beat the Wallabies 12-7 at Ballymore in Brisbane. The key to the win was a change in the defensive pattern with Calder marking the dangerous Mark Ella at stand-off and the back line all moving out as one to counter the Aussies' dangerous running skills. The ploy worked perfectly and Irvine was able to celebrate his 50th cap, equalling Sandy Carmichael's record, in fine style.

A week later it was a different story as the Australians outwitted the Scottish defence running in three tries for a 33-9 win at Sydney Cricket Ground. It was a disappointing way to end the tour and, as it turned out, it was Irvine's final Test. In a glittering career he finished with a world-record

301 points (including 28 for the Lions) and left thrilling memories around the world for all those fortunate enough to see him play.

### The Ball doesn't Bounce for the Scots

The improvements of the previous two seasons were not as pronounced in 1993 because Jim Telfer had been appointed Lions coach to New Zealand and a new coaching partnership of Colin Telfer and Derrick Grant was put in charge. Telfer was promoted to head coach with Grant, a hard nosed Borderer who had coached Hawick to their first five successive Scottish titles, moving up from the Scotland B team as forwards coach. By no means a disastrous season, it could be said, to use a favourite sporting cliché, that the ball didn't bounce for the Scots who lost successively to Ireland 15-13, France 19-15 and Wales 19-15. They badly missed the presence of Rutherford in these three matches and the captaincy did not sit easily on Laidlaw's willing shoulders. Happily, Rutherford was restored to full fitness for the Calcutta Cup match and the captaincy was handed for the first time to Gala skipper Jim Aitken.

Aitken was a very confident man who had enjoyed great success at club level with Gala and away from rugby was a very successful businessman. His confidence rubbed off on the other players and his seven matches at the helm brought an extraordinary sequence of results for Scotland. The team travelled south in the knowledge that England were also experiencing a difficult season with a loss and a draw to their name as their 1980 Grand Slam side began to break up. Their coach Mike Davis, who had inspired them to that success, came out with a nice self-deprecating line before the match stating that: 'I have turned wine into water.'

With confidence reborn and facing a despondent England, the Scots won a rare but famous victory at Twickenham, triumphing for only the fourth time at their traditional graveyard of ambition. The English were rucked off the pitch allowing Rutherford and Laidlaw to run the show. Early in the second half a rejuvenated Laidlaw scored a characteristic try, retrieving a rapid heel from a scrum to arc round the blind side, evading the clutches of the English back row for a crucial score. And a try from debutant Tom Smith, a former basketball international, from a line-out, wrapped up a deserved win for the ecstatic Scots.

Eight of the team accompanied coach Telfer to New Zealand with the Lions but it was not a successful tour and most of the players and the coach returned home in very frustrated mood. Whereas Baird, Paxton and Laidlaw played a full part in the Test series, Beattie, Calder and Rutherford were reduced to bit parts and most astonishingly neither

*Roy Laidlaw en route to his marvellous opening try against England in 1983.*

Deans nor Milne had any active involvement in the Test series at all. Deans was vying with captain Ciaran Fitzgerald for the hooking spot and was the form hooker on the tour but the skipper kept his spot and Milne, also in rumbustious form, could not force his way into the Test front row.

## Scots Bounce Back

Despite the frustrations endured on the Lions tour the Scots in the party returned home with a new-found confidence and self-belief as they realised that they were at least the equal, if not better than, many of their fellow tourists. In the past, many Scottish sides suffered an irrational inferiority complex perceiving players from other nations as somehow superior. Having been up close and personal with the best of British rugby for over two months the Scots were confident that they had the ability, the fitness levels and the willpower to do well in the forthcoming 1984 Five Nations. They also had a coach in Telfer who had been pilloried in the press for his part in the 4-0 Test whitewash and was determined to prove that he was a coach of the highest order.

The bookies were not privy to this inner belief, and would probably have discounted it had they been aware, making France favourites for the Grand Slam and, somewhat oddly, England for the Triple Crown. This largely on the basis that England had recently beaten the All Blacks whilst ignoring their failure to win a match in the previous championship season.

The season started well with a 25-25 draw against the All Blacks, a result the Lions could not achieve in the summer, and an indication of better things to come. Interestingly, in the two B internationals played this season Scotland beat both Ireland at home and, more significantly, France away. The feelgood factor was developing north of the Border.

Wales were first up in the Five Nations and having won well there last time out there was no Cardiff fear factor. The game plan for the season was based on the team's real strength, an outstanding middle five. The back row of Calder, Leslie and Paxton were given a solid platform by the front five to implement Telfer's favoured dynamic rucking game and the quick clean ball was intelligently used by Rutherford and Laidlaw to keep Scotland moving forward. They mixed their game up beautifully, combining clever tactical

**50 Greatest Players**

**DAVID LESLIE Flanker**

**Club:** Dundee High School FP, Gala, West of Scotland

**Debut:** v Ireland, 1 February 1975

**No. of Caps:** 32 **No. of Points:** 8

After winning his first ten caps in a row, Leslie missed 17 of the next 19 internationals as his promising Test career was apparently killed stone dead through injury. Although they did not always see eye to eye, Jim Telfer rates Leslie as the best forward he has ever coached, which is praise indeed. Undoubtedly a world-class open side at his peak, he showed his best form during the 1984 Grand Slam season. He missed out on three Lions tours for various reasons but it is felt in many quarters that his 1984 form was in part a reaction to not being selected for the 1983 Lions tour to New Zealand. Outstanding against Wales in what was known as 'Leslie's Match', he made an immense contribution in the Grand Slam decider and it was his crunching collision with Jerome Gallion which helped turn the match Scotland's way.

kicking with Laidlaw's sniping use of the blind side and Rutherford's open field running to keep opposing loose forwards on their toes.

Although Scotland were criticised for adhering to a limited game plan they emerged as the top try scorers in the campaign with ten scores and played some marvellous adventurous rugby at times, and against Ireland in particular. Their success was also based on a very disciplined approach, a frugal defence conceding fewest penalties in the tournament.

It was a most experienced Scotland side which took the pitch at Cardiff, containing eight Lions to Wales' two and boasting four times as many caps. Scotland's unrelenting offensive defence gave Wales no chance to settle and when in possession their textbook rucking simply wore the Welsh down. For all their advantages, Scotland led by just 6-3 at half-time and Paxton's try owed something to good fortune with one if not two passes in the build up which could have been judged as forward by another referee. Wales scored first in the second half to make it 6-6 and a further exchange of penalties made it 9-9 going into the final 12 minutes. Then Scotland won a line-out in the Welsh half and Deans, whose throwing to Leslie at the tail had tormented Wales all afternoon, once again found his tail gunner with unerring accuracy. The ball was worked to Rutherford and his beautifully weighted chip found touch near the Welsh try line. Scotland managed to disrupt the Welsh throw and first Milne and then Laidlaw made inroads before Aitken, 'Big Daddy' himself, was driven over the line by Gala colleague Leslie to secure an unprecedented second win in three seasons in Cardiff.

Having beaten New Zealand 11 weeks before, the Auld Enemy arrived at Murrayfield confident of opening their championship account with a win. The Scots original game plan had been to bring the three-quarters into play far more than they had done against Wales, thus moving the powerful but heavy England forwards around the pitch. However, Telfer was in the habit of going to the ground on the morning of a match to get a feel for the conditions. On this occasion a lot of rain had fallen and more was forecast for the afternoon making the ball and the pitch slippery.

*Flanker David Leslie made a huge contribution to Scotland's Grand Slam season in 1984.*

The strategy was altered and Rutherford cleverly varied his kicking game to give England full-back Dusty Hare's defensive skills a thorough examination, much in the way he had tormented J.P.R. Williams in 1981. The Scotland wings also put pressure on the hapless full-back who endured a torrid afternoon and whose normally impeccable place kicking suffered as a result, missing six from eight kicks at goal.

The first try came from a line-out when Deans found Leslie at the tail again and the flanker managed to get a hand to the ball deflecting it into Paxton's path. The No. 8 hacked it into England's 22 and Johnston reacted quickest dribbling it over the line to beat Hare, Woodward and Cusworth for an opportunist try. Dods made the conversion but Hare pulled a penalty back and Scotland led 6-3 at half-time. As against Wales, Scotland, with first use of the elements, dominated the half but had only a narrow lead to show for it.

But they got the crucial first score after half-time, winning ball from an English drop-out. From the resultant ruck, Laidlaw punted into space, Calder was first to the bouncing ball and he was driven on by Tomes and Leslie. From the quick ruck ball, Laidlaw linked with Rutherford who drew Woodward before releasing Kennedy through a gaping hole and in for a key score. Dods' conversion made it 12-3 and he kicked two further penalties to

**50 Greatest Players**

**COLIN DEANS Hooker**

**Club:** Hawick

**Debut:** v France, 4 February 1978

**No. of Caps:** 52 **No. of Points:** 8

First capped at the tender age of 22, Deans was Scotland's first-choice hooker for over a decade, led his country 13 times and was captain in the inaugural Rugby World Cup. Blisteringly quick for a hooker, his mobility was a huge asset and made up for a lack of bulk particularly in his early years. And having won a place on the 1983 Lions tour he was desperately frustrated to miss out on the Test slot as he was in direct competition with tour captain Ciaran Fitzgerald. However, in 1986 he was accorded the great honour of captaining the Lions in a home match against the Barbarians in Cardiff, which went some way for making up for the disappointment in New Zealand. He retired from international rugby at the end of the Rugby World Cup and missed Roy Laidlaw's presentation speech to him as he was dealing with the press. Roy had to do it again but apparently his first effort was far better.

Hare's one for Scotland to win 18-6. The win had not been without its casualties, as both Cuthbertson and Kennedy were injured. However, Beattie and Pollock, their replacements, slotted in well during the match and for the rest of the campaign, showing the importance of the squad system.

### 'Laidlaw's Match'

For the sixth time since 1938 Scotland were in a position to win a Triple Crown. Usually it was against England at Twickenham, but on this occasion it was Ireland at Lansdowne Road. Champions for the last two seasons, but successive defeats to France, Wales and England left the Irish needing to beat Scotland to avoid a whitewash and the wooden spoon.

In what was to be called 'Laidlaw's Match' although he only played for 40 minutes, the Irish handed the initiative straight to the Scots before kick-off when skipper Willie Duggan won the toss and elected to play into the elements. Aitken was delighted with the decision as he was always keen to take full advantage of the conditions at the earliest opportunity. And what an advantage Scotland gained. After just four minutes Scotland won a line-out in the Irish 22. From the resultant ruck just enough space had been created on the blind side for Laidlaw to dart right and, unleashing a devastating sidestep, he wrongfooted four Irishmen to score a try to treasure. Dods' conversion and two subsequent penalties stretched the score to 12-0 which quickly became 18-0 when Scotland were awarded a penalty try. On the half-hour mark, Laidlaw again exploited the narrow side, this time from a scrum to touch down almost exactly where he had for the first try. To many Scots this part of the ground will always be known as 'Laidlaw's Corner'. Unfortunately, the Jed maestro received a blow to the head and was replaced at half-time.

At the start of the second half Scotland were 22-0 ahead and they proceeded to produce a marvellously disciplined performance, being prepared to concede possession rather than penalties which might allow Ireland the chance of kicking their way back into the match. They did reduce the gap to 22-9 but Scotland closed them out with two well-worked tries. First Robertson followed Rutherford's clever break to take the scoring pass and then Dods appeared outside the unselfish Baird who timed his pass beautifully for Scotland to win the Triple Crown in great style.

## The Grand Slam

By now Scottish thoughts were on the Grand Slam, something they had not won since 1925. Scottish fans were also delighted that the decider was going to be a winner takes all, head-to-head clash with France who also had three wins under their belt. Despite the Scots' home advantage France started as favourites. They had played some outstanding rugby in beating Ireland 25-12, Wales 21-16 and England 32-18, scoring nine tries in the process.

Both sides had injury worries though it was revealed that Roy Laidlaw had not been concussed against Ireland but had suffered 'athlete's migraine' and so was deemed fit to play. This was a relief as Gordon Hunter, his deputy in Dublin, had survived the second half intact only to fracture a cheekbone colliding with an excited fan when leaving the pitch at full time. France recalled Francis Haget, a Biarritz croupier, who had not played international rugby for four years. He replaced the injured Alain Lorieux in the second row.

*Jim Aitken leaves the pitch to rapturous acclaim as Scotland win a first Grand Slam for 59 years.*

## Great Matches

**FIVE NATIONS CHAMPIONSHIP** **Murrayfield, 17 March 1984**

**Scotland 21 France 12** **Attendance: 62,000**

So, on Jim Telfers' 44th birthday everything was nicely poised. France opened brilliantly and despite getting on the wrong side of the referee from the kick-off – they conceded nine penalties to none in one spell – it looked as if the Grand Slam was theirs for the taking. Scrum-half Gallion scored a Laidlaw-esque try, but Dods' penalty pegged the half-time score to 6-3, the first time Scotland had been behind at the break all season.

Lescarboura extended the lead to 9-3 with a well-struck penalty but then, with the Scots hanging on, came the turning point. Leslie and Gallion collided chasing the ball off a line-out and the Frenchman was knocked out and stretchered off. The injury seemed to knock the French out of their stride as they had lost their most influential player. They also started to lose their discipline and twice talked back to the referee conceding further yardage, thus enabling Dods to kick the resultant goals. Telfer himself felt the turning point was with the scores tied at 12-12 claiming, 'Blanco was caught under a high ball and we carried him 25 yards. I've never seen that before, and we scored immediately afterwards.' From the resulting line-out, Deans threw to Paxton at the tail but Joinel got a hand to the ball. Calder, the arch poacher, anticipating that there might indeed be a ricochet, was perfectly placed to collect the free ball and plunge over for another famous score.

*Jim Calder grounds the ball to score the Grand Slam-winning try.*

Dods' conversion made it 18-12 and he added a late penalty to ensure that the players and the whole of Scotland had an afternoon to remember.

**Scotland:** P.W. Dods; J.A. Pollock, K.W. Robertson, D.I. Johnston, G.R.T. Baird; J.Y. Rutherford, R.J. Laidlaw; J. Aitken (captain), C.T. Deans, I.G. Milne, A.J. Campbell, A.J. Tomes, J.H. Calder, I.A.M. Paxton, D.G. Leslie
**Scorers: Try** Calder **Conversion** Dods **Penalty Goals** Dods 5

**France:** S. Blanco; J. Begu, P.Sella, D. Codorniou, P. Esteve; J.P. Lescarboura, J. Gallion; P. Dospital, P. Dintrans, D. Dubroca, F. Haget, J. Condom, J.P. Rives (captain), J.C. Orso, J.L. Joinel
**Replacement:** Gallion replaced by P. Berbizier
**Scorers: Try** Gallion **Conversion** Lescarboura **Penalty Goal** Lescarboura **Drop Goal** Lescarboura

**Referee:** Mr W. Jones (Wales)

## The Hangover

The lift the Grand Slam gave to Scottish rugby and the nation as a whole was enormous but over the years the Scots have grown accustomed to coming back down to earth with a big bump. A massive high is almost inevitably followed by a swingeing low and that indeed is what followed the Grand Slam success. However, few can have foreseen that it would happen just nine weeks after the greatest moment in Scottish rugby history for 59 years and in Romania of all places. True, a number of key players could not make the trip to Bucharest for a one-off Test match and the impoverished lifestyle of the Romanians and the debilitating conditions badly affected the players. Nevertheless, the European champions crashed 28-22 to one of the up-and-coming nations and were knocked well and truly off their perch.

The 1985 season started with another new coaching combination. Jim Telfer had proved to himself and the rest of the rugby world that he was a winning coach and with a new job as Rector of Hawick High School he needed to channel his energies into his new role. Colin Telfer and Derrick Grant once again were paired as the coaching team and Aitken, at the age of 37, was dropped confirming that there is no sentiment in rugby. Both Laidlaw and Leslie were tried as captain as Scotland defended their Five Nations crown.

Unfortunately, the Scots went from Grand Slam to Grand Slump as they lost all five matches in the season. Australia inflicted the heaviest defeat winning 37-12 to complete their own Grand Slam and win all four Tests on their tour of the UK. In attempting to console the Scots, Australian coach Alan Jones brilliantly encapsulated the vagaries of international sport in one sentence, 'One day you are the rooster, the next a feather duster.' Depressingly the season did not improve in terms of results and although no heavy defeats were sustained, Scotland did not get the breaks which perhaps came their way the previous season, turning glittering prizes into a wooden spoon to go with that infernal feather duster.

## A New Dawn

A bold fresh approach was required for the 1986 season but none could have suspected how bold the selectors would be or what a spectacular return they would receive on their gamble. Derrick Grant was now head coach with his assistant Ian McGeechan who had played Test rugby as recently as 1979 when he was a team-mate of current stalwarts Laidlaw, Rutherford and the newly appointed captain Deans. Grant and McGeechan shared a vision of playing a more expansive and ambitious game and their boldness was rewarded with four wins from the five matches played.

Six new caps were awarded for the championship opener against France. The Hastings brothers, Gavin and Scott, became the first to win their first caps together since Willie and George Neilson against Wales in 1891. The other debutants were Finlay Calder, David Sole, Matt Duncan and Jeremy Campbell-Lamerton. Remarkably four of these players, the Hastings, Calder and Sole, became world-class players integral to the success of Scotland and the British Lions with Calder and Gavin Hastings both captaining the Lions.

However, the brave new world got off to a disastrous start at Murrayfield when Gavin Hastings kicked the ball straight into touch from the kick-off against France. Assuming the French would opt for a scrum, the Scots relaxed momentarily and it was enough for the wily Pierre Berbizier to take a quick throw to hooker Daniel Dubroca, collect the return pass and sprint 50 yards for a shock score. Thankfully, the Scots recovered their composure and in a thrilling match with the lead changing hands seven times Hastings senior more than made up for his early mistake, landing six out of six penalties to equal the world record and help earn Scotland an 18-17 victory.

Despite outscoring Wales by three tries to one in Cardiff in another pulsating match and with the match delicately poised at 16-15, Paul Thorburn's 70-yard penalty knocked the stuffing out of the Scots and Wales went on to win 22-15. But, encouraged by their performance against Wales, the Scots turned their attentions to England. They too entered the match in good heart after a good performance against Wales having beaten them 21-18. But it was to prove to be a remarkable afternoon for Scotland who led 12-6 at half-time, Hastings having won the penalty count 4-2 over Andrew. Gradually the Scottish scrummage got on top and England found themselves unable to win any quality ball. Three second-half tries from Duncan, Rutherford and Scott Hastings steered Scotland to an immensely satisfying and record 33-6 win in a Calcutta Cup match.

*A clearly delighted John Rutherford threads his way through England's defence for Scotland's second try in the 1986 Calcutta Cup match.*

The final match of the championship in Dublin was a letdown following the glorious events at Murrayfield but another try from Laidlaw, at surely his favourite venue, and two Hastings penalties, thereby setting a new individual Scottish record of 52 points in the championship, were enough for Scotland to win 10-9 and share the championship with France.

## 'Good Stuff This, Isn't It?'

There is an old adage which says that a player's second season at international level is often the most difficult. It is likely that it is also true of a team and in 1987 the new Scottish team was in its second, difficult year. Undoubtedly Scotland's fixtures were more difficult than in 1986 as the France and England matches were both away from home and, as it happens, both were lost, but there was much to admire in Scotland's performances that season which put them in contention for a Triple Crown, and much to build on for the forthcoming Rugby World Cup in New Zealand and Australia.

Severe weather caused the postponement of the England match so the Scots did not play their first championship match until late February. Ireland, on the other hand, had the considerable advantage of a warm-up match against Romania and had comfortably despatched England 17-0 in Dublin. However, an early drop goal from Rutherford got the match off to a good start and on a personal level it was to be a wonderful season for the Selkirk playmaker who was voted European Player of the Season. And it was Rutherford who was instrumental in sealing the match, making the initial break which led to Tukalo's try.

In Paris, the Scots found themselves 22-7 down early in the second half as the French had hit their stride early and were in simply irresistible form. Their wingers were in devastating mood, particularly Eric Bonneval who scored a hat-trick and Scotland's only response was when Beattie charged down Blanco's attempted clearance for a try, and a Hastings penalty. The outlook was pretty bleak. But in the final quarter the Scots clicked with the Hastings boys weighing in with 15 points between them and the scoreline read 28-22 to France as full time loomed. Finally, a wicked bounce of the ball with the try line beckoning evaded Calder's clutches and the French were relieved to hear the whistle.

Scotland's 21-15 win over Wales at home suggests a close match but in reality Scotland destroyed Wales particularly in the scrummage which had been outstanding all season, and with a little more composure would have scored over 40 points. At one stage after a wonderful sustained period of pressure which finished near the Welsh line Calder, clearly revelling in the occasion, turned to the Welsh players saying, 'Good stuff this, isn't it?'

The win over Wales set up another chance for a Triple Crown against an England side which had struggled for form all season and was seeking to avoid a whitewash. Although the match was at Twickenham over half the team had won there in 1983 and therefore there was no real fear factor. The English, however, had done their homework on Scottish weaknesses, dominated the line-outs, and adapted to and exploited the wet conditions far better than the Scots. The result: yet another disappointment courtesy of the English.

### The First Rugby World Cup

The inaugural Rugby World Cup, played in 1987, was the result of constant lobbying from the leading southern hemisphere nations, New Zealand and Australia. They did not have the hang-ups or fears that existed particularly in the home nations about the dangers of the over-commercialisation or possible professionalisation of the game. As recently as 1982 the proposal of a World Cup was rejected out of hand not only by the SRU Committee who were 'totally against the proposal', but also the IB.

However, just five years later the first Rugby World Cup was staged in New Zealand and Australia with the Final played at Eden Park, Auckland. The 16 nations taking part were: Argentina, Australia, Canada, England, Fiji, France, Ireland, Italy, Japan, New Zealand, Romania, Scotland, Tonga, USA, Wales and Zimbabwe.

New Zealand, Australia and France were the favourites to win the tournament but one bookie at least made Scotland fourth favourites quoting them at 16-1 to win the William Webb Ellis Trophy. Heady days indeed. There was one major stumbling block for the Scots, namely France. They had been drawn in the same pool as the Grand Slam champions, along with Romania and Zimbabwe, and what is more faced them in the opening tie in Christchurch.

Scotland suffered three major injury blows before the tournament started. Beattie, who had been stretchered off against England with a severe knee injury, was in plaster and could not be considered. Rutherford had also sustained ligament damage to his left knee playing in an end-of-season tournament in Bermuda against SRU wishes. As the Rugby World Cup was so close it was decided not to operate and he was prescribed an intensive course of rehabilitation and exercise. The knee responded well and Rutherford was passed fit to join the Scotland party. The third body blow was when Scott Hastings, who had missed the Calcutta Cup with a fractured cheekbone, pulled a hamstring in training and was ruled out of the first match.

Despite these setbacks, Scotland started against France with 14 of the 15 players who finished the Calcutta Cup match, the only new face being

Dougie Wyllie who took Baird's position in the centre. France too were little changed and the match was a cracker, setting light to the fledgling tournament as the 'Auld Allies' served up a five-try bonanza.

Arguably the match was decided in the opening seven minutes although the result was in doubt until deep into injury time. Scotland were ahead after less than two minutes when Deans found Calder at the back of the line-out. The flanker burst through the French defence and his long pass found White in space who ploughed over for a dramatic start. Hastings missed the conversion which proved to be significant, but Scotland were off to a terrific start.

Tragically, after seven minutes, Scotland's chances were severely dented and Rutherford's playing career was in tatters. Challenging for a high ball near his own line he landed awkwardly and departed the tournament on a stretcher with a recurrence of his knee injury. A brilliant career was brutally terminated. The injury necessitated a reshuffle in the back line with Alan Tait coming on for his first cap at centre and Wyllie moving to stand-off. Both slotted in well and Scotland coped admirably despite the disruption. The set scrum was performing like a dream, winning the tight head count 3-1, and the line-out was functioning impressively. Hastings and Blanco exchanged penalties for Scotland to lead 13-6 at the interval.

Immediately after the restart came one of those moments which could have won the match for Scotland as Robertson just failed to gather a bobbling ball short of the try line. If he had scored then, the Scots would have gained a real psychological advantage as the French had already started to bicker amongst themselves. Nevertheless, Hastings extended the lead to 16-6 before tries by Sella, Berbizier and a controversial effort from Blanco two minutes from time appeared to have won the match for the French 20-16.

But Scotland's magnificent never-say-die attitude enabled them to conjure a marvellous try deep into injury time. Calder reached a Laidlaw chip-ahead first and with Tomes and Wyllie in support they set up a dynamic ruck. From the quick ball Laidlaw linked with White for Duncan to squeeze over at the corner to tie the scores. Hastings' conversion attempt from the touchline was agonisingly close but 20-20 it remained.

It had been a magnificent performance in a magnificent match, but because France had outscored Scotland by three tries to two should the teams finish equal on points, the tournament rules decreed that the French would win the pool and face the easier quarter-final. Of course, that is exactly what happened, and in the event Scotland faced New Zealand in the last eight.

The remaining pool matches were won comfortably enough, scoring 11 tries in beating Zimbabwe 60-21 and in the 55-28 win over Romania.

## 50 Greatest Players

**JOHN RUTHERFORD Stand-off**

**Club:** Selkirk

**Debut:** v Wales, 20 January 1979

**No. of Caps:** 42 **No. of Points:** 64

A world-class stand-off admired and feared throughout the rugby world. A runner when he first appeared on the international scene, he matured into an all-rounder with all the attributes: good hands, a prodigious boot, pace, elusiveness and a sound tackler. But, perhaps most importantly, he formed a formidable partnership with Roy Laidlaw. He toured with the 1983 Lions but only won one cap appearing in the centre for the third Test. He had an excellent match and opened the scoring after five minutes with a superb solo try. His form reached its peak in 1987 when, in a fabulous Five Nations Championship, he enjoyed a terrific season for which he was voted European Player of the Year. Sadly, within a few weeks, his career was over having sustained a knee injury in Barbados. It was a sad end to a glittering career.

Hastings bagged 27 points to set a new individual points-scoring world record (although it was short lived as Didier Camberabero scored 30 points for France against Zimbabwe later that same day). Scotland suffered further injury blows in these matches as Scott Hastings' Rugby World Cup lasted just 30 seconds as he pulled his hamstring against Romania and Jeffrey suffered a chest injury. Both key players missed the quarter-final against the Kiwis.

The All Blacks had been very impressed by the Scots' scrummaging prowess and had worked hard on this most technical aspect of the game. The extra sessions paid off as they laid the platform for a powerful performance in which they completely outplayed, but never overran, Scotland in winning 30-3. Skipper Deans said later, 'This was the best All Blacks side I have played against and I cannot see anyone stopping them.' And he was proved right as they beat Wales 49-6 in the semi-final and France 29-9 in the Final.

### Rebuilding

After a creditable World Cup campaign, the 1988 season was one of rebuilding as the selectors had to face up to replacing such outstanding players as Deans (retired), Rutherford (who was forced to retire at the end

**50 Greatest Players**

**IAIN MILNE Prop**

**Club:** Heriot's FP, Harlequins

**Debut:** v Ireland, 3 March 1979

**No. of Caps:** 44 **No. of Points:** 0

Known as the 'Bear', Iain Milne was one of three brothers (all caps) who made up Heriot's front row for a number of seasons. One of the best tight-head props in the world, he contributed enormously to the good scrummaging pack of the 1980s. For such a huge man, weighing around 20 stones, he was very comfortable with ball in hand and surprisingly mobile. Absolutely outstanding in 1984, he almost single handedly laid the foundations for Scotland's success against France. He soaked up an incredible amount of punishment and provocation from opposite number Pierre Dospital, but never wavered. His supreme self-discipline and superb technique eventually broke the Frenchman and he was singled out for special praise by Jim Telfer after the match. Milne enhanced his reputation further at the 1987 Rugby World Cup but subsequent seasons were ravaged by injuries and finally a neck injury forced him out of the international set-up.

of the season) and Milne who missed much of the season through injury. Unsurprisingly, there were no ready-made replacements for three of Scotland's greatest practitioners in their respective positions.

In the Five Nations, Scotland's only scalp, somewhat ironically, was France, their nemesis in the World Cup. They played very well against Les Bleus beating them 23-12, but lost narrowly to Wales, in a thrilling match in Cardiff, and Ireland. They lost too against England by 9-6 in a drab, dreary Calcutta Cup match where England looked to kill the game at every opportunity. This brought an uncharacteristic outburst from coach Grant who at the post-match press conference said, 'England may have been the birthplace of rugby but today they effectively killed the game stone dead. When the ball should have come back, England killed it on many occasions that were not picked up by the referee.'

The following year Grant stood down as head coach but was persuaded to continue as a selector. McGeechan replaced him and a group of senior forwards persuaded Telfer, who had remained as a selector, to return to the international fold. The McGeechan/Telfer partnership received a severe jolt in their first match together when Scotland went down 32-13 to a marvellous Australian side coached by Bob Dwyer who was still smarting from losing 28-19 to England.

Filling Laidlaw (who had retired) and Rutherford's boots was a priority for the Five Nations and they opted for Laidlaw's Jedforest club-mate Gary Armstrong, who won his first cap against Australia, at scrum-half, and the precocious 20-year-old Craig Chalmers of Melrose at stand-off. Elsewhere they solved Gavin Hastings' absence with a groin injury by recalling Peter Dods and paired New Zealander Sean Lineen with Hastings junior in the centre. Kenny Milne was introduced at hooker alongside elder brother Iain, Damian Cronin and Chris Gray formed the new boiler house and Jeffrey, Calder and White were tried together for the first time in a new-look back row.

Finally, in a surprise but inspired move, the captaincy was handed to Finlay Calder who had never skippered a team of note in his life. But he had proved himself an able lieutenant in battle, was well respected by the other players and was never short of a word or two. The reshaped side was to provide the basis for a further burst of Scottish international success forming the nucleus of the 1990 Grand Slam and 1991 Rugby World Cup semi-final sides.

Full of confidence they opened with an excellent win over Wales 23-7 having led 19-0 at the interval. Chalmers had made a very impressive and confident debut capping it with a try and linking, as if to the manor born, with fellow Borderer Armstrong. The Calcutta Cup match once again ended in rancour and an unsatisfactory 12-12 draw. If Grant was quick to condemn England last year, England manager Geoff Cooke did not miss this year describing Scotland as 'scavengers'. After the press conference, an Irish journalist added some levity to the occasion saying, 'If England think Scotland are good scavengers just wait until they meet Ireland in Dublin in a fortnight's time.'

*Finlay Calder was never short of a word or two.*

The 'scavengers' tag hurt deeply but convenor of selectors Bob Munro was able to draw a line under the episode when Scotland and Ireland served up a super match full of excitement and incident with Scotland triumphing 37-21 in an eight-try thriller at Murrayfield. 'Not bad for a pair of scavengers, eh?', he quipped in the afterglow of the match of the championship.

It was therefore a Scottish party full of good spirit that made the journey to Paris for the decider. But France's research had been careful, considered and thorough and having

**50 Greatest Players**

**ROY LAIDLAW Scrum-half**

**Club:** Jedforest

**Debut:** v Ireland, 2 February 1980

**No. of Caps:** 47 **No. of Points:** 28

Roy Laidlaw, in tandem with John Rutherford for a record 35 occasions, was one of the key components in the successful Scotland sides of the 1980s. Not as extravagantly gifted as his partner, he turned himself into a player of the highest quality and his breaking abilities were much feared by opposition back rows, particularly Irish ones. Indeed, Jim Telfer considers him to be the best breaking scrum-half he has ever seen, rating him ahead of the likes of Edwards, Going, Gallion and Holmes. A tough and durable character, he missed just two matches in his nine seasons at international level. And to emphasise the importance of Laidlaw and Rutherford as a pair, of the eight matches that they did not play together between 1980-87, Scotland lost seven of them. A Lion in 1983, he made the Test spot his own, replacing the injured Terry Holmes.

targeted skipper Calder as the man to stop they did not allow him to take the game to them and Scotland were on the back foot for most of the contest. The French were good value for their 19-3 win.

Naturally the Scots were disappointed to finish the season in such a fashion but eight of them were rewarded for their sterling efforts gaining selection for the Lions tour to Australia. Finlay Calder was named captain and with Ian McGeechan as coach there was a strong Caledonian influence on the tour party. Despite losing the first Test, the Lions responded brilliantly under Calder's admirable leadership to come back and win the series 2-1. A great result not just for British and Irish rugby but Scottish rugby and a portent of further success to come.

# Chapter Thirteen: 1990-95
# Grand Slam Fever

The amount and the speed of change have been constant themes throughout the history of Scottish rugby, but in the 1990s the sport did truly change out of all recognition as the last vestiges of amateurism were cast off and the sport finally and fully embraced professionalism at the highest level of the game.

The 90s were a decade of some considerable success for Scotland with the highlights being a Grand Slam and an impressive tour of New Zealand in 1990, a Rugby World Cup semi-final appearance the following year, tilts at a Triple Crown in 1993 and at Grand Slams in 1995 and 1996; and winning the final Five Nations Championship in 1999.

The seeds for Scotland's remarkable Grand Slam in 1990 were sown on the 1989 Lions tour to Australia. Coach Ian McGeechan and the Scottish players returned boosted by how well the entire squad had fared in Australia against one of the best sides in the world and took that confidence into the new season. Scotland did not have the bulk to compete up front in the Five Nations but compensated by using forwards with mobility and aggression in attack and defence. Once again the middle five of back row and half-backs was to be the key to Scotland's success.

The season started with warm-up matches against Fiji and Romania who provided contrasting challenges. The matches were both satisfying wins as the dangerous, free-spirited Fijians were despatched 38-17 and even more pleasingly the formidable Romanians succumbed 32-0. David Sole was appointed captain for the season in succession to Finlay Calder. McGeechan knew that this was to be Calder's last season of international rugby and had been impressed with the way the younger Sole had captained Scotland in Calder's absence against Fiji.

### The Centenary Quaich

Ireland at Lansdowne Road was the formidable opening challenge in what was the 101st match between the two nations and in recognition of the long and rich history of the fixture, the Centenary Quaich was put up as an annual prize for the winning team. Scotland had sat out the first round of matches and Ireland, although having been humbled by England, had the advantage of a championship match under their belts. The match was played in difficult conditions and Scotland were down 7-0 at half-time. Sole felt that Scotland should attack more through the back row and the tactical switch worked a treat. Jeffrey was in outstanding form and No. 8 White scored two tries, with his pick and drive from channel one ball for his second with ten minutes to go proving to be the match winner. A narrow 13-10 win got the season off to a good start but the players were very disappointed with the performance. Jim Telfer, who was in charge of the team as McGeechan was at home with flu, compared the changing room's atmosphere to being like a morgue and had to remind the players that they had won away from home, a rare feat for Scotsmen.

The self-critical approach was to serve Scotland well during the season and responding to the players' mood a short debrief was held back at the team hotel after each match. Their weaknesses were identified and constructive comments taken on board which helped the coaches tailor the make-up of the squad sessions throughout the rest of the season.

France arrived at Murrayfield having shown distinctly mixed form in their two matches, an away win over Wales and a home defeat to England. Despite taking first use of the wind and creating a number of chances, Scotland turned round just 3-0 ahead having missed a few kicks at goal. Fortune favoured the Scots too as the wind swung round to blow across the pitch and when early in the second half Gavin Hastings launched a huge clearance from his own line the French heads visibly dropped. Scotland sustained their pressure on the French and were helped when referee Fred Howard sent French flanker Alain Carmanati off for stamping on Jeffrey's head. Down to 14 men the French cracked and tries by Calder and Tukalo helped the Scots to an impressive 21-0 win.

Having sat out the first round, Scotland found that their opponents in each of the next three rounds had all been beaten by England in their previous match. England had beaten Ireland 23-0, France 26-7 and Wales 34-6 to put an impressive sequence together. From the Scottish perspective it could be viewed in two ways: firstly England had done them a favour and softened their opponents up, or alternatively, England had made their job a whole lot harder as sides that have been beaten often react furiously.

Wales in Cardiff was their next confrontation and they faced a Welsh side desperate to put on a show at the Arms Park. Scotland were very wary of a backlash and planned to play a controlled game to nullify any Welsh threat. They had lost close, exciting matches on their previous two visits to South Wales; this time it was close again but the Scots were always in control. They dominated the scrum, did well at the line-out and the defence was absolutely first class. In the end each team scored a try apiece with Cronin's try following Armstrong's break round the front of the line-out being countered by an excellent team score finished by Arthur Emyr. Both scores were converted and it was left to Chalmers to outscore Thorburn by three penalties to one to separate the sides and Scotland were happy to depart the Principality with a priceless 13-9 win.

## Grand Slam Fever

The Grand Slam appetite having been whetted six years previously, the entire Scottish nation was positively salivating at the prospect of another one so soon and with the added spice of the opponents being the 'Auld Enemy', at Murrayfield. Furthermore, as against France, it was a head-to-head, winner-takes-all clash as England had swept all before them in their three matches. On paper it was no contest, at least in the minds of the English media. But as they say, nobody has ever won a sporting contest on paper. With two weeks until the match, the build-up was unprecedented as the media on either side of the border went into overdrive. It was quickly agreed that only McGeechan and four of his senior pros, Sole, Calder, Jeffrey and Hastings, would speak to the press, thus keeping the pressure and the spotlight off some of the younger and less experienced players in the party. And it proved to be a very wise move as these five were in constant demand for interviews and comment.

Scotland enjoyed excellent preparations in the run-up to the match and several players, most notably the back row, did not turn out for their clubs the week before the match as they wanted to give themselves every opportunity to be at their absolute peak for such a special opportunity which they reckoned would not come their way again.

*John Jeffrey was the victim of a marvellous wind-up in the run-up to the Grand Slam match against England in 1990.*

As the big day approached and anxiety levels rose some of the senior players got together to plot a wind-up of brutal proportions, with John Jeffrey as the unwitting stooge, to relieve the tension. On the Wednesday evening before the match a small group of players went to a nearby bar for a

**50 Greatest Players**

**JOHN JEFFREY Flanker**

**Club**: Kelso

**Debut:** v Australia, 8 December 1984

**No. of Caps:** 40 **No. of Points**: 44

First capped in 1984 against Australia with the euphoria of the Grand Slam still hanging in the Murrayfield air, his debut was an inauspicious one as Scotland crashed 37-12. Jeffrey did not fully establish himself in the national set-up until 1986 when the decision to play him at blind side flanker in tandem with Finlay Calder paid rich dividends. In all the pair played 30 times together during a highly successful era. Jeffrey, always better at going forward than back and very comfortable with ball in hand, nevertheless worked hard on his defence and produced some stirring defensive performances in the 1990 Grand Slam season. An arch try-poacher he rattled up an impressive 11 international tries and with back row partner Derek White was a valuable alternative source of tries. Although a Lion in 1989, a knee injury hampered his form on tour and he unfortunately failed to make the Test side.

blether and a quiet drink. An attractive blonde then confronted Calder and said, 'Finlay, the test is positive, we must talk.' Having delivered the devastating news she turned on her heels with an apparently mortified Calder, a happily married man with young kids, in hot pursuit. A shocked 'pregnant' pause followed as the players did their best to look suitably aghast and Jeffrey was genuinely appalled with what he had heard.

When the group returned to the hotel, a planted player blurted out that an upset-looking Calder had stormed upstairs to his room. Sole then warned the group not to breathe a word about this situation because if the press got wind of Calder's predicament they would have a field day and it would hamper their chances of winning. Wickedly, a squad member who had not been to the pub, but knew what was happening, wandered by and, seeing an anxious group of players, 'innocently' asked what was wrong. Jeffrey jumped straight in with an emphatic denial of any problem.

Poor Jeffrey had a night to worry about it and on the coach to Thursday's training session a letter appeared addressed to Calder in what someone loudly exclaimed looked like a woman's handwriting. Sean Lineen immediately opened it with Jeffrey charging down the coach in a vain attempt to prevent him from reading it. Worse was to follow as the centre read out aloud the contents with a positively puce Jeffrey physically trying to

**50 Greatest Players**

**FINLAY CALDER Flanker**

**Club**: Stewart's/Melville FP

**Debut:** v France, 18 January 1986

**No. of Caps**: 34 **No. of Points**: 8

A comparative latecomer to the international scene, winning his first cap at the age of 28, Calder had been on the fringes of the national set-up for four years. From a remarkable set of rugby brothers, Gavin, John, Jim and Finlay all played for Scottish Schools and John, Jim and Finlay toured Australia together in 1982 with Scotland. Twin Jim won 27 caps from 1981-85, was a Lion in 1983 and was a key member of the 1984 Grand Slam side. Astonishingly, their international careers did not overlap but Finlay emulated Jim's feats and then went further by captaining both Scotland and the Lions. But this late flourish to his career nearly did not happen as he was on the brink of giving up on his cherished ambition of playing for Scotland when in 1985 Jim Telfer suggested he switch to open-side flanker. And what a move it turned out to be as he enjoyed five years at the very top of the world game.

stop him. The contents literally begged Calder to do the decent thing and stand by the poor woman in her time of need. Lineen then read out the postscript, 'JJ you've been had'.

The brilliant wind-up was a masterstroke, helping release tension and bonding an already close unit even more firmly together in readiness for the Grand Slam encounter with England.

## European Champions v World Champions

A short tour of New Zealand followed in the summer of 1990. Scotland's arrival as Grand Slam champions created enormous interest and the marketing men had a field day billing the Test series as a contest between the World Champions and the European Champions. The Scots played their part and emerged unbeaten in the provincial matches with five wins and a draw and were awfully unlucky not to share the series. Despite losing the first Test 31-16 they went into the second in good heart and led 18-12 at half-time thanks to tries from Stanger and Alex Moore on his debut. A clinical second half from the Blacks in which goal-kicking machine Grant Fox landed three penalties to Hastings' two close misses from long range earned them a narrow 21-18 win.

The 1991 Five Nations was seen as preparation for the Rugby World Cup to be staged in Europe later in the year. Almost inevitably it proved

## Great Matches

**FIVE NATIONS CHAMPIONSHIP** **Murrayfield, 17 March 1990**

**Scotland 13 England 7** **Attendance: 50,000**

Sole led his troops out to a packed Murrayfield at walking pace, throwing down the gauntlet to the English already out on the pitch. The gesture was greeted by an explosion of cheers and a chorus of 'Flower of Scotland' sung with a passion and at a volume never before experienced. Feeding off the atmosphere Scotland set the tone right from the first whistle. From a line-out Lineen took the ball up the middle and as he was checked the back-row arrived in unison to drive him a further 10 yards forward deep into English territory. A penalty was awarded to the Scots, to tumultuous cheers, and England had yet to touch the ball. Chalmers missed but all the pressure was on England.

*David Sole is lifted in triumph by an ecstatic Scottish crowd.*

Next came Calder's famous tap and go from a penalty award in midfield. Bristling with aggression, knees pumping, elbows flailing, socks round his ankles he charged into Skinner who hit him hard. But this time the pack arrived as one to drive their talisman relentlessly forward, rocking England to their core. Another penalty to Scotland, more deafening cheers and yet more greeted Chalmers' successful strike. First blood Scotland: 3-0.

And after 10 minutes it was 6-0 as the stand-off landed penalty number two. Five minutes later and for the only time in the match the Scottish defence was breached as Carling's break was superbly finished by Guscott who glided outside Scott Hastings to score. Sole took the opportunity to gather his men together behind the posts and told them that was to be the last missed tackle of the day and such was the response from his men that it just about was. Chalmers' third penalty made the half-time score Scotland 9 England 4.

The first action of the second half brought a loud groan as Gavin Hastings kicked the ball straight into touch on the full. Advantage England. However, from the scrum England No. 8 Teague decided to pick it up and make some yardage. But instead he knocked it on. Advantage Scotland. From the resultant scrum Jeffrey, who had been switched to No. 8 when White went off injured, showed Teague how it should be done. His pick-up and quick feed to Armstrong was textbook stuff and sent the scrum-half

*Craig Chalmers kicks a goal (left) and Tony Stanger scores the winning try (right).*

away. He drew two men beautifully to put Hastings into space and the big full-back made ground up the touchline before kicking ahead. The ball pitched and bounced high in the English 22 with the chasing Stanger arriving first and, needing every inch of his 6 foot 2 inch frame to pluck the ball out of the air, he scored superbly in the right corner: 13-4.

Scotland were now in the driving seat and made every tackle on their own terms as wave after wave of English attacks were not just repelled but knocked back yards. All they had to show on the board was a Hodgkinson penalty. As the climax of the match approached, the crowd greeted every Scotland tackle and every favourable refereeing decision with eardrum splitting roars of delight. It was a two-way deal. The crowd fed off the players' heroic efforts and the players fed off the deafening levels of support. Murrayfield had never experienced anything like this level of committed and passionate support in 65 years of staging international matches.

When the full-time whistle went the scenes of joy were just incredible as the players were engulfed by many of their supporters before they had a chance to congratulate each other. Edinburgh was the place to be that night as proud Scots celebrated the ultimate triumph, beating England in a Grand Slam decider at Murrayfield.

**Scotland:** A.G.Hastings; A.G Stanger, S. Hastings, S.R.P. Lineen, I. Tukalo; C.M. Chalmers, G. Armstrong; D.M.B. Sole (captain), K.S. Milne, A.P. Burnell, C.A. Gray, D.F. Cronin, J. Jeffrey, D.B. White, F. Calder
**Replacement:** White replaced by D.J. Turnbull
**Scorers: Try** Stanger **Penalty Goals** Chalmers 3

**England:** S.D. Hodgkinson; S.J. Halliday, W.D.C. Carling (captain), J.C. Guscott, R. Underwood; C.R. Andrew, R.J. Hill; P.A.G. Rendall, B.C. Moore, J.A. Probyn, P.J. Ackford, W.A. Dooley, M.G. Skinner, M.C. Teague, P.J. Winterbottom
**Scorers: Try** Guscott **Penalty Goal** Hodgkinson

**Referee:** Mr D. Bishop (New Zealand)

*The lion-hearted Gary Armstrong feeds Craig Chalmers against Wales in 1991.*

impossible to repeat the heroics of 1990. For one, the away matches were against France and England and as McGeechan stated, 'Winning away from home remains the key to winning championships while winning at home produces credibility.'

Calder had retired from the international fold but the squad remained largely intact and just 17 players were used all season indicating that performances were not too far off the pace. The away matches were duly lost as the Scots stuttered badly at the line-out. A tryless encounter in Paris was edged by France thanks largely to three drop goals from Camberabero (2) and Blanco. And England ground out a 21-12 win at Twickenham.

The highlight of the season was a crushing 32-12 win over Wales in which Scotland managed to dominate from start to finish. They so overwhelmed Wales that it was not until the 36th minute that they first set foot in the Scotland 22 and a try score of 4-1 gives an indication of how comprehensive a win it was. Once again the Ireland match was a thriller won 28-25 but the coach and his charges were very despondent afterwards about the quality of performance.

### The Greatest Show on Earth

Despite a poor dress rehearsal in the run-up to the tournament in which Scotland failed to win any of their four warm-up matches, a 16-16 draw against the Barbarians being their best effort, the team played a leading role in what was a magnificent tournament.

Blessed with the great fortune of a sequence of five matches, all played at Murrayfield, the whole nation got behind the team as they embarked on their quest to win the Webb Ellis Trophy. There was huge media interest in the tournament with the tabloids leading the way featuring posed topless photos of some of the better looking squad members. The backs!

With Japan, Zimbabwe and Ireland in their pool there was a great deal of confidence that the Scots could win it. After an under-par first half against Japan where first-night nerves were clearly evident, they comprehensively thrashed them after the break, winning 47-9. An injury to Sole enabled David

Milne, the 'Middle Bear', to make his long-awaited Scotland debut, joining brother Kenny in the front row. He was named for the following match too but had to withdraw owing to injury.

*Derek White on the rampage against Ireland in the 1991 Rugby World Cup.*

A side with eight changes, led by stalwart Peter Dods for the first time, struggled against Zimbabwe early on and were just 15-12 ahead with the halfway mark in sight. However, their form picked up markedly and the Scots were good value for a 51-12 win.

Despite not having produced a complete performance the Scots had won their two openers, scoring 100 points and 15 tries in the process, and could be satisfied with a solid start. But old foes Ireland awaited and although the formbook favoured Scotland most of the recent encounters with the men from Erin had been close and this one was to be no exception. The first half was extremely tough and tight. But the Irish stand-off Ralph Keyes was in splendid goal-kicking mood and kicked four penalties to edge his side ahead by 12-9 which immediately after half-time he extended to 15-9. All of a sudden Scotland looked to be in a bit of bother. What is more, Chalmers had injured his hip and had limped off to be replaced by club-mate Graham Shiel, normally a centre, making his full debut in the most tense of situations.

The turning point came when Calder, who had been persuaded out of retirement for the tournament by McGeechan, chased a high ball and absolutely smashed into Ireland full-back Jim Staples, dislodging the ball but also completely disorientating the full-back. After treatment he bravely continued but Armstrong put up another high ball tester and when he guddled the ball, Stanger was on hand to link with Shiel who scored a try in a fairytale start to his international career. The game had swung Scotland's way and, roared on by their fans, they ran out worthy winners by 24-15 to win the pool and successfully complete part one of this top-level examination.

## Knock-out Agony

The win was not without its cost, however, as both Chalmers (hip) and Lineen (knee) were major doubts for the quarter-final against Western

Samoa, the surprise package of the tournament. The match was a week away and both injuries were rated in the 7-10 day recovery category placing both in the doubtful column. In addition to intensive physiotherapy, modern technology was embraced to aid recovery and the pair underwent daily 90-minute sessions in a hyperbaric-oxygen chamber as high-pressure oxygen helped heal injuries quickly.

The effort was well worthwhile for although Lineen just missed out on the Western Samoa match, Chalmers was fit to start in a reshaped midfield with Shiel slotting into Lineen's place at inside centre. The Samoans could not be treated lightly having finished runners-up in Pool Three, sensationally beating host nation Wales in Cardiff 16-13, losing narrowly by 9-3 to pool winners Australia and finally despatching the formidable Argentinians 35-12. Their hard-nosed, no-nonsense approach was straight from the New Zealand textbook where so many of them were based, but their aggressive chest-high tackling was very much their calling card and Scotland needed to be wary of dangerous opponents who so relished physical confrontation.

McGeechan devised a clever game plan to subdue the South Sea Islanders, in effect taking the game to them and not allowing them to dictate the pace. Gavin Hastings moved up to the stand-off position early in the game and was used as a battering ram to test the Samoan fringe defence. It worked a treat and the clever tactics were implemented comprehensively and impressively for Scotland to win by the satisfying margin of 28-6 against a side who always threatened to explode into action.

The quarter-final in Paris between France and England was a brutal affair and England's win brought a dream semi-final clash between the auldest of enemies at Murrayfield. It was 1990 all over again in another winner-takes-all clash, but this time if anything the stakes were higher as a place in the Rugby World Cup final was the prize.

Sadly, the match was a huge disappointment and far from the glamorous spectacle you would hope, if not expect, a World Cup semi-final to be. England, badly psychologically scarred from Murrayfield 1990, had reverted to a dull, unimaginative approach which undoubtedly played to their considerable physical strengths as they strangled the life out of the match.

In a largely one-sided affair it said as much for the great spirit, fight and pride of the Scots, as it did for their opponents' paucity of ambition, that they were still in with a chance of winning the match with the score 6-6 as full-time drew near. Indeed, Hastings had a great chance to put Scotland ahead and heap real pressure on England when Scotland were awarded a late penalty from almost in front of the posts in England's 22. Agonisingly for the hushed crowd, Scotland's leading points scorer squirted the kick wide and when Andrew sneaked over a drop goal minutes later there was no way back.

It was a gut-wrenching way to exit the World Cup but the Scots had no time to feel sorry for themselves as they faced New Zealand at Cardiff in a play-off to decide third and fourth place. In an exciting but mistake-ridden match, where both teams played positive entertaining rugby, the All Blacks won 13-6.

## The Grand Slam Side Breaks Up

The Grand Slam side broke up over the next two seasons, with Jeffrey retiring immediately after the World Cup and Calder also drawing a line under his Test career. Gray won no more caps after 1991 and White joined his back- row buddies in retirement at the end of the 1992 championship season. Sole and Lineen delayed their retirements by just a couple of months, signing off after the Scotland tour to Australia. And just as significantly, McGeechan left the Test arena after the 1993 Lions tour to try his hand at club level with Northampton.

Having lost some top-notch players and an influential coach in quick succession, it is not surprising that the period produced a decidedly mixed batch of results. In 1992, Scotland won two and lost two matches in the Five Nations without really challenging for honours. An early loss to England was followed by back-to-back wins over Ireland and France before losing narrowly to Wales in a disappointing match in Cardiff.

A frustrating tour of Australia concluded the season with the tourists unable to post their first win until the fifth match of the tour, and the Test series was won comfortably by the newly crowned world champions.

Following Sole's retirement, Gavin Hastings was appointed Scotland captain for 1993 and the players responded to his infectious enthusiasm and confidence to put themselves in position to challenge for a Triple Crown after good wins over Ireland and Wales. The line-out turned out to be a source of plentiful ball this season as a rejuvenated Cronin, new cap Andy Reed and Doddie Weir proved to be a potent blend. Wales were comprehensively beaten 20-0 which sent the Scots south to Twickenham once again in search of a Triple Crown. However, Scotland and Chalmers suffered a painful blow in the 24th minute when the Melrose stand-off broke his right forearm in two places. His replacement was the 19-year-old Gregor Townsend, who became Scotland's youngest cap for over 20 years. The disruption did little to help the team for Stuart Barnes, who had been recalled after a five-year absence to an England side that had struggled all season, provided the creative spark that had been missing as they won 26-12.

**50 Greatest Players**

**DAVID SOLE Prop**

**Clubs:** Bath, Edinburgh Academicals

**Debut:** v France, 18 January 1986

**No. of Caps:** 44 **No. of Points:** 12

A key member of the class of 1986, Sole was one of six new caps against France and, along with Finlay Calder and the Hastings brothers, matured into a player of the highest class. Capped out of Glenalmond for Scottish Schools, he served early notice of his promise in the senior game when he established himself in the formidable Bath front row while a student at Exeter University. Just 23 when he won his first cap, he quickly became a permanent fixture in the Scotland front row, his uncompromising scrummaging and athletic ball-handling abilities in the loose ideally suited to the modern game. He toured Australia in 1989 with the Lions and played in all three Tests and would have been a hot favourite to captain the 1993 Lions had he not retired prematurely from the Test scene. His greatest moment unquestionably was leading Scotland to a third Grand Slam, and his hard-nosed leadership and ferocious will to win ensured he got the very best out of his men.

A season that had hinted at great promise ultimately fizzled out but the charismatic Hastings was rightly rewarded with the Lions captaincy, being one of seven Scots to tour New Zealand (Andy Nicol was called up later as a replacement) while McGeechan was head coach. Hastings enjoyed an outstanding tour and led the side splendidly, scoring a record 38 points in the Test series which was narrowly lost 2-1.

## All Black Gloom

It was all change off the pitch as a new coaching partnership of Dougie Morgan and Richie Dixon, who had been Scotland's coaches on the summer tour to Fiji, Tonga and Western Samoa, was put in charge. Furthermore, Jim Telfer had been lured away from a successful career in education and had been appointed to a new post within the SRU as director of rugby.

The touring All Blacks' impact in Scotland was stunning and their performances cruelly exposed what many believed were shortcomings in the domestic game. In the Test match the All Blacks ruthlessly and clinically took

## 50 Greatest Players

**GAVIN HASTINGS Full-back**

**Clubs**: Watsonians, Cambridge University, London Scottish

**Debut:** v France, 18 January 1986

**No. of Caps**: 61 **No. of Points**: 667

Gavin Hastings achieved just about all there is to achieve in the game. He equalled the world record of six penalty goals on his debut and by the end of the season his haul of 52 points was a new Scottish individual championship record. He finished his career having played in a record 61 internationals, scoring a record 667 points for Scotland and a further 66 points for the Lions in six Tests, another record. But he was more than just a points-gatherer, he was a vital member of the Scotland and Lions teams of his era. In defence he was brilliant under the high ball, safe in the tackle and a prodigious punter of the ball; in attack, although not blessed with startling pace, he timed his runs well and used every ounce of his physical presence to create space and to score 17 tries. Having succeeded Sole as Scotland captain in 1993 he did the job so impressively in his first season that he was appointed Lions captain and was an outstanding leader on the tour to New Zealand.

Scotland apart and won 51-15, scoring seven tries in the process including a hat-trick for 20-year-old Jeff Wilson on his debut. Their skipper Sean Fitzpatrick commented afterwards that it was 'the most satisfying performance in which I have been involved in terms of commitment, total aggression and mental hardness for 15 guys to play for 80 minutes'.

The performance sent shock waves throughout the world of rugby which were, of course, felt most acutely in Scotland. But worse was to follow as the All Blacks' second string destroyed the South in a tour match by 84-5. Telfer said in the aftermath, 'We tend to think in our own little midden that we are good. But we are not.'

And it was this defeat which provided Telfer with a catalyst to drive forward change in the way the game was run in Scotland, diverting the focus away from club rugby and establishing district level rugby for the elite players to give them regular exposure to a higher grade of rugby week in and week out. The results rocked Scottish confidence to its very core and unsurprisingly a difficult Five Nations Championship followed with a draw against Ireland being the best result. Wales sensed blood and handed Scotland a 29-6 beating in Cardiff. In three successive matches Scotland had failed to score a try. Morgan was moved to say after the match, 'Too many of our players have gone soft from living in the First Division comfort zone'. The innovative national leagues which had helped give Scotland a competitive edge in the 1970s and 1980s were now being cited as being counter-productive, particularly having been expanded to 14 teams and providing too many meaningless matches.

The great sides of previous seasons contained some genuine hard men who helped galvanise and bring out the best in those around them. Scotland were struggling desperately to find replacements but it was proving to be very difficult. One added bonus, however, was in persuading Armstrong back from a self-imposed exile in the international wilderness for the Calcutta Cup match, and his impact on proceedings was immense. Scotland produced a display long on guts and determination which restored their credibility in the eyes of their supporters and boosted their own flagging self-confidence.

The match was nip and tuck all the way through and the lead changed hands a staggering seven times. With six minutes to go, Jon Callard kicked his fourth penalty of the afternoon to put England 12-11 in front. As the time ticked away it looked as if England would sneak a one-point win. However, right on the stroke of full time, Townsend dropped a clever goal to apparently win the match. But two minutes later, deep into injury time, England were awarded a kickable penalty for handling in the ruck by a Scotsman. Callard duly kicked the goal and won the match in heartbreaking fashion for the home support.

Hastings, showing how much the defeat hurt, was moved to tears in his post-match interview with Dougie Donnelly immediately after the full-time whistle. But worse was to follow when video evidence showed that it had in fact been an Englishman who had handled the ball in the ruck. England at that time had a navy blue cuff on their long-sleeved shirts and the referee had mistaken Andrew's English shirt for a Scotland one. The incident was quickly dubbed the 'Hand of Rob' but the Englishman remained unrepentant. Once again a Scotland versus England match ended in acrimony and left a sour taste, in Scottish mouths at least.

An away draw against Ireland was a further sign of recovery and once again Armstrong was immense although a thumb injury sidelined him for the final match of the season. Against France the Hastings brothers each made their 50th appearance for Scotland, a remarkable feat from a remarkable pair whose contributions to international rugby have been enormous.

Sadly for the Watsonians duo their special day was spoiled by France, who won 20-12 to record their first win at Murrayfield since 1978.

Reflecting on the season as a whole Gavin Hastings said, 'I'm not proud of the way of the way the season's gone. It's not been through lack of effort. I hope to be back next year. Whether as captain or not.'

## Happier Times

Hastings was indeed back as captain for the 1994-95 season in what was to be a glorious swansong to a long, illustrious and successful career. He led Scotland in 11 internationals, winning eight and personally scoring a staggering 201 points to bow out after the Rugby World Cup quarter-final against New Zealand.

Murrayfield's redevelopment into an all-seater stadium was completed in time for the season and South Africa were invited to officially reopen the ground. They put on an awesome performance of power rugby and ran out worthy winners by 34-10. With a free weekend at the start of the Five Nations, Scotland also played a warm-up match against Canada which helped build confidence for the long season ahead. In appalling conditions the Scots produced a workmanlike performance to win 22-6. Two weeks later Scotland started the championship well, converting a narrow 9-8 half-time lead into a comfortable 26-13 win and for rejuvenated skipper Hastings an individual haul of 16 points, taking him past 500 Test match points, the first European to reach this major milestone.

Two weeks later Scotland finally won in Paris, having waited 26 years for the privilege. Only five Scots had played in the French capital before, so for most of the team there was no 'losers' baggage to contend with. Allied to Hastings' massive self-belief the team overcame a disastrous start to outplay France for long periods. Nevertheless when French captain Philippe Saint-André scored his second try with seven minutes left to give France an undeserved lead of 21-16, it looked as if the battling performance would end in defeat. With full-time looming a sublime slip of the ball from Townsend to Hastings, forever known as the 'Toonie flip', paved the way for the captain to storm half the length of the pitch to score a sensational try. The scores were level at 21-21 and Hastings made the conversion confidently to win the match and pen yet another 'Boys Own' chapter in his life story.

The sunshine of Paris was swapped for the driving snow of Edinburgh as Wales were overcome 26-13. As in Paris they went behind to an early try, only to come roaring back to score one of Scotland's best ever victories. Rob Wainwright fielded a Welsh kick-ahead deep in the Scotland half. He

*Gavin Hastings' dramatic late try and conversion ensured that Scotland beat France in Paris in 1995 for the first time in 26 years.*

passed to Hastings who fed Weir, who put Kenny Logan in space. The winger exploded up the touchline and then swerved infield to hand on to No. 8 Eric Peters, who galloped 20 metres to finish off a marvellous move. Peters' Bath team-mate David Hilton scored a second try minutes later and at 20-7 Scotland were in the driving seat and went on to win comfortably to set up a second winner-takes-all Grand Slam clash with England; but this time the venue was Twickenham.

Once again the media interest was immense as fate had once more brought the sport's oldest and, at the time, bitterest protagonists together in a splendid finale to the season. This time the hype was far better than the actuality and a disjointed, disappointing, penalty-strewn encounter ensued. The back divisions cancelled each other out and in the battle of the boots Andrew's seven penalties and one drop goal proved too much for Hastings' two penalties and Chalmers' two drop goals.

## The World Cup Goes to Africa

Although disappointed there was none of the despondency experienced after losing to England in the World Cup semi-final in 1991. Scotland had exceeded all expectations during the season and to have a chance at a Grand Slam so soon after ending a dismal run of nine successive defeats was beyond everybody's wildest imaginings. Furthermore, there was no chance to dwell on what might have been, with the third Rugby World Cup in South Africa looming. Scottish rugby had been restored to rude health and, what is more, the exciting brand of rugby being played, moving away from the successful rucking game to a more fluid style of total rugby, was proving popular with players and supporters alike.

The very confrontational nature of rugby often results in depriving teams of key players because of injury. This tournament was to prove no exception. The biggest blow was losing Armstrong and the absence of Townsend, Nicol, Reed, Sharp and Munro deprived the squad of some real depth.

However, following an encouraging warm-up match against Romania and a short team-building tour to Spain, Scotland arrived in South Africa in fine fettle and confident that they were genuine contenders for the title. Placed in Pool 4, France were the obvious danger but the Paris result had given the Scottish squad a renewed self-belief. Unlike in the first World Cup, the French match was the final one in the pool and the hope and expectation was that the first two pool matches against Ivory Coast and Tonga would afford the Scots an early opportunity to get into their stride.

And that is exactly how it worked out. Ivory Coast were simply outclassed as Scotland ran riot, scoring 13 tries to win 89-0. It was another colossal triumph for Hastings who set another points-scoring record with a massive 44 points. He even had Ivory Coast players queuing up for his autograph after the match. Although Tonga was an altogether tougher affair, Scotland were happy enough with a 41-5 win and again Hastings stole the show, scoring 31 points.

And so to the final pool match in Pretoria against France. A win for Scotland would put them into a quarter-final against Ireland and a fair chance of making it to the semi-final stage. But a loss and the dark shadow of the All Blacks loomed.

*Gavin Hastings scores five of his 31 points against Tonga.*

Scotland started very well and led 13-3 at half-time having played positively throughout the first half. Maybe the Scots tried to protect their lead too much rather than continue to pressurise their opponents. France ground their way back into contention and five Thierry Lacroix penalties narrowed the gap to 19-15 as the match boiled to an exciting climax. Harshly penalised for bringing the scrum down going forward in their own 22, France took a quick penalty and worked the ball left to Emile Ntamack, the 'Black Pearl', who forced his muscular frame over for the

## 50 Greatest Players

**SCOTT HASTINGS Centre/Wing**

**Club**: Watsonians

**Debut:** v France, 18 January 1986

**No. of Caps**: 65 **No. of Points**: 43

Scott Hastings inherited the family self-confidence gene and the infectious enthusiasm of the Hastings brothers never failed but to lift any flagging spirits. His first appearance for Scotland in 1986 was also Colin Deans' first match as captain of Scotland. Deans recalls the precocious young Scott shouting to him across the team room before the match, 'I say, Deano, could you get me a cup of hot chocolate and some sandwiches before you sit down.' Always determined to enjoy life, Hastings was a magnificent tackler and he and Sean Lineen formed a very effective centre partnership, appearing together on a world record 28 occasions. But he was also committed to playing open expansive rugby whenever possible and much enjoyed the total rugby approach adopted by Scotland in the mid-1990s. After missing the first Test on the 1989 Lions tour to Australia through injury, he played an important part in the second and third Test victories and was unlucky to shatter a cheekbone on the 1993 Lions tour and miss the series.

winning score. Having led for the entire match it was a cruel and painful way to lose and although still in the tournament, the quarter-final against the All Blacks, spearheaded by their new teenage sensation the awesome Jonah Lomu, was a fearsome prospect.

In a typically gritty performance, Scotland were well in contention having played commendably well in the first half, largely nullifying the Lomu threat. New Zealand led 17-9 at half-time but characteristically stepped up a few gears at the start of the second to kill off the game. And if they did not quite run away with the result, their 48-30 win was nevertheless more than enough to earn a semi-final berth and end Scotland's interest at the quarter-final stage for the second time in three tournaments.

# Chapter Fourteen: 1996-2003
# The Professional Era

The 1987 Rugby World Cup, as many bastions of the amateur game had feared, paved the way for the professional game. Scotland players were incensed when they saw All Blacks captain Andy Dalton advertising a farmyard buggy on television during the tournament. The Kiwis were driving a horse and cart through the amateur regulations and Dalton's claim that he was advertising the product in his capacity as a farmer, and not the All Blacks captain, did not wash. Dalton was allowed to benefit commercially from his status with the full blessing of the NZRFU and although an extreme example of 'shamateurism' it was not an isolated incident in a sport which had fought a long but losing battle in its efforts to remain true to its amateur roots and principles.

The history of the sport had been frequently punctuated by money matters: broken-time payments and the formation of the Northern Union in the late 19th century; expenses payments made to touring teams from the southern hemisphere; gifts from Welsh clubs to their players; boot money as match payments; and even in Scotland, players paid to wear certain brands of footwear. The relationship between commerce and top-class sport was nothing new and with a glamorous product with global appeal, the IB had some serious thinking to do if it was to remain in control of the sport it had run since 1886.

Partial concessions had been made during the 1990s to allow players to benefit from off-pitch endorsements. Trust funds could be set up for players, and provision was made to allow them to benefit from limited commercial activities: some Scotland players, for example, modelled leisurewear. And in the 1991 Rugby World Cup each Scotland squad member was paid the princely sum of £368.80 for his participation in the tournament.

Rumours of 'extra' payments were rife in the game. In the UK, for example, it was common knowledge that at club level there were rewards for key players and leading coaches alike, sometimes in the form of hard cash, but often in kind with benefits such as the provision of a car, accommodation or a holiday as reward for success. In France, rugby had been semi-professional for many years and although of Italian descent David Campese was not spending his Australian summers in the land of his forefathers just because of a love of pasta and red wine. It was getting more and more difficult to police these activities and in 1994 the IB set up a four-man working party, chaired by Vernon Pugh and including Fred McLeod of the SRU, to investigate what substance there was to these rumours.

The working party confirmed the worst fears of many and concluded that the IB needed to act and act quickly if it wished to properly regulate the game and control the introduction of professionalism. But although accepting these findings, the IB delayed any decisions until after the 1995 Rugby World Cup.

This decision almost proved calamitous as sporting entrepreneurs were already circling rugby, sensing rich pickings. A sport with global appeal, its own World Cup every four years and players who were keen to make money out of the sport they had put so much into, was ripe for exploitation. Two heavyweight media moguls, Kerry Packer, who had transformed cricket in the 1970s with his 'cricket circus', and Rupert Murdoch, who similarly transformed Australian rugby league to create Super League, emerged centre stage to slug it out. Packer's man Ross Turnbull narrowly failed to pull off the creation of a rugby circus having signed many of the leading players in the world including 18 of Scotland's 1995 World Cup squad. But Murdoch had more success and his News Corporation signed a 10-year £370 million deal with the southern hemisphere nations, which included the rights to broadcast the Tri-Nations and Super-12 series.

Jolted into action, the IB met in Paris and on 27 August 1995 finally announced the end of amateurism in rugby union in the following statement: 'Subsequent to the repeal of the amateur regulations, rugby will become an open game, and there will be no prohibition on payment or the provision of other material benefit to any person involved in the game. Payment may be made at any level of participation. There should be no pay ceiling. Payment for result is not prohibited.'

## The Professional Game in Scotland

The introduction of the professional game in Scotland has not been easy, indeed it has been very painful and at times traumatic. The SRU quickly decided to create a professional structure based on the traditional four Districts – Edinburgh, Glasgow, North and Midlands (Caledonia) and the South and, although it met voluble opposition, a special general meeting approved the new structure.

Players were contracted centrally to the SRU and spread between the four Districts to play in the newly created European competitions: the Heineken Cup and the European Shield. They also played an inter-district championship but represented their clubs during the rest of the season.

In 1997 a power battle ensued between some of the leading clubs who felt that they should be the vehicle for the elite game and the SRU and four former Scotland captains – Jim Aitken, Finlay Calder, Gavin Hastings and David Sole – emerged to put forward the case for an independent review of the SRU. Although they failed to convince enough clubs of the need for such a review, the SRU did ask Lord Mackay of Clashfern to conduct an independent study into all aspects of Scottish rugby in 1998. His findings were broadly supportive of the SRU's policy but there still remain many bridges to build between the SRU and the club game as the sport continues to evolve.

The last few seasons of the 20th century saw some real highs and lows for Scottish rugby, probably more peaks and troughs than at any other time in history. With the introduction of the professional era, expectations, rightly or wrongly, are far higher than ever and media scrutiny has never been more intense. Players are paid, coaches and support staff are paid, administrators are paid and good results are not so much expected as demanded. These pressures have seen the sackings of national and district coaches as the resources are constantly shuffled. Specialist coaches and advisers are engaged in a constant search for a winning formula. Sometimes it comes together over a season, most unexpectedly but pleasingly in the 1996 and 1999 Five Nations campaigns. And sometimes it all comes together in one match, so stunningly against England in 2000, with Duncan Hodge scoring all 19 points, in Ireland in 2001 and the defeat of South Africa in 2002.

*Doddie Weir (left) was one of the outstanding line-out jumpers of his generation whose 61 caps are a record for a Scottish forward.*

In 1996 after a promising World Cup, a home 15-15 draw against Samoa and Scotland A's (a full-strength Scotland in all but name) 29-17 loss to Italy gave little cause for optimism in the Five Nations. But a 16-10 away win against Ireland, a wonderful display to beat the French 19-14 and a second away win by 16-14 over Wales gave Scotland a real chance of winning a Grand Slam for the second time in successive seasons. The strength of the team was once again in the middle five, comprising new captain Rob Wainwright, Ian Smith, Eric

Peters, Bryan Redpath and Gregor Townsend. England, however, brought back Dean Richards and he limited the supply of loose ball to prevent Scotland from playing their exciting, fluid brand of rugby and they went down 18-9.

But this success could not be replicated and seasons 1997 and 1998 yielded single championship victories and cost coaches Richie Dixon and David Johnston their jobs. Jim Telfer returned once more to take charge of the national squad.

## A Fine Line

The 1999 season proved how fine a line there is between success and failure in the championship and the Rugby World Cup. Scotland started well against Wales as John Leslie scored a try after nine seconds. But they were struggling in the second half until Duncan Hodge unfortunately broke his leg. Alan Tait came on as replacement and Gregor Townsend moved to stand-off. The reshaped midfield of Townsend, Leslie and Tait clicked immediately and Scotland went on to win the match comfortably. Tait and Townsend scored three tries between them against England in a narrow defeat at Twickenham and the momentum continued to build as Ireland were comfortably beaten in some style. Against France, Scotland produced some breathtaking rugby to win in exhilarating fashion, and the result left them handily placed to collect the final Five Nations trophy of the century when Wales unexpectedly beat England at Wembley.

If the ball bounced in Scotland's favour in the Five Nations, it evaded their clutches in the Rugby World Cup. They entered the tournament as one of the favourites and as reigning European champions. But their first opponents were South Africa, reigning world champions, who had taken over 100 points off them in their previous two meetings at Murrayfield. It was a daunting prospect for the Scots.

*Gary Armstrong fends off Joost van der Westhuizen in Scotland's Rugby World Cup opener, Murrayfield, 1999.*

But led by rugby warrior Gary Armstrong, Scotland played marvellously well in the first half and led 16-13 at the interval. The Springboks hit back with an early try to edge ahead 18-16. Stung, Townsend hoisted a high ball which John Leslie caught brilliantly in the lee of the South African posts. A great tackle not only deprived him of a try but also badly injured his ankle and he played no further

## Great Matches

**FIVE NATIONS CHAMPIONSHIP** **Stade de France, Paris, 10 April 1999**

**France 22 Scotland 36** **Attendance: 80,000**

This was a truly breathtaking encounter. Scotland arrived in Paris buoyant with confidence having comfortably beaten Wales and Ireland and narrowly lost to England in a thrilling encounter at Twickenham. France, on the other hand, were struggling for form but with the Parisian sunshine on their backs were expected to be a handful for the Scots who had lost two key players in Smith and Peters to injury. The match seemed to start to script when Ntamack scored after two minutes but playmaker Castaignede was injured in the move and went off. Scotland responded in the most positive fashion possible, producing a most glorious display of running rugby full of adventure, daring, flair and panache.

They hit France with a triple whammy of tries. Logan was the creator for the first one, setting off on a long run to set up Martin Leslie for his first try for Scotland. Then Metcalfe made a scintillating burst for that arch try poacher Tait to get on the end of and score by the posts. Then Scotland scored again. This time Townsend, sensing a gap, broke through on the right and as he headed for the posts raised the ball in celebration of scoring his fourth try in successive championship matches. All of a sudden Scotland were 19-5 ahead, and the French defence was in tatters. Finally, France hit back with a converted try by Juillet but Metcalfe's initial thrust combined with Tait's clever support running ensured the Scots returned the compliment and restored Scotland's 14-point lead. And the Scottish supporters had barely drawn breath before Martin Leslie notched his second of the afternoon and Logan's conversion stretched the lead to an astonishing 33-12.

Just before half-time a Dominici try was converted and an Aucagne penalty narrowed the gap, but nevertheless, the remarkable half-time scoreline read France 22 Scotland 33.

Understandably, the two teams could not maintain the thrilling entertainment value in the second half. Mindful of the respective coaches' urgings to tighten up their defence the second period was a tight affair with Logan's second penalty of the match the only score.

**France:** E. Ntamack; X. Garbajosa, F. Comba, P. Giordani, C. Dominici; T. Castaignede, P. Carbonneau; F. Tournaire, R. Ibanez (captain), C. Califano, T. Cleda, O. Brouzet, R. Castel, C. Juillet, C. Labit
**Replacements:** D. Aucagne for Castaignede; C. Laussucq for Carbonneau; P. Benetton for Castel; S. Marconnet for Califano
**Scorers: Tries** Ntamack, Juillet, Dominici **Conversions** Aucagne 2 **Penalty Goal** Aucagne

**Scotland:** G.H. Metcalfe; C.A. Murray, A.V. Tait, J.A. Leslie, K.M. Logan; G.P.J. Townsend, G. Armstrong (captain); D.I.W. Hilton, G.C. Bulloch, A.P. Burnell, S. Murray, S.B. Grimes, A.C. Pountney, S.J. Reid, M.D. Leslie
**Replacements:** G. Graham for Hilton; P. Walton for Pountney; A.I. Reed for S. Murray
**Scorers: Tries** Leslie 2, Tait 2, Townsend **Conversions** Logan 4 **Penalty Goal** Logan

**Referee:** Mr C. Thomas (Wales)

part in the tournament. Although Scotland edged ahead from a Kenny Logan penalty, Leslie's loss disrupted the rhythm of the team and they went down 46-29.

That put Scotland on course for another quarter-final encounter with New Zealand and ultimately out of the tournament. As much as the enforced change of Tait for the injured Hodge against Wales had inspired Scotland in the Five Nations, the opposite had happened in the Rugby World Cup when they lost Leslie to injury. There truly is a fine line between success and failure.

## The New Millennium

The real challenge for Scottish rugby is to achieve a level of consistently high performances and results over a long period of time. Only in the 1990s has the Scotland side won over 50 per cent of its matches, winning 21 of 40 games played in a decade which brought the country's biggest successes of the modern era. In four of those ten seasons Scotland won all four matches once and three out of four matches on three other occasions. In the 1980s, Scotland won four matches once and three matches once but you have to go back to 1964 for the previous time Scotland won three matches in a season. And before that it was in 1938.

Since the introduction of the Six Nations Championship in 2000, Scotland have won seven out of 20 matches, a 35 per cent success rate. Just one match was won in 2000 and if Scotland have found a level of consistency in the last

*Tom Smith's handling and passing abilities mark him out as a world-class player.*

**50 Greatest Players**

**ALAN TAIT Centre**

**Clubs:** Kelso, Newcastle Falcons, Edinburgh Reivers

**Debut:** v France, 23 May 1987

**No. of Caps:** 27 **No. of Points:** 81

After winning the first of eight Scotland caps in the 1987 World Cup as a replacement for John Rutherford, Tait switched to rugby league, signing a contract with Widnes in 1988. He enjoyed a highly successful career with Widnes, being twice voted Man of the Match in the Premiership final in 1989 and 1990 and appearing in the Challenge Cup final in 1994 for Leeds. In all he won 16 caps for Great Britain before returning to union in 1996 with Newcastle. He was welcomed back into the international fold after a nine-year absence when he was capped against Ireland later in the year. His organisational and communication skills brought a steadying influence to the midfield defence and his clever angles of running and a priceless gift for taking chances brought him an impressive total of 17 tries in 27 internationals. One of six former rugby league players on the Lions tour to South Africa in 1997 he was moved to the wing and scored the winning try in the Cape Town Test. His midfield partnership with Gregor Townsend and John Leslie gave Scotland a real cutting edge in the 1999 championship-winning season.

three seasons it is in winning only two out of five matches each campaign to finish fourth in the table each time.

Ian McGeechan's second period in charge has so far not been a particularly successful one, winning 14 of the 35 matches played to date. There has been much tinkering with the personnel at his disposal but that elusive winning blend has yet to materialise. There has been no core of real world-class players in the first years of the new millennium, with Tom Smith the only one currently in that category. But there is a sprinkling of talent in the squad. On his day Scott Murray is one of the best line-out jumpers in the world, Nathan Hines can mix it with the best and Simon Taylor is fast maturing into one of the best No. 8s in the business. Behind the scrum, skipper Bryan Redpath had a good season in 2002-03 and is being hard pressed by Mike Blair, another youngster with a real future. Chris Paterson's best position has yet to be decided, but the promise of Blair and Paterson at half-back for club and country is an exciting one.

*Jim Telfer, who retires as the SRU's director of rugby after the World Cup, having been a magnificent servant to Scottish rugby as player, coach and administrator for almost 40 years.*

McGeechan will step down as head coach after the Rugby World Cup in Australia and will take over Jim Telfer's post as director of rugby when he finally retires. There were very encouraging signs in the summer Tests against South Africa that McGeechan has found a style and pattern of play which could yet enable him to finish his international coaching career with a flourish. Matt Williams, his successor as national coach, will be an interested observer during the Rugby World Cup as he finds out at first hand what raw material he has at his disposal for the next four seasons.

## Domestic Flaws

The professional era has not been kind to Scottish rugby. The domestic flaws and weaknesses identified by Telfer in the aftermath of heavy defeats at the hands of the All Blacks for both Scotland and the South in 1993 have, if anything, been exacerbated in recent seasons. As Scottish players endeavour to get to grips with the demands of being professional sportsmen, other nations are not standing still waiting for Scotland to catch up. The advantages gained in previous seasons, whereby clever and innovative coaching, the assiduous use of video analysis and high levels of fitness all helped compensate for other weaknesses, have been largely nullified in the professional era. Other countries, with bigger playing populations, healthier financial resources and, perhaps most importantly, a positive sporting culture geared to success, have used these advantages to create a widening gulf between the top nations and the rest of the world.

The challenge is huge but there are healthy signs that young players coming through from club level are better prepared both physically and mentally for the demands of professional rugby than ever before. Excellent work is being done to identify players from as young as 14 or 15 through the Pathways system and afford them an early opportunity to get on the representative ladder. The very cream of these youngsters are then invited to join the Scottish Institute of Sport where they work with the national high performance coach to prepare them for a life in the professional game. Some are already professionals but most are club

**50 Greatest Players**

**GARY ARMSTRONG Scrum-half**

**Clubs:** Jedforest, Newcastle Falcons

**Debut:** v Australia, 19 November 1988

**No. of Caps:** 51 **No. of Points:** 21

In an extraordinary international career which started as a 22-year-old against Australia in 1988 and ended almost 11 years later against New Zealand in the World Cup at Murrayfield, Armstrong is still playing top-level rugby. The lorry driver from Jedburgh first of all usurped club-mate Roy Laidlaw from the Jedforest side and then succeeded him in the Scotland team.

A Lion in 1989 and a vital member of the Grand Slam team, Armstrong's unbelievable courage and strength of will helped him overcome two career-threatening injuries in 1993 and 1994. He enjoyed a new lease of life in 1995 when he joined Newcastle and helped them into Division One in 1997 and was part of the championship-winning side in 1998. Jim Telfer's favourite player, he led Scotland in 1998 and to the famous Five Nations Championship victory in 1999, winning his milestone 50th cap, against Samoa, during the World Cup. His current form and fitness for the Borders are such that he could still do a job for Scotland at the age of 37.

players and over half a dozen of them have won professional contracts for the 2002-03 season.

Providing the professional players with good quality, regular, high-grade rugby has been a problem in recent years. The four district teams were quickly cut to two, Edinburgh Reivers and Glasgow Caledonians, and in their first season the only competitive matches they played were in the European Cup and a domestic Tri-Series. The following season the teams played in the cross-border Scottish/Welsh league, an imaginative concept designed to help both countries prepare their players for international rugby.

The league, which received mixed reviews, lasted for three seasons but its main legacy was in paving the way for the Celtic league, as the three Celtic nations look for ways to bridge the gap between the middle and elite levels of world rugby. For 2003-04, a 22-match Celtic league, running throughout the season, will form the main plank of competitive rugby for the three Scottish professional teams (The Borders, Edinburgh Rugby and Glasgow

## 50 Greatest Players

**GREGOR TOWNSEND Stand-off/Centre**

**Clubs:** Gala, Northampton, Brive, Castres, Borders

**Debut:** v England, 6 March 1993

**No. of Caps:** 76 **No. of Points:** 157

One of the most gifted players to be capped by Scotland, Townsend was a 19-year-old when he was first called up for the 1992 tour to Australia. Capped within a year, he has gone on to become Scotland's record cap-holder with a total of 76 currently to his name. At his best he is a world-class, game-breaking player and Ian McGeechan deployed his unique attacking instincts to the full in the Lions series win over South Africa in 1997. His best season for Scotland came after he had been left out of the starting XV for the Five Nations opener against Wales in 1999. Unfortunately, Duncan Hodge broke his leg during the match and Townsend came on, scored a try and turned the game. He went on to score a try in each match that year becoming only the second Scotsman to achieve the feat since Johnnie Wallace in 1925.

Rugby), supplemented by European competition. The Celtic League has the potential to rival the Zurich Premiership in England and represents a great opportunity for Scottish players for the first time to test themselves against tough opposition week in, week out in a meaningful tournament. This can only benefit the prospects for the national side.

However, the SRU, having been the among the first nations to embrace professionalism by contracting players directly, has to make sufficient resources available to enable Scottish teams to be truly competitive. Admittedly, there has been a reduction in the revenue from TV and sponsorship deals for the Six Nations but the recent support staff redundancies and the releasing of key players will have an adverse affect on prospects, at least in the short term.

When Edinburgh signed former All Blacks captain Todd Blackadder in 2001 it was envisaged that he would be the first of a selective band of top-class players to be brought to Scotland to help raise standards. Blackadder has been truly outstanding and his influence and the values and standards he has brought with him from New Zealand have had a noticeable affect on Edinburgh. But what happens when he goes back

**50 Greatest Players**

**TOM SMITH Prop**

**Clubs:** Caledonia Reds, Glasgow Caledonians, Brive, Northampton

**Debut:** v England, 1 February 1997

**No. of Caps:** 45 **No. of Points:** 25

Another Telfer favourite and without question one of the world's leading loose-head props. A solid scrummager, it is his ability in the loose that sets him apart and he is regarded as the best passer of the ball in the current Scotland squad. An excellent Sevens player, his athleticism and ball-playing skills earned him a Melrose winner's medal with Watsonians in 1996 and little over a year later, with just three Scotland caps to his name, he was a key member of the all-Celtic front row which made such a magnificent contribution to the Lions series win over the Springboks. Injury disrupted his career in 1998 and a broken leg sustained against Ireland in 1999 cost him a place in Scotland's sensational win over France. However, he has been a virtual ever-present since and was one of four Scots, along with Scott Murray, Simon Taylor and Gordon Bulloch, who toured with the 2001 Lions to Australia. And once again he was the only Scot to play in all three Tests in a series that was narrowly lost.

home? Will he be replaced? Will the SRU provide the resources to attract another Blackadder for each of the teams?

In a country with just 40,000 players, compared for example to the 60,000 in Ireland or the 250,000 in England and France, it is vital that every effort is made and every opportunity taken to ensure that Scotland can continue to enjoy success at international level.

## Providing the Memories of Tomorrow

Since the formation of the first Scottish team in 1871, its success has been sporadic; sometimes it erupts into glorious purple passages and at other times descends into deeply depressing, dark moments. But for most of the first 132 years of international rugby, Scotland has held a position around mid-table.

There have been some wondrous moments: three Grand Slams, ten Triple Crowns and 14 outright championships. There have been some fantastic results: the first ever international, any win against England, beating South Africa in 1906, Wales in 1951, a 'Triple Crown' against New Zealand, South

Africa and Australia in the 1960s, France in Paris in 1995 and 1999 and Ireland in 2001. Brilliant players have graced the blue shirt throughout the ages: inspiring leaders such as 'Bulldog' Irvine, Charles Reid, Mark Morrison, Jim Telfer, Ian McLauchlan, Jim Aitken, David Sole and Gavin Hastings. Flair players such as Ken MacLeod, Phil Macpherson, Ian Smith, Wilson Shaw, Arthur Smith, Ken Scotland, Jim Renwick, Andy Irvine, John Rutherford and Gregor Townsend. And our share of hard men: David Bedell-Sivright, John Bannerman, Doug Elliot, Hugh McLeod, Gordon Brown, John Jeffrey, Finlay Calder and Gary Armstrong.

It is said that rugby is 90 per cent about memories. If that is so, can I just say finally, thank you for the memories to every single player who has been talented enough and fortunate enough to play for Scotland over the years. You have given us much to look back on with great pride and fondness and good luck to all your successors in this brave new world as we look forward to generations to come providing the memories of tomorrow.

*Andy Nicol was the first Scottish captain to lift the Calcutta Cup for 10 long years. The win gave the nation an enormous lift and he recalls 'that people came up to me in the street afterwards simply to say thank you'.*

THE ESSENTIAL HISTORY OF RUGBY UNION

# SCOTLAND

## STATISTICS

# The Scotland Directory

## Scottish Rugby Union

- Founded 1873

## Honours

- International Championship winners (outright) 1887, 1891, 1895, 1901, 1903, 1904, 1907, 1925, 1929, 1933, 1938, 1984, 1990, 1999
  (shared) 1886, 1890, 1920, 1926, 1927, 1964, 1973, 1986
- Grand Slam winners 1925, 1984, 1990
- Triple Crown winners 1891, 1895, 1901, 1903, 1907, 1925, 1933, 1938, 1984, 1990
- Rugby World Cup fourth place 1991
- International record (cap matches only)

OVERALL P516 W222 D31 L262 Abandoned 1
v Argentina P5 W1 D0 L4
v Australia P19 W7 D0 L12
v Canada P2 W1 D0 L1
v England P120 W40 D17 L63
v Fiji P3 W2 D0 L1
v France P75 W33 D3 L39
v Ireland P115 W61 D5 L48 Abandoned 1
v Italy P7 W5 D0 L2
v Ivory Coast P1 W1 D0 L0
v Japan P1 W1 D0 L0
v New Zealand P24 W0 D2 L22
v Romania P9 W7 D0 L2
v Samoa P4 W3 D1 L0
v South Africa P15 W4 D0 L11
v Spain P1 W1 D0 L0
v SRU President's XV P1 W1 D0 L0
v Tonga P2 W2 D0 L0
v United States P2 W2 D0 L0
v Uruguay P1 W1 D0 L0
v Wales P107 W47 D3 L57
v Zimbabwe P2 W2 D0 L0

## Top Tens

- CAPS

Gregor Townsend 76
Scott Hastings 65
Kenny Logan 63
Gavin Hastings 61
Doddie Weir 61
Craig Chalmers 60
Bryan Redpath 55
Jim Renwick 52
Colin Deans 52
Tony Stanger 52
Paul Burnell 52

- POINTS-SCORERS

Gavin Hastings 667
Andy Irvine 273
Kenny Logan 220
Peter Dods 210
Craig Chalmers 166
Gregor Townsend 157
Chris Paterson 138
Brendan Laney 127
Duncan Hodge 123
Tony Stanger 106

- HIGHEST SCORES

89-0 v Ivory Coast 1995
65-23 v United States 2002
60-21 v Zimbabwe 1987
60-19 v Romania 1999
55-28 v Romania 1987
53-6 v United States 2000
51-12 v Zimbabwe 1991
49-3 v Argentina 1990
49-16 v Romania 1995
48-0 v Spain 1999

- HEAVIEST DEFEATS

10-68 v South Africa 1997
20-69 v New Zealand 2000
0-44 v South Africa 1951
3-45 v Australia 1998
3-43 v England 2001
15-51 v New Zealand 1993
16-51 v France 1998
3-38 v France 2003
14-48 v New Zealand 2000
31-62 v New Zealand 1996
6-37 v New Zealand 2001
9-40 v England 2003

# 50 Greatest Players

Selecting the 50 greatest Scottish international rugby union players is an impossible task and it would be astonishing if anyone agreed entirely with my choice and the order of inclusion. Trying to compare the merits of Scotland's greatest players who played in a range of different positions, under varying laws and conditions across a period of 130-plus years however, is a guaranteed way to provoke heated debate. But one thing is for sure: if these players had been available to the selectors at the same time, with their collective pride, passion, bravery and skills, Scotland could have fielded one hell of a side.

**No. 1 Andy Irvine (Full-back/Wing)** – Caps: 51 Points: 273. The most exciting, charismatic and thrilling runner Scotland has produced. A 'superstar' before the term was invented (see page 137).

**No. 2 Gavin Hastings (Full-back)** – Caps: 61 Points: 667. In his final seven months of Test rugby he rewrote the record books scoring a phenomenal 201 points in 11 matches (see page 171).

**No. 3 Douglas Elliot (Wing-forward)** – Caps: 29 Points: 6. The outstanding back row forward of his generation, his pace, size and ability would have been well suited to the modern game (see page 104).

**No. 4 Phil Macpherson (Centre/Stand-off)** – Caps: 26 Points: 12. The most brilliant attacking back of his era whose profitable partnership with Ian Smith yielded 25 tries in 17 matches (see page 76).

**No. 5 David Bedell-Sivright (Wing-forward)** – Caps: 22 Points: 6. Described as the hardest man ever to play rugby for Scotland, his presence in the blue shirt struck terror into the hearts of the opposition (see page 57).

**No. 6 Gary Armstrong (Scrum-half)** – Caps: 51 Points: 21. The tough Borderer bounced back from serious injury to fight off the stiff challenges of Nicol and Redpath to re-invent himself as number one (see page 185).

**No. 7 Jim Renwick (Centre)** – Caps: 52 Points: 67. A dazzling talent who could cut opposing defences to ribbons with a shimmy, a swerve and an injection of pace (see page 136).

**No. 8 Ian McLauchlan (Prop)** – Caps: 43 Points: 0. The 'Mighty Mouse' who defied concerns about his size to establish himself as one of the hardest and most ferocious prop forwards of any era (see page 130).

**No. 9 Charles Reid (Forward)** – Caps: 21 Points: 4 tries (before scoring by points was introduced). First capped as a schoolboy, at 6 foot 3 inches and 15-16 stones he was a giant amongst men with the ability to match his impressive physique (see page 36).

**No. 10 John Bannerman (Second row)** – Caps: 37 Points: 6. A great enthusiast and powerful personality he made a huge impact on rugby, setting a world record of 37 consecutive appearances (see page 74).

*Phil Macpherson, captain of Scotland's first Grand Slam side in 1925.*

**No. 11 Ian Smith (Wing)** – Caps: 32 Points: 72. His world record total of 24 tries stood until 1987 when David Campese (Australia) broke it in the inaugural Rugby World Cup (see page 88).

**No. 12 Ken Scotland (Full-back/Stand-off)** – Caps: 27 Points: 71. A genuine world-class footballer who could play anywhere in the back division, he blossomed as an attacking full-back with the 1959 Lions (see page 119).

**No. 13 Hugh McLeod (Prop)** – Caps: 40 Points: 0. A fitness fanatic and a double Lion he was an automatic choice from the age of 21, winning 40 consecutive caps to break Bannerman's cap record (see page 107).

**No. 14 Andrew Don Wauchope (Quarter-back)** – Caps: 12 Points: 6 tries (before scoring by points was introduced). One of the greatest attacking players of his era his blinding pace and elusive running skills wreaked havoc in opposing defences (see page 41).

*Jim Greenwood, the pick of the 1955 Lions Test pack.*

**No. 15 John Rutherford (Stand-off)** – Caps: 42 Points: 64. A gifted runner who matured into an outstanding all-round player, he was voted European Player of the Year in 1987 (see page 155).
**No. 16 Roy Laidlaw (Scrum-half)** – Caps: 47 Points: 28. With Rutherford he played in a record 35 internationals and was one of the finest breaking scrum-halves in the world game (see page 158).
**No. 17 Ninian Finlay (Half-back)** – Caps: 9 Points: 3 drop goals (before scoring by points was introduced). The youngest man to play international rugby, he was rated the finest exponent of his era in the art of drop kicking (see page 27).
**No. 18 Wilson Shaw (Stand-off/Centre/Wing)** – Caps: 19 Points: 26. One of the most brilliant backs of all time, pace was his greatest weapon reputedly hitting top speed within a couple of strides (see page 102).
**No. 19 Gordon Brown (Second row)** – Caps: 30 Points: 0. A ruthless competitor who demonstrated on Lions tours in particular that he was a world-class tight five forward (see page 131).
**No. 20 Tom Smith (Prop)** – Caps: 45 Points: 25. One of the world's leading props. On the 1997 Lions tour to South Africa he played a vital role in subduing the Springbok scrummage (see page 187).
**No. 21 Arthur Smith (Wing)** – Caps: 33 Points: 58. A beautifully balanced runner with a devastating change of pace, he scored a sensational solo try on his debut v Wales in 1955 (see page 112).
**No. 22 Harry Stevenson (Centre/Full-back)** – Caps: 15 Points: 2 drop goals (before scoring by points was introduced). Aggressive in defence and a belligerent attacking force, he was once described as 'the greatest footballer in the world' (see page 47).
**No. 23 David Sole (Prop)** – Caps: 44 Points: 12. An uncompromising scrummager and an athletic ball-handler, he achieved everlasting fame captaining Scotland to the Grand Slam in 1990 (see page 170).
**No. 24 David Leslie (Flanker)** – Caps: 32 Points: 8. At his peak a world-class flanker who enjoyed an outstanding season in 1984 to help Scotland to a Grand Slam (see page 145).
**No. 25 Jim Telfer (Flanker\No. 8)** – Caps: 25 Points: 9. Ostensibly a No. 8 he was an abrasive and enthusiastic tackler whose bravery knew no bounds when putting his body on the line in search of securing ball (see page 123).
**No. 26 Robert Irvine (Forward)** – Caps: 13 Points 1 try (before scoring by points was introduced). Capped as a teenager in the first international, quite remarkably he played in the first 13 matches and was captain in the first Calcutta Cup match in 1879 (see page 26).
**No. 27 Finlay Calder (Flanker)** – Caps: 34 Points: 8. First capped at 28 he went on to become a key component in the successful sides of his era and led the 1989 Lions to a remarkable Test series victory (see page 163).
**No. 28 Jim Greenwood (Flanker/No. 8)** – Caps: 20 Points: 0. Selected as captain for his second international, he became a key member of the team and had an outstanding tour of South Africa with the 1955 Lions (see page 106).
**No. 29 Norman Bruce (Hooker)** – Caps: 31 Points: 9. Ahead of his time as a mobile, dynamic hooker, in effect an auxiliary back rower, in an era when a hooker's main function was to win scrummage ball (see page 120).
**No. 30 Mark Morrison (Forward)** – Caps: 23 Points: 0. Captain on 15 occasions, he is the only Scot to have led his country to two Triple Crowns and also led the 1903 Lions to South Africa (see page 54).
**No. 31 John Jeffrey (Flanker)** – Caps: 40 Points: 44. Part of the remarkable back row of Jeffrey, Calder and White, he was an arch try poacher notching up 11 tries in 40 internationals (see page 162).
**No. 32 Colin Deans (Hooker)** – Caps: 52 Points: 8. A mobile, dynamic hooker, he was first choice for a decade, led his country in 13 internationals and was captain for the inaugural Rugby World Cup (see page 147).
**No. 33 Bill Kyle (Forward)** – Caps: 21 Points: 6. An outstanding all-round player such was his line-out ability that the All Blacks deputed two men to sort him out at Inverleith in 1905 (see page 64).
**No. 34 Bill Maclagan (Full-back/Wing)** – Caps: 26 Points: 3 tries and 4 conversions (before scoring by points was introduced). A very aggressive and demanding player he was famed for the ferocity of his tackling (see page 32).

*Scott Hastings, whose 28 appearances at centre with Sean Lineen set a new world record.*

**No. 35 Scott Hastings (Centre/Wing)** – Caps: 65 Points: 43. A magnificent tackler who formed a highly effective centre partnership with Sean Lineen appearing together on a world record 28 occasions (see page 176).
**No. 36 Herbert Waddell (Stand-off)** – Caps: 15 Points: 45. Tactically very astute he also was an invaluable source of points contributing 7 tries and 5 drop goals in just 15 matches (see page 87).
**No. 37 Alan Tait (Centre/Wing)** – Caps: 27 Points: 81. Blessed with the priceless gift of scoring tries, his midfield partnership with Leslie and Townsend was crucial in the 1999 Five Nations (see page 183).
**No. 38 David Chisholm (Stand-off)** – Caps: 14 Points: 15. A genuinely two-footed player he revelled in his defensive duties as much as seeking out or exploiting holes in the opposition defence (see page 124).
**No. 39 Dan Drysdale (Full-back)** – Caps: 26 Points: 45. The best British full-back of his generation he was a committed runner of the ball as well as performing his defensive duties with great aplomb (see page 84).
**No. 40 David Rollo (Prop)** – Caps: 40 Points: 0. A hard uncompromising prop who always played with his socks rolled down, he equalled McLeod's cap record in his final season (see page 122).
**No. 41 Iain Milne (Prop)** – Caps: 44 Points: 0. A remarkably mobile and gifted ball player for such a big man his formidable presence in the front row anchored the scrummage for much of the 1980s (see page 156).
**No. 42 Ian McGeechan (Stand-off/Centre)** – Caps: 32 Points: 21. Excellent all-round player and master tactician with a penchant for dropping vital goals (see page 138).
**No. 43 Gregor Townsend (Stand-off/Centre)** – Caps: 76 Points: 157. At his best one of the most gifted and mercurial attacking talents in the world game. Scotland's cap record-holder (see page 186).
**No. 44 Ross Logan (Scrum-half)** – Caps: 20 Points: 6. A big man for a scrum-half he used his power and strength to telling effect and possessed a devastating break from the base of the scrum (see page 100).
**No. 45 Matthew McEwan (Forward)** – Caps: 15 Points: 3 tries, 2 conversions and 1 drop goal (before scoring by points was introduced) The first player to captain Scotland to the Triple Crown in 1891 (see page 45).
**No. 46 Wattie Sutherland (Wing/Centre)** – Caps: 13 Points: 12. First capped as a teenager he so impressed in his debut season that he was selected to tour with the British Isles to South Africa (see page 66).
**No. 47 Jock Beattie (Second row)** – Caps: 23 Points: 0. A real powerhouse in the scrum, he was a gifted two-handed catcher in the line-out with sufficient skill to play for the Barbarians at Sevens (see page 97).
**No. 48 Charles Usher (Forward)** – Caps: 16 Points: 6. In a career which spanned the First World War, he made a try-scoring debut in 1912 and led Scotland in seven post-war internationals (see page 70).
**No. 49 Harry Lind (Stand-off/Centre)** – Caps: 16 Points: 7. A mercurial talent he was a bit unfortunate that the selectors could not decide in which position to play him for Scotland (see page 91).
**No. 50 Angus Cameron (Centre/Stand-off/Full-back)** – Caps: 17 Points: 18. A versatile footballer he captained Scotland to an unexpected win against Wales in 1955 (see page 105).

*Angus Cameron, who had his best and worst international moments in matches against the Springboks.*

# Results and Tables 1871-2003

Team line-ups are given in blocks to show clearly, in any formation from 20- to 15-a-side, the full-backs, three-quarters, halves and forwards in that order. Where possible three-quarters are given from wing to wing, the fly-half precedes the scrum-half, and forwards are listed from front row to back row. Specialisation has not always existed, so it is only since the 1920s that the familiar prop/hooker/prop/lock/lock/flanker/No. 8/flanker formation is given with any certainty.

It should be noted that until 1875 international matches were decided by a majority of goals, but from 1876 the try-count was employed to decide a match when teams were level on goals. Scoring by points was not introduced until the late 1880s, a try scoring 1 point, a conversion 2 points and a drop goal 3 points. Various experiments were made until 1890-91 when the International Board system was adopted to make scoring uniform in international matches. Since 1890-91, official scoring values have been as follows:

| | Try (T) | Conversion (C) | Drop Goal (DG) | Penalty Goal (PG) | Goal from Mark (GM) |
|---|---|---|---|---|---|
| 1891 | 1 | 2 | 3 | 2 | 3 |
| 1892 to 1893 | 2 | 3 | 4 | 3 | 4 |
| 1894 to 1905 | 3 | 2 | 4 | 3 | 4 |
| 1906 to 1948 | 3 | 2 | 4 | 3 | 3 |
| 1949 to 1971 | 3 | 2 | 3 | 3 | 3 |
| 1972 to 1977 | 4 | 2 | 3 | 3 | 3 |
| 1978 to 1992 | 4 | 2 | 3 | 3 | Void |
| 1993 to date | 5 | 2 | 3 | 3 | Void |

The penalty goal did not become a scoring device until 1891 and the goal from a mark ceased to exist when the Free Kick clause entered the Law Book in 1977-78. Traditionally, a converted try has been referred to as a goal (G). Penalty tries (‡), where appropriate, are credited to players.

The symbol (†) is used to indicate a new cap and (*) shows the player captaining the side. Replacements were sanctioned in 1968-69. Full replacements are denoted using numerical indices (3) and temporary substitutes are shown with lettered indices (a).

The International Championship competition began as a four-nations tournament in 1883. The championship became five nations in 1910 when Scotland played France for the first time, but reverted to four between 1932 and 1939 when the French were temporarily excluded. Italy became full championship members in 2000, making it a six-nation tournament.

Scotland's Tests against overseas sides began in 1905 but only matches against the former Dominions – New Zealand, Australia and South Africa – were recognised as official cap games before 1981, when the International Board ruled that their senior members could award official caps against whom they liked.

The first of the four Rugby World Cups to date was in Australia and New Zealand in 1987.

These statistics are correct up to 31 July 2003.

# 1871-74

## Friendlies

### v ENGLAND

**WON**
Scotland: 1G 1T
England: 1T
Raeburn Place, 27 Mar 1871

† W.D. Brown
† T. Chalmers
† A.C. Ross

† T.R. Marshall
† W. Cross 1C 1T
† J.W. Arthur

*† F.J. Moncreiff
† W.J.C. Lyall
† J.S. Thomson
† R.W. Irvine
† A.H. Robertson
† J.F. Finlay
† G. Ritchie
† A. Buchanan 1T
† R. Munro
† A.G. Colville
† D. Drew
† J.L.H. Macfarlane
† J. Forsyth
† J.A.W. Mein

### v ENGLAND

**LOST**
England: 1G 1DG 2T
Scotland: 1DG
Kennington Oval, 5 Feb 1872

W.D. Brown
T. Chalmers
† L.M. Balfour

T.R. Marshall
† R.P. Maitland

J.W. Arthur
* F.J. Moncreiff
W. Cross

† H.W. Renny-Tailyour
R.W. Irvine
† W. Marshall
J.F. Finlay
† F.T. Maxwell
† E.M. Bannerman
† J.H. McClure
A.G. Colville
† C.W. Cathcart 1DG
J.L.H. Macfarlane
† J. Anderson
J.A.W. Mein

### v ENGLAND

**DRAWN**
Scotland: Nil
England: Nil
Glasgow, 3 Mar 1873

W.D. Brown
T. Chalmers
† J.P.L. Sanderson

† G.B. McClure
J.L.H. Macfarlane

† W. St Clair-Grant
T.R. Marshall

* F.J. Moncreiff
† H.W. Allen
R.W. Irvine
† A.G. Petrie
† P. Anton
† A.T. Wood
E.M. Bannerman
† C.C. Bryce
† T.P. Whittington
C.W. Cathcart
† R.W. Wilson
† J.P. Davidson
J.A.W. Mein

### v ENGLAND

**LOST**
England: 1DG
Scotland: 1T
Kennington Oval, 23 Feb 1874

* W.D. Brown
T. Chalmers

† H.M. Hamilton
T.R. Marshall
† W.H. Kidston

W. St Clair-Grant
† A.K. Stewart

† G. Heron
† A.H. Young
R.W. Irvine
A.G. Petrie
J.F. Finlay 1T
A.T. Wood
† J. Reid
C.C. Bryce
† T. Neilson
† J.K. Todd
R.W. Wilson
J.P. Davidson
J.A.W. Mein

### FACT FILE

- An unofficial association football match between England and Scotland had been played at the Oval in November 1870, but its arrangement and result caused rancour north of the border. Consequently, a challenge inviting England to a match in Edinburgh led to the 1871 international at Raeburn Place.
- The first try in international rugby was a pushover credited to Angus Buchanan.

## 1874-77

### Friendlies

**v ENGLAND**

**DRAWN**
Scotland: Nil
England: Nil
Raeburn Place, 8 Mar 1875

* W.D. Brown
T. Chalmers

† M. Cross
† N.J. Finlay
H.M. Hamilton

† J.R. Hay-Gordon
J.K. Todd

G. Heron
† D. Robertson
R.W. Irvine
A.G. Petrie
J.F. Finlay
A.T. Wood
J. Reid
† A. Marshall
† A. Arthur
† G.R. Fleming
† A.B. Finlay
† J.W. Dunlop
J.A.W. Mein

**v ENGLAND**

**LOST**
England: 1G 1T
Scotland: Nil
Kennington Oval, 6 Mar 1876

† J.S. Carrick
T. Chalmers

M. Cross
N.J. Finlay

A.K. Stewart
† G.Q. Paterson

† D.H. Watson
† D. Lang
† C. Villar
* R.W. Irvine
A.G. Petrie
† J.H.S. Graham
† N.T. Brewis
J. Reid
† J.E. Junor
A. Arthur
G.R. Fleming
C.W. Cathcart
D. Drew
† W.H. Bolton

**v IRELAND**

**WON**
Ireland: Nil
Scotland: 4G 2DG 2T
Belfast, 19 Feb 1877

† H.H. Johnston

M. Cross 4C
† R.C. Mackenzie 2DG 3T

† E.J. Pocock 1T
J.R. Hay-Gordon

† S.H. Smith
D.H. Watson
D. Lang
C. Villar
* R.W. Irvine 1T
A.G. Petrie
J.H.S. Graham
† H.M. Napier
J. Reid 1T
J.E. Junor

**v ENGLAND**

**WON**
Scotland: 1DG
England: Nil
Raeburn Place, 5 Mar 1877

J.S. Carrick
H.H. Johnston

M. Cross 1DG
R.C. Mackenzie

E.J. Pocock
J.R. Hay-Gordon

D.H. Watson
† T.J. Torrie
C. Villar
* R.W. Irvine
A.G. Petrie
J.H.S. Graham
H.M. Napier
J. Reid
J.E. Junor

**FACT FILE**

- Scotland had to wait until international teams were reduced to 15s in 1877 before a second win was registered.
- Whereas the 1871 victory had helped to establish the game in Scotland, the triumph of 1877 led to the high public regard for the English international as the major event of the sporting calendar.

## 1877-80

### Friendlies

**v ENGLAND**

**DRAWN**
England: Nil
Scotland: Nil
Kennington Oval, 4 Mar 1878

† W.E. Maclagan

M. Cross
N.J. Finlay

† J.A. Neilson
† J.A. Campbell

S.H. Smith
† D.R. Irvine
† G. Macleod
† L.C. Auldjo
* R.W. Irvine
A.G. Petrie
J.H.S. Graham
H.M. Napier
N.T. Brewis
J.E. Junor

**v IRELAND**

**WON**
Ireland: Nil
Scotland: IG IDG IT
Belfast, 17 Feb 1879

W.E. Maclagan

M. Cross 1C 1DG
N.J. Finlay

† W.H. Masters
J.A. Campbell

† R. Ainslie
D.R. Irvine
† J.B. Brown 1T
† D. Somerville 1T
* R.W. Irvine
A.G. Petrie
J.H.S. Graham
H.M. Napier
N.T. Brewis
† E.R. Smith

**v ENGLAND**

**DRAWN**
Scotland: 1DG
England: IG
Raeburn Place, 10 Mar 1879

W.E. Maclagan

M. Cross
N.J. Finlay 1DG

J.A. Neilson
J.A. Campbell

R. Ainslie
D.R. Irvine
J.B. Brown
† E.N. Ewart
* R.W. Irvine
A.G. Petrie
J.H.S. Graham
H.M. Napier
N.T. Brewis
J.E. Junor

**v IRELAND**

**WON**
Scotland: 1G 2DG 2T
Ireland: Nil
Glasgow, 14 Feb 1880

W.E. Maclagan

M. Cross 1C
N.J. Finlay 2DG

W.H. Masters 1T
† W.S. Brown

R. Ainslie
† C.A.R. Stewart
J.B. Brown
E.N. Ewart 2T
* R.W. Irvine
A.G. Petrie
J.H.S. Graham
† D. McCowan
N.T. Brewis
† J.G. Tait

**v ENGLAND**

**LOST**
England: 2G 3T
Scotland: 1G
Manchester, 28 Feb 1880

W.E. Maclagan

M. Cross 1C
N.J. Finlay

W.H. Masters
W.S. Brown 1T

R. Ainslie
C.A.R. Stewart
J.B. Brown
E.N. Ewart
* R.W. Irvine
A.G. Petrie
J.H.S. Graham
D. McCowan
N.T. Brewis
† D.Y. Cassels

**FACT FILE**

- Scotland enjoyed an unbeaten run of six matches between 1877 and 1880, defeat at Manchester in the first international played in the north of England ending the sequence and coinciding with the retirement of R.W. 'Bulldog' Irvine.
- The 1879 match with England was the first match for the Calcutta Cup.

## 1880-82

### Friendlies

**v IRELAND**

**LOST**
Ireland: 1DG
Scotland: 1T
Belfast, 19 Feb 1881

† T.A. Begbie

W.E. Maclagan
N.J. Finlay
R.C. Mackenzie

† P.W. Smeaton
J.A. Campbell

D. McCowan
† C. Reid
D.Y. Cassels
* J.H.S. Graham 1T
† B. Allan
J.E. Junor
† G.H. Robb
† A. Walker
J.B. Brown

**v ENGLAND**

**DRAWN**
Scotland: 1G 1T
England: 1DG 1T
Raeburn Place, 19 Mar 1881

T.A. Begbie 1C

W.E. Maclagan
N.J. Finlay
R.C. Mackenzie

† A.R. Don Wauchope
J.A. Campbell

R. Ainslie 1T
C. Reid
† J.W. Fraser
* J.H.S. Graham
D. McCowan
† R. Maitland
† T. Ainslie
† W.A. Peterkin
J.B. Brown 1T

**v IRELAND**

**WON**
Scotland: 2T
Ireland: Nil
Glasgow, 18 Feb 1882

† T. Anderson

W.E. Maclagan
† F. Hunter

W.S. Brown 1T
† A.G. Grant-Asher

G. Macleod
* R. Ainslie
C. Reid
D.Y. Cassels
D. Somerville
D. McCowan 1T
R. Maitland
T. Ainslie
† A.F.C. Gore
J.B. Brown

**v ENGLAND**

**WON**
England: Nil
Scotland: 2T
Manchester, 4 Mar 1882

† J.P. Veitch

W.E. Maclagan
† A. Philp

A.R. Don Wauchope
W.S. Brown

A. Walker
R. Ainslie 2T
C. Reid
* D.Y. Cassels
† W.A. Walls
D. McCowan
R. Maitland
T. Ainslie
† J.G. Walker
J.B. Brown

**FACT FILE**

- Bill Maclagan, Ninian Finlay and Campbell Mackenzie made history in Belfast in 1881, forming the first three-man three-quarter line to appear in an international match.
- In 1881 Charles Reid, a teenager at Edinburgh Academy, became the first schoolboy forward to appear in an international when he played in Scotland's defeat in Belfast.
- Victory at Manchester in 1882 was Scotland's first on English soil.

## 1882-83

### Four Nations Championship

**v WALES**

**WON**
Scotland: 3G
Wales: 1G
Raeburn Place, 8 Jan 1883

† D.W. Kidston

W.E. Maclagan 3C
† D.J. McFarlan 2T

A.R. Don Wauchope 1T
W.S. Brown

A. Walker
D. Somerville
C. Reid
* D.Y. Cassels
W.A. Walls
† J.G. Mowat
† J. Jamieson
T. Ainslie
J.G. Walker
J.B. Brown

**v IRELAND**

**WON**
Ireland: Nil
Scotland: 1G 1T
Belfast, 17 Feb 1883

J.P. Veitch

W.E. Maclagan 1C
† M.F. Reid

P.W. Smeaton
† G.R. Aitchison

A. Walker
D. Somerville 1T
C. Reid 1T
* D.Y. Cassels
W.A. Walls
W.A. Peterkin
J. Jamieson
T. Ainslie
D. McCowan
J.B. Brown

**v ENGLAND**

**LOST**
Scotland: 1T
England: 2T
Raeburn Place, 3 Mar 1883

D.W. Kidston

W.E. Maclagan
M.F. Reid

P.W. Smeaton
W.S. Brown

A. Walker
D. Somerville
C. Reid 1T
* D.Y. Cassels
W.A. Walls
J.G. Mowat
J. Jamieson
T. Ainslie
D. McCowan
J.B. Brown

### FACT FILE

- England deprived the Scots of a Triple Crown in 1883 but controversy surrounded the match at Raeburn Place. Patrick Smeaton and Sorley Brown claimed to have scored tries that would have been sufficient to give Scotland victory.

### FINAL TABLE

| | P | W | D | L | Pts |
|---|---|---|---|---|---|
| England | 3 | 3 | 0 | 0 | 6 |
| **Scotland** | **3** | **2** | **0** | **1** | **4** |
| Ireland | 2 | 0 | 0 | 2 | 0 |
| Wales | 2 | 0 | 0 | 2 | 0 |

*Ireland and Wales did not meet*

*Bill Maclagan was an international for 13 seasons between 1878 and 1890 – a career span unbeaten for 60 years.*

## 1883-84

### Four Nations Championship

**v WALES**

**WON**
Wales: Nil
Scotland: 1DG 1T
Newport, 12 Jan 1884

J.P. Veitch

* W.E. Maclagan
D.J. McFarlan
† G.C. Lindsay

A.R. Don Wauchope
A.G. Grant-Asher 1DG

D. Somerville
C. Reid
† J. Tod
W.A. Walls
W.A. Peterkin
J. Jamieson
T. Ainslie 1T
R. Maitland
J.B. Brown

**v IRELAND**

**WON**
Scotland: 2G 2T
Ireland: 1T
Raeburn Place, 16 Feb 1884

J.P. Veitch

* W.E. Maclagan
D.J. McFarlan
† E.T. Roland

A.R. Don Wauchope 1T
A.G. Grant-Asher 1T

† C.W. Berry 2C
C. Reid
J. Tod 1T
W.A. Walls
W.A. Peterkin 1T
J. Jamieson
T. Ainslie
D. McCowan
J.B. Brown

**v ENGLAND**

**LOST**
England: 1G
Scotland: 1T
Blackheath, 1 Mar 1884

J.P. Veitch

* W.E. Maclagan
D.J. McFarlan
E.T. Roland

A.R. Don Wauchope
A.G. Grant-Asher

C.W. Berry
C. Reid
J. Tod
W.A. Walls
W.A. Peterkin
J. Jamieson 1T
T. Ainslie
D. McCowan
J.B. Brown

**FACT FILE**

- Scotland was again deprived of the Triple Crown in 1884, the match with England being noted for the contentious knock-back which led to the winning English goal.
- The following season Scotland did not meet England, twice beat Ireland – though the first match in Belfast was abandoned after 30 minutes – and played a drawn game with Wales.

**FINAL TABLE**

| | P | W | D | L | Pts |
|---|---|---|---|---|---|
| England | 3 | 3 | 0 | 0 | 6 |
| **Scotland** | **3** | **2** | **0** | **1** | **4** |
| Wales | 3 | 1 | 0 | 2 | 2 |
| Ireland | 3 | 0 | 0 | 3 | 0 |

## 1884-85

### Four Nations Championship

**v WALES**

**DRAWN**
Scotland: Nil
Wales: Nil
Glasgow, 10 Jan 1885

† P.R. Harrower

* W.E. Maclagan
† A.E. Stephen
† G. Maitland

A.R. Don Wauchope
A.G. Grant-Asher

C.W. Berry
C. Reid
J. Tod
† J.G. Mitchell
W.A. Peterkin
J. Jamieson
T. Ainslie
R. Maitland
G.H. Robb

**v IRELAND**

**ABANDONED**
Ireland: Nil
Scotland: 1T
Belfast, 21 Feb 1885

J.P. Veitch

* W.E. Maclagan
G.C. Lindsay
† H.L. Evans

A.R. Don Wauchope
† P.H. Don Wauchope

C.W. Berry
C. Reid
J. Tod
J.G. Mitchell
W.A. Peterkin
J. Jamieson 1T
T. Ainslie
† T.W. Irvine
J.B. Brown

**v IRELAND**

**WON**
Scotland: 1G 2T
Ireland: Nil
Raeburn Place, 7 Mar 1885

J.P. Veitch 1C

* W.E. Maclagan
H.L. Evans
G. Maitland

A.R. Don Wauchope 1T
P.H. Don Wauchope

J.G. Tait
C. Reid 1T
J. Tod
J.G. Mitchell
W.A. Peterkin 1T
J. Jamieson
T. Ainslie
T.W. Irvine
J.B. Brown

### FACT FILE

- Among the four new caps for the Welsh match was a London Scot named Pat Harrower. He gained the unique distinction (for a rugby player) of refereeing an FA Cup final. In 1905 Harrower controlled the final between Aston Villa and Newcastle United.

### FINAL TABLE

| | P | W | D | L | Pts |
|---|---|---|---|---|---|
| England | 2 | 2 | 0 | 0 | 4 |
| **Scotland** | **2** | **1** | **1** | **0** | **3** |
| Wales | 2 | 0 | 1 | 1 | 1 |
| Ireland | 2 | 0 | 0 | 2 | 0 |

*Ireland and Wales did not meet; Scotland and England did not meet*

## 1885-86

### Four Nations Championship

**v WALES**

**WON**
Wales: Nil
Scotland: 2G 1T
Cardiff Arms Park, 9 Jan 1886

† F. McIndoe

† R.H. Morrison
D.J. McFarlan
† W.F. Holms

A.R. Don Wauchope 1T
P.H. Don Wauchope

† C.J.B. Milne
C. Reid
J. Tod 1T
† J. French
† A.T. Clay 1T
W.A. Walls
† W.M. Macleod 2C
T.W. Irvine
* J.B. Brown

**v IRELAND**

**WON**
Scotland: 3G 1DG 2T
Ireland: Nil
Raeburn Place, 20 Feb 1886

F. McIndoe

R.H. Morrison 2T
D.J. McFarlan 1T 3C
A.E. Stephen

A.G. Grant-Asher 1DG
A.R. Don Wauchope 2T

C.J.B. Milne
C. Reid
J. Tod
† D.A. Macleod
A.T. Clay
W.A. Walls
W.M. Macleod
T.W. Irvine
* J.B. Brown

**v ENGLAND**

**DRAWN**
Scotland: Nil
England: Nil
Raeburn Place, 13 Mar 1886

J.P. Veitch

R.H. Morrison
† G.R. Wilson
W.F. Holms

A.G. Grant-Asher
A.R. Don Wauchope

C.J.B. Milne
C. Reid
J. Tod
D.A. Macleod
A.T. Clay
W.A. Walls
† M.C. McEwan
T.W. Irvine
* J.B. Brown

**FACT FILE**

- John Brown led Scotland to a share of the championship. This was his last season in international rugby and he retired with 18 caps to set a new Scottish record.

**FINAL TABLE**

| | P | W | D | L | Pts |
|---|---|---|---|---|---|
| **Scotland** | **3** | **2** | **1** | **0** | **5** |
| England | 3 | 2 | 1 | 0 | 5 |
| Wales | 2 | 0 | 0 | 2 | 0 |
| Ireland | 2 | 0 | 0 | 2 | 0 |

*Ireland and Wales did not meet*

## 1886-87

### Four Nations Championship

**v IRELAND**

**WON**
Ireland: Nil
Scotland: 1G 1GM 2T
Belfast, 19 Feb 1887

W.F. Holms

W.E. Maclagan 1T
D.J. McFarlan
† A.N. Woodrow

† C.E. Orr
P.H. Don Wauchope

C.W. Berry 1C 1GM
* C. Reid
† H.T. Ker
J. French
A.T. Clay
† D.S. Morton 1T
M.C. McEwan 1T
T.W. Irvine
† R.G. MacMillan

**v WALES**

**WON**
Scotland: 4G 8T
Wales: Nil
Raeburn Place, 26 Feb 1887

† A.W.C. Cameron

W.E. Maclagan 1T
G.C. Lindsay 5T
A.N. Woodrow 2C

C.E. Orr 1T
P.H. Don Wauchope 1T

C.W. Berry 2C
* C. Reid 1T
H.T. Ker
J. French
A.T. Clay
D.S. Morton 1T
M.C. McEwan 1T
T.W. Irvine
R.G. MacMillan 1T

**v ENGLAND**

**DRAWN**
England: 1T
Scotland: 1T
Manchester, 5 Mar 1887

W.F. Holms

W.E. Maclagan
G.C. Lindsay
A.N. Woodrow

C.E. Orr
P.H. Don Wauchope

C.W. Berry
* C. Reid
H.T. Ker
J. French
A.T. Clay
D.S. Morton 1T
M.C. McEwan
T.W. Irvine
R.G. MacMillan

### FACT FILE

- New skipper Charles Reid led an experienced side to win the championship, Scotland's first outright title success. The pack was unchanged.
- The first score in the Irish match was Scotland's first goal from a mark in an international. Against Wales, George Lindsay set a world record by running in five tries.
- Douglas Morton scored tries in his first three internationals, a unique record for a Scottish forward.

### FINAL TABLE

| | P | W | D | L | Pts |
|---|---|---|---|---|---|
| **Scotland** | **3** | **2** | **1** | **0** | **5** |
| Wales | 3 | 1 | 1 | 1 | 3 |
| Ireland | 3 | 1 | 0 | 2 | 2 |
| England | 3 | 0 | 2 | 1 | 2 |

## 1887-88

### Three Nations Championship

**v WALES**

**LOST**
Wales: 1T
Scotland: Nil
Newport, 4 Feb 1888

† H.F.T. Chambers

W.E. Maclagan
† H.J. Stevenson
† M.M. Duncan

C.E. Orr
† C.F.P. Fraser

C.W. Berry
* C. Reid
† L.E. Stevenson
† A. Duke
A.T. Clay
D.S. Morton
M.C. McEwan
T.W. Irvine
† T.B. White

**v IRELAND**

**WON**
Scotland: 1G
Ireland: Nil
Raeburn Place, 10 Mar 1888

H.F.T. Chambers

W.E. Maclagan
H.J. Stevenson
D.J. McFarlan 1T

C.E. Orr
* A.R. Don Wauchope

C.W. Berry 1C
C. Reid
H.T. Ker
A. Duke
† A. Malcolm
D.S. Morton
M.C. McEwan
T.W. Irvine
T.B. White

**FACT FILE**

- The international dispute concerning England's participation in the proposed IB raged on in 1888 and 1889: consequently there were no games for the Calcutta Cup.
- Charles Reid ended his international career in Scotland's win over Ireland in 1888. A doctor, Reid played 21 times for Scotland to set a record for a forward.

**FINAL TABLE**

| | P | W | D | L | Pts |
|---|---|---|---|---|---|
| Ireland | 2 | 1 | 0 | 1 | 2 |
| **Scotland** | **2** | **1** | **0** | **1** | **2** |
| Wales | 2 | 1 | 0 | 1 | 2 |

*England did not compete*

## 1888-1889

### Three Nations Championship

**v WALES**

**WON**
Scotland: 2T
Wales: Nil
Raeburn Place, 2 Feb 1889

H.F.T. Chambers

† J.H. Marsh
H.J. Stevenson
W.F. Holms

C.E. Orr 1T
C.F.P. Fraser

† A. Methuen
† J.D. Boswell
H.T. Ker 1T
A. Duke
† W. Auld
* D.S. Morton
M.C. McEwan
† W.A. McDonald
T.B. White

**v IRELAND**

**WON**
Ireland: Nil
Scotland: 1DG
Belfast, 16 Feb 1889

H.F.T. Chambers

J.H. Marsh
H.J. Stevenson 1DG
W.F. Holms

C.E. Orr
† D.G. Anderson

A. Methuen
J.D. Boswell
† J.G. McKendrick
A. Duke
† J.E. Orr
* D.S. Morton
M.C. McEwan
T.W. Irvine
† A.I. Aitken

**FACT FILE**

- James Marsh, who first appeared as a three-quarter in 1889, became the first Scotland player to turn out for two countries when he later played for England.
- Scotland were unbeaten in 1889.

**FINAL TABLE**

| | P | W | D | L | Pts |
|---|---|---|---|---|---|
| **Scotland** | **2** | **2** | **0** | **0** | **4** |
| Ireland | 2 | 1 | 0 | 1 | 2 |
| Wales | 2 | 0 | 0 | 2 | 0 |

*England did not compete*

## 1889-90

### Four Nations Championship

**v WALES**

**WON 5-1**
Wales: 1T
Scotland: 1G 2T
Cardiff Arms Park, 1 Feb 1890

† G. MacGregor

* W.E. Maclagan 1T
H.J. Stevenson
G.R. Wilson

C.E. Orr
D.G. Anderson 1T

† F.W.J. Goodhue
J.D. Boswell
W. Auld
A. Duke
J.E. Orr
† A. Dalgleish
M.C. McEwan 1C 1T
† I. MacIntyre
R.G. MacMillan

**v IRELAND**

**WON 4-0**
Scotland: 1DG 1T
Ireland: Nil
Raeburn Place, 22 Feb 1890

G. MacGregor

* W.E. Maclagan
H.J. Stevenson
G.R. Wilson

C.E. Orr
D.G. Anderson

F.W.J. Goodhue
J.D. Boswell 1DG
H.T. Ker
A. Duke
J.E. Orr 1T
D.S. Morton
M.C. McEwan
I. MacIntyre
R.G. MacMillan

**v ENGLAND**

**LOST 0-4**
Scotland: Nil
England: 1G 1T
Raeburn Place, 1 Mar 1890

G. MacGregor

* W.E. Maclagan
H.J. Stevenson
G.R. Wilson

C.E. Orr
D.G. Anderson

F.W.J. Goodhue
J.D. Boswell
H.T. Ker
D.S. Morton
J.E. Orr
A. Dalgleish
M.C. McEwan
I. MacIntyre
R.G. MacMillan

**FACT FILE**

- Bill Maclagan returned to skipper the side and win the last of his 26 caps, thus creating a new record.
- Adam Dalgleish was the first playing member of a Border club to be capped.

**FINAL TABLE**

| | P | W | D | L | Pts |
|---|---|---|---|---|---|
| England | 3 | 2 | 0 | 1 | 4 |
| **Scotland** | **3** | **2** | **0** | **1** | **4** |
| Wales | 3 | 1 | 1 | 1 | 3 |
| Ireland | 3 | 0 | 1 | 2 | 1 |

## 1890-91

### Four Nations Championship

**v WALES**

**WON 15-0**
Scotland: 1G 2DG 6T
Wales: Nil
Raeburn Place, 7 Feb 1891

H.J. Stevenson 1DG

† P.R. Clauss 2T
G. MacGregor
† W. Neilson 1DG

C.E. Orr 1T
D.G. Anderson

F.W.J. Goodhue 1T
J.D. Boswell 1T
† H.T.O. Leggatt 1T
† G.T. Neilson
J.E. Orr 1T
A. Dalgleish
* M.C. McEwan 1C
I. MacIntyre
R.G. MacMillan

**v IRELAND**

**WON 14-0**
Ireland: Nil
Scotland: 3G 1DG 2T
Belfast, 21 Feb 1891

H.J. Stevenson

P.R. Clauss 1T
G. MacGregor 1T
G.R. Wilson

C.E. Orr
† W. Wotherspoon 3T

F.W.J. Goodhue
J.D. Boswell 3C
H.T.O. Leggatt
G.T. Neilson
J.E. Orr
A. Dalgleish
* M.C. McEwan 1DG
I. MacIntyre
† W.R. Gibson

**v ENGLAND**

**WON 9-3**
England: 1G
Scotland: 1DG 2G
Richmond, 7 Mar 1891

H.J. Stevenson

P.R. Clauss 1DG
G. MacGregor 2C
W. Neilson 1T

C.E. Orr
D.G. Anderson

F.W.J. Goodhue
J.D. Boswell
H.T.O. Leggatt
G.T. Neilson
J.E. Orr 1T
W.R. Gibson
* M.C. McEwan
I. MacIntyre
R.G. MacMillan

*Willie (left) and George Neilson, the former Merchiston School brothers, who helped Scotland win the Triple Crown for the first time in 1891.*

**FACT FILE**

- Two pairs of brothers appeared in the Scottish XVs of 1891. The Neilsons made their debuts against Wales and the Orrs, who had appeared together in 1889, were key members of a side which won the Triple Crown for the first time.

**FINAL TABLE**

| | P | W | D | L | F | A | Pts |
|---|---|---|---|---|---|---|---|
| **Scotland** | **3** | **3** | **0** | **0** | **38** | **3** | **6** |
| England | 3 | 2 | 0 | 1 | 19 | 12 | 4 |
| Wales | 3 | 1 | 0 | 2 | 9 | 26 | 2 |
| Ireland | 3 | 0 | 0 | 3 | 4 | 29 | 0 |

## 1891-92

### Four Nations Championship

**v WALES**

**WON 7-2**
Wales: 1T
Scotland: 1G 1T
Swansea, 6 Feb 1892

H.J. Stevenson

P.R. Clauss
† G.T. Campbell 1T
W. Neilson

* C.E. Orr
D.G. Anderson

F.W.J. Goodhue
J.D. Boswell 1T 1C
H.T.O. Leggatt
G.T. Neilson
J.E. Orr
A. Dalgleish
W.R. Gibson
† J.N. Millar
R.G. MacMillan

**v IRELAND**

**WON 2-0**
Scotland: 1T
Ireland: Nil
Raeburn Place, 20 Feb 1892

H.J. Stevenson

† J.C. Woodburn
G.T. Campbell
W. Neilson

* C.E. Orr
W. Wotherspoon

F.W.J. Goodhue
J.D. Boswell
H.T.O. Leggatt
† N.F. Henderson
J.E. Orr
W.A. McDonald
W.R. Gibson
J.N. Millar 1T
R.G. MacMillan

**v ENGLAND**

**LOST 0-5**
Scotland: Nil
England: 1G
Raeburn Place, 5 Mar 1892

H.J. Stevenson

P.R. Clauss
G.T. Campbell
W. Neilson

* C.E. Orr
D.G. Anderson

F.W.J. Goodhue
J.D. Boswell
M.C. McEwan
G.T. Neilson
J.E. Orr
W.A. McDonald
W.R. Gibson
J.N. Millar
R.G. MacMillan

*Early rugby action-photography. Scotland against England at Raeburn Place, Edinburgh, in March 1892.*

**FACT FILE**

- The forwards were responsible for all but one of Scotland's scores this season.

**FINAL TABLE**

| | P | W | D | L | F | A | Pts |
|---|---|---|---|---|---|---|---|
| England | 3 | 3 | 0 | 0 | 29 | 0 | 6 |
| **Scotland** | **3** | **2** | **0** | **1** | **9** | **7** | **4** |
| Ireland | 3 | 1 | 0 | 2 | 9 | 9 | 2 |
| Wales | 3 | 0 | 0 | 3 | 2 | 33 | 0 |

## 1892-93

### Four Nations Championship

**v WALES**

**LOST 0-9**
Scotland: Nil
Wales: 1PG 3T
Raeburn Place, 4 Feb 1893

A.W.C. Cameron

† D.D. Robertson
G. MacGregor
† J.J. Gowans

† R.C. Greig
W. Wotherspoon

† H.F. Menzies
† T.L. Hendry
H.T.O. Leggatt
G.T. Neilson
† W.B. Cownie
A. Dalgleish
W.R. Gibson
J.N. Millar
* R.G. MacMillan

**v IRELAND**

**DRAWN 0-0**
Ireland: Nil
Scotland: Nil
Belfast, 18 Feb 1893

H.J. Stevenson

G.T. Campbell
G. MacGregor
W. Neilson

† J.W. Simpson
† W.P. Donaldson

H.F. Menzies
T.L. Hendry
* J.D. Boswell
† J.M. Bishop
W.B. Cownie
J.E. Orr
W.R. Gibson
† D. Fisher
† J.R. Ford

**v ENGLAND**

**WON 8-0**
England: Nil
Scotland: 2DG
Leeds, 4 Mar 1893

H.J. Stevenson

G.T. Campbell 1DG
G. MacGregor
W. Neilson

J.W. Simpson
W. Wotherspoon

H.T.O. Leggatt
T.L. Hendry
* J.D. Boswell 1DG
† R.S. Davidson
W.B. Cownie
J.E. Orr
W.R. Gibson
† T.M. Scott
R.G. MacMillan

**FACT FILE**

- Scotland were beaten by the Welsh, who employed the four three-quarter system to good effect.
- Bill Donaldson was one of the first half-backs to perfect the screw kick back to touch.

**FINAL TABLE**

| | P | W | D | L | F | A | Pts |
|---|---|---|---|---|---|---|---|
| Wales | 3 | 3 | 0 | 0 | 23 | 11 | 6 |
| **Scotland** | **3** | **1** | **1** | **1** | **8** | **9** | **3** |
| England | 3 | 1 | 0 | 2 | 15 | 20 | 2 |
| Ireland | 3 | 0 | 1 | 2 | 0 | 6 | 1 |

## 1893-94

### Four Nations Championship

**v WALES**

**LOST 0-7**
Wales: 1DG 1T
Scotland: Nil
Newport, 3 Feb 1894

† J. Rogerson

J.J. Gowans
* G. MacGregor
G.T. Campbell
† H.T.S. Gedge

J.W. Simpson
W. Wotherspoon

H.F. Menzies
† J.B. Wright
† W.M.C. McEwan
W.B. Cownie
A. Dalgleish
W.R. Gibson
G.T. Neilson
R.G. MacMillan

**v IRELAND**

**LOST 0-5**
Ireland: 1G
Scotland: Nil
Lansdowne Road, 24 Feb 1894

A.W.C. Cameron

G. MacGregor
W. Wotherspoon
G.T. Campbell
H.T.S. Gedge

J.W. Simpson
W.P. Donaldson

H.T.O. Leggatt
* J.D. Boswell
† A.H. Anderson
W.B. Cownie
A. Dalgleish
W.R. Gibson
G.T. Neilson
R.G. MacMillan

**v ENGLAND**

**WON 6-0**
Scotland: 2T
England: Nil
Raeburn Place, 17 Mar 1894

G. MacGregor

J.J. Gowans
W. Neilson
G.T. Campbell
H.T.S. Gedge

J.W. Simpson
W. Wotherspoon

H.T.O. Leggatt
* J.D. Boswell **2T**
W.M.C. McEwan
W.B. Cownie
H.F. Menzies
W.R. Gibson
† W.G. Neilson
R.G. MacMillan

**FACT FILE**

- Scotland joined the other home unions in employing four three-quarters in 1894.
- Bill McEwan and Walter Neilson, brothers of former caps, were capped as schoolboys. McEwan later played for South Africa.

**FINAL TABLE**

| | P | W | D | L | F | A | Pts |
|---|---|---|---|---|---|---|---|
| Ireland | 3 | 3 | 0 | 0 | 15 | 5 | 6 |
| England | 3 | 1 | 0 | 2 | 29 | 16 | 2 |
| Wales | 3 | 1 | 0 | 2 | 10 | 27 | 2 |
| **Scotland** | **3** | **1** | **0** | **2** | **6** | **12** | **2** |

## 1894-95

### Four Nations Championship

**v WALES**

**WON 5-4**
Scotland: 1G
Wales: 1GM
Raeburn Place, 26 Jan 1895

† A.R. Smith

J.J. Gowans 1T
W. Neilson
G.T. Campbell
† R. Welsh

J.W. Simpson
† M. Elliot

† J.H. Dods
† H.O. Smith 1C
W.M.C. McEwan
W.B. Cownie
T.M. Scott
* W.R. Gibson
G.T. Neilson
R.G. MacMillan

**v IRELAND**

**WON 6-0**
Scotland: 2T
Ireland: Nil
Raeburn Place, 2 Mar 1895

A.R. Smith

J.J. Gowans
W. Neilson
G.T. Campbell 1T
R. Welsh 1T

J.W. Simpson
P.R. Clauss

J.H. Dods
J.N. Millar
T.L. Hendry
W.B. Cownie
T.M. Scott
W.R. Gibson
G.T. Neilson
* R.G. MacMillan

**v ENGLAND**

**WON 6-3**
England: 1PG
Scotland: 1PG 1T
Richmond, 9 Mar 1895

A.R. Smith

J.J. Gowans
W. Neilson
G.T. Campbell
R. Welsh

J.W. Simpson
W.P. Donaldson

J.H. Dods
J.N. Millar
W.M.C. McEwan
W.B. Cownie
T.M. Scott
W.R. Gibson
G.T. Neilson 1T 1PG
* R.G. MacMillan

**FACT FILE**

- Robert MacMillan, a 29-year-old former pupil of Merchiston, led Scotland to their second Triple Crown in 1895.
- The penalty goal against England by George Neilson was Scotland's first in an international match.

**FINAL TABLE**

| | P | W | D | L | F | A | Pts |
|---|---|---|---|---|---|---|---|
| **Scotland** | **3** | **3** | **0** | **0** | **17** | **7** | **6** |
| England | 3 | 2 | 0 | 1 | 23 | 15 | 4 |
| Wales | 3 | 1 | 0 | 2 | 15 | 22 | 2 |
| Ireland | 3 | 0 | 0 | 3 | 6 | 17 | 0 |

## 1895-96

### Four Nations Championship

**v WALES**

**LOST 0-6**
Wales: 2T
Scotland: Nil
Cardiff Arms Park, 25 Jan 1896

A.R. Smith

G.T. Campbell
† A.B. Timms
† T. Scott
R. Welsh

J.W. Simpson
† D. Patterson

J.H. Dods
H.O. Smith
W.M.C. McEwan
† J.H. Coupar
T.M. Scott
† M.C. Morrison
* G.T. Neilson
† A. Balfour

**v IRELAND**

**DRAWN 0-0**
Ireland: Nil
Scotland: Nil
Lansdowne Road, 15 Feb 1896

A.R. Smith

G.T. Campbell
J.J. Gowans
† C.J.N. Fleming
W. Neilson

J.W. Simpson
W.P. Donaldson

J.H. Dods
H.O. Smith
W.M.C. McEwan
J.H. Coupar
† G.O. Turnbull
M.C. Morrison
* G.T. Neilson
A. Balfour

**v ENGLAND**

**WON 11-0**
Scotland: 1G 2T
England: Nil
Hampden Park, 14 Mar 1896

G. MacGregor

G.T. Campbell
J.J. Gowans 1T
C.J.N. Fleming 1T
H.T.S. Gedge 1T

M. Elliot
W.P. Donaldson

J.H. Dods
H.O. Smith
W.M.C. McEwan
T.M. Scott 1C
G.O. Turnbull
M.C. Morrison
* G.T. Neilson
A. Balfour

**FACT FILE**

- Mark Morrison was to play in 23 internationals, captaining the side on 15 occasions – a Scottish record which lasted for 70 years. He was first capped as an 18 year old.

**FINAL TABLE**

| | P | W | D | L | F | A | Pts |
|---|---|---|---|---|---|---|---|
| Ireland | 3 | 2 | 1 | 0 | 18 | 8 | 5 |
| **Scotland** | **3** | **1** | **1** | **1** | **11** | **6** | **3** |
| England | 3 | 1 | 0 | 2 | 29 | 21 | 2 |
| Wales | 3 | 1 | 0 | 2 | 10 | 33 | 2 |

## 1896-97

### Four Nations Championship

**v IRELAND**

**WON 8-3**
Scotland: IG 1PG
Ireland: 1T
Powderhall Gds, 20 Feb 1897

A.R. Smith

G.T. Campbell
W. Neilson
C.J.N. Fleming
T. Scott

R.C. Greig
M. Elliot

J.H. Dods
† A.S. Laidlaw
W.M.C. McEwan
T.M. Scott 1PG 1C
G.O. Turnbull 1T
M.C. Morrison
† R.C. Stevenson
* R.G. MacMillan

**v ENGLAND**

**LOST 3-12**
England: 1G 1DG 1T
Scotland: 1T
Manchester, 13 Mar 1897

A.R. Smith

† A.M. Bucher 1T
W. Neilson
† A.W. Robertson
T. Scott

J.W. Simpson
M. Elliot

J.H. Dods
A. Balfour
W.M.C. McEwan
T.M. Scott
G.O. Turnbull
M.C. Morrison
R.C. Stevenson
* R.G. MacMillan

**FACT FILE**

- Only two matches were played in 1897, the SRU refusing to play the Welsh.
- Alex Laidlaw, capped against Ireland in 1897, became the first Scottish international to join the Northern Union. He signed professional for Bradford two years after gaining his cap.

**FINAL TABLE**

| | P | W | D | L | F | A | Pts |
|---|---|---|---|---|---|---|---|
| **England** | **3** | **1** | **0** | **2** | **21** | **27** | **2** |
| Ireland | 2 | 1 | 0 | 1 | 16 | 17 | 2 |
| Wales | 1 | 1 | 0 | 0 | 11 | 0 | 2 |
| Scotland | 2 | 1 | 0 | 1 | 11 | 15 | 2 |

*CHAMPIONSHIP UNRESOLVED*
*Wales did not meet Ireland or Scotland*

## 1897-98

### Four Nations Championship

**v IRELAND**

**WON 8-0**
Ireland: Nil
Scotland: 1G 1T
Belfast, 19 Feb 1898

† J.M. Reid

† R.T. Neilson
† E. Spencer
* A.R. Smith
T. Scott 2T

† J.T. Mabon
M. Elliot

† A. MacKinnon
H.O. Smith
W.M.C. McEwan
T.M. Scott 1C
† J.M. Dykes
M.C. Morrison
† R. Scott
† G.C. Kerr

**v ENGLAND**

**DRAWN 3-3**
Scotland: 1T
England: 1T
Powderhall Gds, 12 Mar 1898

J.M. Reid

R.T. Neilson
† T.A. Nelson
* A.R. Smith
T. Scott

J.T. Mabon
M. Elliot

A. MacKinnon
H.O. Smith
W.M.C. McEwan 1T
T.M. Scott
J.M. Dykes
M.C. Morrison
R.C. Stevenson
G.C. Kerr

**FACT FILE**

- Scotland refused to play the Welsh again in 1898.

**FINAL TABLE**

| | P | W | D | L | F | A | Pts |
|---|---|---|---|---|---|---|---|
| England | 3 | 1 | 1 | 1 | 23 | 19 | 3 |
| **Scotland** | **2** | **1** | **1** | **0** | **11** | **3** | **3** |
| Wales | 2 | 1 | 0 | 1 | 18 | 17 | 2 |
| Ireland | 3 | 1 | 0 | 2 | 12 | 25 | 2 |

*CHAMPIONSHIP UNRESOLVED*
*Wales and Scotland did not meet*

## 1898-99

### Four Nations Championship

**v IRELAND**

**LOST 3-9**
Scotland: 1PG
Ireland: 3T
Inverleith, 18 Feb 1899

J.M. Reid

G.T. Campbell
R.T. Neilson
† D.B. Monypenny
T. Scott

J.T. Mabon
* W.P. Donaldson 1PG

A. MacKinnon
H.O. Smith
W.M.C. McEwan
J.H. Coupar
† L. Harvey
M.C. Morrison
R.C. Stevenson
G.C. Kerr

**v WALES**

**WON 21-10**
Scotland: 1GM 2DG 3T
Wales: 2G
Inverleith, 4 Mar 1899

† H. Rottenburg

H.T.S. Gedge 1DG 1T
† G.A.W. Lamond 1DG
D.B. Monypenny 1T
T. Scott

J.W. Simpson
R.T. Neilson

A. MacKinnon
H.O. Smith 1T
W.M.C. McEwan
† W.J. Thomson 1GM
J.M. Dykes
R.C. Stevenson
* M.C. Morrison
G.C. Kerr

**v ENGLAND**

**WON 5-0**
England: Nil
Scotland: 1G
Blackheath, 11 Mar 1899

H. Rottenburg

H.T.S. Gedge
G.A.W. Lamond
D.B. Monypenny
T. Scott

J.W. Simpson
† J.I. Gillespie 1T

A. MacKinnon
H.O. Smith
W.M.C. McEwan
W.J. Thomson 1C
J.M. Dykes
R.C. Stevenson
* M.C. Morrison
G.C. Kerr

**FACT FILE**

- The highlight of 1899 was the opening of Inverleith, Scotland's national ground. The Welsh match was postponed until March because of poor weather, so the Irish were the SFU's first guests at the ground.

**FINAL TABLE**

| | P | W | D | L | F | A | Pts |
|---|---|---|---|---|---|---|---|
| Ireland | 3 | 3 | 0 | 0 | 18 | 3 | 6 |
| **Scotland** | **3** | **2** | **0** | **1** | **29** | **19** | **4** |
| Wales | 3 | 1 | 0 | 2 | 36 | 27 | 2 |
| England | 3 | 0 | 0 | 3 | 3 | 37 | 0 |

## 1899-1900

### Four Nations Championship

**v WALES**

**LOST 3-12**
Wales: 4T
Scotland: 1T
St Helens, 27 Jan 1900

H. Rottenburg

† J.E. Crabbie
A.B. Timms
† W.H. Morrison
T. Scott

† F.H. Fasson
J.I. Gillespie

T.M. Scott
† F.W. Henderson
W.M.C. McEwan
† D.R. Bedell-Sivright
J.M. Dykes 1T
* M.C. Morrison
W.J. Thomson
G.C. Kerr

**v IRELAND**

**DRAWN 0-0**
Ireland: Nil
Scotland: Nil
Lansdowne Road, 24 Feb 1900

H. Rottenburg

† W.H. Welsh
A.B. Timms
A.R. Smith
T. Scott

J.T. Mabon
R.T. Neilson

* T.M. Scott
F.W. Henderson
† J.R.C. Greenlees
R. Scott
J.M. Dykes
† J.A. Campbell
† W.P. Scott
G.C. Kerr

**v ENGLAND**

**DRAWN 0-0**
Scotland: Nil
England: Nil
Inverleith, 10 Mar 1900

H. Rottenburg

W.H. Welsh
G.T. Campbell
A.R. Smith
T. Scott

J.I. Gillespie
R.T. Neilson

A. MacKinnon
H.O. Smith
W.M.C. McEwan
R. Scott
† L.H.I. Bell
* M.C. Morrison
W.P. Scott
G.C. Kerr

**FACT FILE**

- Scotland failed to win a match in 1900, but had the unusual record of playing two consecutive scoreless draws.

**FINAL TABLE**

| | P | W | D | L | F | A | Pts |
|---|---|---|---|---|---|---|---|
| Wales | 3 | 3 | 0 | 0 | 28 | 6 | 6 |
| England | 3 | 1 | 1 | 1 | 18 | 17 | 3 |
| **Scotland** | **3** | **0** | **2** | **1** | **3** | **12** | **2** |
| Ireland | 3 | 0 | 1 | 2 | 4 | 18 | 1 |

*Mark Morrison's Scottish team lines up at Blackheath in 1901 before winning Scotland's third Triple Crown.*

## 1900-01

### Four Nations Championship

**v WALES**

**WON 18-8**
Scotland: 3G 1T
Wales: 1G 1T
Inverleith, 9 Feb 1901

† A.W. Duncan

W.H. Welsh
A.B. Timms
† P. Turnbull 1T
† A.N. Fell 1T

F.H. Fasson
J.I. Gillespie 2C 2T

† J. Ross
† A.B. Flett 1C
† A. Frew
D.R. Bedell-Sivright
J.M. Dykes
* M.C. Morrison
† R.S. Stronach
† J.A. Bell

**v IRELAND**

**WON 9-5**
Scotland: 3T
Ireland: 1G
Inverleith, 23 Feb 1901

A.W. Duncan

W.H. Welsh 2T
A.B. Timms
P. Turnbull
A.N. Fell

F.H. Fasson
J.I. Gillespie 1T

J. Ross
A.B. Flett
A. Frew
D.R. Bedell-Sivright
J.M. Dykes
* M.C. Morrison
† F.P. Dods
J.A. Bell

**v ENGLAND**

**WON 18-3**
England: 1T
Scotland: 3G 1T
Blackheath, 9 Mar 1901

A.W. Duncan

W.H. Welsh 1T
A.B. Timms 1T
P. Turnbull
A.N. Fell 1T

† R.M. Neill
J.I. Gillespie 1T 3C

J. Ross
A.B. Flett
A. Frew
D.R. Bedell-Sivright
J.M. Dykes
* M.C. Morrison
R.S. Stronach
J.A. Bell

### FACT FILE

- Eight new caps appeared at the start of the Scots' Triple Crown season. All of the backs and nine of the side against Wales were from Edinburgh clubs.
- Scotland used only 17 players during the season.

### FINAL TABLE

| | P | W | D | L | F | A | Pts |
|---|---|---|---|---|---|---|---|
| **Scotland** | **3** | **3** | **0** | **0** | **45** | **16** | **6** |
| Wales | 3 | 2 | 0 | 1 | 31 | 27 | 4 |
| Ireland | 3 | 1 | 0 | 2 | 24 | 25 | 2 |
| England | 3 | 0 | 0 | 3 | 9 | 41 | 0 |

## 1901-02

### Four Nations Championship

**v WALES**

**LOST 5-14**
Wales: 1G 3T
Scotland: 1G
Cardiff Arms Park, 1 Feb 1902

A.W. Duncan

W.H. Welsh 1T
A.B. Timms
P. Turnbull
A.N. Fell

F.H. Fasson
J.I. Gillespie 1C

† W.E. Kyle
A.B. Flett
J.R.C. Greenlees
D.R. Bedell-Sivright
J. Ross
* M.C. Morrison
† J.V. Bedell-Sivright
J.A. Bell

**v IRELAND**

**LOST 0-5**
Ireland: 1G
Scotland: Nil
Belfast, 22 Feb 1902

A.W. Duncan

W.H. Welsh
† A.S. Drybrough
P. Turnbull
J.E. Crabbie

R.M. Neill
J.I. Gillespie

W.E. Kyle
A.B. Flett
J.R.C. Greenlees
D.R. Bedell-Sivright
† H.H. Bullmore
* M.C. Morrison
W.P. Scott
J.A. Bell

**v ENGLAND**

**LOST 3-6**
Scotland: 1T
England: 2T
Inverleith, 15 Mar 1902

A.W. Duncan

W.H. Welsh
A.B. Timms
P. Turnbull
A.N. Fell 1T

F.H. Fasson
† E.D. Simson

W.E. Kyle
H.O. Smith
J.R.C. Greenlees
D.R. Bedell-Sivright
J.M. Dykes
* M.C. Morrison
W.P. Scott
J.A. Bell

**FACT FILE**

- Scotland's demise in 1902 was their first whitewash in the championship.

**FINAL TABLE**

| | P | W | D | L | F | A | Pts |
|---|---|---|---|---|---|---|---|
| Wales | 3 | 3 | 0 | 0 | 38 | 13 | 6 |
| England | 3 | 2 | 0 | 1 | 20 | 15 | 4 |
| Ireland | 3 | 1 | 0 | 2 | 8 | 21 | 2 |
| **Scotland** | **3** | **0** | **0** | **3** | **8** | **25** | **0** |

## 1902-03

### Four Nations Championship

**v WALES**

**WON 6-0**
Scotland: 1PG 1T
Wales: Nil
Inverleith, 7 Feb 1903

† W.T. Forrest

A.N. Fell
A.B. Timms 1PG
† H.J. Orr
J.E. Crabbie

† J. Knox
E.D. Simson

W.E. Kyle 1T
† L. West
J.R.C. Greenlees
D.R. Bedell-Sivright
† N. Kennedy
* M.C. Morrison
W.P. Scott
† A.G. Cairns

**v IRELAND**

**WON 3-0**
Scotland: 1T
Ireland: Nil
Inverleith, 28 Feb 1903

W.T. Forrest

J.E. Crabbie 1T
A.S. Drybrough
H.J. Orr
† C. France

J. Knox
E.D. Simson

W.E. Kyle
L. West
J.R.C. Greenlees
D.R. Bedell-Sivright
N. Kennedy
* M.C. Morrison
W.P. Scott
A.G. Cairns

**v ENGLAND**

**WON 10-6**
England: 2T
Scotland: 1DG 2T
Richmond, 21 Mar 1903

W.T. Forrest

A.N. Fell
A.B. Timms 1DG
H.J. Orr
† J.S. MacDonald

J. Knox
E.D. Simson 1T

W.E. Kyle
L. West
* J.R.C. Greenlees
J. Ross
N. Kennedy
† J.D. Dallas 1T
W.P. Scott
A.G. Cairns

*John Dallas (right) touches down to score a debut try for Scotland in the match against England at Richmond.*

**FACT FILE**

- The Scots won the Triple Crown for the fourth time in 1903.

**FINAL TABLE**

| | P | W | D | L | F | A | Pts |
|---|---|---|---|---|---|---|---|
| **Scotland** | **3** | **3** | **0** | **0** | **19** | **6** | **6** |
| Wales | 3 | 2 | 0 | 1 | 39 | 11 | 4 |
| Ireland | 3 | 1 | 0 | 2 | 6 | 21 | 2 |
| England | 3 | 0 | 0 | 3 | 11 | 37 | 0 |

## 1903-04

### Four Nations Championship

**v WALES**

**LOST 3-21**
Wales: 3G 1PG 1T
Scotland: 1T
St Helens, 6 Feb 1904

W.T. Forrest

† G.E. Crabbie
† L.M. MacLeod
H.J. Orr 1T
J.S. MacDonald

E.D. Simson
† A.A. Bissett

W.E. Kyle
G.O. Turnbull
† E.J. Ross
D.R. Bedell-Sivright
L.H.I. Bell
* M.C. Morrison
W.P. Scott
A.G. Cairns

**v IRELAND**

**WON 19-3**
Ireland: 1T
Scotland: 2G 3T
Lansdowne Road, 27 Feb 1904

W.T. Forrest

A.B. Timms 1T
L.M. MacLeod
H.J. Orr 1T
J.S. MacDonald 2C 1T

E.D. Simson 1T
J.I. Gillespie

W.E. Kyle
† J.B. Waters
† W.M. Milne
D.R. Bedell-Sivright 1T
L.H.I. Bell
* M.C. Morrison
W.P. Scott
A.G. Cairns

**v ENGLAND**

**WON 6-3**
Scotland: 2T
England: 1T
Inverleith, 19 Mar 1904

W.T. Forrest

A.B. Timms
L.M. MacLeod
J.S. MacDonald 1T
J.E. Crabbie 1T

E.D. Simson
J.I. Gillespie

W.E. Kyle
J.B. Waters
W.M. Milne
D.R. Bedell-Sivright
† H.N. Fletcher
* M.C. Morrison
W.P. Scott
A.G. Cairns

**FACT FILE**

- Mark Morrison, in his last year as an international, led Scotland to the championship.

**FINAL TABLE**

| | P | W | D | L | F | A | Pts |
|---|---|---|---|---|---|---|---|
| **Scotland** | **3** | **2** | **0** | **1** | **28** | **27** | **4** |
| Wales | 3 | 1 | 1 | 1 | 47 | 31 | 3 |
| England | 3 | 1 | 1 | 1 | 36 | 20 | 3 |
| Ireland | 3 | 1 | 0 | 2 | 17 | 50 | 2 |

## 1904-05

### Four Nations Championship

**v WALES**

**LOST 3-6**
Scotland: 1T
Wals: 2T
Inverleith, 4 Feb 1905

W.T. Forrest

J.E. Crabbie
L.M. MacLeod
† J.L. Forbes
J.S. MacDonald

E.D. Simson
† P. Munro

W.E. Kyle
† A.W. Little 1T
W.M. Milne
R.S. Stronach
H.N. Fletcher
† A. Ross
* W.P. Scott
A.G. Cairns

**v IRELAND**

**LOST 5-11**
Scotland: 1G
Ireland: 1G 2T
Inverleith, 25 Feb 1905

W.T. Forrest 1C

† W.T. Ritchie
L.M. MacLeod
A.B. Timms 1T
† R.H. McCowat

E.D. Simson
P. Munro

W.E. Kyle
L. West
W.M. Milne
R.S. Stronach
† M.R. Dickson
A. Ross
* W.P. Scott
A.G. Cairns

**v ENGLAND**

**WON 8-0**
England: Nil
Scotland: 1G 1T
Richmond, 18 Mar 1905

† D.G. Schulze

W.T. Ritchie
G.A.W. Lamond
* A.B. Timms
† T. Elliot

E.D. Simson 1T
P. Munro

W.E. Kyle
L. West
† J.C. MacCallum
R.S. Stronach 1T
† H.G. Monteith
A. Ross
W.P. Scott 1C
A.G. Cairns

**FACT FILE**

- There were four new caps for the English match. Douglas Schulze played 13 times to become Scotland's most-capped full-back before the war; Tom Elliot was only the second Border back capped for Scotland.

**FINAL TABLE**

| | P | W | D | L | F | A | Pts |
|---|---|---|---|---|---|---|---|
| Wales | 3 | 3 | 0 | 0 | 41 | 6 | 6 |
| Ireland | 3 | 2 | 0 | 1 | 31 | 18 | 4 |
| **Scotland** | **3** | **1** | **0** | **2** | **16** | **17** | **2** |
| England | 3 | 0 | 0 | 3 | 3 | 50 | 0 |

## 1905-06

### Tour Match

**v NEW ZEALAND**

**LOST 7-12**
Scotland: 1DG 1T
NZ: 4T
Inverleith, 18 Nov 1905

† J.G. Scoular

† T. Sloan
L.M. MacLeod
† K.G. MacLeod
† J.T. Simson

E.D. Simson 1DG
P. Munro
† L.L. Greig

L. West
J.C. MacCallum 1T
* D.R. Bedell-Sivright
W.E. Kyle
† W.L. Russell
W.P. Scott
† J.M. Mackenzie

### Four Nations Championship

**v WALES**

**LOST 3-9**
Wales: 3T
Scotland: 1PG
Cardiff Arms Park, 3 Feb 1906

J.G. Scoular

T. Sloan
† W.C. Church
K.G. MacLeod 1PG
† A.B.H.L. Purves

E.D. Simson
P. Munro

H.G. Monteith
* L. West
J.C. MacCallum
D.R. Bedell-Sivright
W.E. Kyle
W.L. Russell
W.P. Scott
A.G. Cairns

**v IRELAND**

**WON 13-6**
Ireland: 2T
Scotland: 2G 1GM
Lansdowne Road, 24 Feb 1906

J.G. Scoular

A.B.H.L. Purves
J.L. Forbes
† M.W. Walter
K.G. MacLeod 1GM

E.D. Simson
P. Munro 1T

H.G. Monteith
* L. West
J.C. MacCallum 2C
D.R. Bedell-Sivright 1T
W.E. Kyle
W.L. Russell
W.P. Scott
A.G. Cairns

**v ENGLAND**

**LOST 3-9**
Scotland: 1T
England: 3T
Inverleith, 17 Mar 1906

J.G. Scoular

A.B.H.L. Purves 1T
J.L. Forbes
M.W. Walter
K.G. MacLeod

E.D. Simson
P. Munro

H.G. Monteith
* L. West
J.C. MacCallum
D.R. Bedell-Sivright
W.E. Kyle
W.L. Russell
W.P. Scott
A.G. Cairns

### FACT FILE

- 1905-06 was a disappointing season with just one win from four matches. The highlight of the winter was the encounter with the first New Zealand team.
- The Scottish selectors had decided to counter the New Zealanders' unusual formation by fielding eight backs and seven forwards. Kenneth MacLeod was a teenager at the time.

### FINAL TABLE

| | P | W | D | L | F | A | Pts |
|---|---|---|---|---|---|---|---|
| Wales | 3 | 2 | 0 | 1 | 31 | 17 | 4 |
| Ireland | 3 | 2 | 0 | 1 | 33 | 25 | 4 |
| **Scotland** | **3** | **1** | **0** | **2** | **19** | **24** | **2** |
| England | 3 | 1 | 0 | 2 | 18 | 35 | 2 |

## 1906-07

### Tour Match

**v SOUTH AFRICA**

**WON 6-0**
Scotland: 2T
SA: Nil
Hampden Park, 17 Nov 1906

J.G. Scoular

K.G. MacLeod 1T
T. Sloan
M.W. Walter
A.B.H.L. Purves 1T

* L.L. Greig
P. Munro

H.G. Monteith
† I.C. Geddes
J.C. MacCallum
D.R. Bedell-Sivright
† G.M. Frew
† L.M. Spiers
W.P. Scott
† W.H. Thomson

### Four Nations Championship

**v WALES**

**WON 6-3**
Scotland: 2T
Wales: 1PG
Inverleith, 2 Feb 1907

T. Sloan

K.G. MacLeod
† D.G. MacGregor
M.W. Walter
A.B.H.L. Purves 1T

E.D. Simson
* L.L. Greig

H.G. Monteith 1T
I.C. Geddes
J.C. MacCallum
D.R. Bedell-Sivright
G.M. Frew
L.M. Spiers
W.P. Scott
† G.A. Sanderson

**v IRELAND**

**WON 15-3**
Scotland: 3G
Ireland: 1PG
Inverleith, 23 Feb 1907

D.G. Schulze

K.G. MacLeod
D.G. MacGregor
M.W. Walter
A.B.H.L. Purves 1T

E.D. Simson
* P. Munro

H.G. Monteith
I.C. Geddes 3C
J.C. MacCallum
D.R. Bedell-Sivright
G.M. Frew 1T
L.M. Spiers
W.P. Scott
G.A. Sanderson 1T

**v ENGLAND**

**WON 8-3**
England: 1T
Scotland: 1G 1T
Blackheath, 16 Mar 1907

D.G. Schulze

K.G. MacLeod
D.G. MacGregor
T. Sloan
A.B.H.L. Purves 1T

E.D. Simson 1T
* P. Munro

† J.M.B. Scott
I.C. Geddes 1C
J.C. MacCallum
D.R. Bedell-Sivright
G.M. Frew
L.M. Spiers
W.P. Scott
G.A. Sanderson

### FACT FILE

- The touring Springboks were beaten by two second-half tries on a muddy pitch at Hampden Park, and in front of a record crowd of 30,000.
- The Triple Crown was added to the famous South Africa victory to give Scotland four wins from four matches. Alec Purves, playing on the left wing (another former pupil of Fettes), scored tries in each of the matches.

### FINAL TABLE

| | P | W | D | L | F | A | Pts |
|---|---|---|---|---|---|---|---|
| **Scotland** | **3** | **3** | **0** | **0** | **29** | **9** | **6** |
| Wales | 3 | 2 | 0 | 1 | 54 | 6 | 4 |
| Ireland | 3 | 1 | 0 | 2 | 20 | 53 | 2 |
| England | 3 | 0 | 0 | 3 | 12 | 47 | 0 |

## 1907-08

## Four Nations Championship

**v WALES**

**LOST 5-6**
Wales: 2T
Scotland: 1G
St Helens, 1 Feb 1908

D.G. Schulze

A.B.H.L. Purves 1T
M.W. Walter
T. Sloan
† H. Martin

* L.L. Greig
† G. Cunningham

D.R. Bedell-Sivright
J.C. MacCallum
L.M. Spiers
I.C. Geddes 1C
† G.C. Gowlland
J.M.B. Scott
† J.A. Brown
G.M. Frew

**v IRELAND**

**LOST 11-16**
Ireland: 2G 2T
Scotland: 1G 1PG 1T
Lansdowne Road, 29 Feb 1908

D.G. Schulze

A.B.H.L. Purves
M.W. Walter
K.G. MacLeod 1PG 1C 1T
H. Martin 1T

* L.L. Greig
G. Cunningham

D.R. Bedell-Sivright
J.C. MacCallum
L.M. Spiers
† J.S. Wilson
G.A. Sanderson
J.M.B. Scott
J.A. Brown
G.M. Frew

**v ENGLAND**

**WON 16-10**
Scotland: 1G 2DG 1T
England: 2G
Inverleith, 21 Mar 1908

D.G. Schulze 1DG

A.B.H.L. Purves 1DG
† C.M. Gilray
K.G. MacLeod 2T
H. Martin

† J. Robertson
† A.L. Wade

W.E. Kyle
J.C. MacCallum
L.M. Spiers
* I.C. Geddes 1C
H.G. Monteith
J.M.B. Scott
† A.L. Robertson
G.M. Frew

### FACT FILE

- Purves' try in the opening game of 1908 gave him an unusual record for Scotland: he had scored tries in six consecutive matches stretching back to the English game of 1906.

### FINAL TABLE

| | P | W | D | L | F | A | Pts |
|---|---|---|---|---|---|---|---|
| Wales | 3 | 3 | 0 | 0 | 45 | 28 | 6 |
| England | 3 | 1 | 0 | 2 | 41 | 47 | 2 |
| **Scotland** | **3** | **1** | **0** | **2** | **32** | **32** | **2** |
| Ireland | 3 | 1 | 0 | 2 | 24 | 35 | 2 |

## 1908-09

### Four Nations Championship

**v WALES**

**LOST 3-5**
Scotland: 1PG
Wales: 1G
Inverleith, 6 Feb 1909

D.G. Schulze

H. Martin
C.M. Gilray
† A.W. Angus
J.T. Simson

G. Cunningham 1PG
† J.M. Tennent

W.E. Kyle
J.C. MacCallum
A. Ross
J.S. Wilson
G.C. Gowlland
* J.M.B. Scott
J.M. Mackenzie
G.M. Frew

**v IRELAND**

**WON 9-3**
Scotland: 3T
Ireland: 1PG
Inverleith, 27 Feb 1909

D.G. Schulze

J.T. Simson
T. Sloan
† J. Pearson
† R.H. Lindsay-Watson 1T

J.M. Tennent
† J.R. McGregor 1T

W.E. Kyle 1T
J.C. MacCallum
A. Ross
† C.D. Stuart
† W.G. Lely
* J.M.B. Scott
J.M. Mackenzie
G.M. Frew

**v ENGLAND**

**WON 18-8**
England: 1G 1T
Scotland: 3G 1T
Richmond, 20 Mar 1909

D.G. Schulze

H. Martin
C.M. Gilray 1T
J. Pearson
J.T. Simson 1T

* G. Cunningham 3C
J.M. Tennent 2T

W.E. Kyle
J.C. MacCallum
† J. Reid-Kerr
† A.R. Moodie
G.C. Gowlland
J.M.B. Scott
J.M. Mackenzie
G.M. Frew

*James Pearson, the Watsonians three-quarter, won the first of his dozen Scottish caps in 1909. He was killed in action at Hooge in Belgium in 1915, aged 26.*

**FACT FILE**

- Sir George Cunningham, as he became, was one of the first Scottish international halves to specialise at fly-half.

**FINAL TABLE**

| | P | W | D | L | F | A | Pts |
|---|---|---|---|---|---|---|---|
| Wales | 3 | 3 | 0 | 0 | 31 | 8 | 6 |
| **Scotland** | **3** | **2** | **0** | **1** | **30** | **16** | **4** |
| England | 3 | 1 | 0 | 2 | 19 | 31 | 2 |
| Ireland | 3 | 0 | 0 | 3 | 13 | 38 | 0 |

# 1909-10

## Five Nations Championship

### v FRANCE

**WON 27-0**
Scotland: 3G 4T
France: Nil
Inverleith, 22 Jan 1910

† F.G. Buchanan

J.T. Simson
A.W. Angus 1T
J. Pearson
† I.P.M. Robertson 2T

* G. Cunningham
J.M. Tennent 3T

† R.C. Stevenson
J.C. MacCallum 3C
L.M. Spiers
C.D. Stuart
G.C. Gowlland 1T
J.M.B. Scott
A.R. Moodie
G.M. Frew

### v WALES

**LOST 0-14**
Wales: 1G 3T
Scotland: Nil
Cardiff Arms Park, 5 Feb 1910

D.G. Schulze

J.T. Simson
A.W. Angus
J. Pearson
† W.R. Sutherland

J.M. Tennent
† E. Milroy

W.E. Kyle
J.C. MacCallum
L.M. Spiers
C.D. Stuart
G.C. Gowlland
J.M.B. Scott
J.M. Mackenzie
* G.M. Frew

### v IRELAND

**WON 14-0**
Ireland: Nil
Scotland: 1G 3T
Belfast, 26 Feb 1910

D.G. Schulze

† D.G. Macpherson
M.W. Walter 2T
J. Pearson
† J.D. Dobson 1T

* G. Cunningham
† A.B. Lindsay

R.C. Stevenson
J.C. MacCallum 1C
† C.H. Abercrombie
C.D. Stuart 1T
G.C. Gowlland
J.M.B. Scott
J.M. Mackenzie
G.M. Frew

### v ENGLAND

**LOST 5-14**
Scotland: 1G
England: 1G 3T
Inverleith, 19 Mar 1910

D.G. Schulze

D.G. Macpherson 1T
A.W. Angus
J. Pearson
W.R. Sutherland

* G. Cunningham
J.M. Tennent

R.C. Stevenson
J.C. MacCallum 1C
C.H. Abercrombie
C.D. Stuart
G.C. Gowlland
J.M.B. Scott
J.M. Mackenzie
L.M. Spiers

### FACT FILE

- Scotland opened the season with their first international against France. Although the side is regarded as a full Scotland team the SFU did not award caps to the players. Nevertheless, the match has always been included in international records.
- The Watsonians club, one of the strongest in Scotland at the time, supplied the entire three-quarter line against the French.

### FINAL TABLE

| | P | W | D | L | F | A | Pts |
|---|---|---|---|---|---|---|---|
| England | 4 | 3 | 1 | 0 | 36 | 14 | 7 |
| Wales | 4 | 3 | 0 | 1 | 88 | 28 | 6 |
| **Scotland** | **4** | **2** | **0** | **2** | **46** | **28** | **4** |
| Ireland | 4 | 1 | 1 | 2 | 11 | 36 | 3 |
| France | 4 | 0 | 0 | 4 | 20 | 95 | 0 |

## 1910-11

### Five Nations Championship

**v FRANCE**

**LOST 15-16**
France: 2G 2T
Scotland: 1G 1DG 2T
Stade Colombes, 2 Jan 1911

† H.B. Tod

W.R. Sutherland
F.G. Buchanan
† T.E.B. Young
J. Pearson 1DG

* P. Munro 1T
† F.L. Osler

R.C. Stevenson
† F.H. Turner 1C
† R. Fraser
C.H. Abercrombie 1T
† A.M. Stevenson
J.M.B. Scott
A.R. Moodie
J.C. MacCallum 1T

**v WALES**

**LOST 10-32**
Scotland: 1DG 2T
Wales: 2G 1DG 6T
Inverleith, 4 Feb 1911

D.G. Schulze

† D.M. Grant
F.G. Buchanan
A.W. Angus
† J.M. Macdonald

* P. Munro 1DG
F.L. Osler

R.C. Stevenson
F.H. Turner 1T
R. Fraser
C.H. Abercrombie
† A.R. Ross
J.M.B. Scott 1T
J.M. Mackenzie
A.L. Robertson

**v IRELAND**

**LOST 10-16**
Scotland: 1DG 2T
Ireland: 2G 2T
Inverleith, 25 Feb 1911

† A. Greig

D.M. Grant
† C. Ogilvy
A.W. Angus 1T
J.T. Simson 1T

* P. Munro 1DG
A.B. Lindsay

R.C. Stevenson
F.H. Turner
R. Fraser
C.D. Stuart
G.M. Frew
J.M.B. Scott
J.M. Mackenzie
J.C. MacCallum

**v ENGLAND**

**LOST 8-13**
England: 2G 1T
Scotland: 1G 1T
Twickenham, 18 Mar 1911

C. Ogilvy

† S.S.L. Steyn
† R.F. Simson 1T
G. Cunningham 1C
W.R. Sutherland 1T

† J.Y.M. Henderson
E. Milroy

† D.McL. Bain
F.H. Turner
R. Fraser
C.D. Stuart
G.M. Frew
† W.R. Hutchison
† J. Dobson
* J.C. MacCallum

**FACT FILE**

- 1911 was a season of unmitigated disaster. For a start there was the humiliation of defeat against a young French team in Paris, and this was followed by Scotland's heaviest defeat (until then) by Wales, at Inverleith. The remaining matches were also lost, leaving Scotland with four losses from four games for the first time.
- The Calcutta Cup match was Scotland's first trip to Twickenham.

**FINAL TABLE**

| | P | W | D | L | F | A | Pts |
|---|---|---|---|---|---|---|---|
| Wales | 4 | 4 | 0 | 0 | 78 | 21 | 8 |
| Ireland | 4 | 3 | 0 | 1 | 44 | 31 | 6 |
| England | 4 | 2 | 0 | 2 | 61 | 26 | 4 |
| France | 4 | 1 | 0 | 3 | 21 | 92 | 2 |
| **Scotland** | **4** | **0** | **0** | **4** | **43** | **77** | **0** |

## 1911-12

## Five Nations Championship

### v FRANCE

**WON 31-3**
Scotland: 5G 1PG 1T
France: 1T
Inverleith, 20 Jan 1912

† W.M. Dickson

W.R. Sutherland 2T
A.W. Angus
J. Pearson 1PG 1T
† J.G. Will 1T

† A.W. Gunn 1T
† J. Hume

* J.C. MacCallum
† R.D. Robertson
† W.D.C.L. Purves
† D.D. Howie
D. McL. Bain
† C.C.P. Hill
J. Dobson
F.H. Turner 1T 5C

### v WALES

**LOST 6-21**
Wales: 2G 2DG 1T
Scotland: 2T
St Helens, 3 Feb 1912

W.M. Dickson

W.R. Sutherland
A.W. Angus
J. Pearson
J.G. Will 2T

A.W. Gunn
E. Milroy

* J.C. MacCallum
A.L. Robertson
W.D.C.L. Purves
D.D. Howie
D. McL. Bain
J.M.B. Scott
J. Dobson
F.H. Turner

### v IRELAND

**LOST 8-10**
Ireland: 1DG 1PG 1T
Scotland: 1G 1T
Lansdowne Road, 24 Feb 1912

C. Ogilvy

S.S.L. Steyn
A.W. Angus
C.M. Gilray
J.G. Will 1T

A.W. Gunn
E. Milroy

* J.C. MacCallum 1C
A.L. Robertson
W.D.C.L. Purves
D.D. Howie
C.C.P. Hill
J.M.B. Scott
J. Dobson
F.H. Turner 1T

### v ENGLAND

**WON 8-3**
Scotland: 1G 1T
England: 1T
Inverleith 16 Mar 1912

W.M. Dickson

W.R. Sutherland 1T
† W. Burnet
A.W. Angus
J.G. Will

† J.L. Boyd
E. Milroy

* J.C. MacCallum 1C
A.L. Robertson
† C.M. Usher 1T
D.D. Howie
D. McL. Bain
J.M.B. Scott
J. Dobson
F.H. Turner

### FACT FILE

- John Will was a fast, determined runner who scored tries in each of his first three internationals. Turner converted five of the tries against the French to set a new Scottish record.
- Captain John MacCallum, was one of the strongest all-round Scottish forwards of the era. Described as a 'gifted player', he played the last of his 26 internationals against England this season, passing the cap record held by Bill Maclagan.

### FINAL TABLE

| | P | W | D | L | F | A | Pts |
|---|---|---|---|---|---|---|---|
| England | 4 | 3 | 0 | 1 | 44 | 16 | 6 |
| Ireland | 4 | 3 | 0 | 1 | 33 | 34 | 6 |
| **Scotland** | **4** | **2** | **0** | **2** | **53** | **37** | **4** |
| Wales | 4 | 2 | 0 | 2 | 40 | 34 | 4 |
| France | 4 | 0 | 0 | 4 | 25 | 74 | 0 |

## 1912-13

### Tour Match

**v SOUTH AFRICA**

**LOST 0-16**
Scotland: Nil
SA: 2G 2T
Inverleith 23 Nov 1912

W.M. Dickson

W.R. Sutherland
A.W. Angus
A.W. Gunn
J. Pearson

J.L. Boyd
E. Milroy

† P.C.B. Blair
A.L. Robertson
W.D.C.L. Purves
D.D. Howie
D. McL. Bain
J.M.B. Scott
J. Dobson
* F.H. Turner

### Five Nations Championship

**v FRANCE**

**WON 21-3**
France: 1T
Scotland: 3G 2T
Parc des Princes, 1 Jan 1913

W.M. Dickson

† W.A. Stewart **3T**
A.W. Angus
† R.E. Gordon **2T**
W.R. Sutherland

A.W. Gunn
E. Milroy

P.C.B. Blair
† G.A. Ledingham
C.M. Usher
D.D. Howie
D. McL. Bain
† J.B. McDougall
C.H. Abercrombie
* F.H. Turner **3C**

**v WALES**

**LOST 0-8**
Scotland: Nil
Wales: 1G 1T
Inverleith, 1 Feb 1913

W.M. Dickson

W.A. Stewart
A.W. Angus
R.E. Gordon
W.R. Sutherland

† J.H. Bruce-Lockhart
E. Milroy

P.C.B. Blair
A.L. Robertson
C.M. Usher
D.D. Howie
D. McL. Bain
J.M.B. Scott
C.H. Abercrombie
* F.H. Turner

**v IRELAND**

**WON 29-14**
Scotland: 4G 3T
Ireland: 2G 1DG
Inverleith, 22 Feb 1913

W.M. Dickson

W.A. Stewart **4T**
J. Pearson
R.E. Gordon
W.R. Sutherland

† T.C. Bowie **1T**
E. Milroy

P.C.B. Blair
A.L. Robertson
C.M. Usher **1T**
W.D.C.L. Purves **1T**
D.McL. Bain
J.M.B. Scott
† G.H.H.P. Maxwell
* F.H. Turner **4C**

**v ENGLAND**

**LOST 0-3**
England: 1T
Scotland: Nil
Twickenham, 15 Mar 1913

† W.M. Wallace

† J.B. Sweet
J. Pearson
† E.G. Loudon-Shand
W.R. Sutherland

T.C. Bowie
E. Milroy

P.C.B. Blair
A.L. Robertson
C.M. Usher
W.D.C.L. Purves
D. McL. Bain
J.M.B. Scott
G.H.H.P. Maxwell
* F.H. Turner

### FACT FILE

- William Stewart, a Tasmanian born at Launceston, burst on to the scene in the game with France, scoring three tries on the wing.

### FINAL TABLE

| | P | W | D | L | F | A | Pts |
|---|---|---|---|---|---|---|---|
| England | 4 | 4 | 0 | 0 | 50 | 4 | 8 |
| Wales | 4 | 3 | 0 | 1 | 35 | 33 | 6 |
| **Scotland** | **4** | **2** | **0** | **2** | **50** | **28** | **4** |
| Ireland | 4 | 1 | 0 | 3 | 55 | 60 | 2 |
| France | 4 | 0 | 0 | 4 | 11 | 76 | 0 |

## 1913-14

## Five Nations Championship

### v WALES

**LOST 5-24**
Wales: 2G 2DG 1PG 1T
Scotland: 1G
Cardiff Arms Park, 7 Feb 1914

W.M. Wallace

J.G. Will
W.R. Sutherland
† R.M. Scobie
W.A. Stewart 1T

† A.T. Sloan
† A.S. Hamilton

† A.M. Stewart
† A.D. Laing 1C
† A. Weymss
A.R. Ross
* D. McL. Bain
† A.W. Symington
G.H.H.P. Maxwell
† D.G. Donald

### v IRELAND

**LOST 0-6**
Ireland: 2T
Scotland: Nil
Lansdowne Road, 28 Feb 1914

W.M. Wallace

J.G. Will
† J.R. Warren
R.M. Scobie
J.B. Sweet

T.C. Bowie
* E. Milroy

A.D. Laing
F.H. Turner
A. Weymss
A.R. Ross
D. McL. Bain
J.B. McDougall
G.H.H.P. Maxwell
D.G. Donald

### v ENGLAND

**LOST 15-16**
Scotland: 1G 1DG 2T
Ireland: 2G 2T
Inverleith, 21 Mar 1914

W.M. Wallace

J.G. Will 2T
A.W. Angus
R.M. Scobie
† J.L. Huggan 1T

T.C. Bowie 1DG
* E. Milroy

A.D. Laing
F.H. Turner 1C
C.M. Usher
A.R. Ross
† I.M. Pender
A.W. Symington
G.H.H.P. Maxwell
† E.T. Young

### FACT FILE

- Scotland were defeated in all three matches in 1914, there being no game with the French.
- Andrew 'Jock' Wemyss won his first cap against Wales. Despite losing an eye in the war, he continued playing for Scotland in the 1920s, along with other 1914 caps Alex Angus, Allen Sloan, Andrew Hamilton, John McDougall, Charles Usher, 'Podger' Laing, John Hume and Patrick Maxwell.

### FINAL TABLE

| | P | W | D | L | F | A | Pts |
|---|---|---|---|---|---|---|---|
| England | 4 | 4 | 0 | 0 | 82 | 49 | 8 |
| Wales | 4 | 3 | 0 | 1 | 75 | 18 | 6 |
| Ireland | 4 | 2 | 0 | 2 | 29 | 34 | 4 |
| **Scotland** | **3** | **0** | **0** | **3** | **20** | **46** | **0** |
| France | 3 | 0 | 0 | 3 | 19 | 78 | 0 |

*Scotland and France did not meet*

## 1919-20

### Five Nations Championship

**v FRANCE**

**WON 5-0**
France: Nil
Scotland: 1G
Parc des Princes, 1 Jan 1920

† G.L. Pattullo

† G.B. Crole 1T
† E.C. Fahmy
* A.W. Angus
A.T. Sloan

A.S. Hamilton
J. Hume

† F. Kennedy
† R.A. Gallie
† D.D. Duncan
† W.A.K. Murray
A.D. Laing 1C
† G. Thom
C.M. Usher
A. Wemyss

**v WALES**

**WON 9-5**
Scotland: 2PG 1T
Wales: 1G
Inverleith, 7 Feb 1920

G.L. Pattullo

G.B. Crole
E.C. Fahmy
A.W. Angus
† E.B. Mackay

A.T. Sloan 1T
† J.A.R. Selby

F. Kennedy 2PG
R.A. Gallie
D.D. Duncan
† N.C. Macpherson
A.D. Laing
G. Thom
* C.M. Usher
G.H.H.P. Maxwell

**v IRELAND**

**WON 19-0**
Scotland: 2G 1PG 2T
Ireland: Nil
Inverleith, 28 Feb 1920

G.L. Pattullo

G.B. Crole 2T
A.T. Sloan
A.W. Angus 1T
† A. Browning 1T

E.C. Fahmy
J.A.R. Selby

F. Kennedy 1PG 2C
R.A. Gallie
D.D. Duncan
N.C. Macpherson
A.D. Laing
G. Thom
* C.M. Usher
W.A.K. Murray

**v ENGLAND**

**LOST 4-13**
England: 2G 1T
Scotland: 1DG
Twickenham, 20 Mar 1920

G.L. Pattullo

G.B. Crole
J.H. Bruce-Lockhart 1DG
A.W. Angus
A.T. Sloan

E.C. Fahmy
† C.S. Nimmo

F. Kennedy
R.A. Gallie
D.D. Duncan
N.C. Macpherson
G.H.H.P. Maxwell
A. Wemyss
* C.M. Usher
G. Thom

**FACT FILE**

- Scotland lost to England and the championship was thus shared with the Welsh and English.
- Patrick Maxwell was one of the largest forwards to play for Scotland before modern times. He measured over 6 foot and his weight exceeded 16 stones. He played 13 times between 1913 and 1922 and was noted for his remarkable kicking powers.

**FINAL TABLE**

| | P | W | D | L | F | A | Pts |
|---|---|---|---|---|---|---|---|
| Wales | 4 | 3 | 0 | 1 | 58 | 23 | 6 |
| **Scotland** | **4** | **3** | **0** | **1** | **37** | **18** | **6** |
| England | 4 | 3 | 0 | 1 | 40 | 37 | 6 |
| France | 4 | 1 | 0 | 3 | 23 | 26 | 2 |
| Ireland | 4 | 0 | 0 | 4 | 22 | 76 | 0 |

## 1920-21

### Five Nations Championship

**v FRANCE**

**LOST 0-3**
Scotland: Nil
France: 1T
Inverleith, 22 Jan 1921

† H.H. Forsayth

† J.H. Carmichael
† A.L. Gracie
† A.E. Thomson
† I.J. Kilgour

* A.T. Sloan
J. Hume

R.A. Gallie
† R.S. Cumming
† J.M. Bannerman
J.B. McDougall
A.D. Laing
W.A.K. Murray
G.H.H.P. Maxwell
N.C. Macpherson

**v WALES**

**WON 14-8**
Wales: 2DG
Scotland: 1G 1PG 2T
St Helens, 5 Feb 1921

H.H. Forsayth

A.T. Sloan 1T
A.L. Gracie
A.E. Thomson 1T
J.H. Carmichael

† R.L.H. Donald
* J. Hume

R.S. Cumming
† J.C.R. Buchanan 1T
J.M. Bannerman
R.A. Gallie
† G. Douglas
C.M. Usher
† J.N. Shaw
G.H.H.P. Maxwell 1C 1PG

**v IRELAND**

**LOST 8-9**
Ireland: 3T
Scotland: 1G 1T
Lansdowne Road, 26 Feb 1921

H.H. Forsayth

† J.W.S. McCrow
A.L. Gracie
A.T. Sloan
J.H. Carmichael

R.L.H. Donald
* J. Hume 2T

R.A. Gallie
J.C.R. Buchanan
J.M. Bannerman
J.B. McDougall
G.H.H.P. Maxwell 1C
† J.L. Stewart
J.N. Shaw
† G.M. Murray

**v ENGLAND**

**LOST 0-18**
Scotland: Nil
England: 3G 1T
Inverleith, 19 Mar 1921

H.H. Forsayth

A.T. Sloan
† C.J.G. Mackenzie
A.E. Thomson
A.L. Gracie

R.L.H. Donald
* J. Hume

R.A. Gallie
J.C.R. Buchanan
J.M. Bannerman
J.B. McDougall
F. Kennedy
C.M. Usher
G.H.H.P. Maxwell
N.C. Macpherson

**FACT FILE**

- The shock caused by the first French victory in Scotland was forgotten after the triumph at Swansea, Scotland's first win in Wales for 29 years.
- John Bannerman was the most illustrious of the Scottish newcomers. A teenager when first capped, he went on to win 37 caps and set a new appearance record for Scotland. A hard tackler and dynamic leader, he was the outstanding Scottish forward between the wars.

**FINAL TABLE**

| | P | W | D | L | F | A | Pts |
|---|---|---|---|---|---|---|---|
| England | 4 | 4 | 0 | 0 | 61 | 9 | 8 |
| France | 4 | 2 | 0 | 2 | 33 | 32 | 4 |
| Wales | 4 | 2 | 0 | 2 | 29 | 36 | 4 |
| **Scotland** | **4** | **1** | **0** | **3** | **22** | **38** | **2** |
| Ireland | 4 | 1 | 0 | 3 | 19 | 49 | 2 |

## 1921-22

### Five Nations Championship

**v FRANCE**

**DRAWN 3-3**
France: 1T
Scotland: 1T
Stade Colombes, 2 Jan 1922

† W.C. Johnston

A. Browning 1T
† G.P.S. Macpherson
A.L. Gracie
† E.H. Liddell

† J.C. Dykes
J. Hume

† A.K. Stevenson
† D.M. Bertram
A. Wemyss
J.M. Bannerman
† D.S. Davies
† J.R. Lawrie
* C.M. Usher
G.H.H.P. Maxwell

**v WALES**

**DRAWN 9-9**
Scotland: 1PG 2T
Wales: 1G 1DG
Inverleith, 4 Feb 1922

H.H. Forsayth

A. Browning 1PG 2T
† R.C. Warren
A.L. Gracie
E.H. Liddell

G.P.S. Macpherson
† W.E. Bryce

† W.G. Dobson
D.M. Bertram
A. Wemyss
J.M. Bannerman
D.S. Davies
J.R. Lawrie
* C.M. Usher
J.C.R. Buchanan

**v IRELAND**

**WON 6-3**
Scotland: 2T
Ireland: 1T
Inverleith, 25 Feb 1922

H.H. Forsayth

A. Browning
R.C. Warren
A.L. Gracie
E.H. Liddell 1T

G.P.S. Macpherson
W.E. Bryce 1T

W.G. Dobson
D.M. Bertram
A. Wemyss
J.M. Bannerman
D.S. Davies
J.R. Lawrie
* C.M. Usher
J.C.R. Buchanan

**v ENGLAND**

**LOST 5-11**
England: 1G 2T
Scotland: 1G
Twickenham, 18 Mar 1922

H.H. Forsayth

E.B. Mackay
G.P.S. Macpherson
A.L. Gracie
† J.M. Tolmie

J.C. Dykes 1T
W.E. Bryce

W.G. Dobson
D.M. Bertram 1C
J.C.R. Buchanan
J.M. Bannerman
D.S. Davies
J.R. Lawrie
* C.M. Usher
G.H.H.P. Maxwell

**FACT FILE**

- Eric Liddell, a notable debutant in the backs, was the subject of the film *Chariots of Fire*.

**FINAL TABLE**

| | P | W | D | L | F | A | Pts |
|---|---|---|---|---|---|---|---|
| Wales | 4 | 3 | 1 | 0 | 59 | 23 | 7 |
| England | 4 | 2 | 1 | 1 | 40 | 47 | 5 |
| **Scotland** | **4** | **1** | **2** | **1** | **23** | **26** | **4** |
| France | 4 | 0 | 2 | 2 | 20 | 33 | 2 |
| Ireland | 4 | 1 | 0 | 3 | 19 | 32 | 2 |

## 1922-23

### Five Nations Championship

**v FRANCE**

**WON 16-3**
Scotland: 2G 2T
France: 1GM
Inverleith, 20 Jan 1923

† D. Drysdale 2C

E.H. Liddell 1T
* A.L. Gracie
† E. McLaren 2T
† A.C. Wallace

† S.B. McQueen
W.E. Bryce 1T

† D.S. Kerr
D.M. Bertram
A.K. Stevenson
J.M. Bannerman
† L.M. Stuart
J.C.R. Buchanan
D.S. Davies
J.R. Lawrie

**v WALES**

**WON 11-8**
Wales: 1G 1PG
Scotland: 1G 2T
Cardiff Arms Park, 3 Feb 1923

D. Drysdale 1C

E.H. Liddell 1T
* A.L. Gracie 1T
E. McLaren
A. Browning

S.B. McQueen
W.E. Bryce

D.S. Kerr
D.M. Bertram
A.K. Stevenson
J.M. Bannerman
L.M. Stuart 1T
J.C.R. Buchanan
D.S. Davies
J.R. Lawrie

**v IRELAND**

**WON 13-3**
Ireland: 1T
Scotland: 2G 1T
Lansdowne Road, 24 Feb 1923

D. Drysdale

E.H. Liddell
* A.L. Gracie 1T
E. McLaren
A. Browning 1T 2C

S.B. McQueen 1T
W.E. Bryce

N.C. Macpherson
D.M. Bertram
J.C.R. Buchanan
J.M. Bannerman
L.M. Stuart
† R.S. Simpson
D.S. Davies
J.R. Lawrie

**v ENGLAND**

**LOST 6-8**
Scotland: 2T
England: 1G 1T
Inverleith, 17 Mar 1923

D. Drysdale

E.H. Liddell
* A.L. Gracie 1T
E. McLaren 1T
A. Browning

S.B. McQueen
W.E. Bryce

N.C. Macpherson
D.M. Bertram
J.C.R. Buchanan
J.M. Bannerman
L.M. Stuart
A.K. Stevenson
D.S. Davies
J.R. Lawrie

**FACT FILE**

- Altogether the backs were responsible for 11 of Scotland's 12 tries during the season.

**FINAL TABLE**

| | P | W | D | L | F | A | Pts |
|---|---|---|---|---|---|---|---|
| England | 4 | 4 | 0 | 0 | 50 | 17 | 8 |
| **Scotland** | **4** | **3** | **0** | **1** | **46** | **22** | **6** |
| Wales | 4 | 1 | 0 | 3 | 31 | 31 | 2 |
| France | 4 | 1 | 0 | 3 | 28 | 52 | 2 |
| Ireland | 4 | 1 | 0 | 3 | 21 | 54 | 2 |

## 1923-24

### Five Nations Championship

**v FRANCE**

**LOST 10-12**
France: 4T
Scotland: 1PG 1DG 1T
Stade Pershing, 1 Jan 1924

D. Drysdale

† C.E.W.C. Mackintosh
A.L. Gracie
E. McLaren
A.C. Wallace 1T

† H. Waddell 1DG
W.E. Bryce

† R.A. Howie
† A. Ross
D.S. Kerr
J.M. Bannerman
L.M. Stuart
† K.G.P. Hendrie
D.S. Davies 1PG
* J.C.R. Buchanan

**v WALES**

**WON 35-10**
Scotland: 4G 1PG 4T
Wales: 2G
Inverleith, 2 Feb 1924

D. Drysdale 1PG 4C

† I.S. Smith 3T
G.P.S. Macpherson 1T
† G.G. Aitken
A.C. Wallace 1T

H. Waddell 1T
W.E. Bryce 1T

R.A. Howie
D.M. Bertram 1T
A. Ross
J.M. Bannerman
* J.C.R. Buchanan
† A.C. Gillies
K.G.P. Hendrie
J.R. Lawrie

**v IRELAND**

**WON 13-8**
Scotland: 2G 1T
Ireland: 1G 1T
Inverleith, 23 Feb 1924

D. Drysdale 2C

I.S. Smith
G.G. Aitken
J.C. Dykes
† R.K. Millar

H. Waddell 2T
W.E. Bryce

R.A. Howie
D.M. Bertram 1T
† R.G. Henderson
J.M. Bannerman
* J.C.R. Buchanan
J.R. Lawrie
K.G.P. Hendrie
A.C. Gillies

**v ENGLAND**

**LOST 0-19**
England: 3G 1DG
Scotland: Nil
Twickenham, 15 Mar 1924

D. Drysdale

I.S. Smith
G.P.S. Macpherson
G.G. Aitken
A.C. Wallace

H. Waddell
W.E. Bryce

R.A. Howie
D.M. Bertram
D.S. Davies
J.M. Bannerman
R.G. Henderson
* J.C.R. Buchanan
A.C. Gillies
J.R. Lawrie

**FACT FILE**

- For the Welsh match at Inverleith Scotland fielded a club three-quarter line, Oxford University supplying Ian Smith (who on his debut romped away for three tries), George Aitken (who had been capped for New Zealand in 1921), 'Johnnie' Wallace (an Australian), and Phil Macpherson.
- Scotland's win over a weak Welsh side stands as the biggest ever Scottish victory over the Welsh.

**FINAL TABLE**

| | P | W | D | L | F | A | Pts |
|---|---|---|---|---|---|---|---|
| England | 4 | 4 | 0 | 0 | 69 | 19 | 8 |
| **Scotland** | **4** | **2** | **0** | **2** | **58** | **49** | **4** |
| Ireland | 4 | 2 | 0 | 2 | 30 | 37 | 4 |
| Wales | 4 | 1 | 0 | 3 | 39 | 71 | 2 |
| France | 4 | 1 | 0 | 3 | 25 | 45 | 2 |

## 1924-25

### Five Nations Championship

**v FRANCE**

**WON 25-4**
Scotland: 2G 5T
France: 1DG
Inverleith, 24 Jan 1925

D. Drysdale 1C

A.C. Wallace 2T
* G.P.S. Macpherson
G.G. Aitken
I.S. Smith 4T

J.C. Dykes
† J.B. Nelson

† W.H. Stevenson
† J. Gilchrist
J.C.R. Buchanan
J.M. Bannerman
† D.J. MacMyn
† J.R. Paterson
A.C. Gillies 1T 1C
† J.W. Scott

**v WALES**

**WON 24-14**
Wales: 1G 1PG 2T
Scotland: 1G 1DG 5T
St Helens, 7 Feb 1925

D. Drysdale 1DG 1C

A.C. Wallace 2T
* G.P.S. Macpherson
G.G. Aitken
I.S. Smith 4T

J.C. Dykes
J.B. Nelson

R.A. Howie
† J.C.H. Ireland
D.S. Davies
J.M. Bannerman
D.J. MacMyn
J.R. Paterson
A.C. Gillies
J.W. Scott

**v IRELAND**

**WON 14-8**
Ireland: 1G 1PG
Scotland: 2G 1DG
Lansdowne Road, 28 Feb 1925

* D. Drysdale 1C

A.C. Wallace 1T
G.G. Aitken
J.C. Dykes 1C
I.S. Smith

H. Waddell 1DG
J.B. Nelson

R.A. Howie
J.C.H. Ireland
D.S. Davies
J.M. Bannerman
D.J. MacMyn 1T
J.R. Paterson
J.C.R. Buchanan
J.W. Scott

**v ENGLAND**

**WON 14-11**
Scotland: 2G 1DG
England: 1G 1PG 1T
Murrayfield, 21 Mar 1925

D. Drysdale 1C

A.C. Wallace 1T
G.G. Aitken
* G.P.S. Macpherson
I.S. Smith

H. Waddell 1DG
J.B. Nelson 1T

R.A. Howie
J.C.H. Ireland
D.S. Davies
J.M. Bannerman
D.J. MacMyn
J.R. Paterson
A.C. Gillies 1C
J.W. Scott

**FACT FILE**

- Scotland won the Grand Slam for the first time in 1924-25.
- Ian Smith scored the last three tries of the French match and first three against Wales.
- The match with England was the first Test staged at Murrayfield.

**FINAL TABLE**

| | P | W | D | L | F | A | Pts |
|---|---|---|---|---|---|---|---|
| **Scotland** | **4** | **4** | **0** | **0** | **77** | **37** | **8** |
| Ireland | 4 | 2 | 1 | 1 | 42 | 26 | 5 |
| England | 4 | 2 | 1 | 1 | 42 | 37 | 5 |
| Wales | 4 | 1 | 0 | 3 | 34 | 60 | 2 |
| France | 4 | 0 | 0 | 4 | 23 | 58 | 0 |

## 1925-26

### Five Nations Championship

**v FRANCE**

**WON 20-6**
France: 1PG 1T
Scotland: 1G 1PG 4T
Stade Colombes, 2 Jan 1926

* D. Drysdale 1C

I.S. Smith
† R.M. Kinnear
J.C. Dykes
A.C. Wallace 3T

H. Waddell
J.B. Nelson

† W.V. Berkeley
J.C.H. Ireland
D.S. Davies
D.J. MacMyn 1T
J.M. Bannerman 1T
J.W. Scott
A.C. Gillies 1PG
J.R. Paterson

**v WALES**

**WON 8-5**
Scotland: 1G 1PG
Wales: 1G
Murrayfield, 6 Feb 1926

* D. Drysdale 1C

I.S. Smith
R.M. Kinnear
J.C. Dykes
† W.M. Simmers

H. Waddell 1T
J.B. Nelson

G.M. Murray
J.C.H. Ireland
D.S. Davies
D.J. MacMyn
J.M. Bannerman
J.W. Scott
A.C. Gillies 1PG
J.R. Paterson

**v IRELAND**

**LOST 0-3**
Scotland: Nil
Ireland: 1T
Murrayfield, 27 Feb 1926

* D. Drysdale

I.S. Smith
R.M. Kinnear
J.C. Dykes
W.M. Simmers

H. Waddell
J.B. Nelson

D.S. Kerr
J.C.H. Ireland
D.S. Davies
D.J. MacMyn
J.M. Bannerman
† J. Graham
J.W. Scott
J.R. Paterson

**v ENGLAND**

**WON 17-9**
England: 3T
Scotland: 2G 1DG 1T
Twickenham, 20 Mar 1926

* D. Drysdale

I.S. Smith 2T
J.C. Dykes 1DG
W.M. Simmers
† G.M. Boyd

H. Waddell 1T 2C
J.B. Nelson

D.S. Kerr
J.C.H. Ireland
D.S. Davies
D.J. MacMyn
J.M. Bannerman
J. Graham
J.W. Scott
J.R. Paterson

**FACT FILE**

- Scotland were champions again in 1926, though Ireland became the first international team to win at Murrayfield, and so prevented the Scots winning the Triple Crown.
- Ian Smith's two tries at Twickenham helped Scotland to their first victory at the ground, and their first win on English soil for 17 years.

**FINAL TABLE**

| | P | W | D | L | F | A | Pts |
|---|---|---|---|---|---|---|---|
| **Scotland** | **4** | **3** | **0** | **1** | **45** | **23** | **6** |
| Ireland | 4 | 3 | 0 | 1 | 41 | 26 | 6 |
| Wales | 4 | 2 | 1 | 1 | 26 | 24 | 5 |
| England | 4 | 1 | 1 | 2 | 38 | 39 | 3 |
| France | 4 | 0 | 0 | 4 | 11 | 49 | 0 |

## 1926-27

### Five Nations Championship

**v FRANCE**

**WON 23-6**
Scotland: 4G 1PG
France: 2T
Murrayfield, 22 Jan 1927

D. Drysdale 1C

I.S. Smith 2T
* G.P.S. Macpherson
J.C. Dykes
W.M. Simmers

H. Waddell 2T
J.B. Nelson

† J.W. Allan
J.C.H. Ireland
D.S. Davies
J.W. Scott
J.M. Bannerman
J.R. Paterson
A.C. Gillies 3C 1PG
J. Graham

**v WALES**

**WON 5-0**
Wales: Nil
Scotland: 1G
Cardiff Arms Park, 5 Feb 1927

D. Drysdale

† E.G. Taylor
* G.P.S. Macpherson
J.C. Dykes
W.M. Simmers

H. Waddell
J.B. Nelson

D.S. Kerr 1T
J.C.H. Ireland
D.S. Davies
J.W. Scott
J.M. Bannerman
J.R. Paterson
A.C. Gillies 1C
J. Graham

**v IRELAND**

**LOST 0-6**
Ireland: 2T
Scotland: Nil
Lansdowne Road, 26 Feb 1927

D. Drysdale

I.S. Smith
* G.P.S. Macpherson
J.C. Dykes
W.M. Simmers

H. Waddell
J.B. Nelson

D.S. Kerr
J.C.H. Ireland
D.S. Davies
J.W. Scott
J.M. Bannerman
J.R. Paterson
A.C. Gillies
J. Graham

**v ENGLAND**

**WON 21-13**
Scotland: 1G 1DG 4T
England: 2G 1PG
Murrayfield, 19 Mar 1927

* D. Drysdale

I.S. Smith 2T
G.P.S. Macpherson 1T
J.C. Dykes 1T
W.M. Simmers

H. Waddell 1DG
J.B. Nelson

D.S. Kerr
J.C.H. Ireland
J.W. Scott 1T
J.M. Bannerman
D.J. MacMyn
J.R. Paterson
A.C. Gillies 1C
J. Graham

**FACT FILE**

- Scotland again shared the championship, winning three matches but failing against Ireland.
- The Irish match in Dublin was played in the most awful conditions, and it was probably Ireland's luck in winning the toss which settled the match – their points coming before the teams were frozen rigid by a stiff wind carrying icy rain.

**FINAL TABLE**

| | P | W | D | L | F | A | Pts |
|---|---|---|---|---|---|---|---|
| **Scotland** | **4** | **3** | **0** | **1** | **49** | **25** | **6** |
| Ireland | 4 | 3 | 0 | 1 | 39 | 20 | 6 |
| England | 4 | 2 | 0 | 2 | 32 | 39 | 4 |
| Wales | 4 | 1 | 0 | 3 | 43 | 42 | 2 |
| France | 4 | 1 | 0 | 3 | 19 | 56 | 2 |

## 1927-28

### Tour Match

**v AUSTRALIA**

**WON 10-8**
Scotland: 2G
Australia: 1G 1T
Murrayfield, 17 Dec 1927

* D. Drysdale 2C

E.G. Taylor
† R.F. Kelly
J.C. Dykes
W.M. Simmers

† H.D. Greenlees
† P.S. Douty

† W.G. Ferguson
† W.N. Roughead
J.W. Scott
J.M. Bannerman
D.J. MacMyn
J. Graham 1T
† W.B. Welsh 1T
J.R. Paterson

### Five Nations Championship

**v FRANCE**

**WON 15-6**
France: 2T
Scotland: 5T
Stade Colombes, 2 Jan 1928

* D. Drysdale

G.P.S. Macpherson
R.F. Kelly
J.C. Dykes 2T
W.M. Simmers

H.D. Greenlees
P.S. Douty 1T

W.G. Ferguson
W.N. Roughead
W.B. Welsh
J.M. Bannerman
D.J. MacMyn
J. Graham
J.W. Scott 1T
J.R. Paterson 1T

**v WALES**

**LOST 0-13**
Scotland: Nil
Wales: 2G 1T
Murrayfield, 4 Feb 1928

D. Drysdale

† J. Goodfellow
G.P.S. Macpherson
R.F. Kelly
W.M. Simmers

H.D. Greenlees
P.S. Douty

W.G. Ferguson
W.N. Roughead
† J.H. Ferguson
* J.M. Bannerman
J.W. Scott
J.R. Paterson
W.B. Welsh
J. Graham

**v IRELAND**

**LOST 5-13**
Scotland: 1G
Ireland: 2G 1T
Murrayfield, 25 Feb 1928

* D. Drysdale 1C

J. Goodfellow
† J.W.G. Hume
J.C. Dykes
W.M. Simmers

† H. Lind
J.B. Nelson

J.W. Allan
W.N. Roughead
D.S. Kerr 1T
J.M. Bannerman
W.G. Ferguson
J. Graham
W.B. Welsh
J.R. Paterson

**v ENGLAND**

**LOST 0-6**
England: 2T
Scotland: Nil
Twickenham, 17 Mar 1928

* D. Drysdale

J. Goodfellow
G.P.S. Macpherson
W.M. Simmers
R.F. Kelly

† A.H. Brown
J.B. Nelson

L.M. Stuart
W.N. Roughead
D.S. Kerr
J.M. Bannerman
W.G. Ferguson
J. Graham
J.W. Scott
J.R. Paterson

**FACT FILE**

- The 'Waratahs', from Australia, captained by former cap 'Johnnie' Wallace, visited Scotland in 1927.
- Max Simmers gained 28 consecutive caps and also had the pleasure of watching his son Brian play for Scotland in the late 1960s.

**FINAL TABLE**

| | P | W | D | L | F | A | Pts |
|---|---|---|---|---|---|---|---|
| England | 4 | 4 | 0 | 0 | 41 | 22 | 8 |
| Ireland | 4 | 3 | 0 | 1 | 44 | 30 | 6 |
| Wales | 4 | 1 | 0 | 3 | 34 | 31 | 2 |
| France | 4 | 1 | 0 | 3 | 30 | 48 | 2 |
| **Scotland** | **4** | **1** | **0** | **3** | **20** | **38** | **2** |

## 1928-29

### Five Nations Championship

**v FRANCE**

**WON 6-3**
Scotland: 1PG 1T
France: 1T
Murrayfield, 19 Jan 1929

* D. Drysdale

I.S. Smith
G.G. Aitken
J.C. Dykes
W.M. Simmers

A.H. Brown 1PG
J.B. Nelson

† R.T. Smith
† H.S. Mackintosh
J.W. Allan
J.M. Bannerman
† J. Beattie
J.R. Paterson 1T
W.V. Berkeley
† K.M. Wright

**v WALES**

**LOST 7-14**
Wales: 1G 3T
Scotland: 1DG 1PG
St Helens, 2 Feb 1929

† T.G. Aitchison

I.S. Smith
† T.G. Brown
J.C. Dykes
W.M. Simmers

A.H. Brown 1DG 1PG
J.B. Nelson

R.T. Smith
H.S. Mackintosh
J.W. Allan
* J.M. Bannerman
J. Beattie
J.R. Paterson
W.V. Berkeley
K.M. Wright

**v IRELAND**

**WON 16-7**
Ireland: 1DG 1T
Scotland: 2G 2T
Lansdowne Road, 23 Feb 1929

T.G. Aitchison

I.S. Smith 1T
G.P.S. Macpherson 1T
J.C. Dykes 1C
W.M. Simmers 1T

H.D. Greenlees
J.B. Nelson

R.T. Smith
H.S. Mackintosh
J.W. Allan 1C
W.V. Berkeley
* J.M. Bannerman 1T
J.R. Paterson
W.B. Welsh
K.M. Wright

**v ENGLAND**

**WON 12-6**
Scotland: 4T
England: 2T
Murrayfield, 16 Mar 1929

T.G. Aitchison

I.S. Smith 2T
G.P.S. Macpherson
W.M. Simmers
† C.H.C. Brown 1T

H.D. Greenlees
J.B. Nelson 1T

R.T. Smith
H.S. Mackintosh
J.W. Allan
J.M. Scott
* J.M. Bannerman
J.R. Paterson
W.B. Welsh
K.M. Wright

**FACT FILE**

- Scotland were the champions again in 1929, though defeat at Swansea cost them the Triple Crown. Four of the forwards were drawn from the competitive teams of the Border league: Jock Beattie of Hawick, John Allan, the Melrose kicking specialist, Robert Smith of Kelso and another Hawick man, William Welsh.

**FINAL TABLE**

| | P | W | D | L | F | A | Pts |
|---|---|---|---|---|---|---|---|
| **Scotland** | **4** | **3** | **0** | **1** | **41** | **30** | **6** |
| Wales | 4 | 2 | 1 | 1 | 30 | 23 | 5 |
| Ireland | 4 | 2 | 1 | 1 | 24 | 26 | 5 |
| England | 4 | 2 | 0 | 2 | 35 | 27 | 4 |
| France | 4 | 0 | 0 | 4 | 12 | 36 | 0 |

## 1929-1930

### Five Nations Championship

**v FRANCE**

**LOST** **3-7**
France: 1DG 1T
Scotland: 1T
Stade Colombes, 1 Jan 1930

† R.W. Langrish

I.S. Smith
* G.P.S. Macpherson
J.W.G. Hume
W.M. Simmers **1T**

† W.D. Emslie
J.B. Nelson

R.T. Smith
H.S. Mackintosh
J.W. Allan
† J. Stewart
J.W. Scott
† F,H. Waters
† R. Rowand
W.B. Welsh

**v WALES**

**WON** **12-9**
Scotland: 1G 1DG 1T
Wales: 1G 1DG
Murrayfield, 1 Feb 1930

R.C. Warren

I.S. Smith
* G.P.S. Macpherson
† T.M. Hart
W.M. Simmers **2T**

H. Waddell **1DG**
J.B. Nelson

R.T. Smith
H.S. Mackintosh
† R.A. Foster
F.H. Waters **1C**
J. Beattie
† W.C.C. Agnew
R. Rowand
W.B. Welsh

**v IRELAND**

**LOST** **11-14**
Scotland: 1G 2T
Ireland: 1G 3T
Murrayfield, 22 Feb 1930

R.C. Warren

I.S. Smith
* G.P.S. Macpherson **1T**
W.M. Simmers
† D.J. St.C. Ford **1T**

T.M. Hart
J.B. Nelson

R.T. Smith
W.N. Roughead
H.S. Mackintosh
L.M. Stuart
W.C.C. Agnew
F.H. Waters **1T 1C**
J. Graham
W.B. Welsh

**v ENGLAND**

**DRAWN** **0-0**
England: Nil
Scotland: Nil
Twickenham, 15 Mar 1930

R.C. Warren

D.J. St.C. Ford
† J.E. Hutton
* G.P.S. Macpherson
W.M. Simmers

H.D. Greenlees
J.B. Nelson

H.S. Mackintosh
W.N. Roughead
J.W. Allan
L.M. Stuart
W.B. Welsh
F.H. Waters
J. Graham
† A.H. Polson

### FACT FILE

- Only one championship victory for Scotland meant that the wooden spoon went north for the first time since 1911.
- Herbert Waddell made a brief return to win his 15th and final cap against Wales. In the final minutes of the match he dropped a goal from in front of the posts to win the game. It was his fifth drop goal in internationals, creating a Scottish record.

### FINAL TABLE

| | P | W | D | L | F | A | Pts |
|---|---|---|---|---|---|---|---|
| England | 4 | 2 | 1 | 1 | 25 | 12 | 5 |
| Wales | 4 | 2 | 0 | 2 | 35 | 30 | 4 |
| Ireland | 4 | 2 | 0 | 2 | 25 | 31 | 4 |
| France | 4 | 2 | 0 | 2 | 17 | 25 | 4 |
| **Scotland** | **4** | **1** | **1** | **2** | **26** | **30** | **3** |

## 1930-31

### Five Nations Championship

**v FRANCE**

**WON 6-4**
Scotland: 2PG
France: 1DG
Murrayfield, 24 Jan 1931

R.W. Langrish

I.S. Smith
J.E. Hutton
† A.W. Wilson
W.M. Simmers

H. Lind
J.B. Nelson

J.W. Allan 2PG
* W.N. Roughead
H.S. Mackintosh
J. Beatie
† A. McLaren
† A.W. Walker
† J.S. Wilson
W.B. Welsh

**v WALES**

**LOST 8-13**
Wales: 2G 1T
Scotland: 1G 1T
Cardiff Arms Park, 7 Feb 1931

R.W. Langrish

I.S. Smith
G.P.S. Macpherson
W.M. Simmers
† G. Wood

H. Lind
J.E. Nelson

J.W. Allan 1C
* W.N. Roughead
H.S. Mackintosh
J. Beattie
A.W. Walker
† D. Crichton-Miller 2T
J.S. Wilson
W.B. Welsh

**v IRELAND**

**LOST 5-8**
Ireland: 1G 1T
Scotland: 1G
Lansdowne Road, 28 Feb 1931

R.W. Langrish

I.S. Smith
W.M. Simmers
A.W. Wilson
G. Wood

H. Lind
J.B. Nelson

J.W. Allan 1C
* W.N. Roughead
H.S. Mackintosh 1T
J. Beattie
A.W. Walker
D. Crichton-Miller
J.S. Wilson
W.B. Welsh

**v ENGLAND**

**WON 28-19**
Scotland: 5G 1T
England: 2G 1PG 2T
Murrayfield, 21 Mar 1931

A.W. Wilson

I.S. Smith 2T
* G.P.S. Macpherson
D.J. St.C. Ford 1T
W.M. Simmers

H. Lind
† W.R. Logan 1T

J.W. Allan 5C
W.N. Roughead
H.S. Mackintosh 2T
J. Beattie
A.W. Walker
D. Crichton-Miller
J.S. Wilson
W.B. Welsh

**FACT FILE**

- A huge crowd of 50,000 at Murrayfield saw the Scots gain a win over the French in perfect conditions.
- John Allan's place-kicking earned him a position in the record books this season, when his seven conversions (five against England) surpassed the previous record for a season. The record stood until Peter Dods kicked eight in 1984.

**FINAL TABLE**

| | P | W | D | L | F | A | Pts |
|---|---|---|---|---|---|---|---|
| Wales | 4 | 3 | 1 | 0 | 74 | 25 | 7 |
| **Scotland** | **4** | **2** | **0** | **2** | **47** | **44** | **4** |
| France | 4 | 2 | 0 | 2 | 24 | 44 | 4 |
| Ireland | 4 | 2 | 0 | 2 | 17 | 28 | 4 |
| England | 4 | 0 | 1 | 3 | 38 | 59 | 1 |

## 1931-32

### Tour Match

**v SOUTH AFRICA**

**LOST 3-6**
Scotland: 1T
SA: 2T
Murrayfield, 16 Jan 1932

† T.H.B. Lawther

I.S. Smith
G.P.S. Macpherson
* W.M. Simmers
† J.E. Forrest

H. Lind 1T
W.R. Logan

J.W. Allan
H.S. Mackintosh
R.A. Foster
J. Beattie
† M.S. Stewart
F.H. Waters
W.B. Welsh
J. Graham

### Four Nations Championship

**v WALES**

**LOST 0-6**
Scotland: Nil
Wales: 1PG 1T
Murrayfield, 6 Feb 1932

T.H.B. Lawther

I.S. Smith
* W.M. Simmers
D.J. St.C. Ford
G. Wood

H. Lind
W.R. Logan

H.S. Mackintosh
W.N. Roughead
J.W. Allan
J. Beattie
M.S. Stewart
F.H. Waters
W.B. Welsh
J. Graham

**v IRELAND**

**LOST 8-20**
Scotland: 1G 1T
Ireland: 4G
Murrayfield, 27 Feb 1932

† A.H.M. Hutton

* W.M. Simmers 1T
D.J. St.C. Ford
G. Wood 1T
I.S. Smith

W.D. Emslie
W.R. Logan

R.A. Foster
H.S. Mackintosh
J.W. Allan 1C
J. Beattie
M.S. Stewart
W.B. Welsh
F.H. Waters
A.W. Walker

**v ENGLAND**

**LOST 3-16**
England: 2G 2T
Scotland: 1T
Twickenham, 19 Mar 1932

† A.S. Dykes

I.S. Smith 1T
* G.P.S. Macpherson
G. Wood
W.M. Simmers

H. Lind
† J.P. Macarthur

R. Rowand
H.S. Mackintosh
R.A. Foster
J. Beattie
† F.A. Wright
J.S. Wilson
† G.F. Ritchie
W.B. Welsh

### FACT FILE

- Concerned about rumours of professionalism in France, the four home unions warned the FFR in February 1931 that unless the game was restored to amateur status France would be expelled from the Five Nations. Having failed to meet this ultimatum, the five nations became four nations from 1931-32 until 1946-47.
- Scotland crashed to their then worst defeat against Ireland, losing 8-20 at Murrayfield.

### FINAL TABLE

| | P | W | D | L | F | A | Pts |
|---|---|---|---|---|---|---|---|
| Ireland | 3 | 2 | 0 | 1 | 40 | 29 | 4 |
| Wales | 3 | 2 | 0 | 1 | 28 | 17 | 4 |
| England | 3 | 2 | 0 | 1 | 32 | 23 | 4 |
| **Scotland** | **3** | **0** | **0** | **3** | **11** | **42** | **0** |

## 1932-33

### Four Nations Championship

**v WALES**

**WON 11-3**
Wales: 1T
Scotland: 1G 1PG 1T
St Helens, 4 Feb 1933

† D.I. Brown

* I.S. Smith 1T
† H.D.B. Lorraine
H. Lind
† K.C. Fyfe 1PG 1C

† K.L.T. Jackson 1T
W.R. Logan

† J.A. Waters
† J.M. Ritchie
† J.R. Thom
J. Beattie
M.S. Stewart
R. Rowand
† J.McL. Henderson
W.B. Welsh

**v ENGLAND**

**WON 3-0**
Scotland: 1T
England: Nil
Murrayfield, 18 Mar 1933

D.I. Brown

* I.S. Smith
H.D.B. Lorraine
H. Lind
K.C. Fyfe 1T

K.L.T. Jackson
W.R. Logan

J.A. Waters
J.M. Ritchie
J.R. Thom
J. Beattie
M.S. Stewart
R. Rowand
J. McL. Henderson
W.B. Welsh

**v IRELAND**

**WON 8-6**
Ireland: 2T
Scotland: 2DG
Lansdowne Road, 1 Apr 1933

D.I. Brown

* I.S. Smith
H.D.B. Lorraine
H. Lind 1DG
† P.M.S. Gedge

K.L.T. Jackson 1DG
W.R. Logan

J.A. Waters
J.M. Ritchie
J.R. Thom
J. Beattie
M.S. Stewart
R. Rowand
J. McL. Henderson
W.B. Welsh

### FACT FILE

- This was Ian Smith's last season in international rugby, and he had the honour of leading the side to the Triple Crown. Smith retired with 24 tries in his 32 internationals, a total which was a world record for matches involving International Board nations for 54 years.
- An appalling blizzard caused the postponement of the Irish match in Dublin. The game was eventually played in April. Harry Lind's late drop goal gave the Scots the Triple Crown for the first time since 1925.

### FINAL TABLE

| | P | W | D | L | F | A | Pts |
|---|---|---|---|---|---|---|---|
| **Scotland** | **3** | **3** | **0** | **0** | **22** | **9** | **6** |
| Ireland | 3 | 1 | 0 | 2 | 22 | 30 | 2 |
| England | 3 | 1 | 0 | 2 | 20 | 16 | 2 |
| Wales | 3 | 1 | 0 | 2 | 15 | 24 | 2 |

## 1933-34

### Four Nations Championship

**v WALES**

**LOST 6-13**
Scotland: 1PG 1T
Wales: 2G 1T
Murrayfield, 3 Feb 1934

† K.W. Marshall

† R.W. Shaw
† R.C.S. Dick
* H. Lind
† J. Park

K.L.T. Jackson
W.R. Logan 1T

† W.A. Burnet
† L.B. Lambie
J.M. Ritchie 1PG
† J.D. Lowe
M.S. Stewart
R. Rowand
J.A. Waters
† D.A. Thom

**v IRELAND**

**WON 16-9**
Scotland: 2G 1PG 1T
Ireland: 3T
Murrayfield, 24 Feb 1934

K.W. Marshall

R.W. Shaw 1C
R.C.S. Dick 2T
H. Lind
† J.A. Crawford 1T

† J.L. Cotter
W.R. Logan

J.W. Allan 1PG 1C
† G.S. Cottington
J.M. Ritchie
J. Beattie
* M.S. Stewart
L.B. Lambie
J.A. Waters
† J.G. Watherston

**v ENGLAND**

**LOST 3-6**
England: 2T
Scotland: 1T
Twickenham, 17 Mar 1934

K.W. Marshall

R.W. Shaw 1T
R.C.S. Dick
H. Lind
K.C. Fyfe

J.L. Cotter
W.R. Logan

J.W. Allan
G.S. Cottington
J.M. Ritchie
J. Beattie
* M.S. Stewart
L.B. Lambie
J.A. Waters
J.G. Watherston

*Mark Stewart (middle row, with ball), in his last international match, leads the team at Twickenham in 1934.*

### FACT FILE

- David Brown had been an outstanding success at full-back during the Triple Crown year, but injuries dogged him in 1934 and he never again played for Scotland. Kenneth Marshall, the Edinburgh Academical who was South African by birth, proved an able deputy.

### FINAL TABLE

| | P | W | D | L | F | A | Pts |
|---|---|---|---|---|---|---|---|
| England | 3 | 3 | 0 | 0 | 28 | 6 | 6 |
| Wales | 3 | 2 | 0 | 1 | 26 | 15 | 4 |
| **Scotland** | **3** | **1** | **0** | **2** | **25** | **28** | **2** |
| Ireland | 3 | 0 | 0 | 3 | 12 | 42 | 0 |

## 1934-35

### Four Nations Championship

**v WALES**

**LOST 6-10**
Wales: 1DG 2T
Scotland: 2T
Cardiff Arms Park, 2 Feb 1935

K.W. Marshall

† W.G.S. Johnston
R.C.S. Dick
R.W. Shaw 1T
* K.C. Fyfe

† C.F. Grieve
W.R. Logan

† R.O. Murray
G.S. Cottington
† R.M. Grieve
J. Beattie
W.A. Burnet
L.B. Lambie
J.A. Waters
D.A. Thom 1T

**v IRELAND**

**LOST 5-12**
Ireland: 4T
Scotland: 1G
Lansdowne Road, 23 Feb 1935

K.W. Marshall

W.G.S. Johnston
R.C.S. Dick
H. Lind
K.C. Fyfe 1C

* R.W. Shaw 1T
W.R. Logan

† A.S.B. McNeil
G.S. Cottington
R.M. Grieve
J. Beattie
W.A. Burnet
L.B. Lambie
J.A. Waters
D.A. Thom

**v ENGLAND**

**WON 10-7**
Scotland: 2G
England: 1DG 1T
Murrayfield, 16 Mar 1935

K.W. Marshall

J.E. Forrest
R.C.S. Dick
† W.C.W. Murdoch
K.C. Fyfe 1T 2C

* R.W. Shaw
W.R. Logan

R.O. Murray
† P.W. Tait
R.M. Grieve
J. Beattie
W.A. Burnet
L.B. Lambie 1T
J.A. Waters
D.A. Thom

**FACT FILE**

- The selectors experimented with Wilson Shaw this season. Previously capped on the wing, he appeared at centre against Wales and was finally chosen in his best position, fly-half, for the two closing matches of the season.

**FINAL TABLE**

| | P | W | D | L | F | A | Pts |
|---|---|---|---|---|---|---|---|
| Ireland | 3 | 2 | 0 | 1 | 24 | 22 | 4 |
| England | 3 | 1 | 1 | 1 | 24 | 16 | 3 |
| Wales | 3 | 1 | 1 | 1 | 16 | 18 | 3 |
| **Scotland** | **3** | **1** | **0** | **2** | **21** | **29** | **2** |

## 1935-36

### Tour Match

**v NEW ZEALAND**

**LOST 8-18**
Scotland: 1G 1T
NZ: 3G 1T
Murrayfield, 23 Nov 1935

† J.M. Kerr

J.E. Forrest
R.C.S. Dick 1T
W.C.W. Murdoch 1C
K.C. Fyfe 1T

* R.W. Shaw
W.R. Logan

R.M. Grieve
† G.L. Gray
† G.D. Shaw
J. Beattie
W.A. Burnet
L.B. Lambie
J.A. Waters
D.A. Thom

### Four Nations Championship

**v WALES**

**LOST 3-13**
Scotland: 1T
Wales: 2G 1T
Murrayfield, 1 Feb 1936

K.W. Marshall

W.C.W. Murdoch
* R.C.S. Dick
† H.M. Murray 1T
K.C. Fyfe

R.W. Shaw
W.R. Logan

R.M. Grieve
† W.A.H. Druitt
J.A. Waters
J. Beattie
W.A. Burnet
† M. McG. Cooper
† P.L. Duff
G.D. Shaw

**v IRELAND**

**LOST 4-10**
Scotland: 1DG
Ireland: 1DG 2T
Murrayfield, 22 Feb 1936

J.M. Kerr

W.C.W. Murdoch 1DG
* R.C.S. Dick
H.M. Murray
† R.J.E. Whitworth

R.W. Shaw
W.R. Logan

R.M. Grieve
W.A.H. Druitt
J.A. Waters
J. Beattie
W.A. Burnet
M. McG. Cooper
P.L. Duff
† V.G. Weston

**v ENGLAND**

**LOST 8-9**
England: 3T
Scotland: 1G 1PG
Twickenham, 21 Mar 1936

J.M. Kerr

R.W. Shaw 1T
R.C.S. Dick
H. Lind
K.C. Fyfe 1PG 1C

C.F. Grieve
W.R. Logan

R.M. Grieve
G.S. Cottington
W.A.H. Druitt
* J. Beattie
W.A. Burnet
† R.W. Barrie
J.A. Waters
V.G. Weston

**FACT FILE**

- Scotland were unable to win a match in 1936.
- Two veterans, Harry Lind and Jock Beattie, played their final internationals against England. Beattie was given the captaincy for the day in the Calcutta Cup match.

**FINAL TABLE**

| | P | W | D | L | F | A | Pts |
|---|---|---|---|---|---|---|---|
| Wales | 3 | 2 | 1 | 0 | 16 | 3 | 5 |
| Ireland | 3 | 2 | 0 | 1 | 16 | 10 | 4 |
| England | 3 | 1 | 1 | 1 | 12 | 14 | 3 |
| **Scotland** | **3** | **0** | **0** | **3** | **15** | **32** | **0** |

## 1936-37

### Four Nations Championship

**v WALES**

**WON 13-6**
Wales: 2T
Scotland: 2G 1T
St Helens, 6 Feb 1937

J.M. Kerr

W.G.S. Johnston
R.C.S. Dick 2T
† D.J. Macrae
R.W. Shaw 1T

† W.A. Ross
* W.R. Logan

† M.M. Henderson
G.L. Gray
† W.M. Inglis
† G.B. Horsburgh
† C.L. Melville
† W.B. Young
J.A. Waters
G.D. Shaw 2C

**v IRELAND**

**LOST 4-11**
Ireland: 1G 2T
Scotland: 1DG
Lansdowne Road, 27 Feb 1937

J.M. Kerr

W.G.S. Johnston
† I. Shaw 1DG
D.J. Macrae
R.W. Shaw

† R.B. Bruce-Lockhart
* W.R. Logan

M.M. Henderson
G.L. Gray
W.M. Inglis
G.B. Horsburgh
C.L. Melville
W.B. Young
J.A. Waters
G.D. Shaw

**v ENGLAND**

**LOST 3-6**
Scotland: 1PG
England: 2T
Murrayfield, 20 Mar 1937

K.W. Marshall

W.G.S. Johnston
R.W. Shaw
D.J. Macrae
† R.H. Dryden

W.A. Ross
* W.R. Logan

M.M. Henderson
G.L. Gray
W.M. Inglis
G.B. Horsburgh
C.L. Melville
W.B. Young
J.A. Waters
G.D. Shaw 1PG

### FACT FILE

- Ross Logan, a veteran scrum-half, was Scotland's captain for 1937. He had succeeded Jimmy Nelson at the base of the scrum way back in 1931 and ended his international career after the English match, having won 20 caps.

### FINAL TABLE

| | P | W | D | L | F | A | Pts |
|---|---|---|---|---|---|---|---|
| England | 3 | 3 | 0 | 0 | 19 | 14 | 6 |
| Ireland | 3 | 2 | 0 | 1 | 24 | 16 | 4 |
| **Scotland** | **3** | **1** | **0** | **2** | **20** | **23** | **2** |
| Wales | 3 | 0 | 0 | 3 | 12 | 22 | 0 |

## 1937-38

### Four Nations Championship

**v WALES**

**WON 8-6**
Scotland: 1G 1PG
Wales: 2T
Murrayfield, 5 Feb 1938

† G. Roberts

† A.H. Drummond
R.C.S. Dick
D.J. Macrae
† J.G.S. Forrest

* R.W. Shaw
† T.F. Dorward

† J.B. Borthwick
† J.D.H. Hastie
W.M. Inglis
G.B. Horsburgh
† A. Roy
W.B. Young
P.L. Duff
† W.H. Crawford **1T 1C 1PG**

**v IRELAND**

**WON 23-14**
Scotland: 2G 1DG 1PG 2T
Ireland: 1G 3T
Murrayfield, 26 Feb 1938

G. Roberts

A.H. Drummond **1PG 1T**
R.C.S. Dick
D.J. Macrae **1T**
J.G.S. Forrest **2T**

* R.W. Shaw
T.F. Dorward **1DG**

J.B. Borthwick
J.D.H. Hastie
W.M. Inglis
G.B. Horsburgh
A. Roy
W.B. Young
P.L. Duff
W.H. Crawford **2C**

**v ENGLAND**

**WON 21-16**
England: 1DG 3PG 1T
Scotland: 2PG 5T
Twickenham, 19 Mar 1938

G. Roberts

† W.N. Renwick **2T**
R.C.S. Dick **1T**
D.J. Macrae
J.G.S. Forrest

* R.W. Shaw **2T**
T.F. Dorward

† W.F. Blackadder
J.D.H. Hastie
W.M. Inglis
G.B. Horsburgh
A. Roy
W.B. Young
P.L. Duff
W.H. Crawford **2PG**

**FACT FILE**

- Wilson Shaw, restored at fly-half, captained Scotland in 1938 and was a key member of the side which regained the Triple Crown.
- The Triple Crown match at Twickenham was played in perfect conditions before a crowd of 70,000 and was the first to be broadcast live on television.

**FINAL TABLE**

| | P | W | D | L | F | A | Pts |
|---|---|---|---|---|---|---|---|
| **Scotland** | **3** | **3** | **0** | **0** | **52** | **36** | **6** |
| Wales | 3 | 2 | 0 | 1 | 31 | 21 | 4 |
| England | 3 | 1 | 0 | 2 | 60 | 49 | 2 |
| Ireland | 3 | 0 | 0 | 3 | 33 | 70 | 0 |

## 1938-39

### Four Nations Championship

**v WALES**

**LOST 3-11**
Wales: 1G 1PG 1T
Scotland: 1PG
Cardiff Arms Park, 4 Feb 1939

G. Roberts

† J.B. Craig
D.J. Macrae
† J.R.S. Innes
W.N. Renwick

* R.W. Shaw
† W.R.C. Brydon

† G.H. Gallie
† R.W.F. Sampson
† W. Purdie
G.B. Horsburgh
A. Roy
W.B. Young
P.L. Duff
W.H. Crawford 1PG

**v IRELAND**

**LOST 3-12**
Ireland: 1PG 1GM 2T
Scotland: 1T
Lansdowne Road, 25 Feb 1939

† W.M. Penman

J.R.S. Innes 1T
D.J. Macrae
* R.W. Shaw
K.C. Fyfe

R.B. Bruce-Lockhart
T.F. Dorward

† I.C. Henderson
† I.N. Graham
W. Purdie
G.B. Horsburgh
A. Roy
W.B. Young
† D.K.A. Mackenzie
G.D. Shaw

**v ENGLAND**

**LOST 6-9**
Scotland: 2T
England: 3PG
Murrayfield, 18 Mar 1939

G. Roberts

J.R.S. Innes
D.J. Macrae
* R.W. Shaw 1T
W.C.W. Murdoch 1T

R.B. Bruce-Lockhart
T.F. Dorward

I.C. Henderson
I.N. Graham
W. Purdie
G.B. Horsburgh
A. Roy
W.B. Young
D.K.A. Mackenzie
W.H. Crawford

**FACT FILE**

- Five of the 1939 side survived to play in post-war official Tests: John Innes, 'Copey' Murdoch, Ralph Sampson, Ian Henderson and William Young.

**FINAL TABLE**

| | P | W | D | L | F | A | Pts |
|---|---|---|---|---|---|---|---|
| Wales | 3 | 2 | 0 | 1 | 18 | 6 | 4 |
| Ireland | 3 | 2 | 0 | 1 | 17 | 10 | 4 |
| England | 3 | 2 | 0 | 1 | 12 | 11 | 4 |
| **Scotland** | **3** | **0** | **0** | **3** | **12** | **32** | **0** |

## 1946-47

### Five Nations Championship

**v FRANCE**

**LOST 3-8**
France: 1G 1T
Scotland: 1PG
Stade Colombes, 1 Jan 1947

*† K.I. Geddes 1PG

† T.G.H. Jackson
† C.W. Drummond
† C.R. Bruce
† W.D. MacLennan

† I.J.M. Lumsden
† A.W. Black

† T.P.L. McGlashan
I.C. Henderson
† A.G.M. Watt
† G.L. Cawkwell
† J.M. Hunter
† W.I.D. Elliot
† D.W. Deas
† J.H. Orr

**v WALES**

**LOST 8-22**
Scotland: 1G 1PG
Wales: 2G 1PG 3T
Murrayfield, 1 Feb 1947

* K.I. Geddes 1C 1PG

T.G.H. Jackson
C.W. Drummond
C.R. Bruce
† D.D. Mackenzie

I.J.M. Lumsden
A.W. Black

I.C. Henderson
R.W.F. Sampson
† R. Aitken
D.W. Deas
† F.H. Coutts
W.I.D. Elliot 1T
A.G.M. Watt
J.H. Orr

**v IRELAND**

**LOST 0-3**
Scotland: Nil
Ireland: 1T
Murrayfield, 22 Feb 1947

K.I. Geddes

W.D. MacLennan
C.W. Drummond
C.R. Bruce
D.D. Mackenzie

*† W.H. Munro
† E. Anderson

T.P.L. McGlashan
† A.T. Fisher
† H.H. Campbell
A.G.M. Watt
F.H. Coutts
† D.D. Valentine
† J.B. Lees
† D.I. McLean

**v ENGLAND**

**LOST 5-24**
England: 4G 1DG
Scotland: 1G
Twickenham, 15 Mar 1947

K.I. Geddes 1C

T.G.H. Jackson 1T
C.W. Drummond
W.H. Munro
D.D. Mackenzie

* C.R. Bruce
E. Anderson

T.P.L. McGlashan
A.T. Fisher
H.H. Campbell
I.C. Henderson
F.H. Coutts
D.D. Valentine
D.I. McLean
W.I.D. Elliot

**FACT FILE**

- A high standard of combined play had made Scotland the outstanding performers in the unofficial 'Victory Internationals' of 1945-46, but they failed to reproduce such form in 1947, and all four matches were lost in the championship.
- Scotland's new wing-forwards were to enjoy successful rugby careers. Douglas Elliot played 29 times up to 1954.

**FINAL TABLE**

| | P | W | D | L | F | A | Pts |
|---|---|---|---|---|---|---|---|
| Wales | 4 | 3 | 0 | 1 | 37 | 17 | 6 |
| England | 4 | 3 | 0 | 1 | 39 | 36 | 6 |
| Ireland | 4 | 2 | 0 | 2 | 33 | 18 | 4 |
| France | 4 | 2 | 0 | 2 | 23 | 20 | 4 |
| **Scotland** | **4** | **0** | **0** | **4** | **16** | **57** | **0** |

## 1947-48

### Tour Match

**v AUSTRALIA**

**LOST 7-16**
Scotland: 1DG 1PG
Australia: 2G 2T
Murrayfield, 22 Nov 1947

I.J.M. Lumsden

T.G.H. Jackson
* J.R.S. Innes
† T. Wright
† C. McDonald 1PG

† D.P. Hepburn 1DG
† W.D. Allardice

† R.M. Bruce
† G.G. Lyall
I.C. Henderson
† L.R. Currie
† J.C. Dawson
W.I.D. Elliot
A.G.M. Watt
J.B. Lees

### Five Nations Championship

**v FRANCE**

**WON 9-8**
Scotland: 2PG 1T
France: 1G 1PG
Murrayfield, 24 Jan 1948

W.C.W. Murdoch 2PG

T.G.H. Jackson 1T
* J.R.S. Innes
C.W. Drummond
D.D. Mackenzie

D.P. Hepburn
W.D. Allardice

R.M. Bruce
G.G. Lyall
† W.P. Black
L.R. Currie
J.C. Dawson
W.I.D. Elliot
A.G.M. Watt
J.B. Lees

**v WALES**

**LOST 0-14**
Wales: 1G 1PG 2T
Scotland: Nil
Cardiff Arms Park, 7 Feb 1948

W.C.W. Murdoch

T.G.H. Jackson
* J.R.S. Innes
† A. Cameron
D.D. Mackenzie

D.P. Hepburn
W.D. Allardice

L.R. Currie
G.G. Lyall
R.M. Bruce
J.C. Dawson
W.P. Black
W.I.D. Elliot
A.G.M. Watt
J.B. Lees

**v IRELAND**

**LOST 0-6**
Ireland: 2T
Scotland: Nil
Lansdowne Road, 28 Feb 1948

W.C.W. Murdoch

T.G.H. Jackson
* J.R.S. Innes
C.W. Drummond
D.D. Mackenzie

D.P. Hepburn
W.D. Allardice

† S. Coltman
G.G. Lyall
I.C. Henderson
H.H. Campbell
L.R. Currie
W.I.D. Elliot
W.P. Black
R.M. Bruce

**v ENGLAND**

**WON 6-3**
Scotland: 2T
England: 1PG
Murrayfield, 20 Mar 1948

W.C.W. Murdoch

T.G.H. Jackson
* J.R.S. Innes
† L. Bruce-Lockhart
C.W. Drummond 1T

D.P. Hepburn
A.W. Black

H.H. Campbell
G.G. Lyall
I.C. Henderson
† R. Finlay
W.P. Black
W.I.D. Elliot
J.B. Lees
W.B. Young 1T

**FACT FILE**

- The assistance of two pre-war caps, John Innes and 'Copey' Murdoch, added experience to the side for the championship matches. Murdoch's international career thus spanned 14 seasons, a record for a Scot.

**FINAL TABLE**

| | P | W | D | L | F | A | Pts |
|---|---|---|---|---|---|---|---|
| Ireland | 4 | 4 | 0 | 0 | 36 | 19 | 8 |
| France | 4 | 2 | 0 | 2 | 40 | 25 | 4 |
| **Scotland** | **4** | **2** | **0** | **2** | **15** | **31** | **4** |
| Wales | 4 | 1 | 1 | 2 | 23 | 20 | 3 |
| England | 4 | 0 | 1 | 3 | 16 | 35 | 1 |

## 1948-49

### Five Nations Championship

**v FRANCE**

**WON 8-0**
France: Nil
Scotland: 1G 1T
Stade Colombes, 15 Jan 1949

I.J.M. Lumsden

T.G.H. Jackson
† L.G. Gloag
D.P. Hepburn
† D.W.C. Smith

C.R. Bruce
W.D. Allardice 1C

J.C. Dawson
† J.G. Abercrombie
S. Coltman
L.R. Currie
† G.A. Wilson
W.I.D. Elliot 1T
† P.W. Kininmonth 1T
*† D.H. Keller

**v WALES**

**WON 6-5**
Scotland: 2T
Wales: 1G
Murrayfield, 5 Feb 1949

I.J.M. Lumsden

T.G.H. Jackson
L.G. Gloag 1T
D.P. Hepburn
D.W.C. Smith 1T

C.R. Bruce
W.D. Allardice

J.C. Dawson
J.G. Abercrombie
S. Coltman
L.R. Currie
G.A. Wilson
W.I.D. Elliot
P.W. Kininmonth
* D.H. Keller

**v IRELAND**

**LOST 3-13**
Scotland: 1PG
Ireland: 2G 1PG
Murrayfield, 26 Feb 1949

I.J.M. Lumsden

T.G.H. Jackson
L.G. Gloag
D.P. Hepburn
D.W.C. Smith

C.R. Bruce
W.D. Allardice 1PG

J.C. Dawson
J.G. Abercrombie
S. Coltman
L.R. Currie
† A.M. Thomson
W.I.D. Elliot
P.W. Kininmonth
* D.H. Keller

**v ENGLAND**

**LOST 3-19**
England: 2G 3T
Scotland: 1PG
Twickenham, 19 Mar 1949

I.J.M. Lumsden

T.G.H. Jackson
L.G. Gloag
D.P. Hepburn
D.W.C. Smith

C.R. Bruce
W.D. Allardice

† S.T.H. Wright
† J.A.R. MacPhail
S. Coltman
L.R. Currie
G.A. Wilson 1PG
W.I.D. Elliot
P.W. Kininmonth
* D.H. Keller

**FACT FILE**

- Doug Keller, an Australian who had played against the Scots the previous season, became the new captain on his debut. Keller had returned to Britain following the 1947-48 Wallabies tour in order to study at Guy's Hospital.

**FINAL TABLE**

| | P | W | D | L | F | A | Pts |
|---|---|---|---|---|---|---|---|
| Ireland | 4 | 3 | 0 | 1 | 41 | 24 | 6 |
| England | 4 | 2 | 0 | 2 | 35 | 29 | 4 |
| France | 4 | 2 | 0 | 2 | 24 | 28 | 4 |
| **Scotland** | **4** | **2** | **0** | **2** | **20** | **37** | **4** |
| Wales | 4 | 1 | 0 | 3 | 17 | 19 | 2 |

## 1949-50

### Five Nations Championship

**v FRANCE**

**WON 8-5**
Scotland: 1G 1T
France: 1G
Murrayfield, 14 Jan 1950

† G. Burrell

D.W.C. Smith
† R. MacDonald 1T
† D.A. Sloan
C.W. Drummond

L. Bruce-Lockhart 1C
† A.F. Dorward

J.C. Dawson
J.G. Abercrombie
† G.M. Budge 1T
† R. Gemmill
† D.E. Muir
* W.I.D. Elliot
P.W. Kininmonth
D.H. Keller

**v WALES**

**LOST 0-12**
Wales: 1DG 1PG 2T
Scotland: Nil
St Helens, 4 Feb 1950

G. Burrell

D.W.C. Smith
R. MacDonald
D.A. Sloan
C.W. Drummond

L. Bruce-Lockhart
A.W. Black

J.C. Dawson
J.G. Abercrombie
G.M. Budge
R. Gemmill
D.E. Muir
* W.I.D. Elliot
P.W. Kininmonth
D.H. Keller

**v IRELAND**

**LOST 0-21**
Ireland: 3G 2PG
Scotland: Nil
Lansdowne Road, 25 Feb 1950

G. Burrell

† D.M. Scott
R. MacDonald
C.W. Drummond
D.W.C. Smith

A. Cameron
A.W. Black

J.C. Dawson
J.G. Abercrombie
G.M. Budge
R. Gemmill
D.E. Muir
* W.I.D. Elliot
P.W. Kininmonth
D.H. Keller

**v ENGLAND**

**WON 13-11**
Scotland: 2G 1T
England: 1G 1PG 1T
Murrayfield, 18 Mar 1950

† T. Gray 2C

D.M. Scott
R. MacDonald
D.A. Sloan 2T
C.W. Drummond

A. Cameron
A.W. Black

J.C. Dawson
J.G. Abercrombie 1T
G.M. Budge
R. Gemmill
D.E. Muir
W.I.D. Elliot
* P.W. Kininmonth
† H. Scott

**FACT FILE**

- George Burrell, who later became an international referee, was appointed manager for the 1977 British and Irish Lions tour, and served as president of the SRU in 1985-86.
- Scotland regained the Calcutta Cup. Tom Gray was a surprise choice as full-back for the match, for he had been playing club rugby for Northampton as a fly-half. Aged 33, he thus became the oldest first cap to play for Scotland.

**FINAL TABLE**

| | P | W | D | L | F | A | Pts |
|---|---|---|---|---|---|---|---|
| Wales | 4 | 4 | 0 | 0 | 50 | 8 | 8 |
| **Scotland** | **4** | **2** | **0** | **2** | **21** | **49** | **4** |
| Ireland | 4 | 1 | 1 | 2 | 27 | 12 | 3 |
| France | 4 | 1 | 1 | 2 | 14 | 35 | 3 |
| England | 4 | 1 | 0 | 3 | 22 | 30 | 2 |

## 1950-51

### Five Nations Championship

**v FRANCE**

**LOST 12-14**
France: 1G 2PG 1T
Scotland: 2PG 2T
Stade Colombes, 13 Jan 1951

T. Gray 2PG

† A.D. Cameron
† I.D.F. Coutts
† F.O. Turnbull
† D.M. Rose 2T

A. Cameron
† I.A. Ross

J.C. Dawson
† N.G.R. Mair
† R.L. Wilson
† H.M. Inglis
R. Gemmill
W.I.D. Elliot
* P.W. Kininmonth
† J.J. Hegarty

**v WALES**

**WON 19-0**
Scotland: 2G 1DG 1PG 1T
Wales: Nil
Murrayfield, 3 Feb 1951

† I.H.M. Thomson 1PG 1C

† R.A. Gordon 2T
D.A. Sloan
D.M. Scott
D.M. Rose

A. Cameron
I.A. Ross

J.C. Dawson 1T
N.G.R. Mair
R.L. Wilson
H.M. Inglis 1C
R. Gemmill
W.I.D. Elliot
* P.W. Kininmonth 1DG
† R.C. Taylor

**v IRELAND**

**LOST 5-6**
Scotland: 1G
Ireland: 1DG 1T
Murrayfield, 24 Feb 1951

I.H.M. Thomson 1C

† K.J. Dalgleish
D.A. Sloan 1T
D.M. Scott
D.M. Rose

A. Cameron
I.A. Ross

J.C. Dawson
N.G.R. Mair
R.L. Wilson
H.M. Inglis
R. Gemmill
W.I.D. Elliot
* P.W. Kininmonth
R.C. Taylor

**v ENGLAND**

**LOST 3-5**
England: 1G
Scotland: 1T
Twickenham, 17 Mar 1951

T. Gray

K.J. Dalgleish
D.A. Sloan
D.M. Scott
D.M. Rose

A. Cameron 1T
I.A. Ross

J.C. Dawson
N.G.R. Mair
R.L. Wilson
H.M. Inglis
W.P. Black
W.I.D. Elliot
* P.W. Kininmonth
R.C. Taylor

**FACT FILE**

- Scotland's sole win of the season, the massacre of Wales, was described as the most famous 'David and Goliath' act in international rugby history.
- Peter Kininmonth dropped a goal from beyond the Welsh 25. It was the turning point of the match and inspired the Scots to win by 19 points.

**FINAL TABLE**

| | P | W | D | L | F | A | Pts |
|---|---|---|---|---|---|---|---|
| Ireland | 4 | 3 | 1 | 0 | 21 | 16 | 7 |
| France | 4 | 3 | 0 | 1 | 41 | 27 | 6 |
| Wales | 4 | 1 | 1 | 2 | 29 | 35 | 3 |
| **Scotland** | **4** | **1** | **0** | **3** | **39** | **25** | **2** |
| England | 4 | 1 | 0 | 3 | 13 | 40 | 2 |

## 1951-52

### Tour Match

**v SOUTH AFRICA**

**LOST 0-44**
Scotland: Nil
SA: 7G 1DG 2T
Murrayfield, 24 Nov 1951

G. Burrell

† J.G.M. Hart
D.M. Scott
F.O. Turnbull
D.M. Rose

* A. Cameron
A.F. Dorward

J.C. Dawson
J.A.R. MacPhail
R.L. Wilson
† J. Johnston
H.M. Inglis
W.I.D. Elliot
P.W. Kininmonth
R.C. Taylor

### Five Nations Championship

**v FRANCE**

**LOST 11-13**
Scotland: 1G 2PG
France: 2G 1PG
Murrayfield, 12 Jan 1952

I.H.M. Thomson 2PG 1C

R.A. Gordon
† I.F. Cordial 1T
† J.L. Allan
D.M. Scott

† J.N.G. Davidson
† A.K. Fulton

J.C. Dawson
† N.M. Munnoch
† J. Fox
J. Johnston
† M. Walker
W.I.D. Elliot
* F.W. Kininmonth
† J.T. Greenwood

**v WALES**

**LOST 0-11**
Wales: 1G 2PG
Scotland: Nil
Cardiff Arms Park, 2 Feb 1952

I.H.M. Thomson

R.A. Gordon
I.F. Cordial
J.L. Allan
D.M. Scott

J.N.G. Davidson
A.F. Dorward

J.C. Dawson
N.M. Munnoch
J. Fox
J. Johnston
D.E. Muir
W.I.D. Elliot
H.M. Inglis
* P.W. Kininmonth

**v IRELAND**

**LOST 8-12**
Ireland: 1PG 3T
Scotland: 1G 1PG
Lansdowne Road, 23 Feb 1952

I.H.M. Thomson 1PG 1C

R.A. Gordon
I.F. Cordial
J.L. Allan
D.M. Scott

J.N.G. Davidson 1T
A.F. Dorward

J.C. Dawson
N.M. Munnoch
J. Fox
J. Johnston
D.E. Muir
W.I.D. Elliot
H.M. Inglis
* P.W. Kininmonth

**v ENGLAND**

**LOST 3-19**
Scotland: 1T
England: 2G 1DG 2T
Murrayfield, 15 Mar 1952

† N.W. Cameron

R.A. Gordon
I.F. Cordial
I.D.F. Coutts
† T.G. Weatherstone

J.N.G. Davidson
* A.F. Dorward

J.C. Dawson
J. Fox
† J.M. Inglis
J. Johnston 1T
D.E. Muir
W.I.D. Elliot
† J.P. Friebe
† D.S. Gilbert-Smith

### FACT FILE

- 1951-52 went down as Scotland's worst season on record. Five matches were lost, 99 points conceded, and Scotland's record defeat by South Africa was a rugby disaster which the nation took several years to overcome.
- John Hart, who won his only cap for Scotland in the match with the Springboks, went on to become honorary secretary of the International Board.

### FINAL TABLE

| | P | W | D | L | F | A | Pts |
|---|---|---|---|---|---|---|---|
| Wales | 4 | 4 | 0 | 0 | 42 | 14 | 8 |
| England | 4 | 3 | 0 | 1 | 34 | 14 | 6 |
| Ireland | 4 | 2 | 0 | 2 | 26 | 33 | 4 |
| France | 4 | 1 | 0 | 3 | 29 | 37 | 2 |
| **Scotland** | **4** | **0** | **0** | **4** | **22** | **55** | **0** |

## 1952-53

### Five Nations Championship

**v FRANCE**

**LOST 5-11**
France: 1G 1DG 1PG
Scotland: 1G
Stade Colombes, 10 Jan 1953

N.W. Cameron 1C

K.J. Dalgleish
D.M. Scott
D.A. Sloan
D.M. Rose 1T

J.N.G. Davidson
* A.F. Dorward

† B.E. Thomson
† J.H.F. King
R.L. Wilson
† J.H. Henderson
J.J. Hegarty
† A.R. Valentine
† D.C. McDonald
† K.H.D. McMillan

**v WALES**

**LOST 0-12**
Scotland: Nil
Wales: 1PG 3T
Murrayfield, 7 Feb 1953

N.W. Cameron

R.A. Gordon
K.J. Dalgleish
J.L. Allan
D.M. Rose

J.N.G. Davidson
* A.F. Dorward

B.E. Thomson
J.H.F. King
R.L. Wilson
J.H. Henderson
J.J. Hegarty
A.R. Valentine
D.C. McDonald
K.H.D. McMillan

**v IRELAND**

**LOST 8-26**
Scotland: 1G 1PG
Ireland: 4G 2T
Murrayfield, 28 Feb 1953

I.H.M. Thomson 1C

T.G. Weatherstone
* A. Cameron
† D. Cameron
D.W.C. Smith

L. Bruce-Lockhart
† K.M. Spence

B.E. Thomson
† G.C. Hoyer-Millar
† J.H. Wilson
J.H. Henderson 1T 1PG
J.J. Hegarty
A.R. Valentine
† E.H. Henriksen
K.H.D. McMillan

**v ENGLAND**

**LOST 8-26**
England: 4G 2T
Scotland: 1G 1T
Twickenham, 21 Mar 1953

I.H.M. Thomson 1C

T.G. Weatherstone 1T
* A. Cameron
D. Cameron
† J.S. Swan

L. Bruce-Lockhart
A.F. Dorward

J.C. Dawson
J.H.F. King
R.L. Wilson
J.H. Henderson 1T
J.J. Hegarty
† W. Kerr
† W.L.K. Cowie
K.H.D. McMillan

### FACT FILE

- Doctor Douglas Smith, a native of Aberdeen who played for London Scottish, won the last of his eight Scottish caps against Ireland. Later, in 1971, he was the manager of the victorious British and Irish Lions team which toured New Zealand.

### FINAL TABLE

| | P | W | D | L | F | A | Pts |
|---|---|---|---|---|---|---|---|
| England | 4 | 3 | 1 | 0 | 54 | 20 | 7 |
| Wales | 4 | 3 | 0 | 1 | 26 | 14 | 6 |
| Ireland | 4 | 2 | 1 | 1 | 54 | 25 | 5 |
| France | 4 | 1 | 0 | 3 | 17 | 38 | 2 |
| **Scotland** | **4** | **0** | **0** | **4** | **21** | **75** | **0** |

## 1953-54

### Five Nations Championship

**v FRANCE**

**LOST 0-3**
Scotland: Nil
France: 1T
Murrayfield, 9 Jan 1954

† J.C. Marshall

J.S. Swan
A.D. Cameron
D. Cameron
T.G. Weatherstone

* J.N.G. Davidson
A.K. Fulton

T.P.L. McGlashan
† R.K.G. MacEwen
† H.F. McLeod
† E.A.J. Fergusson
† E.J.S. Michie
† A. Robson
P.W. Kininmonth
J.H. Henderson

### Tour Match

**v NEW ZEALAND**

**LOST 0-3**
Scotland: Nil
NZ: 1PG
Murrayfield, 13 Feb 1954

J.C. Marshall

J.S. Swan
† M.K. Elgie
D. Cameron
T.G. Weatherstone

† G.T. Ross
† L.P. MacLachlan

T.P.L. McGlashan
R.K.G. MacEwen
H.F. McLeod
E.A.J. Fergusson
E.J.S. Michie
* W.I.D. Elliot
P.W. Kininmonth
J.H. Henderson

### Five Nations Championship

**v IRELAND**

**LOST 0-6**
Ireland: 2T
Scotland: Nil
Ravenhill, 27 Feb 1954

J.C. Marshall

J.S. Swan
M.K. Elgie
D. Cameron
T.G. Weatherstone

G.T. Ross
L.P. MacLachlan

T.P.L. McGlashan
R.K.G. MacEwen
H.F. McLeod
E.A.J. Fergusson
E.J.S. Michie
* W.I.D. Elliot
P.W. Kininmonth
J.H. Henderson

**v ENGLAND**

**LOST 3-13**
Scotland: 1T
England: 2G 1T
Murrayfield, 20 Mar 1954

J.C. Marshall

J.S. Swan
M.K. Elgie 1T
D. Cameron
T.G. Weatherstone

G.T. Ross
L.P. MacLachlan

T.P.L. McGlashan
J.H.F. King
H.F. McLeod
E.A.J. Fergusson
E.J.S. Michie
* W.I.D. Elliot
P.W. Kininmonth
J.H. Henderson

**v WALES**

**LOST 3-15**
Wales: 1PG 4T
Scotland: 1T
St Helens, 10 Apr 1954

J.C. Marshall

J.S. Swan
M.K. Elgie
A.D. Cameron
T.G. Weatherstone

G.T. Ross
L.P. MacLachlan

T.P.L. McGlashan
R.K.G. MacEwen
H.F. McLeod
E.A.J. Fergusson
† J.W.Y. Kemp
* W.I.D. Elliot
P.W. Kininmonth
J.H. Henderson 1T

### FACT FILE

- Kim Elgie, a South African who later played Test cricket against New Zealand, was a hard-running centre with the ability to kick goals.
- Another South African, 'Chick' Henderson, played the last of his nine internationals for Scotland against Wales. He later returned to South Africa and became well known for his broadcasts of South African rugby and cricket matches.

### FINAL TABLE

| | P | W | D | L | F | A | Pts |
|---|---|---|---|---|---|---|---|
| Wales | 4 | 3 | 0 | 1 | 52 | 34 | 6 |
| England | 4 | 3 | 0 | 1 | 39 | 23 | 6 |
| France | 4 | 3 | 0 | 1 | 35 | 22 | 6 |
| Ireland | 4 | 1 | 0 | 3 | 18 | 34 | 2 |
| **Scotland** | **4** | **0** | **0** | **4** | **6** | **37** | **0** |

## 1954-55

### Five Nations Championship

**v FRANCE**

**LOST 0-15**
France: 4T 1PG
Scotland: Nil
Stade Colombes, 8 Jan 1955

A. Cameron

J.S. Swan
M.K. Elgie
† M.L. Grant
T.G. Weatherstone

† J.T. Docherty
A.F. Dorward

H.F. McLeod
† W.K.L. Relph
† I.R. Hastie
J.J. Hegarty
J.W.Y. Kemp
† H. Duffy
* J.T. Greenwood
A. Robson

**v WALES**

**WON 14-8**
Scotland: 1G 1DG 1PG 1T
Wales: 1G 1T
Murrayfield, 5 Feb 1955

* A. Cameron

† A.R. Smith 1T
M.K. Elgie 1PG 1C
† R.G. Charters
J.S. Swan

J.T. Docherty 1DG
† J.A. Nichol 1T

H.F. McLeod
W.K.L. Relph
† T. Elliot
E.J.S. Michie
J.W.Y. Kemp
† W.S. Glen
J.T. Greenwood
A. Robson

**v IRELAND**

**WON 12-3**
Scotland: 1DG 2PG 1T
Ireland: 1PG
Murrayfield, 26 Feb 1955

† R.W.T. Chisholm

A.R. Smith
M.K. Elgie 2PG
R.G. Charters
J.S. Swan 1T

* A. Cameron 1DG
J.A. Nichol

H.F. McLeod
W.K.L. Relph
T. Elliot
E.J.S. Michie
J.W.Y. Kemp
† I.A.A. MacGregor
J.T. Greenwood
A. Robson

**v ENGLAND**

**LOST 6-9**
England: 1PG 2T
Scotland: 1PG 1T
Twickenham, 19 Mar 1955

R.W.T. Chisholm

A.R. Smith
M.K. Elgie
R.G. Charters
J.S. Swan

* A. Cameron 1PG 1T
J.A. Nichol

H.F. McLeod
W.K.L. Relph
T. Elliot
E.J.S. Michie
J.W.Y. Kemp
I.A.A. MacGregor
J.T. Greenwood
A. Robson

**FACT FILE**

- A long, grim series of defeats – 17 in all – ended with a triumph against a strong Welsh XV.
- Arthur Smith, on his debut, scored a brilliant try against the Welsh. He went on to win 33 caps for Scotland, captained the side 15 times, and retired after skippering the 1962 Lions to South Africa.
- Scotland beat Ireland for the first time since 1938.

**FINAL TABLE**

| | P | W | D | L | F | A | Pts |
|---|---|---|---|---|---|---|---|
| Wales | 4 | 3 | 0 | 1 | 48 | 28 | 6 |
| France | 4 | 3 | 0 | 1 | 47 | 28 | 6 |
| **Scotland** | **4** | **2** | **0** | **2** | **32** | **35** | **4** |
| England | 4 | 1 | 1 | 2 | 24 | 31 | 3 |
| Ireland | 4 | 0 | 1 | 3 | 15 | 44 | 1 |

## 1955-56

### Five Nations Championship

**v FRANCE**

**WON 12-0**
Scotland: 2PG 2T
France: Nil
Murrayfield, 14 Jan 1956

R.W.T. Chisholm

A.R. Smith 1PG
* A. Cameron 1PG
† K.R. MacDonald
J.S. Swan

M.L. Grant
† N.M. Campbell

H.F. McLeod
R.K.G. MacEwen
T. Elliot
E.J.S. Michie
J.W.Y. Kemp 2T
I.A.A. MacGregor
J.T. Greenwood
A. Robson

**v WALES**

**LOST 3-9**
Wales: 3T
Scotland: 1PG
Carciff Arms Park, 4 Feb 1956

R.W.T. Chisholm

A.R. Smith
* A. Cameron 1PG
K.R. MacDonald
J.S. Swan

M.L. Grant
N.M. Campbell

H.F. McLeod
R.K.G. MacEwen
T. Elliot
E.J.S. Michie
J.W.Y. Kemp
I.A.A. MacGregor
J.T. Greenwood
A. Robson

**v IRELAND**

**LOST 10-14**
Ireland: 1G 3T
Scotland: 2G
Lansdowne Road, 25 Feb 1956

R.W.T. Chisholm

A.R. Smith 1T
† T. McClung 2C
K.R. MacDonald
J.S. Swan

* A. Cameron
A.F. Dorward

H.F. McLeod
R.K.G. MacEwen
T. Elliot
E.J.S. Michie 1T
J.W.Y. Kemp
I.A.A. MacGregor
J.T. Greenwood
A. Robson

**v ENGLAND**

**LOST 6-11**
Scotland: 1PG 1T
England: 1G 2PG
Murrayfield, 17 Mar 1956

R.W.T. Chisholm

A.R. Smith 1PG
J.T. Docherty
† G.D. Stevenson 1T
J.S. Swan

T. McClung
A.F. Dorward

H.F. McLeod
R.K.G. MacEwen
T. Elliot
E.J.S. Michie
J.W.Y. Kemp
I.A.A. MacGregor
* J.T. Greenwood
A. Robson

**FACT FILE**

- The Scottish forwards, favouring the old-fashioned 3-2-3 scrummage formation, were unchanged throughout the season.

**FINAL TABLE**

| | P | W | D | L | F | A | Pts |
|---|---|---|---|---|---|---|---|
| Wales | 4 | 3 | 0 | 1 | 25 | 20 | 6 |
| England | 4 | 2 | 0 | 2 | 43 | 28 | 4 |
| Ireland | 4 | 2 | 0 | 2 | 33 | 47 | 4 |
| France | 4 | 2 | 0 | 2 | 31 | 34 | 4 |
| **Scotland** | **4** | **1** | **0** | **3** | **31** | **34** | **2** |

## 1956-57

### Five Nations Championship

**v FRANCE**

**WON 6-0**
France: Nil
Scotland: 1DG 1PG
Stade Colombes, 12 Jan 1957

† K.J.F. Scotland 1DG 1PG

A.R. Smith
† E. McKeating
G.D. Stevenson
J.S. Swan

M.L. Grant
A.F. Dorward

H.F. McLeod
R.K.G. MacEwen
T. Elliot
E.J.S. Michie
J.W.Y. Kemp
I.A.A. MacGregor
* J.T. Greenwood
A. Robson

**v WALES**

**WON 9-6**
Scotland: 1DG 1PG 1T
Wales: 1PG 1T
Murrayfield, 2 Feb 1957

K.J.F. Scotland 1PG

A.R. Smith 1T
E. McKeating
K.R. MacDonald
J.S. Swan

T. McClung
A.F. Dorward 1DG

H.F. McLeod
R.K.G. MacEwen
T. Elliot
E.J.S. Michie
J.W.Y. Kemp
I.A.A. MacGregor
* J.T. Greenwood
A. Robson

**v IRELAND**

**LOST 3-5**
Scotland: 1PG
Ireland: 1G
Murrayfield, 23 Feb 1957

K.J.F. Scotland 1PG

* A.R. Smith
T. McClung
K.R. MacDonald
† J.L.F. Allan

† J.M. Maxwell
A.F. Dorward

H.F. McLeod
R.K.G. MacEwen
T. Elliot
E.J.S. Michie
J.W.Y. Kemp
I.A.A. MacGregor
† G.K. Smith
A. Robson

**v ENGLAND**

**LOST 3-16**
England: 2G 1PG 1T
Scotland: 1PG
Twickenham, 16 Mar 1957

K.J.F. Scotland 1PG

A.R. Smith
T. McClung
K.R. MacDonald
J.L.F. Allan

† G.H. Waddell
A.F. Dorward

H.F. McLeod
R.K.G. MacEwen
T. Elliot
E.J.S. Michie
J.W.Y. Kemp
G.K. Smith
* J.T. Greenwood
A. Robson

**FACT FILE**

- Ken Scotland, a full-back from Heriot's FP, scored all of Scotland's points on his debut to become the first Scot since Bill Crawford in 1938 to score all the points in a win.
- The Scottish pack created a record in 1957, too. By playing together against France and Wales, they did so for the sixth time in internationals, a feat never achieved by any side prior to this date.

**FINAL TABLE**

| | P | W | D | L | F | A | Pts |
|---|---|---|---|---|---|---|---|
| England | 4 | 4 | 0 | 0 | 34 | 8 | 8 |
| Wales | 4 | 2 | 0 | 2 | 31 | 30 | 4 |
| **Scotland** | **4** | **2** | **0** | **2** | **21** | **21** | **4** |
| Ireland | 4 | 2 | 0 | 2 | 21 | 27 | 4 |
| France | 4 | 0 | 0 | 4 | 24 | 45 | 0 |

## 1957-58

### Five Nations Championship

**v FRANCE**

**WON 11-9**
Scotland: 1G 1PG 1T
France: 2PG 1T
Murrayfield, 11 Jan 1958

R.W.T. Chisholm 1PG 1C
* A.R. Smith
G.D. Stevenson 1T
J.T. Docherty
J.S. Swan
G.H. Waddell
† J.A.T. Rodd
H.F. McLeod
† N.S. Bruce
I.R. Hastie 1T
† M.W. Swan
J.W.Y. Kemp
G.K. Smith
J.T. Greenwood
† M.A. Robertson

**v WALES**

**LOST 3-8**
Wales: 1G 1T
Scotland: 1PG
Cardiff Arms Park, 1 Feb 1958

R.W.T. Chisholm
* A.R. Smith 1PG
G.D. Stevenson
J.T. Docherty
T.G. Weatherstone
G.H. Waddell
J.A.T. Rodd
H.F. McLeod
R.K.G. MacEwan
T. Elliot
M.W. Swan
J.W.Y. Kemp
G.K. Smith
J.T. Greenwood
A. Robson

### Tour Match

**v AUSTRALIA**

**WON 12-8**
Scotland: 2PG 2T
Australia: 1G 1T
Murrayfield, 15 Feb 1958

R.W.T. Chisholm
* A.R. Smith 2PG
G.D. Stevenson 1T
J.T. Docherty
T.G. Weatherstone 1T
G.H. Waddell
J.A.T. Rodd
H.F. McLeod
N.S. Bruce
T. Elliot
M.W. Swan
J.W.Y. Kemp
G.K. Smith
J.T. Greenwood
A. Robson

### Five Nations Championship

**v IRELAND**

**LOST 6-12**
Ireland: 2PG 2T
Scotland: 2T
Lansdowne Road, 1 Mar 1958

R.W.T. Chisholm
* A.R. Smith 1T
G.D. Stevenson
J.T. Docherty
T.G. Weatherstone 1T
G.H. Waddell
J.A.T. Rodd
H.F. McLeod
N.S. Bruce
T. Elliot
M.W. Swan
J.W.Y. Kemp
J.T. Greenwood
D.C. McDonald
A. Robson

**v ENGLAND**

**DRAWN 3-3**
Scotland: 1PG
England: 1PG
Murrayfield, 15 Mar 1958

K.J.F. Scotland
† C. Elliot 1PG
G.D. Stevenson
J.T. Docherty
T.G. Weatherstone
G.H. Waddell
J.A.T. Rodd
H.F. McLeod
N.S. Bruce
I.R. Hastie
M.W. Swan
J.W.Y. Kemp
* J.T. Greenwood
D.C. McDonald
A. Robson

### FACT FILE

- Arthur Smith's place-kicking changed the course of a close match with Australia. Australia were leading by 8-6 when Smith kicked a tremendous penalty goal from halfway early in the second half.
- Norman Bruce, an army officer, played the first of his 31 matches for Scotland against France. He retired as Scotland's most-capped hooker in 1964.

### FINAL TABLE

| | P | W | D | L | F | A | Pts |
|---|---|---|---|---|---|---|---|
| England | 4 | 2 | 2 | 0 | 26 | 6 | 6 |
| Wales | 4 | 2 | 1 | 1 | 26 | 28 | 5 |
| France | 4 | 2 | 0 | 2 | 36 | 37 | 4 |
| **Scotland** | **4** | **1** | **1** | **2** | **23** | **32** | **3** |
| Ireland | 4 | 1 | 0 | 3 | 24 | 32 | 2 |

## 1958-59

### Five Nations Championship

**v FRANCE**

**LOST 0-9**
France: 2DG 1T
Scotland: Nil
Stade Colombes, 10 Jan 1959

K.J.F. Scotland

A.R. Smith
T. McClung
† I.H.P. Laughland
C. Elliot

G.H. Waddell
† S. Coughtrie

H.F. McLeod
N.S. Bruce
I.R. Hastie
M.W. Swan
J.W.Y. Kemp
G.K. Smith
* J.T. Greenwood
A. Robson

**v WALES**

**WON 6-5**
Scotland: 1PG 1T
Wales: 1G
Murrayfield, 7 Feb 1959

K.J.F. Scotland **1PG**

A.R. Smith
T. McClung
G.D. Stevenson
T.G. Weatherstone

G.H. Waddell
S. Coughtrie

H.F. McLeod
N.S. Bruce **1T**
I.R. Hastie
M.W. Swan
J.W.Y. Kemp
G.K. Smith
* J.T. Greenwood
A. Robson

**v IRELAND**

**LOST 3-8**
Scotland: 1PG
Ireland: 1G 1PG
Murrayfield, 28 Feb 1959

K.J.F. Scotland **1PG**

A.R. Smith
T. McClung
G.D. Stevenson
T.G. Weatherstone

G.H. Waddell
S. Coughtrie

H.F. McLeod
N.S. Bruce
I.R. Hastie
M.W. Swan
J.W.Y. Kemp
G.K. Smith
* J.T. Greenwood
A. Robson

**v ENGLAND**

**DRAWN 3-3**
England: 1PG
Scotland: 1PG
Twickenham, 21 Mar 1959

K.J.F. Scotland **1PG**

A.R. Smith
† J.A.P. Shackleton
G.D. Stevenson
T.G. Weatherstone

* G.H. Waddell
S. Coughtrie

H.F. McLeod
N.S. Bruce
† D.M.D. Rollo
† F.H. ten Bos
J.W.Y. Kemp
G.K. Smith
† J.A. Davidson
A. Robson

**FACT FILE**

- Emergency measures were necessary before the Welsh match. A freeze had gripped the country at the start of February 1959, but thanks to an anti-freeze plan, the Murrayfield pitch was firm but playable on a cold day. At the end of the season the SRU laid an electric blanket at Murrayfield.

**FINAL TABLE**

| | P | W | D | L | F | A | Pts |
|---|---|---|---|---|---|---|---|
| France | 4 | 2 | 1 | 1 | 28 | 15 | 5 |
| Ireland | 4 | 2 | 0 | 2 | 23 | 19 | 4 |
| Wales | 4 | 2 | 0 | 2 | 21 | 23 | 4 |
| England | 4 | 1 | 2 | 1 | 9 | 11 | 4 |
| **Scotland** | **4** | **1** | **1** | **2** | **12** | **25** | **3** |

## 1959-60

### Five Nations Championship

**v FRANCE**

**LOST 11-13**
Scotland: 1G 1PG 1T
France: 2G 1T
Murrayfield, 9 Jan 1960

K.J.F. Scotland

* A.R. Smith 2T
† J.J. McPartlin
I.H.P. Laughland
C. Elliot 1PG 1C

† G. Sharp
J.A.T. Rodd

D.M.D. Rollo
N.S. Bruce
H.F. McLeod
F.H. ten Bos
J.W.Y. Kemp
G.K. Smith
† K.R.F. Bearne
A. Robson

**v WALES**

**LOST 0-8**
Wales: 1G 1PG
Scotland: Nil
Cardiff Arms Park, 6 Feb 1960

K.J.F. Scotland

* A.R. Smith
J.J. McPartlin
I.H.P. Laughland
G.D. Stevenson

T. McClung
J.A.T. Rodd

D.M.D. Rollo
N.S. Bruce
H.F. McLeod
F.H. ten Bos
J.W.Y. Kemp
G.K. Smith
K.R.F. Bearne
† C.E.B. Stewart

**v IRELAND**

**WON 6-5**
Ireland: 1G
Scotland: 1DG 1T
Lansdowne Road, 27 Feb 1960

K.J.F. Scotland 1DG

A.R. Smith
G.D. Stevenson
I.H.P. Laughland
† R.H. Thomson 1T

* G.H. Waddell
† R.B. Shillinglaw

D.M.D. Rollo
N.S. Bruce
H.F. McLeod
† T.O. Grant
J.W.Y. Kemp
G.K. Smith
J.A. Davidson
† D.B. Edwards

**v ENGLAND**

**LOST 12-21**
Scotland: 3PG 1T
England: 3G 1DG 1PG
Murrayfield, 19 Mar 1960

K.J.F. Scotland 3PG

A.R. Smith 1T
G.D. Stevenson
I.H.P. Laughland
R.H. Thomson

* G.H. Waddell
R.B. Shillinglaw

D.M.D. Rollo
N.S. Bruce
H.F. McLeod
T.O. Grant
J.W.Y. Kemp
G.K. Smith
J.A. Davidson
D.B. Edwards

### Tour Match

**v SOUTH AFRICA**

**LOST 10-18**
SA: 3G 1T
Scotland: 2G
Port Elizabeth, 30 Apr 1960

R.W.T. Chisholm

A.R. Smith 2C 1T
G.D. Stevenson
† P.J. Burnet
R.H. Thomson

* G.H. Waddell
R.B. Shillinglaw

D.M.D. Rollo
N.S. Bruce 1T
H.F. McLeod
F.H. ten Bos
J.W.Y. Kemp
† W. Hart
T.O. Grant
D.B. Edwards

**FACT FILE**

- The match in Dublin provided Scotland's second win over Ireland since the war, and it was their first success there since 1933.
- At the end of the season the Scots made a short tour to South Africa, becoming the first home nation to undertake such a trip.

**FINAL TABLE**

| | P | W | D | L | F | A | Pts |
|---|---|---|---|---|---|---|---|
| France | 4 | 3 | 1 | 0 | 55 | 28 | 7 |
| England | 4 | 3 | 1 | 0 | 46 | 26 | 7 |
| Wales | 4 | 2 | 0 | 2 | 32 | 39 | 4 |
| **Scotland** | **4** | **1** | **0** | **3** | **29** | **47** | **2** |
| Ireland | 4 | 0 | 0 | 4 | 25 | 47 | 0 |

## 1960-61

### Five Nations Championship

**v FRANCE**

**LOST 0-11**
France: 1G 1DG 1PG
Scotland: Nil
Stade Colombes, 7 Jan 1961

K.J.F. Scotland

A.R. Smith
† R.C. Cowan
G.D. Stevenson
R.H. Thomson

* G.H. Waddell
R.B. Shillinglaw

H.F. McLeod
N.S. Bruce
D.M.D. Rollo
F.H. ten Bos
† M.J. Campbell-Lamerton
G.K. Smith
† J. Douglas
C.E.B. Stewart

### Tour Match

**v SOUTH AFRICA**

**LOST 5-12**
Scotland: 1G
SA: 2PG 2T
Murrayfield, 21 Jan 1961

K.J.F. Scotland 1C

* A.R. Smith 1T
E. McKeating
G.D. Stevenson
R.H. Thomson

I.H.P. Laughland
R.B. Shillinglaw

H.F. McLeod
N.S. Bruce
D.M.D. Rollo
F.H. ten Bos
M.J. Campbell-Lamerton
G.K. Smith
J. Douglas
† K.I. Ross

### Five Nations Championship

**v WALES**

**WON 3-0**
Scotland: 1T
Wales: Nil
Murrayfield, 11 Feb 1961

K.J.F. Scotland

* A.R. Smith 1T
E. McKeating
G.D. Stevenson
R.H. Thomson

I.H.P. Laughland
† A.J. Hastie

H.F. McLeod
N.S. Bruce
D.M.D. Rollo
F.H. ten Bos
M.J. Campbell-Lamerton
G.K. Smith
J. Douglas
K.I. Ross

**v IRELAND**

**WON 16-8**
Scotland: 2G 1PG 1T
Ireland: 1G 1T
Murrayfield, 25 Feb 1961

K.J.F. Scotland 2C 1PG

* A.R. Smith
E. McKeating
G.D. Stevenson
R.H. Thomson

I.H.P. Laughland
A.J. Hastie

H.F. McLeod
N.S. Bruce
D.M.D. Rollo
F.H. ten Bos
M.J. Campbell-Lamerton
G.K. Smith
J. Douglas 1T
K.I. Ross 2T

**v ENGLAND**

**LOST 0-6**
England: 1PG 1T
Scotland: Nil
Twickenham, 18 Mar 1961

K.J.F. Scotland

* A.R. Smith
E. McKeating
G.D. Stevenson
R.H. Thomson

I.H.P. Laughland
A.J. Hastie

H.F. McLeod
N.S. Bruce
D.M.D. Rollo
F.H. ten Bos
J. Douglas
† J.C. Brash
G.K. Smith
K.I. Ross

### FACT FILE

- Scotland fielded only 20 players this season.
- Back-row forward John Douglas had a remarkable distinction in 1979: he was the owner of the Grand National winner Rubstic.

### FINAL TABLE

| | P | W | D | L | F | A | Pts |
|---|---|---|---|---|---|---|---|
| France | 4 | 3 | 1 | 0 | 39 | 14 | 7 |
| Wales | 4 | 2 | 0 | 2 | 21 | 14 | 4 |
| **Scotland** | **4** | **2** | **0** | **2** | **19** | **25** | **4** |
| England | 4 | 1 | 1 | 2 | 22 | 22 | 3 |
| Ireland | 4 | 1 | 0 | 3 | 22 | 48 | 2 |

## 1961-62

### Five Nations Championship

**v FRANCE**

**LOST 3-11**
Scotland: 1PG
France: IG 2PG
Murrayfield, 13 Jan 1962

K.J.F. Scotland

* A.R. Smith 1PG
J.J. McPartlin
I.H.P. Laughland
R.C. Cowan

G.H. Waddell
J.A.T. Rodd

H.F. McLeod
N.S. Bruce
D.M.D. Rollo
F.H. ten Bos
M.J. Campbell-Lamerton
† R.J.C. Glasgow
J. Douglas
K.I. Ross

**v WALES**

**WON 8-3**
Wales: 1DG
Scotland: IG 1T
Cardiff Arms Park, 3 Feb 1962

K.J.F. Scotland 1C

* A.R. Smith
J.J. McPartlin
I.H.P. Laughland
R.C. Cowan

G.H. Waddell
S. Coughtrie

H.F. McLeod
N.S. Bruce
D.M.D. Rollo
F.H. ten Bos 1T
M.J. Campbell-Lamerton
R.J.C. Glasgow 1T
J. Douglas
K.I. Ross

**v IRELAND**

**WON 20-6**
Ireland: 1PG 1T
Scotland: 1G 1DG 2PG 2T
Lansdowne Road, 24 Feb 1962

K.J.F. Scotland 2PG 1C

* A.R. Smith 2T
J.J. McPartlin
I.H.P. Laughland
R.C. Cowan 1T

G.H. Waddell
S. Coughtrie 1DG

H.F. McLeod
N.S. Bruce
† R. Steven
F.H. ten Bos
M.J. Campbell-Lamerton
R.J.C. Glasgow
J. Douglas
K.I. Ross

**v ENGLAND**

**DRAWN 3-3**
Scotland: 1PG
England: 1PG
Murrayfield, 17 Mar 1962

K.J.F. Scotland 1PG

* A.R. Smith
J.J. McPartlin
I.H.P. Laughland
R.C. Cowan

G.H. Waddell
S. Coughtrie

H.F. McLeod
N.S. Bruce
D.M.D. Rollo
F.H. ten Bos
M.J. Campbell-Lamerton
R.J.C. Glasgow
J. Douglas
K.I. Ross

**FACT FILE**

- Ron Glasgow made a name for himself by scoring Scotland's opening try in a famous victory in the mud at Cardiff where they had not won since 1927. Their five points – two wins and a draw – in the championship was the best Scottish performance in the competition since before the Second World War.
- Hugh McLeod finished his career with 40 caps to set a new Scottish cap record.

**FINAL TABLE**

| | P | W | D | L | F | A | Pts |
|---|---|---|---|---|---|---|---|
| France | 4 | 3 | 0 | 1 | 35 | 6 | 6 |
| **Scotland** | **4** | **2** | **1** | **1** | **34** | **23** | **5** |
| England | 4 | 1 | 2 | 1 | 19 | 16 | 4 |
| Wales | 4 | 1 | 2 | 1 | 9 | 11 | 4 |
| Ireland | 4 | 0 | 1 | 3 | 9 | 50 | 1 |

## 1962-63

### Five Nations Championship

**v FRANCE**

**WON 11-6**
France: 1DG 1PG
Scotland: 1G 1DG 1PG
Stade Colombes, 12 Jan 1963

* K.J.F. Scotland 1DG 1PG 1C

R.H. Thomson 1T
J.A.P. Shackleton
† D.M. White
G.D. Stevenson

I.H.P. Laughland
S. Coughtrie

† A.C.W. Boyle
N.S. Bruce
D.M.D. Rollo
F.H. ten Bos
M.J. Campbell-Lamerton
† W.R.A. Watherston
J. Douglas
K.I. Ross

**v WALES**

**LOST 0-6**
Scotland: Nil
Wales: 1DG 1PG
Stade Colombes, 2 Feb 1963

* K.J.F. Scotland

R.H. Thomson
J.A.P. Shackleton
D.M. White
G.D. Stevenson

I.H.P. Laughland
S. Coughtrie

A.C.W. Boyle
N.S. Bruce
D.M.D. Rollo
F.H. ten Bos
M.J. Campbell-Lamerton
W.R.A. Watherston
J. Douglas
K.I. Ross

**v IRELAND**

**WON 3-0**
Scotland: 1PG
Ireland: Nil
Murrayfield, 23 Feb 1963

† C.F. Blaikie

R.H. Thomson
I.H.P. Laughland
D.M. White
G.D. Stevenson

* K.J.F. Scotland
S. Coughtrie 1PG

A.C.W. Boyle
N.S. Bruce
D.M.D. Rollo
F.H. ten Bos
M.J. Campbell-Lamerton
W.R.A. Watherston
J. Douglas
R.J.C. Glasgow

**v ENGLAND**

**LOST 8-10**
England: 2G
Scotland: 1G 1DG
Twickenham, 16 Mar 1963

C.F. Blaikie

C. Elliot
† B.C. Henderson
D.M. White
R.H. Thomson

* K.J.F. Scotland 1DG
S. Coughtrie 1C

† J.B. Neill
N.S. Bruce
D.M.D. Rollo
F.H. ten Bos
M.J. Campbell-Lamerton
K.I. Ross
† J.P. Fisher
R.J.C. Glasgow 1T

**FACT FILE**

- There were seven London Scottish players in the side which gained a belated victory in Paris, Scotland's first there since 1957.

**FINAL TABLE**

| | P | W | D | L | F | A | Pts |
|---|---|---|---|---|---|---|---|
| England | 4 | 3 | 1 | 0 | 29 | 19 | 7 |
| France | 4 | 2 | 0 | 2 | 40 | 25 | 4 |
| **Scotland** | **4** | **2** | **0** | **2** | **22** | **22** | **4** |
| Ireland | 4 | 1 | 1 | 2 | 19 | 33 | 3 |
| Wales | 4 | 1 | 0 | 3 | 21 | 32 | 2 |

## 1963-64

### Five Nations Championship

**v FRANCE**

**WON 10-0**
Scotland: 2G
France: Nil
Murrayfield, 4 Jan 1964

† S. Wilson 2C

C. Elliot
B.C. Henderson
I.H.P. Laughland 1T
R.H. Thomson 1T

G. Sharp
J.A.T. Rodd

D.M.D. Rollo
N.S. Bruce
* J.B. Neill
† W.J. Hunter
† P.C. Brown
† J.W. Telfer
T.O. Grant
J.P. Fisher

### Tour Match

**v NEW ZEALAND**

**DRAWN 0-0**
Scotland: Nil
NZ: Nil
Murrayfield, 18 Jan 1964

S. Wilson

C. Elliot
J.A.P. Shackleton
I.H.P. Laughland
R.H. Thomson

G. Sharp
J.A.T. Rodd

D.M.D. Rollo
N.S. Bruce
* J.B. Neill
W.J. Hunter
P.C. Brown
J.W. Telfer
T.O. Grant
J.P. Fisher

### Five Nations Championship

**v WALES**

**LOST 3-11**
Wales: 1G 1PG 1T
Scotland: 1T
Cardiff Arms Park, 1 Feb 1964

S.Wilson

C.Elliot
J.A.P.Shackleton
I.H.P.Laughland 1T
R.H.Thomson

G.Sharp
J.A.T.Rodd

D.M.D.Rollo
N.S.Bruce
* J.B.Neill
W.J.Hunter
P.C.Brown
J.W.Telfer
T.O.Grant
J.P.Fisher

**v IRELAND**

**WON 6-3**
Ireland: 1PG
Scotland: 2PG
Lansdowne Road, 22 Feb 1964

S. Wilson 2PG

C. Elliot
B.C. Henderson
I.H.P. Laughland
† W.D. Jackson

† D.H. Chisholm
A.J. Hastie

D.M.D. Rollo
N.S. Bruce
* J.B. Neill
P.C. Brown
M.J. Campbell-Lamerton
J.W. Telfer
J.P. Fisher
R.J.C. Glasgow

**v ENGLAND**

**WON 15-6**
Scotland: 3G
England: 1PG 1T
Murrayfield, 21 Mar 1964

S. Wilson 3C

C. Elliot
B.C. Henderson
I.H.P. Laughland
G.D. Stevenson

D.H. Chisholm
A.J. Hastie

D.M.D. Rollo
N.S. Bruce 1T
* J.B. Neill
P.C. Brown
M.J. Campbell-Lamerton
J.P. Fisher
J.W. Telfer 1T
R.J.C. Glasgow 1T

### FACT FILE

- This was Scotland's most successful season since 1938. The Fifth All Blacks were held to a scoreless draw and the Scots also shared the championship with Wales.
- Scotland's 15-6 win at Murrayfield was their first against England since 1950.

### FINAL TABLE

| | P | W | D | L | F | A | Pts |
|---|---|---|---|---|---|---|---|
| Wales | 4 | 2 | 2 | 0 | 43 | 26 | 6 |
| **Scotland** | **4** | **3** | **0** | **1** | **34** | **20** | **6** |
| France | 4 | 1 | 1 | 2 | 41 | 33 | 3 |
| England | 4 | 1 | 1 | 2 | 23 | 42 | 3 |
| Ireland | 4 | 1 | 0 | 3 | 33 | 53 | 2 |

## 1964-65

### Five Nations Championship

**v FRANCE**

**LOST 8-16**
France: 2G 2T
Scotland: 1G 1T
Stade Colombes, 9 Jan 1965

K.J.F. Scotland 1C

C. Elliot
B.C. Henderson 2T
I.H.P. Laughland
G.D. Stevenson

† B.M. Simmers
J.A.T. Rodd

D.M.D. Rollo
† F.A.L. Laidlaw
* J.B. Neill
† P.K. Stagg
M.J. Campbell-Lamerton
J.P. Fisher
J.W. Telfer
† D. Grant

**v WALES**

**LOST 12-14**
Scotland: 2DG 2PG
Wales: 1G 2PG 1T
Murrayfield, 6 Feb 1965

S. Wilson 2PG

C. Elliot
B.C. Henderson
I.H.P. Laughland
† D.J. Whyte

B.M. Simmers 2DG
J.A.T. Rodd

D.M.D. Rollo
F.A.L. Laidlaw
† N. Suddon
P.K. Stagg
* M.J. Campbell-Lamerton
J.P. Fisher
J.W. Telfer
R.J.C. Glasgow

**v IRELAND**

**LOST 6-16**
Scotland: 1DG 1PG
Ireland: 2G 1DG 1T
Murrayfield, 27 Feb 1965

S. Wilson 1PG

C. Elliot
B.C. Henderson
J.A.P. Shackleton
D.J. Whyte

I.H.P. Laughland 1DG
J.A.T. Rodd

D.M.D. Rollo
F.A.L. Laidlaw
N. Suddon
P.C. Brown
* M.J. Campbell-Lamerton
J.P. Fisher
J.W. Telfer
R.J.C. Glasgow

**v ENGLAND**

**DRAWN 3-3**
England: 1T
Scotland: 1DG
Twickenham, 20 Mar 1965

* S. Wilson

D.J. Whyte
B.C. Henderson
I.H.P. Laughland
W.D. Jackson

D.H. Chisholm 1DG
A.J. Hastie

D.M.D. Rollo
F.A.L. Laidlaw
N. Suddon
P.K. Stagg
M.J. Campbell-Lamerton
J.P. Fisher
P.C. Brown
D. Grant

### Tour Match

**v SOUTH AFRICA**

**WON 8-5**
Scotland: 1G 1DG
SA: 1G
Murrayfield, 17 Apr 1965

* S. Wilson 1C

D.J. Whyte
J.A.P. Shackleton 1T
I.H.P. Laughland
W.D. Jackson

D.H. Chisholm 1DG
A.J. Hastie

D.M.D. Rollo
F.A.L. Laidlaw
N. Suddon
P.K. Stagg
M.J. Campbell-Lamerton
J.P. Fisher
P.C. Brown
D. Grant

**FACT FILE**

- David Chisholm and Alex Hastie confirmed their promise as Scotland's finest half-back pair in 1964-65. The Melrose club pair were selected on 13 occasions: twice more than the Glasgow Academical pair of Jimmy Nelson and Herbert Waddell in the 1920s. Chisholm's winning drop goal against South Africa gave Scotland their first win over the Springboks since 1906.
- At 6 foot 10 inches Peter Stagg became the tallest man ever to play Test rugby.

**FINAL TABLE**

| | P | W | D | L | F | A | Pts |
|---|---|---|---|---|---|---|---|
| Wales | 4 | 3 | 0 | 1 | 55 | 45 | 6 |
| France | 4 | 2 | 1 | 1 | 47 | 33 | 5 |
| Ireland | 4 | 2 | 1 | 1 | 32 | 23 | 5 |
| England | 4 | 1 | 1 | 2 | 15 | 28 | 3 |
| **Scotland** | **4** | **0** | **1** | **3** | **29** | **49** | **1** |

## 1965-66

### Five Nations Championship

**v FRANCE**

**DRAWN 3-3**
Scotland: 1T
France: 1PG
Murrayfield, 15 Jan 1966

* S. Wilson

† A.J.W. Hinshelwood
B.C. Henderson
I.H.P. Laughland
D.J. Whyte 1T

D.H. Chisholm
A.J. Hastie

D.M.D. Rollo
F.A.L. Laidlaw
† J.D. MacDonald
P.K. Stagg
M.J. Campbell-Lamerton
J.P. Fisher
J.W. Telfer
D. Grant

**v WALES**

**LOST 3-8**
Wales: 1G 1T
Scotland: 1PG
Cardiff Arms Park, 5 Feb 1966

* S. Wilson 1PG

A.J.W. Hinshelwood
B.C. Henderson
I.H.P. Laughland
D.J. Whyte

† J.W.C. Turner
A.J. Hastie

D.M.D. Rollo
F.A.L. Laidlaw
J.D. MacDonald
P.K. Stagg
M.J. Campbell-Lamerton
J.P. Fisher
J.W. Telfer
D. Grant

**v IRELAND**

**WON 11-3**
Ireland: 1PG
Scotland: 1G 2T
Lansdowne Road, 26 Feb 1966

S. Wilson 1C

A.J.W. Hinshelwood 2T
B.C. Henderson
* I.H.P. Laughland
D.J. Whyte

D.H. Chisholm
A.J. Hastie

D.M.D. Rollo
F.A.L. Laidlaw
J.D. MacDonald
P.K. Stagg
M.J. Campbell-Lamerton
J.P. Fisher
J.W. Telfer
D. Grant 1T

**v ENGLAND**

**WON 6-3**
Scotland: 1PG 1T
England: 1DG
Murrayfield, 19 Mar 1966

C.F. Blaikie 1PG

A.J.W. Hinshelwood
B.C. Henderson
* I.H.P. Laughland
D.J. Whyte 1T

D.H. Chisholm
A.J. Hastie

D.M.D. Rollo
F.A.L. Laidlaw
J.D. MacDonald
P.K. Stagg
M.J. Campbell-Lamerton
J.P. Fisher
J.W. Telfer
D. Grant

**FACT FILE**

- The Scottish pack was unchanged during the championship for the first time since 1956.

**FINAL TABLE**

| | P | W | D | L | F | A | Pts |
|---|---|---|---|---|---|---|---|
| Wales | 4 | 3 | 0 | 1 | 34 | 26 | 6 |
| France | 4 | 2 | 1 | 1 | 35 | 18 | 5 |
| **Scotland** | **4** | **2** | **1** | **1** | **23** | **17** | **5** |
| Ireland | 4 | 1 | 1 | 2 | 24 | 34 | 3 |
| England | 4 | 0 | 1 | 3 | 15 | 36 | 1 |

## 1966-67

### Tour Match

**v AUSTRALIA**

**WON 11-5**
Scotland: 1G 1PG 1T
Australia: 1G
Murrayfield, 17 Dec 1966

S. Wilson 1PG 1C

A.J.W. Hinshelwood
J.W.C. Turner
B.M. Simmers
D.J. Whyte

D.H. Chisholm 1T
A.J. Hastie

N. Suddon
F.A.L. Laidlaw
D.M.D. Rollo
P.K. Stagg
P.C. Brown
* J.P. Fisher
† A.H.W. Boyle 1T
D. Grant

### Five Nations Championship

**v FRANCE**

**WON 9-8**
France: 1G 1T
Scotland: 2PG 1DG
Stade Colombes, 14 Jan 1967

S. Wilson 2PG

A.J.W. Hinshelwood
J.W.C. Turner
B.M. Simmers 1DG
D.J. Whyte

D.H. Chisholm
A.J. Hastie

J.D. MacDonald
F.A.L. Laidlaw
D.M.D. Rollo
P.K. Stagg
W.J. Hunter
* J.P. Fisher
A.H.W. Boyle
D. Grant

**v WALES**

**WON 11-5**
Scotland: 1G 1PG 1T
Wales: 1G
Murrayfield, 4 Feb 1967

S. Wilson 1C

A.J.W. Hinshelwood 1T
J.W.C. Turner
B.M. Simmers
D.J. Whyte

D.H. Chisholm 1DG
A.J. Hastie

J.D. MacDonald
F.A.L. Laidlaw
D.M.D. Rollo
P.K. Stagg
W.J. Hunter
* J.P. Fisher
J.W. Telfer 1T
D. Grant

**v IRELAND**

**LOST 3-5**
Scotland: 1PG
Ireland: 1G
Murrayfield, 25 Feb 1967

S. Wilson 1PG

A.J.W. Hinshelwood
J.W.C. Turner
† R.B. Welsh
D.J. Whyte

B.M. Simmers
A.J. Hastie

J.D. MacDonald
F.A.L. Laidlaw
† A.B. Carmichael
P.K. Stagg
W.J. Hunter
* J.P. Fisher
J.W. Telfer
D. Grant

**v ENGLAND**

**LOST 14-27**
England: 3G 2PG 1DG 1T
Scotland: 1G 2PG 1T
Twickenham, 18 Mar 1967

S. Wilson 2PG 1C

A.J.W. Hinshelwood 1T
J.W.C. Turner 1T
R.B. Welsh
D.J. Whyte

I.H.P. Laughland
† I.G. McCrae

J.D. MacDonald
F.A.L. Laidlaw
D.M.D. Rollo
P.K. Stagg
W.J. Hunter
* J.P. Fisher
J.W. Telfer
D. Grant

### FACT FILE

- Scotland's loose trio of Pringle Fisher, Jim Telfer and Derek Grant were an experienced unit who played together through eight internationals.

### FINAL TABLE

| | P | W | D | L | F | A | Pts |
|---|---|---|---|---|---|---|---|
| France | 4 | 3 | 0 | 1 | 55 | 41 | 6 |
| England | 4 | 2 | 0 | 2 | 68 | 67 | 4 |
| **Scotland** | **4** | **2** | **0** | **2** | **37** | **45** | **4** |
| Ireland | 4 | 2 | 0 | 2 | 17 | 22 | 4 |
| Wales | 4 | 1 | 0 | 3 | 53 | 55 | 2 |

## 1967-68

### Tour Match

**v NEW ZEALAND**

**LOST 3-14**
Scotland: 1DG
NZ: 1G 2PG 1T
Murrayfield, 2 Dec 1967

S.Wilson

A.J.W. Hinshelwood
J.W.C. Turner
† J.N.M. Frame
† R.R. Keddie

D.H. Chisholm 1DG
A.J. Hastie

A.B. Carmichael
F.A.L. Laidlaw
D.M.D. Rollo
P.K. Stagg
† G.W.E. Mitchell
* J.P. Fisher
A.H.W. Boyle
D. Grant

### Five Nations Championship

**v FRANCE**

**LOST 6-8**
Scotland: 1PG 1T
France: 1G 1T
Murrayfield, 13 Jan 1968

S. Wilson 1PG

A.J.W. Hinshelwood
J.W.C. Turner
J.N.M. Frame
† G.J. Keith 1T

D.H. Chisholm
A.J. Hastie

A.B. Carmichael
F.A.L. Laidlaw
D.M.D. Rollo
P.K. Stagg
G.W.E. Mitchell
* J.P. Fisher
A.H.W. Boyle
D. Grant

**v WALES**

**LOST 0-5**
Wales: 1G
Scotland: Nil
Cardiff Arms Park, 3 Feb 1968

S. Wilson

A.J.W. Hinshelwood
J.W.C. Turner
J.N.M. Frame
G.J. Keith

D.H. Chisholm
A.J. Hastie

A.B. Carmichael
F.A.L. Laidlaw
D.M.D. Rollo
P.K. Stagg
G.W.E. Mitchell
* J.P. Fisher
A.H.W. Boyle
† T.G. Elliot

**v IRELAND**

**LOST 6-14**
Ireland: 1G 1PG 2T
Scotland: 2PG
Lansdowne Road, 24 Feb 1968

S. Wilson 2PG

A.J.W. Hinshelwood
J.W.C. Turner
J.N.M. Frame
† C.G. Hodgson

D.H. Chisholm
I.G. McCrae

A.B. Carmichael
F.A.L. Laidlaw
D.M.D. Rollo
P.K. Stagg
† A.F. McHarg
* J.P. Fisher
A.H.W. Boyle
† R.J. Arneil

**v ENGLAND**

**LOST 6-8**
Scotland: 1PG 1DG
England: 1G 1PG
Murrayfield, 16 Mar 1968

S. Wilson 1PG

A.J.W. Hinshelwood
J.W.C. Turner
J.N.M. Frame
C.G. Hodgson

† I. Robertson
† G.C. Connell 1DG

A.B. Carmichael
† D.T. Deans
N. Suddon
P.K. Stagg
A.F. McHarg
J.P. Fisher
* J.W. Telfer
R.J. Arneil

### FACT FILE

- This was Scotland's most disappointing season for 14 years. All five matches were lost, there were 11 new caps introduced during the season, and altogether 26 different players appeared in Scotland's internationals.
- David Rollo, a durable farmer from the Howe of Fife club, appeared in the last of his 40 internationals for Scotland when he played against Ireland. He thus equalled Hugh McLeod's record number of caps for Scotland.

### FINAL TABLE

| | P | W | D | L | F | A | Pts |
|---|---|---|---|---|---|---|---|
| France | 4 | 4 | 0 | 0 | 52 | 30 | 8 |
| Ireland | 4 | 2 | 1 | 1 | 38 | 37 | 5 |
| England | 4 | 1 | 2 | 1 | 37 | 40 | 4 |
| Wales | 4 | 1 | 1 | 2 | 31 | 34 | 3 |
| **Scotland** | **4** | **0** | **0** | **4** | **18** | **35** | **0** |

## 1968-69

### Tour Match

**v AUSTRALIA**

**WON 9-3**
Scotland: 2PG 1T
Australia: 1PG
Murrayfield, 2 Nov 1968

C.F. Blaikie **2PG**

A.J.W. Hinshelwood **1T**
J.W.C. Turner
† C.W.W. Rea
W.D. Jackson

† C.M. Telfer
G.C. Connell

N. Suddon
F.A.L. Laidlaw
A.B. Carmichael
P.K. Stagg
A.F. McHarg
T.G. Elliot
* J.W. Telfer
R.J. Arneil

### Five Nations Championship

**v FRANCE**

**WON 6-3**
France: 1PG
Scotland: 1PG 1T
Stade Colombes, 11 Jan 1969

C.F. Blaikie **1PG**

A.J.W. Hinshelwood
J.W.C. Turner
C.W.W. Rea
W.D. Jackson

C.M. Telfer
G.C. Connell [1]

N. Suddon
F.A.L. Laidlaw
A.B. Carmichael
P.K. Stagg
A.F. McHarg
T.G. Elliot
* J.W. Telfer **1T**
R.J. Arneil

1 Rep by I.G. McCrae

**v WALES**

**LOST 3-17**
Scotland: 1PG
Wales: 1G 2PG 2T
Murrayfield, 1 Feb 1969

C.F. Blaikie **1PG**

A.J.W. Hinshelwood
J.N.M. Frame
C.W.W. Rea
W.D. Jackson

C.M. Telfer
I.G. McCrae

N. Suddon
F.A.L. Laidlaw
A.B. Carmichael
P.K. Stagg
A.F. McHarg
T.G. Elliot
* J.W. Telfer
R.J. Arneil

**v IRELAND**

**LOST 0-16**
Scotland: Nil
Ireland: 2G 2T
Murrayfield, 22 Feb 1969

C.F. Blaikie

A.J.W. Hinshelwood
J.N.M. Frame
C.W.W. Rea [1]
W.D. Jackson

C.M. Telfer
† R.C. Allan

N. Suddon
F.A.L. Laidlaw
A.B. Carmichael
P.C. Brown
A.F. McHarg
† W. Lauder
* J.W. Telfer [2]
R.J. Arneil

1 Rep by † W.G. McDonald
2 Rep by P.K. Stagg

**v ENGLAND**

**LOST 3-8**
England: 1G 1T
Scotland: 1PG
Twickenham, 15 Mar 1969

C.F. Blaikie

† W.C.C. Steele
J.N.M. Frame
I. Robertson
W.D. Jackson

C.M. Telfer
G.C. Connell

† J. McLauchlan
F.A.L. Laidlaw
A.B. Carmichael
P.C. Brown **1PG**
A.F. McHarg
W. Lauder
* J.W. Telfer
R.J. Arneil

### FACT FILE

- In the match against Australia, Scotland brought to an end a sequence of seven consecutive international defeats.
- Gordon McCrae became the first replacement used by Scotland when he substituted for Connell in the first half against France.

### FINAL TABLE

| | P | W | D | L | F | A | Pts |
|---|---|---|---|---|---|---|---|
| Wales | 4 | 3 | 1 | 0 | 79 | 31 | 7 |
| Ireland | 4 | 3 | 0 | 1 | 61 | 48 | 6 |
| England | 4 | 2 | 0 | 2 | 54 | 58 | 4 |
| **Scotland** | **4** | **1** | **0** | **3** | **12** | **44** | **2** |
| France | 4 | 0 | 1 | 3 | 28 | 53 | 1 |

## 1969-70

### Tour Match

**v SOUTH AFRICA**

**WON 6-3**
Scotland: 1T 1PG
S.Africa: 1PG
Murrayfield, 6 Dec 1969

† I.S.G. Smith 1PG 1T

† A.G. Biggar
J.N.M. Frame
C.W.W. Rea
A.J.W. Hinshelwood

I. Robertson
† D.S. Paterson

J. McLauchlan
F.A.L. Laidlaw
A.B. Carmichael
P.K. Stagg
† G.L. Brown
W. Lauder
* J.W. Telfer
R.J. Arneil

### Five Nations Championship

**v FRANCE**

**LOST 9-11**
Scotland: 2PG 1T
France: 1G 1DG 1T
Murrayfield, 10 Jan 1970

I.S.G. Smith 1T

A.G. Biggar
J.N.M. Frame
C.W.W. Rea
A.J.W. Hinshelwood

I. Robertson
G.C. Connell

J. McLauchlan
F.A.L. Laidlaw
A.B. Carmichael
P.K. Stagg
G.L. Brown
W. Lauder 2PG
* J.W. Telfer
R.J. Arneil

**v WALES**

**LOST 9-18**
Wales: 3G 1T
Scotland: 1DG 1PG 1T
Cardiff Arms Park, 7 Feb 1970

I.S.G. Smith

† M.A. Smith
J.N.M. Frame
C.W.W. Rea
A.J.W. Hinshelwood

I. Robertson 1T 1DG
† R.G. Young

J. McLauchlan
F.A.L. Laidlaw
A.B. Carmichael
P.K. Stagg
P.C. Brown [1]
W. Lauder 1PG
* J.W. Telfer
R.J. Arneil

1 Rep by G.L. Brown

**v IRELAND**

**LOST 11-16**
Ireland: 2G 2T
Scotland: 1G 1DG 1T
Lansdowne Road, 28 Feb 1970

I.S.G. Smith 1C

M.A. Smith 1T
J.N.M. Frame
C.W.W. Rea
A.G. Biggar

I. Robertson 1DG
D.S. Paterson

N. Suddon
F.A.L. Laidlaw
A.B. Carmichael
P.K. Stagg
G.L. Brown
W. Lauder 1T
* J.W. Telfer
R.J. Arneil

**v ENGLAND**

**WON 14-5**
Scotland: 1G 2PG 1T
England: 1G
Murrayfield, 21 Mar 1970

I.S.G. Smith

M.A. Smith
J.N.M. Frame
J.W.C. Turner 1T
A.G. Biggar 1T

I. Robertson
D.S. Paterson

N. Suddon
* F.A.L. Laidlaw
A.B. Carmichael
P.K. Stagg
G.L. Brown
T.G. Elliot
P.C. Brown 2PG 1C
R.J. Arneil

### FACT FILE

- Scotland shared the wooden spoon in 1970, despite beating the Sixth Springboks. Ian Smith gained the distinction of becoming the first full-back to score a try for Scotland.
- Gordon Brown had the unusual distinction of coming on as a replacement for his brother Peter in Cardiff.
- Scotland made a short tour of Australia in the summer of 1970.

### FINAL TABLE

| | P | W | D | L | F | A | Pts |
|---|---|---|---|---|---|---|---|
| France | 4 | 3 | 0 | 1 | 60 | 33 | 6 |
| Wales | 4 | 3 | 0 | 1 | 46 | 42 | 6 |
| Ireland | 4 | 2 | 0 | 2 | 33 | 28 | 4 |
| **Scotland** | **4** | **1** | **0** | **3** | **43** | **50** | **2** |
| England | 4 | 1 | 0 | 3 | 40 | 69 | 2 |

## 1969-70 continued

### Tour Match

**v AUSTRALIA**

**LOST 3-23**
Australia: 1G 1PG 5T
Scotland: 1PG
Sydney C.G., 6 Jun 1970

J.W.C. Turner

M.A. Smith
J.N.M. Frame
C.W.W. Rea
A.G. Biggar

I. Robertson
D.S. Paterson

N. Suddon
* F.A.L. Laidlaw
A.B. Carmichael
P.K. Stagg
G.L. Brown
W. Lauder 1PG
† G.K. Oliver
R.J. Arneil

*Billy Steele (left) and Ian McLauchlan, who made their international debuts against England at Twickenham in 1969.*

## 1970-71

### Five Nations Championship

**v FRANCE**

**LOST 8-13**
France: 2G 1PG
Scotland: 1G 1PG
Stade Colombes, 16 Jan 1971

I.S.G. Smith 1PG [1]

W.C.C. Steele 1T
J.N.M. Frame
C.W.W. Rea
A.G. Biggar

J.W.C. Turner
D.S. Paterson

J. McLauchlan
F.A.L. Laidlaw
A.B. Carmichael
A.F. McHarg
G.L. Brown
† N.A. MacEwan
* P.C. Brown 1C
R.J. Arneil

1 Rep by B.M. Simmers

**v WALES**

**LOST 18-19**
Scotland: 4PG 2T
Wales: 2G 1PG 2T
Murrayfield, 6 Feb 1971

I.S.G. Smith

W.C.C. Steele
J.N.M. Frame
C.W.W. Rea 1T
A.G. Biggar

J.W.C. Turner
D.S. Paterson

J. McLauchlan
F.A.L. Laidlaw
A.B. Carmichael 1T
A.F. McHarg
G.L. Brown
N.A. MacEwan
* P.C. Brown 4PG
R.J. Arneil

**v IRELAND**

**LOST 5-17**
Scotland: 1G
Ireland: 1G 2PG 2T
Murrayfield, 27 Feb 1971

I.S.G. Smith

W.C.C. Steele
J.N.M. Frame 1T
A.G. Biggar
† R.S.M. Hannah

J.W.C. Turner
D.S. Paterson

J. McLauchlan
F.A.L. Laidlaw
A.B. Carmichael
A.F. McHarg
G.L. Brown
N.A. MacEwan
* P.C. Brown 1C
R.J. Arneil

## 1970-71 continued

### Five Nations Championship

**1st v ENGLAND**

**WON 16-15**
England: 3PG 2T
Scotland: 2G 1DG 1T
Twickenham, 20 Mar 1971

† A.R.Brown

W.C.C.Steele
J.N.M.Frame [1]
C.W.W.Rea 1T
A.G.Biggar

J.W.C.Turner
D.S.Paterson 1T 1DG

J.McLauchlan
† Q.Dunlop
A.B.Carmichael
A.F.McHarg
G.L.Brown
N.A.MacEwan
* P.C.Brown 1T 2C
R.J.Arneil

1 Rep by † A.S. Turk

### Centenary Match

**2nd v ENGLAND**

**WON 26-6**
Scotland: 4G 1PG 1T
England: 1DG 1PG
Murrayfield, 27 Mar 1971

A.R.Brown 4C

W.C.C.Steele 1T
J.N.M.Frame 2T
C.W.W.Rea 1T
A.G.Biggar

J.W.C.Turner
D.S.Paterson

J.McLauchlan
Q.Dunlop
A.B.Carmichael
A.F.McHarg
G.L.Brown [1]
N.A.MacEwan
* P.C.Brown 1T 1PG
R.J.Arneil

1 Rep by † G.M. Strachan

**FACT FILE**

- At Twickenham, Chris Rea's last-minute try was converted by Brown for the Scots to secure their first win in England since 1938. To prove that this win was no fluke, the Scots hammered England a week later in a celebration match to mark the centenary of international rugby.

**FINAL TABLE**

| | P | W | D | L | F | A | Pts |
|---|---|---|---|---|---|---|---|
| Wales | 4 | 4 | 0 | 0 | 73 | 38 | 8 |
| France | 4 | 1 | 2 | 1 | 41 | 40 | 4 |
| England | 4 | 1 | 1 | 2 | 44 | 58 | 3 |
| Ireland | 4 | 1 | 1 | 2 | 41 | 46 | 3 |
| **Scotland** | **4** | **1** | **0** | **3** | **47** | **64** | **2** |

## 1971-72

### Five Nations Championship

**v FRANCE**

**WON 20-9**
Scotland: 1G 1PG 1DG 2T
France: 1G 1PG
Murrayfield, 15 Jan 1972

A.R. Brown 1C

W.C.C. Steele
J.N.M. Frame 1T
† J.M. Renwick 1T
A.G. Biggar

C.M. Telfer 1T 1DG
I.G. McCrae [1]

J. McLauchlan
† R.L. Clark
A.B. Carmichael
A.F. McHarg
G.L. Brown
N.A. MacEwan
* P.C. Brown 1PG
R.J. Arneil

1 Rep by † A.J.M. Lawson

**v WALES**

**LOST 12-35**
Wales: 3G 3PG 2T
Scotland: 1G 2PG
Cardiff Arms Park, 5 Feb 1972

A.R. Brown

W.C.C. Steele
J.N.M. Frame
J.M. Renwick 1PG
A.G. Biggar [1]

C.M. Telfer
D.S. Paterson

J. McLauchlan
R.L. Clark 1T
A.B. Carmichael
† I.A. Barnes
G.L. Brown
N.A. MacEwan
* P.C. Brown 1PG 1C
R.J. Arneil

1 Rep by † L.G. Dick

**v ENGLAND**

**WON 23-9**
Scotland: 1DG 4PG 2T
England: 3PG
Murrayfield, 18 Mar 1972

A.R. Brown 1PG

W.C.C. Steele
J.N.M. Frame
J.M. Renwick
L.G. Dick

C.M. Telfer 1DG
A.J.M. Lawson

J. McLauchlan
R.L. Clark
A.B. Carmichael
A.F. McHarg
G.L. Brown
N.A. McEwan 1T
* P.C. Brown 3PG 1T
R.J. Arneil

## 1971-72 continued

### Five Nations Championship

**FACT FILE**

- The internal political problems in Ireland caused the SRU to cancel their visit to Dublin.
- Jim Renwick went on to become Scotland's most-capped player, appearing in 52 internationals.
- Peter Brown led Scotland to victory against England, becoming the first captain to beat them three times since Mark Morrison at the turn of the century.

**FINAL TABLE**

| | P | W | D | L | F | A | Pts |
|---|---|---|---|---|---|---|---|
| Wales | 3 | 3 | 0 | 0 | 67 | 21 | 6 |
| **Scotland** | **3** | **2** | **0** | **1** | **55** | **53** | **4** |
| Ireland | 2 | 2 | 0 | 0 | 30 | 21 | 4 |
| France | 4 | 1 | 0 | 3 | 61 | 66 | 2 |
| England | 4 | 0 | 0 | 4 | 36 | 88 | 0 |

*CHAMPIONSHIP UNRESOLVED*
*Ireland did not meet Wales or Scotland*

## 1972-73

### Tour Match

**v NEW ZEALAND**

**LOST 9-14**
Scotland: 2PG 1DG
NZ: 1G 2T
Murrayfield, 16 Dec 1972

† A.R. Irvine 2PG

W.C.C. Steele
† I.W. Forsyth
J.M. Renwick
† D. Shedden

† I.R. McGeechan 1DG
I.G. McCrae

J. McLauchlan
R.L. Clark
A.B. Carmichael
A.F. McHarg
G.L. Brown
N.A. McEwan
* P.C. Brown
R.J. Arneil

### Five Nations Championship

**v FRANCE**

**LOST 13-16**
France: 3PG 1DG 1T
Scotland: 2PG 1DG 1T
Parc des Princes, 13 Jan 1973

A.R. Irvine

W.C.C. Steele
I.W. Forsyth
J.M. Renwick
D. Shedden

I.R. McGeechan 1DG
A.J.M. Lawson 1T

J. McLauchlan
R.L. Clark
A.B. Carmichael
A.F. McHarg
† R.W.J. Wright
N.A. McEwan
* P.C. Brown 2PG
W. Lauder

**v WALES**

**WON 10-9**
Scotland: 1G 1T
Wales: 3PG
Murrayfield, 3 Feb 1973

A.R. Irvine

W.C.C. Steele 1T
I.R. McGeechan
I.W. Forsyth
D. Shedden

C.M. Telfer 1T
† D.W. Morgan 1C

* J. McLauchlan
R.L. Clark
A.B. Carmichael
A.F. McHarg
P.C. Brown
N.A. McEwan
G.M. Strachan
† J.G. Millican

## 1972-73 continued

## Five Nations Championship

### v IRELAND

**WON 19-14**
Scotland: 1T 2PG 3DG
Ireland: 2T 2PG
Murrayfield, 24 Feb 1973

A.R. Irvine

W.C.C. Steele
I.R.McGeechan 1DG
I.W. Forsyth 1T
D. Shedden

C.M. Telfer
D.W. Morgan 2DG 2PG

* J. McLauchlan [1]
R.L. Clark
A.B. Carmichael
A.F. McHarg
P.C. Brown
N.A. McEwan
G.M. Strachan
J.G. Millican

1 Rep by † R.D.H. Bryce

### v ENGLAND

**LOST 13-20**
England: 2G 2T
Scotland: 1G 1PG 1T
Twickenham, 17 Mar 1973

A.R. Irvine 1C

W.C.C. Steele 2T
I.R. McGeechan
I.W. Forsyth
D. Shedden

C.M. Telfer
D.W. Morgan 1PG

* J. McLauchlan
R.L. Clark
A.B. Carmichael
A.F. McHarg
P.C. Brown
N.A. McEwan
G.M. Strachan
J.G. Millican [1]

1 Rep by G.L. Brown

## SRU Centenary Match

### v OVERSEAS XV

**WON 27-16**
Scotland: 2G 1PG 3T
O/s XV: 2G 1T
Murrayfield, 31 Mar 1973

A.R. Irvine 1PG 2C

† A.D. Gill 2T
I.R. McGeechan [1]
I.W. Forsyth
D. Shedden 1T

C.M. Telfer 1T
D.W. Morgan

* J. McLauchlan
R.L. Clark
A.B. Carmichael
A.F. McHarg 1T
G.L. Brown
N.A. McEwan
P.C. Brown
G.M. Strachan

1 Rep by J.N.M. Frame

### FACT FILE

- This was the centenary season of the SRU, and it was celebrated with an extra international against the SRU president's Overseas XV.

### FINAL TABLE

| | P | W | D | L | F | A | Pts |
|---|---|---|---|---|---|---|---|
| Wales | 4 | 2 | 0 | 2 | 53 | 43 | 4 |
| Ireland | 4 | 2 | 0 | 2 | 50 | 48 | 4 |
| France | 4 | 2 | 0 | 2 | 38 | 36 | 4 |
| **Scotland** | **4** | **2** | **0** | **2** | **55** | **59** | **4** |
| England | 4 | 2 | 0 | 2 | 52 | 62 | 4 |

*Same again: the Scotland team which beat Wales 10-9 take a break from training before the Ireland match at Murrayfield in February 1973.*

## 1973-74

### Five Nations Championship

**v WALES**

**LOST 0-6**
Wales: 1G
Scotland: Nil
Cardiff Arms Park, 19 Jan 1974

A.R. Irvine

A.D. Gill
J.M. Renwick
I.R. McGeechan
L.G. Dick

C.M. Telfer
A.J.M. Lawson

* J. McLauchlan
† D.F. Madsen
A.B. Carmichael
G.L. Brown
A.F. McHarg
N.A. McEwan
† W.S. Watson
W. Lauder

**v ENGLAND**

**WON 16-14**
Scotland: 1G 2PG 1T
England: 2T 1DG 1PG
Murrayfield, 2 Feb 1974

A.R. Irvine **1C 1T 2PG**

A.D. Gill
J.M. Renwick
I.R. McGeechan
L.G. Dick

C.M. Telfer
A.J.M. Lawson

* J. McLauchlan
D.F. Madsen
A.B. Carmichael
G.L. Brown
A.F. McHarg
N.A. McEwan
W.S. Watson
W. Lauder **1T**

**v IRELAND**

**LOST 6-9**
Ireland: 1G 1PG
Scotland: 2PG
Lansdowne Road, 2 Mar 1974

A.R. Irvine **2PG**

A.D. Gill
J.M. Renwick
I.R. McGeechan
L.G. Dick

C.M. Telfer
D.W. Morgan

* J. McLauchlan
D.F. Madsen
A.B. Carmichael
G.L. Brown
A.F. McHarg
N.A. McEwan
W.S. Watson
W. Lauder

**v FRANCE**

**WON 19-6**
Scotland: 1G 3PG 1T
France: 1PG 1DG
Murrayfield, 16 Mar 1974

A.R. Irvine **2PG 1C**

A.D. Gill
J.M. Renwick
† M.D. Hunter
L.G. Dick **1T**

I.R. McGeechan
D.W. Morgan **1PG**

* J. McLauchlan
D.F. Madsen
A.B. Carmichael
G.L. Brown
A.F. McHarg **1T**
N.A. McEwan [1]
W.S. Watson
W. Lauder

1 Rep by † I.A. Barnes

**FACT FILE**

- By winning their two home matches, Scotland were able to feature as joint runners-up in the championship.
- The game against England produced a last-minute victory for the Scots. England were leading 14-13, going into injury time. Then, from 40 yards and near touch, Andy Irvine converted a penalty to thwart the visitors.

**FINAL TABLE**

| | P | W | D | L | F | A | Pts |
|---|---|---|---|---|---|---|---|
| Ireland | 4 | 2 | 1 | 1 | 50 | 45 | 5 |
| Wales | 4 | 1 | 2 | 1 | 43 | 41 | 4 |
| France | 4 | 1 | 2 | 1 | 43 | 53 | 4 |
| **Scotland** | **4** | **2** | **0** | **2** | **41** | **35** | **4** |
| England | 4 | 1 | 1 | 2 | 63 | 66 | 3 |

# 1974-75

## Five Nations Championship

### v IRELAND

**WON 20-13**
Scotland: 2PG 2DG 2T
Ireland: 1G 1PG 1T
Murrayfield, 1 Feb 1975

A.R. Irvine 2PG

W.C.C. Steele 1T
J.M. Renwick 1T
† D.L. Bell
L.G. Dick

I.R. McGeechan 1DG
D.W. Morgan 1DG

* J. McLauchlan
D.F. Madsen
A.B. Carmichael
A.F. McHarg
G.L. Brown
† M.A. Biggar
† D.G. Leslie
W. Lauder

### v FRANCE

**LOST 9-10**
France: 1PG 1DG 1T
Scotland: 3PG
Parc des Princes, 15 Feb 1975

A.R. Irvine 3PG

W.C.C. Steele
J.M. Renwick
D.L. Bell
L.G. Dick

I.R. McGeechan
D.W. Morgan

* J. McLauchlan
D.F. Madsen
A.B. Carmichael
A.F. McHarg
G.L. Brown
M.A. Biggar
D.G. Leslie
W. Lauder

### v WALES

**WON 12-10**
Scotland: 3PG 1DG
Wales: 2PG 1T
Murrayfield, 1 Mar 1975

A.R. Irvine

W.C.C. Steele
J.M. Renwick
D.L. Bell
L.G. Dick

I.R. McGeechan 1DG
D.W. Morgan 3PG

* J. McLauchlan
D.F. Madsen
A.B. Carmichael
A.F. McHarg
G.L. Brown
M.A. Biggar
D.G. Leslie
N.A. MacEwan

### v ENGLAND

**LOST 6-7**
England: 1PG 1T
Scotland: 2PG
Twickenham, 15 Mar 1975

A.R. Irvine

W.C.C. Steele
J.M. Renwick
D.L. Bell
L.G. Dick

I.R. McGeechan
D.W. Morgan 2PG

* J. McLauchlan
D.F. Madsen
A.B. Carmichael
A.F. McHarg
G.L. Brown
M.A. Biggar
D.G. Leslie
N.A. MacEwan [1]

1 Rep by I.A. Barnes

## Tour Match

### v NEW ZEALAND

**LOST 0-24**
NZ: 4G
Scotland: Nil
Auckland, 14 June 1975

† B.H. Hay [1]

A.R. Irvine
J.M. Renwick
† G.A. Birkett
L.G. Dick

I.R. McGeechan
D.W. Morgan

* J. McLauchlan
† C.D. Fisher
A.B. Carmichael
I.A. Barnes
A.F. McHarg
D.G. Leslie
W.S. Watson
W. Lauder

1 Rep by W.C.C. Steele

### FACT FILE

- For the fourth time since the war, England prevented Scotland gaining the Triple Crown at Twickenham.
- A world record crowd of 104,000 saw the match against Wales.
- Scotland toured New Zealand in the summer of 1975, winning four of the seven matches played.

### FINAL TABLE

| | P | W | D | L | F | A | Pts |
|---|---|---|---|---|---|---|---|
| Wales | 4 | 3 | 0 | 1 | 87 | 30 | 6 |
| Ireland | 4 | 2 | 0 | 2 | 54 | 67 | 4 |
| France | 4 | 2 | 0 | 2 | 53 | 79 | 4 |
| **Scotland** | **4** | **2** | **0** | **2** | **47** | **40** | **4** |
| England | 4 | 1 | 0 | 3 | 40 | 65 | 2 |

## 1975-76

### Tour Match

#### v AUSTRALIA

**WON 10-3**
Scotland: 1G 1T
Australia: 1PG
Murrayfield, 6 Dec 1975

B.H. Hay

A.R. Irvine
J.M. Renwick 1T
I.R. McGeechan
L.G. Dick 1T

C.M. Telfer
D.W. Morgan 1C

* J. McLauchlan
C.D. Fisher
A.B. Carmichael
A.F. McHarg
G.L. Brown
W. Lauder
† G.Y. Mackie
D.G. Leslie

### Five Nations Championship

#### v FRANCE

**LOST 6-13**
Scotland: 1PG 1DG
France: 3PG 1T
Murrayfield, 10 Jan 1976

B.H. Hay

A.R. Irvine
J.M. Renwick 1PG
I.R. McGeechan
L.G. Dick

C.M. Telfer
D.W. Morgan 1DG

* J. McLauchlan
D.F. Madsen
A.B. Carmichael
A.F. McHarg
G.L. Brown
W. Lauder
G.Y. Mackie
D.G. Leslie

#### v WALES

**LOST 6-28**
Wales: 2G 3PG 1DG 1T
Scotland: 1G
Cardiff Arms Park, 7 Feb 1976

A.R. Irvine 1T

W.C.C. Steele
J.M. Renwick
† A.G. Cranston
D. Shedden

I.R. McGeechan
D.W. Morgan 1C

* J. McLauchlan
C.D. Fisher
A.B. Carmichael
A.F. McHarg
G.L. Brown
M.A. Biggar
G.Y. Mackie
D.G. Leslie

#### v ENGLAND

**WON 22-12**
Scotland: 2G 2PG 1T
England: 1G 2PG
Murrayfield, 21 Feb 1976

A.R. Irvine 2PG 2C

W.C.C. Steele
A.G. Cranston
I.R. McGeechan
D. Shedden 1

† R. Wilson
A.J.M. Lawson 2T

* J. McLauchlan
C.D. Fisher
A.B. Carmichael
† A.J. Tomes
G.L. Brown
M.A. Biggar
A.F. McHarg
D.G. Leslie 1T

1 Rep by J.M. Renwick

#### v IRELAND

**WON 15-6**
Ireland: 2PG
Scotland: 4PG 1DG
Lansdowne Road, 20 Mar 1976

A.R. Irvine 4PG

W.C.C. Steele
A.G. Cranston
I.R. McGeechan
D. Shedden

R. Wilson 1DG
A.J.M. Lawson

* J. McLauchlan
C.D. Fisher
A.B. Carmichael
A.J. Tomes
G.L. Brown
M.A. Biggar
A.F. McHarg
D.G. Leslie

#### FACT FILE

- The win in Dublin gave Scotland their first away victory since 1971.

#### FINAL TABLE

| | P | W | D | L | F | A | Pts |
|---|---|---|---|---|---|---|---|
| Wales | 4 | 4 | 0 | 0 | 102 | 37 | 8 |
| France | 4 | 3 | 0 | 1 | 82 | 37 | 6 |
| **Scotland** | **4** | **2** | **0** | **2** | **49** | **59** | **4** |
| Ireland | 4 | 1 | 0 | 3 | 31 | 87 | 2 |
| England | 4 | 0 | 0 | 4 | 42 | 86 | 0 |

# 1976-77

## Five Nations Championship

### v ENGLAND

**LOST 6-26**
England: 2G 2PG 2T
Scotland: 2PG
Twickenham, 15 Jan 1977

A.R. Irvine **2PG**

W.C.C. Steele
* I.R. McGeechan
A.G. Cranston
L.G. Dick

R. Wilson
A.J.M. Lawson

† J. Aitken
D.F. Madsen
A.B. Carmichael
A.J. Tomes
A.F. McHarg
W. Lauder
† D.S.M. MacDonald
† A.K. Brewster

### v IRELAND

**WON 21-18**
Scotland: 2PG 1DG 3T
Ireland: 1G 3PG 1DG
Murrayfield, 19 Feb 1977

A.R. Irvine **2PG**

† W.B.B. Gammell **2T**
* I.R. McGeechan
J.M. Renwick
D. Shedden

R. Wilson
D.W. Morgan **1DG**

J. Aitken
D.F. Madsen **1T**
† N.E.K. Pender [1]
I.A. Barnes
A.F. McHarg
M.A. Biggar
D.S.M. MacDonald
W.S. Watson

1 Rep by A.B. Carmichael

### v FRANCE

**LOST 3-23**
France: 2G 1PG 2T
Scotland: 1PG
Parc des Princes, 5 Mar 1977

A.R. Irvine **1PG**

W.B.B. Gammell
* I.R. McGeechan
J.M. Renwick
D. Shedden

R. Wilson
D.W. Morgan

J. Aitken
D.F. Madsen
A.B. Carmichael
I.A. Barnes
A.F. McHarg
M.A. Biggar
D.S.M. MacDonald
W.S. Watson

### v WALES

**LOST 9-18**
Scotland: 1G 1DG
Wales: 2G 2PG
Murrayfield, 19 Mar 1977

A.R. Irvine **1T 1C**

W.B.B. Gammell
J.M. Renwick
A.G. Cranston
D. Shedden

* I.R. McGeechan **1DG**
D.W. Morgan

J. McLauchlan
D.F. Madsen
A.B. Carmichael
I.A. Barnes
A.F. McHarg
M.A. Biggar
D.S.M. MacDonald
W.S. Watson

### FACT FILE

- Two events before the start of the international season affected Scotland's fortunes in 1977. In October David Leslie injured his back and was out of contention. Then Gordon Brown, Scotland's key lock, was sent off in December while playing in an inter-district match and later banned.
- The heavy defeats at Twickenham and Parc des Princes were Scotland's biggest losing points margins against England and France respectively.

### FINAL TABLE

| | P | W | D | L | F | A | Pts |
|---|---|---|---|---|---|---|---|
| France | 4 | 4 | 0 | 0 | 58 | 21 | 8 |
| Wales | 4 | 3 | 0 | 1 | 66 | 43 | 6 |
| England | 4 | 2 | 0 | 2 | 42 | 24 | 4 |
| **Scotland** | **4** | **1** | **0** | **3** | **39** | **85** | **2** |
| Ireland | 4 | 0 | 0 | 4 | 33 | 65 | 0 |

## 1977-78

### Five Nations Championship

**v IRELAND**

**LOST 9-12**
Ireland: 1G 2PG
Scotland: 3PG
Lansdowne Road, 21 Jan 1978

B.H. Hay

A.R. Irvine
J.M. Renwick
I.R. McGeechan
D. Shedden

R. Wilson
* D.W. Morgan 3PG

J. McLauchlan
D.F. Madsen
A.B. Carmichael
A.J. Tomes
A.F. McHarg
M.A. Biggar
D.S.M. MacDonald
† C.B. Hegarty

**v FRANCE**

**LOST 16-19**
Scotland: 1G 1PG 1DG 1T
France: 1G 3PG 1T
Murrayfield, 4 Feb 1978

A.R. Irvine 1T 1

B.H. Hay
J.M. Renwick
I.R. McGeechan
D. Shedden 1T 2

R. Wilson
* D.W. Morgan 1DG 1PG 1C

J. McLauchlan
† C.T. Deans
N.E.K. Pender
A.J. Tomes
A.F. McHarg
M.A. Biggar
G.Y. Mackie
C.B. Hegarty

1 Rep by A.G. Cranston
2 Rep by † C.G. Hogg

**v WALES**

**LOST 14-22**
Wales: 1PG 1DG 4T
Scotland: 2PG 2T
Cardiff Arms Park, 18 Feb 1978

B.H. Hay

W.B.B. Gammell
J.M. Renwick 1T
A.G. Cranston
D. Shedden 1

I.R. McGeechan
* D.W. Morgan 2PG

J. McLauchlan
C.T. Deans
N.E.K. Pender
A.F. McHarg
A.J. Tomes 1T
M.A. Biggar
D.S.M. MacDonald
C.B. Hegarty

1 Rep by C.G. Hogg

**v ENGLAND**

**LOST 0-15**
Scotland: Nil
England: 2G 1PG
Murrayfield, 4 Mar 1978

A.R. Irvine

W.B.B. Gammell
J.M. Renwick
A.G. Cranston
B.H. Hay

† R.W. Breakey
* D.W. Morgan

J. McLauchlan
C.T. Deans
N.E.K. Pender
A.J. Tomes
† D. Gray
M.A. Biggar
D.S.M. MacDonald
C.B. Hegarty

**FACT FILE**

- This was Scotland's worst international season since 1968.
- Sandy Carmichael's international career ended after the Irish match. He played in 50 international matches, retiring as the most-capped Scottish player and the world's most-capped prop.

**FINAL TABLE**

| | P | W | D | L | F | A | Pts |
|---|---|---|---|---|---|---|---|
| Wales | 4 | 4 | 0 | 0 | 67 | 43 | 8 |
| France | 4 | 3 | 0 | 1 | 51 | 47 | 6 |
| England | 4 | 2 | 0 | 2 | 42 | 33 | 4 |
| Ireland | 4 | 1 | 0 | 3 | 46 | 54 | 2 |
| **Scotland** | **4** | **0** | **0** | **4** | **39** | **68** | **0** |

## 1978-79

### Tour Match

**v NEW ZEALAND**

**LOST 9-18**
Scotland: 1G 1DG
NZ: 2G 2PG
Murrayfield, 9 Dec 1978

A.R. Irvine 1C

† K.W. Robertson
J.M. Renwick
A.G. Cranston
B.H. Hay 1T

* I.R. McGeechan 1DG
A.J.M. Lawson

J. McLauchlan
C.T. Deans
† R.F. Cunningham
A.J. Tomes
A.F. McHarg
M.A. Biggar
D.G. Leslie[1]
† G. Dickson

1 Rep by † I.K. Lambie

### Five Nations Championship

**v WALES**

**LOST 13-19**
Scotland: 3PG 1T
Wales: 1G 3PG 1T
Murrayfield, 20 Jan 1979

A.R. Irvine 3PG 1T

K.W. Robertson
J.M. Renwick
* I.R. McGeechan
B.H. Hay

† J.Y. Rutherford
A.J.M. Lawson

J. McLauchlan
C.T. Deans
R.F. Cunningham
A.J. Tomes
A.F. McHarg
M.A. Biggar
I.K. Lambie
G. Dickson

**v ENGLAND**

**DRAWN 7-7**
England: 1PG 1T
Scotland: 1PG 1T
Twickenham, 3 Feb 1979

A.R. Irvine 1PG

K.W. Robertson
J.M. Renwick
* I.R. McGeechan
B.H. Hay

J.Y. Rutherford 1T
A.J.M. Lawson

J. McLauchlan
C.T. Deans
R.F. Cunningham
A.J. Tomes
A.F. McHarg
M.A. Biggar
I.K. Lambie
G. Dickson

**v IRELAND**

**DRAWN 11-11**
Scotland: 1PG 2T
Ireland: 1PG 2T
Murrayfield, 3 Mar 1979

A.R. Irvine 1PG 1T

K.W. Robertson 1T
J.M. Renwick
* I.R. McGeechan
B.H. Hay

J.Y. Rutherford
A.J.M. Lawson

J. McLauchlan
C.T. Deans
† I.G. Milne
A.J. Tomes
D. Gray
M.A. Biggar
W.S. Watson
G. Dickson

**v FRANCE**

**LOST 17-21**
France: 2PG 1DG 3T
Scotland: 1G 1PG 2T
Parc des Princes, 17 Mar 1979

A.R. Irvine 1PG 1C 1T

K.W. Robertson 1T
J.M. Renwick
* I.R. McGeechan
B.H. Hay

J.Y. Rutherford
A.J.M. Lawson

J. McLauchlan
C.T. Deans
I.G. Milne
A.J. Tomes
D. Gray
M.A. Biggar
W.S. Watson
G. Dickson 1T

### FACT FILE

- Andy Irvine became the second full-back in international history to score three tries in a season (equalling Bob Hiller's record of 1971). He took his haul of tries to seven, more than any other international full-back.
- Alastair McHarg retired as Scotland's most-capped lock. He played the last of his 44 games against England (though two of his appearances had been at No. 8).

### FINAL TABLE

| | P | W | D | L | F | A | Pts |
|---|---|---|---|---|---|---|---|
| Wales | 4 | 3 | 0 | 1 | 83 | 51 | 6 |
| France | 4 | 2 | 1 | 1 | 50 | 46 | 5 |
| Ireland | 4 | 1 | 2 | 1 | 53 | 51 | 4 |
| England | 4 | 1 | 1 | 2 | 24 | 52 | 3 |
| **Scotland** | **4** | **0** | **2** | **2** | **48** | **58** | **2** |

## 1979-80

### Tour Match

#### v NEW ZEALAND

**LOST 6-20**
Scotland: 2PG
NZ: 2G 2T
Murrayfield, 10 Nov 1979

A.R. Irvine **2PG**

K.W. Robertson
J.M. Renwick
† D.I. Johnston
B.H. Hay

J.Y. Rutherford
A.J.M. Lawson

* J. McLauchlan
C.T. Deans
I.G. Milne
A.J. Tomes
D. Gray
M.A. Biggar
I.K. Lambie
G. Dickson

### Five Nations Championship

#### v IRELAND

**LOST 15-22**
Ireland: 1G 1DG 3PG 1T
Scotland: 2G 1PG
Lansdowne Road, 2 Feb 1980

A.R. Irvine **1PG 2C**

† S. Munro
J.M. Renwick
D.I. Johnston **2T**
B.H. Hay

J.Y. Rutherford
† R.J. Laidlaw

† J.N. Burnett
C.T. Deans
I.G. Milne
† W. Cuthbertson
D. Gray
* M.A. Biggar
† J.R. Beattie
A.K. Brewster

#### v FRANCE

**WON 22-14**
Scotland: 2G 2PG 1T
France: 1PG 1DG 2T
Murrayfield, 16 Feb 1980

A.R. Irvine **2T 2PG 1C**

S. Munro
J.M. Renwick **1C**
D.I. Johnston
B.H. Hay

J.Y. Rutherford **1T**
R.J. Laidlaw

J.N. Burnett
C.T. Deans [1]
I.G. Milne
A.J. Tomes
D. Gray
* M.A. Biggar
J.R. Beattie
A.K. Brewster

1 Rep by † K.G. Lawrie

#### v WALES

**LOST 6-17**
Wales: 1G 1PG 2T
Scotland: 1G
Cardiff Arms Park, 1 Mar 1980

A.R. Irvine **1C**

K.W. Robertson
J.M. Renwick **1T**
D.I. Johnston
B.H. Hay

† B.M. Gossman
R.J. Laidlaw [1]

J.N. Burnett
K.G. Lawrie
† N.A. Rowan
A.J. Tomes
D. Gray
* M.A. Biggar
J.R. Beattie
G. Dickson

1 Rep by A.J.M. Lawson

#### v ENGLAND

**LOST 18-30**
Scotland: 2G 2PG
England: 2G 2PG 3T
Murrayfield, 15 Mar 1980

* A.R. Irvine **2PG 2C**

K.W. Robertson
J.M. Renwick
D.I. Johnston
B.H. Hay [1]

J.Y. Rutherford **1T**
R.J. Laidlaw

J.N. Burnett
K.G. Lawrie
N.A. Rowan
A.J. Tomes **1T**
D. Gray
D.G. Leslie
J.R. Beattie
M.A. Biggar

1 Rep by † J.S. Gossman

#### FACT FILE

- Scotland shared the wooden spoon with France in 1980. The long run without success ended in a win, the first for 13 matches, against the French.
- Ian McLauchlan played the last of his 43 internationals for Scotland against the All Blacks in November. His career spanned 12 seasons and he captained Scotland a then record number of times (19).

#### FINAL TABLE

| | P | W | D | L | F | A | Pts |
|---|---|---|---|---|---|---|---|
| England | 4 | 4 | 0 | 0 | 80 | 48 | 8 |
| Ireland | 4 | 2 | 0 | 2 | 70 | 65 | 4 |
| Wales | 4 | 2 | 0 | 2 | 50 | 45 | 4 |
| **Scotland** | **4** | **1** | **0** | **3** | **61** | **83** | **2** |
| France | 4 | 1 | 0 | 3 | 55 | 75 | 2 |

# 1980-81

## Five Nations Championship

### v FRANCE

**LOST 9-16**
France: 1G 2PG 1T
Scotland: 1G 1PG
Parc des Princes, 17 Jan 1981

* A.R. Irvine 1PG

S. Munro
J.M. Renwick 1C
K.W. Robertson
B.H. Hay

J.Y. Rutherford 1T
R.J. Laidlaw

J. Aitken
C.T. Deans
N.A. Rowan
A.J. Tomes
D. Gray
† J.H. Calder
J.R. Beattie
G. Dickson

### v WALES

**WON 15-6**
Scotland: 2G‡ 1PG
Wales: 2PG
Murrayfield, 7 Feb 1981

* A.R. Irvine 1T‡

S. Munro
J.M. Renwick 1PG 2C
K.W. Robertson
B.H. Hay

J.Y. Rutherford
R.J. Laidlaw

J. Aitken
C.T. Deans
N.A. Rowan
W. Cuthbertson
A.J. Tomes 1T
J.H. Calder
J.R. Beattie
D.G. Leslie

‡includes penalty try

### v ENGLAND

**LOST 17-23**
England: 1G 3PG 2T
Scotland: 1G 1PG 2T
Twickenham, 21 Feb 1981

* A.R. Irvine 1C 1PG

S. Munro 2T
J.M. Renwick
K.W. Robertson
B.H. Hay

J.Y. Rutherford
R.J. Laidlaw

J. Aitken
C.T. Deans
N.A. Rowan
W. Cuthbertson
A.J. Tomes
J.H. Calder 1T
J.R. Beattie
D.G. Leslie

### v IRELAND

**WON 10-9**
Scotland: 1PG 1DG 1T
Ireland: 1G 1PG
Murrayfield, 21 Mar 1981

* A.R. Irvine 1PG

S. Munro
J.M. Renwick
K.W. Robertson
B.H. Hay 1T

J.Y. Rutherford 1DG
R.J. Laidlaw

J. Aitken
C.T. Deans
N.A. Rowan
W. Cuthbertson
A.J. Tomes
J.H. Calder
J.R. Beattie
D.G. Leslie

### FACT FILE

- Jim Telfer was Scotland's new coach for 1981.
- Andy Irvine has been credited with the penalty try scored by the Scots against Wales, the first ever scored in the long history of the International Championship and the first ever awarded to Scotland.

### FINAL TABLE

| | P | W | D | L | F | A | Pts |
|---|---|---|---|---|---|---|---|
| France | 4 | 4 | 0 | 0 | 70 | 49 | 8 |
| England | 4 | 2 | 0 | 2 | 64 | 60 | 4 |
| **Scotland** | **4** | **2** | **0** | **2** | **51** | **54** | **4** |
| Wales | 4 | 2 | 0 | 2 | 51 | 61 | 4 |
| Ireland | 4 | 0 | 0 | 4 | 36 | 48 | 0 |

## 1980-81 continued

### Tour Matches

#### 1st v NEW ZEALAND

**LOST 4-11**
NZ: 1PG 2T
Scotland: 1T
Dunedin, 13 Jun 1981

* A.R. Irvine

S. Munro
A.G. Cranston
J.M. Renwick
B.H. Hay

J.Y. Rutherford
R.J. Laidlaw

J. Aitken
C.T. Deans 1T
I.G. Milne
W. Cuthbertson
A.J. Tomes
D.G. Leslie
† I.A.M. Paxton
J.H. Calder

#### 2nd v NEW ZEALAND

**LOST 15-40**
NZ: 6G 1T
Scotland: 1G 2PG 1DG
Auckland, 20 Jun 1981

* A.R. Irvine 1C 2PG

S. Munro
A.G. Cranston
J.M. Renwick 1DG
B.H. Hay 1T

J.Y. Rutherford
R.J. Laidlaw

J. Aitken
C.T. Deans
I.G. Milne
W. Cuthbertson
A.J. Tomes
D.G. Leslie
I.A.M. Paxton
J.H. Calder

## 1981-82

### Tour Matches

#### v ROMANIA

**WON 12-6**
Scotland: 4PG
Romania: 2PG
Murrayfield, 26 Sept 1981

* A.R. Irvine 4PG

S. Munro
J.M. Renwick
D.I. Johnston
K.W. Robertson

R. Wilson
R.J. Laidlaw

J. Aitken
C.T. Deans
I.G. Milne
W. Cuthbertson
A.J. Tomes
J.H. Calder
I.A.M. Paxton
D.G. Leslie

#### v AUSTRALIA

**WON 24-15**
Scotland: 1G 5PG 1DG
Australia: 1PG 3T
Murrayfield, 19 Dec 1981

* A.R. Irvine 1C 5PG

K.W. Robertson
J.M. Renwick 1T
D.I. Johnston
† G.R.T. Baird

J.Y. Rutherford 1DG
R.J. Laidlaw

J. Aitken
C.T. Deans
I.G. Milne
W. Cuthbertson
A.J. Tomes
J.H. Calder
I.A.M. Paxton
D.G. Leslie

### Five Nations Championship

#### v ENGLAND

**DRAWN 9-9**
Scotland: 2PG 1DG
England: 3PG
Murrayfield, 16 Jan 1982

* A.R. Irvine 2PG

K.W. Robertson
J.M. Renwick
D.I. Johnston
G.R.T. Baird

J.Y. Rutherford 1DG
R.J. Laidlaw

J. Aitken
C.T. Deans
I.G. Milne
W. Cuthbertson
A.J. Tomes
J.H. Calder
I.A.M. Paxton
D.G. Leslie

## 1981-82 continued

## Five Nations Championship

### v IRELAND

**LOST 12-21**
Ireland: 6PG 1DG
Scotland: 1G 2PG
Lansdowne Road, 20 Feb 1982

* A.R. Irvine 1C

K.W. Robertson
J.M. Renwick 2PG
D.I. Johnston
G.R.T. Baird

J.Y. Rutherford 1T
R.J. Laidlaw

J. Aitken
C.T. Deans
I.G. Milne
W. Cuthbertson
A.J. Tomes
J.H. Calder
I.A.M. Paxton
† R.E. Paxton

### v FRANCE

**WON 16-7**
Scotland: 3PG 1DG 1T
France: 1PG 1T
Murrayfield, 6 Mar 1982

* A.R. Irvine 3PG

K.W. Robertson
J.M. Renwick 1DG
D.I. Johnston
G.R.T. Baird

J.Y. Rutherford 1T
R.J. Laidlaw

J. Aitken
C.T. Deans
I.G. Milne
W. Cuthbertson
A.J. Tomes
J.H. Calder
I.A.M. Paxton
† D.B. White

### v WALES

**WON 34-18**
Wales: 1G 4PG
Scotland: 4G 2DG 1T
Cardiff Arms Park, 20 Mar 1982

* A.R. Irvine 4C

† J.A. Pollock 1T
J.M. Renwick 1DG 1T
D.I. Johnston 1T
G.R.T. Baird

J.Y. Rutherford 1DG
R.J. Laidlaw

J. Aitken
C.T. Deans
I.G. Milne
W. Cuthbertson
A.J. Tomes
J.H. Calder 1T
I.A.M. Paxton [1]
D.B. White 1T

1 Rep by G. Dickson

### FACT FILE

- In the second Test against Australia, Andy Irvine made his last appearance for Scotland and thus retired as the most-capped Scottish international, having played 51 times and scored 273 points – another Scottish (and world) record.
- Scotland's win at Cardiff was their first there in 20 years.

### FINAL TABLE

| | P | W | D | L | F | A | Pts |
|---|---|---|---|---|---|---|---|
| Ireland | 4 | 3 | 0 | 1 | 66 | 61 | 6 |
| **Scotland** | **4** | **2** | **1** | **1** | **71** | **55** | **5** |
| England | 4 | 2 | 1 | 1 | 68 | 47 | 5 |
| Wales | 4 | 1 | 0 | 3 | 59 | 83 | 2 |
| France | 4 | 1 | 0 | 3 | 56 | 74 | 2 |

## Tour Matches

### 1st v AUSTRALIA

**WON 12-7**
Australia: 1PG 1T
Scotland: 1G 1PG 1DG
Ballymore, 4 Jul 1982

* A.R. Irvine 1PG 1C

K.W. Robertson 1T
† R.J. Gordon
D.I. Johnston
G.R.T. Baird

J.Y. Rutherford 1DG
R.J. Laidlaw

† G.M. McGuiness
C.T. Deans
I.G. Milne
W. Cuthbertson
A.J. Tomes
J.H. Calder
I.A.M. Paxton
D.B. White

### 2nd v AUSTRALIA

**LOST 9-33**
Australia: 3G 5PG
Scotland: 3PG
Sydney C.G., 10 Jul 1982

* A.R. Irvine 3PG

K.W. Robertson
R.J. Gordon
D.I. Johnston
G.R.T. Baird

J.Y. Rutherford
R.J. Laidlaw

G.M. McGuiness
C.T. Deans
I.G. Milne
W. Cuthbertson
A.J. Tomes
J.H. Calder
I.A.M. Paxton [1]
D.B. White

1 Rep by R.E. Paxton

## 1982-83

### Five Nations Championship

**v IRELAND**

**LOST 13-15**
Scotland: 2PG 1DG 1T
Ireland: 1G 3PG
Murrayfield, 15 Jan 1983

† P.W. Dods 2PG

K.W. Robertson
J.M. Renwick 1DG
D.I. Johnston
G.R.T. Baird

R. Wilson
* R.J. Laidlaw 1T

G.M. McGuiness
C.T. Deans
I.G. Milne
W. Cuthbertson
A.J. Tomes
J.H. Calder
I.A.M. Paxton
D.G. Leslie

**v FRANCE**

**LOST 15-19**
France: 1G 3PG 1T
Scotland: 1G 1PG 2DG
Parc des Princes, 5 Feb 1983

P.W. Dods 1PG 1C

K.W. Robertson 1T
J.M. Renwick
D.I. Johnston
G.R.T. Baird

B.M. Gossman 2DG
* R.J. Laidlaw

J. Aitken
C.T. Deans
I.G. Milne
W. Cuthbertson
A.J. Tomes
J.H. Calder
J.R. Beattie
D.G. Leslie

**v WALES**

**LOST 15-19**
Scotland: 1G 3PG
Wales: 1G 3PG 1T
Murrayfield, 19 Feb 1983

P.W. Dods 3PG 1C

K.W. Robertson
J.M. Renwick 1T
D.I. Johnston
G.R.T. Baird

B.M. Gossman
* R.J. Laidlaw

J. Aitken
C.T. Deans
I.G. Milne
W. Cuthbertson
A.J. Tomes
J.H. Calder
J.R. Beattie
D.G. Leslie

**v ENGLAND**

**WON 22-12**
England: 3PG 1DG
Scotland: 1G 3PG 1DG 1T
Twickenham, 5 Mar 1983

P.W. Dods 3PG 1C

J.A. Pollock
J.M. Renwick
K.W. Robertson 1DG
G.R.T. Baird

J.Y. Rutherford
R.J. Laidlaw 1T

* J. Aitken
C.T. Deans
I.G. Milne
† T.J. Smith 1T
I.A.M. Paxton
J.H. Calder
J.R. Beattie
D.G. Leslie

**FACT FILE**

- Scotland's best performance of the season was against England, when they registered their fourth ever win at Twickenham.

**FINAL TABLE**

| | P | W | D | L | F | A | Pts |
|---|---|---|---|---|---|---|---|
| France | 4 | 3 | 0 | 1 | 70 | 61 | 6 |
| Ireland | 4 | 3 | 0 | 1 | 71 | 67 | 6 |
| Wales | 4 | 2 | 1 | 1 | 64 | 53 | 5 |
| **Scotland** | **4** | **1** | **0** | **3** | **65** | **65** | **2** |
| England | 4 | 0 | 1 | 3 | 55 | 79 | 1 |

## 1983-84

### Tour Match

#### v NEW ZEALAND

**DRAWN 25-25**
Scotland: 5PG 2DG 1T
NZ: 2G 3PG 1T
Murrayfield, 12 Nov 1983

P.W. Dods 5PG

J.A. Pollock 1T
† A.E. Kennedy
D.I. Johnston
G.R.T. Baird

J.Y. Rutherford 2DG
R.J. Laidlaw

* J. Aitken
C.T. Deans
I.G. Milne
W. Cuthbertson
T.J. Smith
J.H. Calder
I.A.M. Paxton
J.R. Beattie

### Five Nations Championship

#### v WALES

**WON 15-9**
Wales: 1G 1PG
Scotland: 2G 1PG
Cardiff Arms Park, 21 Jan 1984

P.W. Dods 1PG 2C

S. Munro
D.I. Johnston
A.E. Kennedy
G.R.T. Baird

J.Y. Rutherford
R.J. Laidlaw

* J. Aitken 1T
C.T. Deans
I.G. Milne
W. Cuthbertson
A.J. Tomes
J.H. Calder
I.A.M. Paxton 1T
D.G. Leslie

#### v ENGLAND

**WON 18-6**
Scotland: 2G 2PG
England: 2PG
Murrayfield, 4 Feb 1984

P.W. Dods 2PG 2C

K.W. Robertson
A.E. Kennedy 1T [1]
D.I. Johnston 1T
G.R.T. Baird

J.Y. Rutherford
R.J. Laidlaw

* J. Aitken
C.T. Deans
I.G. Milne
W. Cuthbertson [2]
A.J. Tomes
J.H. Calder
I.A.M. Paxton
D.G. Leslie

1 Rep by J.A. Pollock
2 Rep by J.R. Beattie

#### v IRELAND

**WON 32-9**
Ireland: 1G 1PG
Scotland: 3G‡ 2PG 2T
Lansdowne Road, 3 Mar 1984

P.W. Dods 3C 2PG 1T

J.A. Pollock
K.W. Robertson 1T
D.I. Johnston
G.R.T. Baird

J.Y. Rutherford
R.J. Laidlaw 2T [1]

* J. Aitken
C.T. Deans
I.G. Milne
† A.J. Campbell
A.J. Tomes
J.H. Calder
I.A.M. Paxton
D.G. Leslie

1 Rep by † I.G. Hunter
‡includes penalty try

#### v FRANCE

**WON 21-12**
Scotland: 1G 5PG
France: 1G 1PG 1DG
Murrayfield, 17 Mar 1984

P.W. Dods 5PG 1C

J.A. Pollock
K.W. Robertson
D.I. Johnston
G.R.T. Baird

J.Y. Rutherford
R.J. Laidlaw

* J. Aitken
C.T. Deans
I.G. Milne
A.J. Campbell
A.J. Tomes
J.H. Calder 1T
I.A.M. Paxton
D.G. Leslie

#### FINAL TABLE

| | P | W | D | L | F | A | Pts |
|---|---|---|---|---|---|---|---|
| **Scotland** | **4** | **4** | **0** | **0** | **86** | **36** | **8** |
| France | 4 | 3 | 0 | 1 | 90 | 67 | 6 |
| Wales | 4 | 2 | 0 | 2 | 67 | 60 | 4 |
| England | 4 | 1 | 0 | 3 | 51 | 83 | 2 |
| Ireland | 4 | 0 | 0 | 4 | 39 | 87 | 0 |

## 1983-84 continued

### Tour Match

**v ROMANIA**

**LOST 22-28**
Romania: 2G 3PG 1DG 1T
Scotland: 1G 3PG 1DG 1T
Bucharest, 20 May 1984

P.W. Dods 1T 1C 3PG

J.A. Pollock
J.M. Renwick
D.I. Johnston
K.W. Robertson 1DG

J.Y. Rutherford
R.J. Laidlaw

* J. Aitken
† G.J. Callander
N.A. Rowan
A.J. Campbell
A.J. Tomes
† S.K. McGaughey
J.R. Beattie
D.G. Leslie 1T

**FACT FILE**

- Scotland's busiest domestic season for years started with a hectic 25-25 draw against the All Blacks – at the time the highest-scoring draw ever between International Board countries. Then the Scots went on to their first Grand Slam since 1925, and their first Triple Crown triumph since 1938.
- Peter Dods kicked 50 points in the championship, creating a new Scottish record.
- The side was well beaten in Bucharest in the spring. Jim Renwick returned to win his 52nd cap, thus becoming Scotland's most-capped player.

## 1984-85

### Tour Match

**v AUSTRALIA**

**LOST 12-37**
Scotland: 4PG
Australia: 3G 5PG 1T
Murrayfield, 8 Dec 1984

P.W. Dods 4PG

† P.D. Steven
A.E. Kennedy
K.W. Robertson
G.R.T. Baird

† D.S. Wyllie
* R.J. Laidlaw

† A.D.G. Mackenzie
C.T. Deans
I.G. Milne
W. Cuthbertson
A.J. Tomes
J.H. Calder
J.R. Beattie
† J. Jeffrey

### Five Nations Championship

**v IRELAND**

**LOST 15-18**
Scotland: 4PG 1DG
Ireland: 2G 1DG 1PG
Murrayfield, 2 Feb 1985

P.W. Dods 4PG

G.R.T. Baird
† K.T. Murray
K.W. Robertson 1DG
† I. Tukalo

J.Y. Rutherford
* R.J. Laidlaw

G.M. McGuinness
C.T. Deans
N.A. Rowan
A.J. Campbell
T.J. Smith
J.H. Calder
J.R. Beattie [1]
J. Jeffrey

1 Rep by I.A.M. Paxton

**v FRANCE**

**LOST 3-11**
France: 1PG 2T
Scotland: 1PG
Parc des Princes, 16 Feb 1985

P.W. Dods 1PG

P.D. Steven
K.T. Murray
K.W. Robertson
J.A. Pollock

J.Y. Rutherford
R.J. Laidlaw [1]

G.M. McGuinness
C.T. Deans
I.G. Milne
A.J. Campbell
T.J. Smith
J.H. Calder
I.A.M. Paxton
* D.G. Leslie

1 Rep by I.G. Hunter

## 1984-85 continued

### Five Nations Championship

**v WALES**

**LOST 21-25**
Scotland: 2G 2DG 1PG
Wales: 1G 1DG 4PG 1T
Murrayfield, 2 Mar 1985

P.W. Dods 1PG 2C

P.D. Steven
K.T. Murray [1]
K.W. Robertson
G.R.T. Baird

J.Y. Rutherford 2DG
I.G. Hunter

G.M. McGuinness
C.T. Deans
I.G. Milne
A.J. Campbell
A.J. Tomes
J.H. Calder
I.A.M. Paxton 2T
* D.G. Leslie

1 Rep by D.S. Wyllie

**v ENGLAND**

**LOST 7-10**
England: 2PG 1T
Scotland: 1PG 1T
Twickenham, 16 Mar 1985

P.W. Dods 1PG

P.D. Steven
D.S. Wyllie
K.W. Robertson 1T
G.R.T. Baird

J.Y. Rutherford
I.G. Hunter

G.M. McGuinness
C.T. Deans
I.G. Milne
A.J. Campbell
A.J. Tomes
J. Jeffrey
I.A.M. Paxton
* D.G. Leslie

**FACT FILE**

- Scotland went from the Grand Slam to the wooden spoon. Colin Telfer succeeded Jim Telfer as Scottish coach.
- John Rutherford's two drop goals against Wales took him ahead of Ian McGeechan's Scottish career record.

**FINAL TABLE**

| | P | W | D | L | F | A | Pts |
|---|---|---|---|---|---|---|---|
| Ireland | 4 | 3 | 1 | 0 | 67 | 49 | 7 |
| France | 4 | 2 | 2 | 0 | 49 | 30 | 6 |
| Wales | 4 | 2 | 0 | 2 | 61 | 71 | 4 |
| England | 4 | 1 | 1 | 2 | 44 | 53 | 3 |
| **Scotland** | **4** | **0** | **0** | **4** | **46** | **64** | **0** |

## 1985-86

### Five Nations Championship

**v FRANCE**

**WON 18-17**
Scotland: 6PG
France: 2PG 1DG 2T
Murrayfield, 18 Jan 1986

† A.G. Hastings 6PG

† M.D.F. Duncan
D.I. Johnston
† S. Hastings
G.R.T. Baird

J.Y. Rutherford
R.J. Laidlaw

† D.M.B. Sole
* C.T. Deans
I.G. Milne
A.J. Campbell
† J.R.E. Campbell-Lamerton
J. Jeffrey
J.R. Beattie
† F. Calder

**v WALES**

**LOST 15-22**
Wales: 5PG 1DG 1T
Scotland: 1PG 3T
Cardiff Arms Park, 1 Feb 1986

A.G. Hastings 1T 1PG

M.D.F. Duncan 1T
D.I. Johnston
S. Hastings
G.R.T. Baird

J.Y. Rutherford
R.J. Laidlaw

D.M.B. Sole
* C.T. Deans
I.G. Milne
A.J. Campbell
I.A.M. Paxton
J. Jeffrey 1T
J.R. Beattie
F. Calder

**v ENGLAND**

**WON 33-6**
Scotland: 3G 5PG
England: 2PG
Murrayfield, 15 Feb 1986

A.G. Hastings 5PG 3C

M.D.F. Duncan 1T
D.I. Johnston
S. Hastings 1T
G.R.T. Baird

J.Y. Rutherford 1T
R.J. Laidlaw

A.K. Brewster
* C.T. Deans
I.G. Milne
A.J. Campbell
I.A.M. Paxton
J. Jeffrey
J.R. Beattie
F. Calder

## 1985-86 continued

### Five Nations Championship

**v IRELAND**

**WON 10-9**
Ireland: 1G 1PG
Scotland: 2PG 1T
Lansdowne Road, 15 Mar 1986

A.G. Hastings 2PG

K.W. Robertson
D.I. Johnston
S. Hastings
G.R.T. Baird

J.Y. Rutherford
R.J. Laidlaw 1T

A.K. Brewster
* C.T. Deans
I.G. Milne
A.J. Campbell
I.A.M. Paxton
J. Jeffrey
J.R. Beattie
F. Calder

### Tour Match

**v ROMANIA**

**WON 33-18**
Romania: 1DG 5PG
Scotland: 3G 5PG
Bucharest, 29 Mar 1986

A.G. Hastings 5PG 3C

M.D.F. Duncan
D.I. Johnston
S. Hastings 1T
G.R.T. Baird

J.Y. Rutherford
R.J. Laidlaw

A.K. Brewster
* C.T. Deans 1T
I.G. Milne
A.J. Campbell
I.A.M. Paxton
J. Jeffrey 1T
J.R. Beattie
F. Calder

### FACT FILE

- Scott Hastings made his debut with his brother Gavin against France. They were the first pair of brothers to play together on their debuts for Scotland since William and George Neilson first appeared in 1891.
- Gavin Hastings equalled the world record of six penalty goals for a match on his debut, and in so doing created a new Scottish record for points in an international.

### FINAL TABLE

| | P | W | D | L | F | A | Pts |
|---|---|---|---|---|---|---|---|
| France | 4 | 3 | 0 | 1 | 98 | 52 | 6 |
| **Scotland** | **4** | **3** | **0** | **1** | **76** | **54** | **6** |
| Wales | 4 | 2 | 0 | 2 | 74 | 71 | 4 |
| England | 4 | 2 | 0 | 2 | 62 | 100 | 4 |
| Ireland | 4 | 0 | 0 | 4 | 50 | 83 | 0 |

*John Beattie (left), Colin Deans (centre) and Roger Baird rush to congratulate team-mate John Rutherford on Scotland's second try against England in February, 1986.*

## 1986-87

### Five Nations Championship

**v IRELAND**

**WON 16-12**
Scotland: 1G 2DG 1T
Ireland: 1G 1DG 1PG
Murrayfield, 21 Feb 1987

A.G. Hastings 1C

M.D.F. Duncan
D.S. Wyllie
S. Hastings
I. Tukalo 1T

J.Y. Rutherford 2DG
R.J. Laidlaw 1T

D.M.B. Sole
* C.T. Deans
I.G. Milne
A.J. Tomes
I.A.M. Paxton
J. Jeffrey
J.R. Beattie
F. Calder

**v FRANCE**

**LOST 22-28**
France: 3PG 1DG 4T
Scotland: 1G 4PG 1T
Parc des Princes, 7 Mar 1987

A.G. Hastings 4PG 1C

M.D.F. Duncan
D.S. Wyllie [1]
S. Hastings 1T
I. Tukalo

J.Y. Rutherford
R.J. Laidlaw

D.M.B. Sole
* C.T. Deans
I.G. Milne
A.J. Tomes
I.A.M. Paxton
J. Jeffrey
J.R. Beattie 1T
F. Calder

1 Rep by K.W. Robertson

**v WALES**

**WON 21-15**
Scotland: 2G 2PG 1DG
Wales: 1G 2PG 1DG
Murrayfield, 21 Mar 1987

A.G. Hastings 2PG 2C

M.D.F. Duncan
K.W. Robertson
S. Hastings
I. Tukalo

J.Y. Rutherford 1DG
R.J. Laidlaw

D.M.B. Sole
* C.T. Deans
I.G. Milne
D.B. White
I.A.M. Paxton
J. Jeffrey 1T
J.R. Beattie 1T
F. Calder

**v ENGLAND**

**LOST 12-21**
England: 2G‡ 3PG
Scotland: 1G 2PG
Twickenham, 4 Apr 1987

A.G. Hastings 2PG 1C

M.D.F. Duncan
K.W. Robertson 1T
G.R.T. Baird
I. Tukalo

J.Y. Rutherford
R.J. Laidlaw

D.M.B. Sole
* C.T. Deans
I.G. Milne
D.B. White
I.A.M. Paxton
J. Jeffrey
J.R. Beattie [1]
F. Calder

‡includes penalty try
1 Rep by A.J. Tomes

**FACT FILE**

- Gavin Hastings brought up his century of points in internationals with a towering early penalty goal against England. Only in his ninth international appearance, Hastings thus became the fastest century-maker for Scotland.

**FINAL TABLE**

| | P | W | D | L | F | A | Pts |
|---|---|---|---|---|---|---|---|
| France | 4 | 4 | 0 | 0 | 82 | 59 | 8 |
| Ireland | 4 | 2 | 0 | 2 | 57 | 46 | 4 |
| **Scotland** | **4** | **2** | **0** | **2** | **71** | **76** | **4** |
| Wales | 4 | 1 | 0 | 3 | 54 | 64 | 2 |
| England | 4 | 1 | 0 | 3 | 48 | 67 | 2 |

# 1987 First Rugby World Cup

## Group Matches

### v FRANCE

**DRAWN 20-20**
Scotland: 4PG 2T
France: 1G 2PG 2T
Christchurch, 23 May 1987

A.G. Hastings 4PG

M.D.F. Duncan 1T
K.W. Robertson
D.S. Wyllie
I. Tukalo

J.Y. Rutherford [1]
R.J. Laidlaw

D.M.B. Sole
* C.T. Deans
I.G. Milne
D.B. White 1T
A.J. Tomes
J. Jeffrey
I.A.M. Paxton
F. Calder

1 Rep by † A.V. Tait

### v ZIMBABWE

**WON 60-21**
Scotland: 8G 3T
Zimbabwe: 1G 5PG
Wellington, 30 May 1987

A.G. Hastings 8C 1T

M.D.F. Duncan 2T
A.V. Tait 2T
K.W. Robertson
I. Tukalo 2T

D.S. Wyllie
† G.H. Oliver 1T

D.M.B. Sole
* C.T. Deans
I.G. Milne
J.R.E. Campbell-Lamerton
A.J. Tomes
J. Jeffrey 1T
I.A.M. Paxton 2T
F. Calder

### v ROMANIA

**WON 55-28**
Romania: 2G 4PG 1T
Scotland: 8G 1PG 1T
Dunedin, 2 Jun 1987

A.G. Hastings 8C 1PG 2T

M.D.F. Duncan 1T
A.V. Tait 2T
S. Hastings [1]
I. Tukalo 1T

D.S. Wyllie
R.J. Laidlaw

D.M.B. Sole
* C.T. Deans
N.A. Rowan
D.B. White
A.J. Tomes [2]
J. Jeffrey 3T
I.A.M. Paxton
F. Calder

1 Rep by † R.I. Cramb
2 Rep by J.R.E. Campbell-Lamerton

## Quarter-final

### v NEW ZEALAND

**LOST 3-30**
NZ: 2G 6PG
Scotland: 1PG
Christchurch, 6 Jun 1987

A.G. Hastings 1PG

M.D.F. Duncan
A.V. Tait
K.W. Robertson
I. Tukalo

D.S. Wyllie
R.J. Laidlaw

D.M.B. Sole
* C.T. Deans
I.G. Milne
D.B. White
A.J. Tomes
† D.J. Turnbull
I.A.M. Paxton
F. Calder

### FACT FILE

- The 60-21 win against Zimbabwe established a new record score for Scotland in a Test. Gavin Hastings set a new Scotland Test record with his 27 points in the pool match against Romania.
- Scotland were beaten by eventual winners New Zealand in the quarter-finals of the first Rugby World Cup, staged in Australia and New Zealand.

## 1987-88

### Five Nations Championship

**v IRELAND**

**LOST 18-22**
Ireland: 2G 1PG 1DG 1T
Scotland: 2G 2PG
Lansdowne Road, 16 Jan 1988

A.G. Hastings 2PG 2C

M.D.F. Duncan
A.V. Tait
S. Hastings 1T
G.R.T. Baird

R.I. Cramb
R.J. Laidlaw 1T

D.M.B. Sole
* G.J. Callander
N.A. Rowan
D.B. White
† D.F. Cronin
J. Jeffrey
I.A.M Paxton
F. Calder

**v FRANCE**

**WON 23-12**
Scotland: 4PG 1DG 2T
France: 1DG 1PG 1G
Murrayfield, 6 Feb 1988

A.G. Hastings 4PG 1T

M.D.F. Duncan
A.V. Tait
S. Hastings
I. Tukalo 1T

R.I. Cramb 1DG
R.J. Laidlaw

D.M.B. Sole
* G.J. Callander
N.A. Rowan
A.J. Campbell
D.F. Cronin
D.J. Turnbull
D.B. White
F. Calder

**v WALES**

**LOST 20-25**
Wales: 2G 2DG 1PG 1T
Scotland: 4PG 2T
Cardiff Arms Park, 20 Feb 1988

A.G. Hastings 4PG

M.D.F. Duncan 1T
A.V. Tait
S. Hastings
I. Tukalo

† A.B.M. Ker
R.J. Laidlaw

D.M.B. Sole
* G.J. Callander
N.A. Rowan
A.J. Campbell
D.F. Cronin
J. Jeffrey
D.B. White
F. Calder 1T

**v ENGLAND**

**LOST 6-9**
Scotland: 2PG
England: 1DG 2PG
Murrayfield, 5 Mar 1988

A.G. Hastings 2PG

M.D.F. Duncan
A.V. Tait
K.W. Robertson
I. Tukalo

A.B.M. Ker
R.J. Laidlaw

D.M.B. Sole
* G.J. Callander
N.A. Rowan
D.B. White
D.F. Cronin
D.J. Turnbull
I.A.M. Paxton
F. Calder

**FACT FILE**

- John Jeffrey, Derek White and Finlay Calder formed the back row for the first time against Wales. They went on to establish a national record by playing 17 times together until Jeffrey and Calder retired after the 1991 Rugby World Cup.

**FINAL TABLE**

| | P | W | D | L | F | A | Pts |
|---|---|---|---|---|---|---|---|
| Wales | 4 | 3 | 0 | 1 | 57 | 42 | 6 |
| France | 4 | 3 | 0 | 1 | 57 | 47 | 6 |
| England | 4 | 2 | 0 | 2 | 56 | 30 | 4 |
| **Scotland** | **4** | **1** | **0** | **3** | **67** | **68** | **2** |
| Ireland | 4 | 1 | 0 | 3 | 40 | 90 | 2 |

## 1988-89

### Tour Match

#### v AUSTRALIA

**LOST 13-32**
Scotland: 1G 1PG 1T
Australia: 3G 2PG 2T
Murrayfield, 19 Nov 1988

A.G. Hastings 1T 1C 1PG

M.D.F. Duncan
S. Hastings
K.W. Robertson 1T
I. Tukalo

R.I. Cramb
† G. Armstrong

D.M.B. Sole
* G.J. Callander
I.G. Milne
A.J. Campbell
D.F. Cronin
D.B. White [1]
I.A.M. Paxton
J. Jeffrey

1 Rep by † G.R. Marshall

### Five Nations Championship

#### v WALES

**WON 23-7**
Scotland: 1G 2PG 1DG 2T
Wales: 1PG 1T
Murrayfield, 21 Jan 1989

P.W. Dods 1C 2PG

M.D.F. Duncan
S. Hastings
† S.R.P. Lineen
I. Tukalo

† C.M. Chalmers 1DG 1T
G. Armstrong 1T

D.M.B. Sole
† K.S. Milne
I.G. Milne
† C.A. Gray
D.F. Cronin
J. Jeffrey
D.B. White 1T
* F. Calder

#### v ENGLAND

**DRAWN 12-12**
England: 4PG
Scotland: 1G 2PG
Twickenham, 4 Feb 1989

P.W. Dods 1C 2PG

K.W. Robertson
S. Hastings
S.R.P. Lineen
I. Tukalo

C.M. Chalmers
G. Armstrong

D.M.B. Sole
K.S. Milne
† A.P. Burnell
C.A. Gray
D.F. Cronin
J. Jeffrey 1T
D.B. White
* F. Calder

#### v IRELAND

**WON 37-21**
Scotland: 4G 3PG 1T
Ireland: 3G 1PG
Murrayfield, 4 Mar 1989

P.W. Dods 4C 3PG

K.W. Robertson
S. Hastings
S.R.P. Lineen
I. Tukalo 3T

C.M. Chalmers
G. Armstrong

D.M.B. Sole
K.S. Milne
A.P. Burnell
C.A. Gray
D.F. Cronin 1T
J. Jeffrey 1T
D.B. White
* F. Calder

#### v FRANCE

**LOST 3-19**
France: 2G 1PG 1T
Scotland: 1PG
Parc des Princes, 18 Mar 1989

P.W. Dods 1PG

K.W. Robertson
S. Hastings
S.R.P. Lineen
I. Tukalo

C.M. Chalmers
G. Armstrong

D.M.B. Sole
K.S. Milne
A.P. Burnell
C.A. Gray
D.F. Cronin
J. Jeffrey
D.B. White
* F. Calder

#### FACT FILE

- Peter Dods fired Scotland to their then highest score against Ireland in the 37-21 win at Murrayfield.

#### FINAL TABLE

| | P | W | D | L | F | A | Pts |
|---|---|---|---|---|---|---|---|
| France | 4 | 3 | 0 | 1 | 76 | 47 | 6 |
| England | 4 | 2 | 1 | 1 | 48 | 27 | 5 |
| **Scotland** | **4** | **2** | **1** | **1** | **75** | **59** | **5** |
| Ireland | 4 | 1 | 0 | 3 | 64 | 92 | 2 |
| Wales | 4 | 1 | 0 | 3 | 44 | 82 | 2 |

## 1989-90

### Tour Matches

**v FIJI**

**WON 38-17**
Scotland: 4G 2PG 2T
Fiji: 3PG 2T
Murrayfield, 28 Oct 1989

A.G. Hastings 4C 2PG 1T
† A.G. Stanger 2T
S. Hastings
S.R.P. Lineen
I. Tukalo 1T
C.M. Chalmers
G. Armstrong
* D.M.B. Sole
K.S. Milne 1T
A.P. Burnell
C.A. Gray 1T
D.F. Cronin
J. Jeffrey
D.B. White
G.R. Marshall [1]

1 Rep by † G.A.E. Buchanan-Smith

**v ROMANIA**

**WON 32-0**
Scotland: 3G 2PG 2T
Romania: Nil
Murrayfield, 9 Dec 1989

A.G. Hastings 3C 2PG
A.G. Stanger 3T
S. Hastings
S.R.P. Lineen
† W.L. Renwick
D.S. Wyllie
G. Armstrong
* D.M.B. Sole 1T
K.S. Milne
A.P. Burnell
C.A. Gray
D.F. Cronin
J. Jeffrey
D.B. White 1T
F. Calder

### Five Nations Championship

**v IRELAND**

**WON 13-10**
Ireland: 2PG 1T
Scotland: 1G 1PG 1T
Lansdowne Road, 3 Feb 1990

A.G. Hastings
A.G. Stanger
S. Hastings
S.R.P. Lineen
I. Tukalo
C.M. Chalmers 1C 1PG
G. Armstrong
* D.M.B. Sole
K.S. Milne
A.P. Burnell
C.A. Gray
D.F. Cronin
J. Jeffrey
D.B. White 2T
F. Calder

**v FRANCE**

**WON 21-0**
Scotland: 2G 3PG
France: Nil
Murrayfield, 17 Feb 1990

A.G. Hastings 1PG
A.G. Stanger
S. Hastings
S.R.P. Lineen
I. Tukalo 1T
C.M. Chalmers 2C 2PG
G. Armstrong
* D.M.B. Sole
K.S. Milne
A.P. Burnell
C.A. Gray
D.F. Cronin
J. Jeffrey
D.B. White
F. Calder 1T

**v WALES**

**WON 13-9**
Wales: 1G 1PG
Scotland: 3PG 1T
Cardiff Arms Park, 3 Mar 1990

A.G. Hastings
A.G. Stanger
S. Hastings
S.R.P. Lineen
I. Tukalo
C.M. Chalmers 3PG
G. Armstrong
* D.M.B. Sole
K.S. Milne
A.P. Burnell
C.A. Gray
D.F. Cronin 1T
J. Jeffrey
D.B. White
F. Calder

**v ENGLAND**

**WON 13-7**
Scotland: 3PG 1T
England: 1PG 1T
Murrayfield, 17 Mar 1990

A.G. Hastings
A.G. Stanger 1T
S. Hastings
S.R.P. Lineen
I. Tukalo
C.M. Chalmers 3PG
G. Armstrong
* D.M.B. Sole
K.S. Milne
A.P. Burnell
C.A. Gray
D.F. Cronin
J. Jeffrey
D.B. White [1]
F. Calder

Rep by D.J. Turnbull

## 1989-90 continued

### FACT FILE

- Victory in the decider with England brought Scotland their third championship Grand Slam and last to date.
- Scotland were unchanged throughout the Five Nations season for the first time.

### FINAL TABLE

| | P | W | D | L | F | A | Pts |
|---|---|---|---|---|---|---|---|
| **Scotland** | **4** | **4** | **0** | **0** | **60** | **26** | **8** |
| England | 4 | 3 | 0 | 1 | 90 | 26 | 6 |
| France | 4 | 2 | 0 | 2 | 61 | 78 | 4 |
| Ireland | 4 | 1 | 0 | 3 | 36 | 75 | 2 |
| Wales | 4 | 0 | 0 | 4 | 42 | 84 | 0 |

### Tour Matches

#### 1st v NEW ZEALAND

**LOST** **16-31**
NZ: 4G 1PG 1T
Scotland: 2G 1T
Dunedin, 16 Jun 1990

A.G. Hastings 2C

A.G. Stanger
S. Hastings
S.R.P. Lineen 1T
I. Tukalo

C.M. Chalmers
G. Armstrong

* D.M.B. Sole 1T
† J. Allan
I.G. Milne
C.A. Gray 1T
D.F. Cronin
J. Jeffrey
D.B. White
F. Calder

#### 2nd v NEW ZEALAND

**LOST** **18-21**
NZ: 1G 5PG
Scotland: 2G 2PG
Auckland, 23 Jun 1990

A.G. Hastings 2C 2PG

A.G. Stanger 1T
S. Hastings
S.R.P. Lineen
† A. Moore 1T

C.M. Chalmers
G. Armstrong [1]

* D.M.B. Sole
K.S. Milne
I.G. Milne
C.A. Gray
D.F. Cronin
J. Jeffrey
D.B. White
F. Calder

1 Rep by G.H. Oliver

## 1990-91

### Tour Match

#### v ARGENTINA

**WON** **49-3**
Scotland: 5G 1PG 4T
Argentina: 1PG
Murrayfield, 10 Nov 1990

A.G. Hastings 5C 1PG 1T

A.G. Stanger 2T
S. Hastings
S.R.P. Lineen
A. Moore 1T

C.M. Chalmers 1T
G. Armstrong 1T

* D.M.B. Sole
K.S. Milne 2T
A.P. Burnell
C.A. Gray 1T
† G.W. Weir
J. Jeffrey
G.R. Marshall
G.A.E. Buchanan-Smith

### Five Nations Championship

#### v FRANCE

**LOST** **9-15**
France: 3DG 2PG
Scotland: 1DG 2PG
Parc des Princes, 19 Jan 1991

A.G. Hastings

A.G. Stanger
S. Hastings
S.R.P. Lineen
A. Moore

C.M. Chalmers 1DG 2PG
G. Armstrong

* D.M.B. Sole
K.S. Milne
A.P. Burnell
C.A. Gray
D.F. Cronin
D.J. Turnbull
D.B. White
J. Jeffrey

#### v WALES

**WON** **32-12**
Scotland: 2G 3PG 1DG 2T
Wales: 1G 2PG
Murrayfield, 2 Feb 1991

A.G. Hastings 1C 2PG

A.G. Stanger
S. Hastings
S.R.P. Lineen
A. Moore

C.M. Chalmers 1DG 1C 1PG 1T
G. Armstrong 1T

* D.M.B. Sole
J. Allan [1]
A.P. Burnell
C.A. Gray
D.F. Cronin
D.J. Turnbull
D.B. White 2T
J. Jeffrey

1 Rep by K.S. Milne

## 1990-91 continued

### Five Nations Championship

**v ENGLAND**

**LOST 12-21**
England: 1G 5PG
Scotland: 4PG
Twickenham, 16 Feb 1991

A.G. Hastings

A.G. Stanger
S. Hastings
S.R.P. Lineen
A. Moore

C.M. Chalmers **4PG**
G. Armstrong

* D.M.B. Sole
K.S. Milne
A.P. Burnell
C.A. Gray
D.F. Cronin
D.J. Turnbull
D.B. White
J. Jeffrey

**v IRELAND**

**WON 28-25**
Scotland: 2G 4PG 1T
Ireland: 3G 1DG 1T
Murrayfield, 16 Mar 1991

A.G. Hastings **1PG 1T**

A.G. Stanger **1T**
S. Hastings **1T**
S.R.P. Lineen
I. Tukalo [1]

C.M. Chalmers **2C 3PG**
G. Armstrong

* D.M.B. Sole
J. Allan
A.P. Burnell
C.A. Gray
D.F. Cronin
D.J. Turnbull
D.B. White
J. Jeffrey

1 Rep by P.W. Dods

### World Cup Warm-up Match

**v ROMANIA**

**LOST 12-18**
Romania: 2G 2PG
Scotland: 1G 2PG
Bucharest, 31 Aug 1991

P.W. Dods **1C 2PG**

A.G. Stanger
S.R.P. Lineen
D.S. Wyllie
I. Tukalo **1T**

C.M. Chalmers
G. Armstrong

* D.M.B. Sole
J. Allan
A.P. Burnell
D.F. Cronin
G.W. Weir
D.J. Turnbull
D.B. White
F. Calder

### FACT FILE

- In the 49-3 win against Argentina at Murrayfield, Gavin Hastings passed Andy Irvine's haul of 273 points to become Scotland's leading points scorer in Tests.
- Craig Chalmers became the first Scot to register a full house of scoring (try, conversion, penalty and drop goal) in a Test with his contributions against Wales.

### FINAL TABLE

| | P | W | D | L | F | A | Pts |
|---|---|---|---|---|---|---|---|
| England | 4 | 4 | 0 | 0 | 83 | 44 | 8 |
| France | 4 | 3 | 0 | 1 | 91 | 46 | 6 |
| **Scotland** | **4** | **2** | **0** | **2** | **81** | **73** | **4** |
| Ireland | 4 | 0 | 1 | 3 | 66 | 86 | 1 |
| Wales | 4 | 0 | 1 | 3 | 42 | 114 | 1 |

*Damien Cronin (5) and John Jeffrey (7) in Five Nations line-out action v Ireland at Murrayfield in 1991.*

# 1991 Second Rugby World Cup

## Group Matches

### v JAPAN

**WON 47-9**
Scotland: 5G‡ 3PG 2T
Japan: 1G 1DG
Murrayfield, 5 Oct 1991

A.G. Hastings **5C 2PG 1T**

A.G. Stanger **1T**
S. Hastings **1T**
S.R.P. Lineen
I. Tukalo **1T**

C.M. Chalmers [1] **1PG 1T**
G. Armstrong

* D.M.B. Sole [2]
J. Allan
A.P. Burnell
C.A. Gray
G.W. Weir
J. Jeffrey
D.B. White **1T**
F. Calder **1T ‡**

‡includes penalty try
1 Rep by D.S. Wyllie
2 Rep by † D.F. Milne

### v ZIMBABWE

**WON 51-12**
Scotland: 5G 2PG 1DG 3T
Zimbabwe: 2G
Murrayfield, 9 Oct 1991

* P.W. Dods **5C 2PG**

A.G. Stanger [1] **1T**
S. Hastings **1T**
S.R.P. Lineen
I. Tukalo **3T**

D.S. Wyllie **1DG**
G.H. Oliver

A.P. Burnell
K.S. Milne
† A.G.J. Watt
D.F. Cronin
G.W. Weir **1T**
D.J. Turnbull **1T**
D.B. White **1T**
G.R. Marshall

1 Rep by C.M. Chalmers

### v IRELAND

**WON 24-15**
Scotland: 2G 3PG 1DG
Ireland: 4PG 1DG
Murrayfield, 12 Oct 1991

A.G. Hastings **2C 3PG**

A.G. Stanger
S. Hastings
S.R.P. Lineen
I. Tukalo

C.M. Chalmers [1] **1DG**
G. Armstrong **1T**

* D.M.B. Sole
J. Allan
A.P. Burnell
C.A. Gray
G.W. Weir
J. Jeffrey
D.B. White
F. Calder

1 Rep by † A.G. Shiel **1T**

## Quarter-final

### v WESTERN SAMOA

**WON 28-6**
Scotland: 2G 4PG 1T
WS: 1PG 1DG
Murrayfield, 19 Oct 1991

A.G. Hastings **2C 4PG**

A.G. Stanger **1T**
S. Hastings
A.G. Shiel
I. Tukalo

C.M. Chalmers
G. Armstrong

* D.M.B. Sole
J. Allan
A.P. Burnell
C.A. Gray
G.W. Weir
J. Jeffrey **2T**
D.B. White
F. Calder

## Semi-final

### v ENGLAND

**LOST 6-9**
Scotland: 2PG
England: 2PG 1DG
Murrayfield, 26 Oct 1991

A.G. Hastings **2PG**

A.G. Stanger
S. Hastings
S.R.P. Lineen
I. Tukalo

C.M. Chalmers
G. Armstrong

* D.M.B. Sole
J. Allan
A.P. Burnell
C.A. Gray
G.W. Weir
J. Jeffrey
D.B. White
F. Calder

## Third/Fourth Place Play-off

### v NEW ZEALAND

**LOST 6-13**
Scotland: 2PG
NZ: 3PG 1T
Cardiff Arms Park, 30 Oct 1991

A.G. Hastings **2PG**

A.G. Stanger [1]
S. Hastings
S.R.P. Lineen
I. Tukalo

C.M. Chalmers
G. Armstrong

* D.M.B. Sole
J. Allan
A.P. Burnell
C.A. Gray
G.W. Weir
J. Jeffrey
D.B. White
F. Calder

1 Rep by P.W. Dods

## 1991-92

### Five Nations Championship

**v ENGLAND**

**LOST 7-25**
Scotland: 1PG 1T
England: 1G 4PG 1DG 1T
Murrayfield, 18 Jan 1992

A.G. Hastings 1PG

A.G. Stanger
S. Hastings
S.R.P. Lineen
I. Tukalo

C.M. Chalmers
† A.D. Nicol

* D.M.B. Sole
K.S. Milne
A.P. Burnell
† N.G.B. Edwards
G.W. Weir
† D.J. McIvor
D.B. White 1T
† I.R. Smith

**v IRELAND**

**WON 18-10**
Ireland: 2PG 1T
Scotland: 2G 2PG
Lansdowne Road, 15 Feb 1992

A.G. Hastings 2PG 2C

A.G. Stanger 1T
S. Hastings
S.R.P. Lineen
I. Tukalo

C.M. Chalmers
A.D. Nicol 1T

* D.M.B. Sole
K.S. Milne
A.P. Burnell
N.G.B. Edwards [1]
G.W. Weir
D.J. McIvor
D.B. White
I.R. Smith

1 Rep by † R.I. Wainwright

**v FRANCE**

**WON 10-6**
Scotland: 2PG 1T
France: 2PG
Murrayfield, 7 Mar 1992

A.G. Hastings 2PG

A.G. Stanger
S. Hastings
S.R.P. Lineen
I. Tukalo

C.M. Chalmers
A.D. Nicol

* D.M.B. Sole
K.S. Milne
A.P. Burnell
N.G.B. Edwards 1T
G.W. Weir
D.J. McIvor
D.B. White
R.I. Wainwright

**v WALES**

**LOST 12-15**
Wales: 1G 3PG
Scotland: 3PG 1DG
Cardiff Arms Park, 21 Mar 1992

A.G. Hastings 1PG

A.G. Stanger
S. Hastings
S.R.P. Lineen
I. Tukalo

C.M. Chalmers 2PG 1DG
A.D. Nicol

* D.M.B. Sole
K.S. Milne
A.P. Burnell [1]
N.G.B. Edwards
G.W. Weir
D.J. McIvor
D.B. White
I.R. Smith

1 Rep by † P.M. Jones

**FACT FILE**

- David Sole passed Ian McLauchlan's record for most matches as Scotland's captain (19) in the opening match of the International Championship, against England.

**FINAL TABLE**

| | P | W | D | L | F | A | Pts |
|---|---|---|---|---|---|---|---|
| England | 4 | 4 | 0 | 0 | 118 | 29 | 8 |
| France | 4 | 2 | 0 | 2 | 75 | 62 | 4 |
| **Scotland** | **4** | **2** | **0** | **2** | **47** | **56** | **4** |
| Wales | 4 | 2 | 0 | 2 | 40 | 63 | 4 |
| Ireland | 4 | 0 | 0 | 4 | 46 | 116 | 0 |

## 1991-92 continued

### Tour Matches

**1st v AUSTRALIA**

**LOST 12-27**
Australia: 1G 3PG 3T
Scotland: 1G 2PG
Sydney, 13 Jun 1992

A.G. Hastings 1C 2PG

A.G. Stanger
S. Hastings
S.R.P. Lineen
I. Tukalo

C.M. Chalmers
A.D. Nicol

* D.M.B. Sole
K.S. Milne [1]
† P.H. Wright
N.G.B. Edwards
G.W. Weir
† C.D. Hogg
R.I. Wainwright 1T
I.R. Smith

1 Rep by † I. Corcoran

**2nd v AUSTRALIA**

**LOST 13-37**
Australia: 1G 5PG 4T
Scotland: 1G 1PG 1T
Brisbane, 21 Jun 1992

† K.M. Logan

A.G. Stanger
S. Hastings
S.R.P. Lineen 1T
I. Tukalo

C.M. Chalmers 1C 1PG
A.D. Nicol

* D.M.B. Sole 1T
† M.W. Scott
P.H. Wright
D.F. Cronin
G.W. Weir
C.D. Hogg
R.I. Wainwright
I.R. Smith

**FACT FILE**

- David Sole ended his Test career with the last score of the Brisbane international. It was also the last Scottish Test try valued at four points.

*Line-out action as Derek White tangles with England's Tim Rodber at Murrayfield in January, 1992.*

## 1992-93

### Five Nations Championship

**v IRELAND**

**WON 15-3**
Scotland: 1G 1PG 1T
Ireland: 1PG
Murrayfield, 16 Jan 1993

* A.G. Hastings 1C 1PG

A.G. Stanger 1T
S. Hastings
A.G. Shiel
† D.A. Stark 1T

C.M. Chalmers
G. Armstrong

A.G.J. Watt
K.S. Milne
A.P. Burnell
† A.I. Reed
D.F. Cronin
D.J. Turnbull
G.W. Weir
† I.R. Morrison

**v FRANCE**

**LOST 3-11**
France: 2PG 1T
Scotland: 1PG
Parc des Princes, 6 Feb 1993

* A.G. Hastings 1PG

A.G. Stanger
S. Hastings
A.G. Shiel
D.A. Stark

C.M. Chalmers
G. Armstrong

P.H. Wright
K.S. Milne
A.P. Burnell
A.I. Reed
D.F. Cronin
D.J. Turnbull
G.W. Weir
I.R. Morrison

**v WALES**

**WON 20-0**
Scotland: 5PG 1T
Wales: Nil
Murrayfield, 20 Feb 1993

* A.G. Hastings 5PG

A.G. Stanger
S. Hastings
A.G. Shiel
D.A. Stark

C.M. Chalmers
G. Armstrong

P.H. Wright
K.S. Milne
A.P. Burnell
A.I. Reed
D.F. Cronin
D.J. Turnbull 1T
G.W. Weir
I.R. Morrison

**v ENGLAND**

**LOST 12-26**
England: 1G 3PG 2T
Scotland: 3PG 1DG
Twickenham, 6 Mar 1993

* A.G. Hastings 3PG

A.G. Stanger
S. Hastings [2]
A.G. Shiel
D.A. Stark

C.M. Chalmers [1] 1DG
G. Armstrong

P.H. Wright
K.S. Milne
A.P. Burnell
A.I. Reed
D.F. Cronin
D.J. Turnbull
G.W. Weir
I.R. Morrison

1 Rep by † G.P.J. Townsend
2 Rep by K.M. Logan

**FACT FILE**

- Gavin Hastings set a new Scotland record for the series against Wales scoring 15 points. Gregor Townsend, the current Scotland cap record holder, made his debut with a cameo appearance as a replacement against England.

**FINAL TABLE**

| | P | W | D | L | F | A | Pts |
|---|---|---|---|---|---|---|---|
| France | 4 | 3 | 0 | 1 | 73 | 35 | 6 |
| **Scotland** | **4** | **2** | **0** | **2** | **50** | **40** | **4** |
| England | 4 | 2 | 0 | 2 | 54 | 54 | 4 |
| Ireland | 4 | 2 | 0 | 2 | 45 | 53 | 4 |
| Wales | 4 | 1 | 0 | 3 | 34 | 74 | 2 |

## 1993-94

### Tour Match

#### v NEW ZEALAND

**LOST 15-51**
Scotland: 5PG
NZ: 5G 2PG 2T
Murrayfield, 20 Nov 1993

* A.G. Hastings [b] **4PG**

A.G. Stanger
† I.C. Jardine
A.G. Shiel
S. Hastings

C.M. Chalmers [1] **1PG**
A.D. Nicol [a]

A.G.J. Watt
K.S. Milne
A.P. Burnell
D.F. Cronin [2]
† A.E.D. Macdonald
D.J. McIvor
G.W. Weir
R.I. Wainwright

1 Rep by D.S. Wyllie
2 Rep by C.D. Hogg
a Rep by † B.W. Redpath
b Rep by K.M. Logan

### Five Nations Championship

#### v WALES

**LOST 6-29**
Wales: 1G 4PG 2T
Scotland: 2PG
Cardiff Arms Park, 15 Jan 1994

* A.G. Hastings **2PG**

A.G. Stanger
G.P.J. Townsend
I.G. Jardine
K.M. Logan

C.M. Chalmers [2]
A.D. Nicol

P.H. Wright
K.S. Milne
A.P. Burnell
N.G.B. Edwards
† D.S. Munro
D.J. Turnbull
R.I. Wainwright
I.R. Morrison [1]

1 Rep by G.W. Weir
2 Rep by D.S. Wyllie

#### v ENGLAND

**LOST 14-15**
Scotland: 2PG 1DG 1T
England: 5PG
Murrayfield, 5 Feb 1994

* A.G. Hastings **2PG**

A.G. Stanger
S. Hastings [2]
D.S. Wyllie
K.M. Logan

G.P.J. Townsend **1DG**
G. Armstrong [a]

† A.V. Sharp
K.S. Milne
A.P. Burnell
D.S. Munro
A.I. Reed
† P. Walton
G.W. Weir
R.I. Wainwright [1] **1T**

1 Rep by I.R. Smith
2 Rep by I.C. Jardine
a Rep by B.W. Redpath

#### v IRELAND

**DRAWN 6-6**
Ireland: 2PG
Scotland: 2PG
Lansdowne Road, 5 Mar 1994

* A.G. Hastings [a] **2PG**

A.G. Stanger
S. Hastings
D.S. Wyllie
K.M. Logan

G.P.J. Townsend
G. Armstrong

A.V. Sharp
K.S. Milne
A.P. Burnell
D.S. Munro
A.I. Reed
P. Walton
G.W. Weir
I.R. Smith

a Rep by † M. Dods

#### v FRANCE

**LOST 12-20**
Scotland: 4PG
Ireland: 2G 2PG
Murrayfield, 19 Mar 1994

* A.G. Hastings **4PG**

A.G. Stanger
S. Hastings
D.S. Wyllie
K.M. Logan

G.P.J. Townsend
B.W. Redpath

A.V. Sharp
K.S. Milne
A.P. Burnell
D.S. Munro
A.I. Reed
P. Walton
G.W. Weir
I.R. Smith

#### FACT FILE

- Scotland conceded 50 points for the first time in a Test when they crashed to the All Blacks in the autumn international.

#### FINAL TABLE

| | P | W | D | L | F | A | Pts |
|---|---|---|---|---|---|---|---|
| Wales | 4 | 3 | 0 | 1 | 78 | 51 | 6 |
| England | 4 | 3 | 0 | 1 | 60 | 49 | 6 |
| France | 4 | 2 | 0 | 2 | 84 | 69 | 4 |
| Ireland | 4 | 1 | 1 | 2 | 49 | 70 | 3 |
| **Scotland** | **4** | **0** | **1** | **3** | **38** | **70** | **1** |

## 1993-94 continued

### Tour Matches

**1st v ARGENTINA**

**LOST 15-16**
Argentina: 1G 3PG
Scotland: 5PG
Buenos Aires, 4 Jun 1994

M. Dods **5PG**

† C.A. Joiner
I.C. Jardine
A.G. Shiel
K.M. Logan

G.P.J. Townsend
B.W. Redpath

A.V. Sharp
† K.D. McKenzie
A.P. Burnell
D.S. Munro
* A.I. Reed
P. Walton
C.D. Hogg
I.R. Smith

**2nd v ARGENTINA**

**LOST 17-19**
Argentina: 1G 3PG 1DG
Scotland: 3PG 1DG 1T
Buenos Aires, 11 Jun 1994

M. Dods **1PG**

C.A. Joiner
I.C. Jardine
A.G. Shiel **2PG**
K.M. Logan [2] **1T**

G.P.J. Townsend **1DG**
B.W. Redpath

A.V. Sharp [1]
K.D. McKenzie
A.P. Burnell
D.S. Munro [a]
* A.I. Reed
P. Walton
C.D. Hogg
I.R. Smith

a/1 Rep by A.G.J. Watt
2 Rep by † S.A. Nichol

## 1994-95

### Tour Matches

**v SOUTH AFRICA**

**LOST 10-34**
Scotland: 1G 1PG
SA: 3G 1PG 2T
Murrayfield, 19 Nov 1994

* A.G. Hastings **1PG 1C**

A.G. Stanger **1T**
S. Hastings
A.G. Shiel
K.M. Logan

C.M. Chalmers
† D.W. Patterson

A.V. Sharp
K.S. Milne
A.P. Burnell
† J.F. Richardson
A.I. Reed
D.J. McIvor
G.W. Weir
I.R. Morrison

**v CANADA**

**WON 22-6**
Scotland: 1G 5PG
Canada: 2PG
Murrayfield, 21 Jan 1995

* A.G. Hastings **5PG 1C**

C.A. Joiner
G.P.J. Townsend
I.C. Jardine
K.M. Logan

C.M. Chalmers
B.W. Redpath

† D.I.W. Hilton
K.S. Milne
P.H. Wright
D.F. Cronin **1T**
† S.J. Campbell
R.I. Wainwright
† E.W. Peters
I.R. Morrison

**FACT FILE**

- Tony Stanger's try in the autumn Test with the Springboks took him ahead of Iwan Tukalo (who scored 15) and into second place behind Ian Smith (24) on the list of leading try-scorers for Scotland.

## 1994-95 continued

### Five Nations Championship

**v IRELAND**

**WON 26-13**
Scotland: 2G 4PG
Ireland: 1PG 2T
Murrayfield, 4 Feb 1995

* A.G. Hastings 4PG 2C

C.A. Joiner 1T
G.P.J. Townsend
I.C. Jardine
K.M. Logan

C.M. Chalmers
B.W. Redpath

D.I.W. Hilton
K.S. Milne
P.H. Wright
D.F. Cronin 1T
S.J. Campbell
R.I. Wainwright
E.W. Peters
I.R. Morrison

**v FRANCE**

**WON 23-21**
France: 1PG 1DG 3T
Scotland: 2G 3PG
Parc des Princes, 18 Feb 1995

* A.G. Hastings 3PG 2C 1T

C.A. Joiner
G.P.J. Townsend 1T
I.C. Jardine
K.M. Logan

C.M. Chalmers
B.W. Redpath

D.I. W.Hilton
K.S. Milne
P.H. Wright
D.F. Cronin [1]
S.J. Campbell
R.I. Wainwright
E.W. Peters
I.R. Morrison

1 Rep by G.W. Weir

**v WALES**

**WON 26-13**
Scotland: 2G 4PG
Wales: 1G 2PG
Murrayfield, 4 Mar 1995

* A.G. Hastings 4PG 2C

C.A. Joiner
G.P.J. Townsend
S. Hastings
K.M. Logan

C.M. Chalmers
B.W. Redpath

D.I.W. Hilton 1T
K.S. Milne
P.H. Wright
G.W. Weir
S.J. Campbell
R.I. Wainwright
E.W. Peters 1T
I.R. Morrison

**v ENGLAND**

**LOST 12-24**
England: 7PG 1DG
Scotland: 2PG 2DG
Twickenham, 18 Mar 1995

* A.G. Hastings 2PG

C.A. Joiner
G.P.J. Townsend
S. Hastings
K.M. Logan

C.M. Chalmers 2DG
B.W. Redpath

D.I.W. Hilton [1]
K.S. Milne
P.H. Wright
G.W. Weir
S.J. Campbell
R.I. Wainwright
E.W. Peters
I.R. Morrison

1 Rep by † J.J. Manson

### World Cup Warm-up Match

**v ROMANIA**

**WON 49-16**
Scotland: 4G 2PG 3T
Romania: 1G 3PG
Murrayfield, 22 Apr 1995

* A.G. Hastings [1] 2PG 4C 1T

C.A. Joiner 1T
A.G. Stanger 2T
A.G. Shiel 1T
K.M. Logan 1T

C.M. Chalmers
B.W. Redpath

D.I.W. Hilton
K.D. McKenzie
P.H. Wright
G.W. Weir
S.J. Campbell
R.I. Wainwright
E.W. Peters 1T
I.R. Morrison

1 Rep by S. Hastings

**FACT FILE**

- There were two new Scotland scoring records for the International Championship. The team totalled 87 points of which Gavin Hastings contributed 56.

**FINAL TABLE**

| | P | W | D | L | F | A | Pts |
|---|---|---|---|---|---|---|---|
| England | 4 | 4 | 0 | 0 | 98 | 39 | 8 |
| **Scotland** | **4** | **3** | **0** | **1** | **87** | **71** | **6** |
| France | 4 | 2 | 0 | 2 | 77 | 70 | 4 |
| Ireland | 4 | 1 | 0 | 3 | 44 | 83 | 2 |
| Wales | 4 | 0 | 0 | 4 | 43 | 86 | 0 |

## 1995 Third Rugby World Cup

### Group Matches

**v IVORY COAST**

**WON 89-0**
Scotland: 9G 2PG 4T
Côte D'Ivoire: Nil
Rustenburg, 26 May 1995

* A.G. Hastings 2PG 9C 4T

C.A. Joiner
A.G. Stanger 1T
A.G. Shiel 1T
K.M. Logan 2T

C.M. Chalmers 1T
B.W. Redpath

A.P. Burnell 1T
K.D. McKenzie
P.H. Wright 1T
G.W. Weir
S.J. Campbell
P. Walton 2T
R.I. Wainwright
I.R. Smith

**v TONGA**

**WON 41-5**
Scotland: 1G 8PG 2T
Tonga: 1T
Pretoria, 30 May 1995

* A.G. Hastings 8PG 1C 1T

C.A. Joiner
S. Hastings 1T
I.C. Jardine
K.M. Logan

C.M. Chalmers
D.W. Patterson

D.I.W. Hilton
K.S. Milne
P.H. Wright [1]
D.F. Cronin
G.W. Weir
R.I. Wainwright
E.W. Peters 1T
I.R. Morrison

1 Rep by A.P. Burnell

**v FRANCE**

**LOST 19-22**
Scotland: 1G 4PG
France: 1G 5PG
Pretoria, 3 Jun 1995

* A.G. Hastings 4PG 1C

C.A. Joiner
S. Hastings
A.G. Shiel [a/1]
K.M. Logan

C.M. Chalmers
B.W. Redpath

D.I.W. Hilton
K.S. Milne
P.H. Wright [2]
D.F. Cronin
G.W. Weir
R.I. Wainwright 1T
E.W. Peters
I.R. Morrison

a/1 Rep by I.C. Jardine
2 Rep by A.P. Burnell

### Quarter-final

**v NEW ZEALAND**

**LOST 30-48**
Scotland: 3G 3PG
NZ: 6G 2PG
Pretoria, 11 Jun 1995

* A.G. Hastings 3PG 3C

C.A. Joiner
S. Hastings 1T
A.G. Shiel
K.M. Logan

C.M. Chalmers [1]
B.W. Redpath

D.I. W.Hilton
K.S. Milne
P.H. Wright
D.F. Cronin [2]
G.W. Weir 2T
R.I. Wainwright
E.W. Peters
I.R. Morrison

1 Rep by I.C. Jardine
2 Rep by S.J. Campbell

**FACT FILE**

- In the opening pool match, against the Ivory Coast, Gavin Hastings scored 44 points and Scotland won 89-0 – still national Test records.
- For the third time, Scotland's final fixture in the Rugby World Cup was against New Zealand. This time the side reached the quarter-finals.

## 1995-96

### Tour Match

**v WESTERN SAMOA**

**DRAWN 15-15**
Scotland: 5PG
WS: 1G 1PG 1T
Murrayfield, 18 Nov 1995

† R.J.S. Shepherd

M. Dods 5PG
G.P.J. Townsend
A.G. Shiel
K.M. Logan

C.M. Chalmers
B.W. Redpath

D.I.W. Hilton
† J.A. Hay
A.P. Burnell
G.W. Weir
D.F. Cronin
* R.I. Wainwright
† S.J. Reid
I.R. Smith [a]

a Rep by S.J. Campbell

### Five Nations Championship

**v IRELAND**

**WON 16-10**
Ireland: 1G 1PG
Scotland: 1PG 1DG 2T
Lansdowne Road, 20 Jan 1996

R.J.S. Shepherd

C.A. Joiner
S. Hastings
I.C. Jardine
M. Dods 1PG 1T

G.P.J. Townsend 1DG
B.W. Redpath

D.I.W. Hilton
K.D. McKenzie 1T
P.H. Wright
S.J. Campbell
G.W. Weir
* R.I. Wainwright
E.W. Peters
I.R. Smith

**v FRANCE**

**WON 19-14**
Scotland: 3PG 2T
France: 3PG 1T
Murrayfield, 3 Feb 1996

R.J.S. Shepherd

C.A. Joiner
S. Hastings
I.C. Jardine
M. Dods 2T 3PG

G.P.J. Townsend
B.W. Redpath

D.I.W. Hilton
K.D. McKenzie
P.H. Wright
S.J. Campbell
G.W. Weir
* R.I. Wainwright
E.W. Peters
I.R. Smith

**v WALES**

**WON 16-14**
Wales: 3PG 1T
Scotland: 1G 3PG
Cardiff Arms Park, 17 Feb 1996

R.J.S. Shepherd

C.A. Joiner [1]
S. Hastings
I.C. Jardine
M. Dods 1C 3PG

G.P.J. Townsend 1T
B.W. Redpath

D.I.W. Hilton
K.D. McKenzie
P.H. Wright
S.J. Campbell
G.W. Weir
* R.I. Wainwright
E.W. Peters
I.R. Smith

1 Rep by K.M. Logan

**v ENGLAND**

**LOST 9-18**
Scotland: 3PG
England: 6PG
Murrayfield, 2 Mar 1996

R.J.S. Shepherd

C.A. Joiner
S. Hastings
I.C. Jardine
M. Dods 3PG

G.P.J. Townsend
B.W. Redpath

D.I.W. Hilton
K.D. McKenzie
P.H. Wright
S.J. Campbell
G.W. Weir
* R.I. Wainwright
E.W. Peters
I.R. Smith

### FACT FILE

- Michael Dods created a new individual scoring record for Scotland against France, collecting all 19 points in the Murrayfield victory.

### FINAL TABLE

| | P | W | D | L | F | A | Pts |
|---|---|---|---|---|---|---|---|
| England | 4 | 3 | 0 | 1 | 79 | 54 | 6 |
| **Scotland** | **4** | **3** | **0** | **1** | **60** | **56** | **6** |
| France | 4 | 2 | 0 | 2 | 89 | 57 | 4 |
| Wales | 4 | 1 | 0 | 3 | 62 | 82 | 2 |
| Ireland | 4 | 1 | 0 | 3 | 65 | 106 | 2 |

## 1995-96 continued

### Tour Matches

**1st v NEW ZEALAND**

**LOST 31-62**
NZ: 7G 1PG 2T
Scotland: 2G 3PG 1DG 1T
Dunedin, 15 Jun 1996

R.J.S. Shepherd 2C 3PG 1DG

C.A. Joiner 1T
I.C. Jardine
† B.R.S. Eriksson
K.M. Logan

G.P.J. Townsend 1T
G. Armstrong

D.I.W. Hilton
K.D. McKenzie
P.H. Wright
G.W. Weir
D.F. Cronin
* R.I. Wainwright
E.W. Peters 1T
I.R. Smith

**2nd v NEW ZEALAND**

**LOST 12-36**
NZ: 4G‡ 1PG 1T
Scotland: 1G 1T
Auckland, 22 Jun 1996

R.J.S. Shepherd 1T 1C

A.G. Stanger
S. Hastings
I.C. Jardine [1]
K.M. Logan

G.P.J. Townsend
G. Armstrong

D.I.W. Hilton
K.D. McKenzie
† B.D. Stewart
G.W. Weir
D.F. Cronin
* R.I. Wainwright
E.W. Peters 1T
I.R. Smith

‡includes penalty try
1 Rep by D.A. Stark

**FACT FILE**

- Scotland conceded their then record number of points in a Test by losing 31-62 to New Zealand.
- Scott Hastings passed brother Gavin's record at Auckland to become Scotland's most-capped player.

## 1996-97

### Tour Match

**v AUSTRALIA**

**LOST 19-29**
Scotland: 3PG 2T
Australia: 2G 5PG
Murrayfield, 9 Nov 1996

R.J.S. Shepherd 3PG

A.G. Stanger 1T
* G.P.J. Townsend
B.R.S. Eriksson
K.M. Logan 1T

C.M. Chalmers
G. Armstrong [1]

D.I.W. Hilton
K.D. McKenzie
B.D. Stewart
D.F. Cronin
G.W. Weir
† M.I. Wallace
E.W. Peters
I.R. Smith

1 Rep by B.W. Redpath

### Friendly

**v ITALY**

**WON 29-22**
Scotland: 3G 1PG 1T
Italy: 1G‡ 4PG 1DG
Murrayfield, 14 Dec 1996

R.J.S. Shepherd [1] 1PG

A.G. Stanger 1T
S. Hastings
* G.P.J. Townsend
K.M. Logan 2T

C.M. Chalmers 3C
B.W. Redpath

D.I.W. Hilton
K.D. McKenzie
† M.J. Stewart
D.F. Cronin [2]
A.I. Reed
M.I. Wallace
E.W. Peters
I.R. Smith

‡includes penalty try
1 Rep by D.A. Stark 1T
2 Rep by G.W. Weir

## 1996-97 continued

### Five Nations Championship

**v WALES**

**LOST 19-34**
Scotland: 1G 3PG 1DG
Wales: 4G 2PG
Murrayfield, 18 Jan 1997

R.J.S. Shepherd 3PG 1C

A.G. Stanger
S. Hastings 1T
G.P.J. Townsend
K.M. Logan

C.M. Chalmers [2] 1DG
G. Armstrong

D.I.W. Hilton
† D.G. Ellis
M.J. Stewart
G.W. Weir
A.I. Reed [1]
P. Walton
* R.I. Wainwright
M.I. Wallace

1 Rep by D.S. Munro
2 Rep by D.A. Stark

**v ENGLAND**

**LOST 13-41**
England: 3G‡ 5PG 1T
Scotland: 1G 2PG
Twickenham, 1 Feb 1997

R.J.S. Shepherd 2PG 1C

D.A. Stark
A.G. Stanger
B.R.S. Eriksson [1] 1T
K.M. Logan

G.P.J. Townsend
B.W. Redpath

† T.J. Smith
D.G. Ellis
M.J. Stewart
G.W. Weir
A.I. Reed
P. Walton
* R.I. Wainwright
I.R. Smith

‡includes penalty try
1 Rep by S. Hastings

**v IRELAND**

**WON 38-10**
Scotland: 5G 1PG
Ireland: 1G 1PG
Murrayfield, 1 Mar 1997

R.J.S. Shepherd 1PG 5C

A.G. Stanger 1T
A.V. Tait 1T
G.P.J. Townsend 1T
K.M. Logan

C.M. Chalmers
B.W. Redpath

T.J. Smith
D.G. Ellis
M.J. Stewart
G.W. Weir 1T
A.I. Reed
* R.I. Wainwright
P. Walton 1T
I.R. Smith

**v FRANCE**

**LOST 20-47**
France: 3G 6PG 1DG 1T
Scotland: 2G 2PG
Parc des Princes, 15 Mar 1997

R.J.S. Shepherd 2PG 2C

A.G. Stanger
A.V. Tait [3] 2T
G.P.J. Townsend
K.M. Logan

C.M. Chalmers [2]
B.W. Redpath

T.J. Smith
D.G. Ellis
M.J. Stewart
G.W. Weir
A.I. Reed
* R.I. Wainwright
P. Walton [1]
I.R. Smith

1 Rep by D.F. Cronin
2 Rep by † D.W. Hodge
3 Rep by † I.C. Glasgow

**FACT FILE**

- The 90 points were a new Scotland team record for an International Championship season.
- The 38-10 result against Ireland set a new record highest score for Scotland in a championship match.
- France's 47-20 Paris win was the highest score then conceded by the Scots in the championship.

**FINAL TABLE**

| | P | W | D | L | F | A | Pts |
|---|---|---|---|---|---|---|---|
| France | 4 | 4 | 0 | 0 | 129 | 77 | 8 |
| England | 4 | 3 | 0 | 1 | 141 | 55 | 6 |
| Wales | 4 | 1 | 0 | 3 | 94 | 106 | 2 |
| **Scotland** | **4** | **1** | **0** | **3** | **90** | **132** | **2** |
| Ireland | 4 | 1 | 0 | 3 | 57 | 141 | 2 |

## 1997-98

### Tour Matches

**v AUSTRALIA**

**LOST 8-37**
Scotland: 1PG 1T
Australia: 3G 2PG 2T
Murrayfield, 22 Nov 1997

D.W. Hodge 1PG

† J.M. Craig
A.G. Stanger [3]
A.V. Tait
K.M. Logan

G.P.J. Townsend
* A.D. Nicol

D.I.W. Hilton [4]
† G. McKelvey
M.J. Stewart [2]
S.J. Campbell
† S. Murray 1T
† A.J. Roxburgh [1]
E.W. Peters
I.R. Smith [a]

1 Rep by † S.B. Grimes
2 Rep by † G. Graham
3 Rep by C.M. Chalmers
a Rep by S.B. Grimes
4 Rep by M.J. Stewart

**v SOUTH AFRICA**

**LOST 10-68**
Scotland: 1G 1PG
SA: 9G 1T
Murrayfield, 6 Dec 1997

R.J.S. Shepherd 1C 1PG

C.A. Joiner
A.G. Stanger [a]
C.M. Chalmers [1]
D.A. Stark 1T

G.P.J. Townsend
A.D. Nicol [2]

D.I.W. Hilton [4]
† G.C. Bulloch
M.J. Stewart
S.J. Campbell
S. Murray
* R.I. Wainwright
E.W. Peters [3]
I.R. Smith

a/1 Rep by D.W. Hodge
2 Rep by G. Armstrong
3 Rep by P. Walton
4 Rep by G. Graham

### Friendly

**v ITALY**

**LOST 21-25**
Italy: 1G 6PG
Scotland: 1G 3PG 1T
Treviso, 24 Jan 1998

R.J.S. Shepherd 1C 3PG 1T

A.G. Stanger
A.V. Tait 1T
C.M. Chalmers
C.A. Joiner

G.P.J. Townsend
G. Armstrong

D.I.W. Hilton
G.C. Bulloch
M.J. Stewart
G.W. Weir
S. Murray
* R.I. Wainwright
A.J. Roxburgh
† S.D. Holmes

### Five Nations Championship

**v IRELAND**

**WON 17-16**
Ireland: 1G‡ 2PG 1DG
Scotland: 4PG 1T
Lansdowne Road, 7 Feb 1998

R.J.S. Shepherd [4] 2PG

C.A. Joiner [1]
A.V. Tait 1T
G.P.J. Townsend
K.M. Logan

C.M. Chalmers 2PG
* G. Armstrong

G. Graham [2]
G.C. Bulloch
M.J. Stewart
D.F. Cronin [3]
G.W. Weir
R.I. Wainwright
P. Walton
S.D. Holmes

‡includes penalty try
1 Rep by A.G. Stanger
2 Rep by D.I.W. Hilton
3 Rep by S.B. Grimes
4 Rep by † D.J. Lee

**v FRANCE**

**LOST 16-51**
Scotland: 1G 3PG
France: 5G 2PG 2T
Murrayfield, 21 Feb 1998

D.J. Lee

A.G. Stanger 1T
A.V. Tait
G.P.J. Townsend
K.M. Logan

C.M. Chalmers [4] 1C 3PG
* G. Armstrong

D.I.W. Hilton [2]
G.C. Bulloch
M.J. Stewart
D.F. Cronin [1]
G.W. Weir
R.I. Wainwright
P. Walton [3]
S.D. Holmes

1 Rep by S.B. Grimes
2 Rep by G. Graham
3 Rep by A.J. Roxburgh
4 Rep by † S.L. Longstaff

**v WALES**

**LOST 13-19**
Wales: 1G 4PG
Scotland: 1PG 2T
Wembley, 7 Mar 1998

D.J. Lee [2]

A.G. Stanger
G.P.J. Townsend 1T
A.V. Tait
S.L. Longstaff

C.M. Chalmers 1PG
* G. Armstrong

D.I.W. Hilton
G.C. Bulloch
M.J. Stewart [3]
D.F. Cronin [1] 1T
G.W. Weir
R.I. Wainwright
E.W. Peters
A.J. Roxburgh

1 Rep by S.B. Grimes
2 Rep by R.J.S. Shepherd
3 Rep by G. Graham

## 1997-98 continued

### Five Nations Championship

**v ENGLAND**

**LOST 20-34**
Scotland: 2G 2PG
England: 4G‡ 1PG 1DG
Murrayfield, 22 Mar 1998

D.J. Lee **2C**

A.G. Stanger **1T**
G.P.J. Townsend
A.V. Tait
S.L. Longstaff **1T**

C.M. Chalmers [2] **2PG**
* G. Armstrong

D.I.W. Hilton
G.C. Bulloch
A.P. Burnell
D.F. Cronin [1]
G.W. Weir
R.I. Wainwright
E.W. Peters
A.J. Roxburgh

‡includes penalty try
1 Rep by S.B. Grimes
2 Rep by † C.A. Murray

### Tour Matches

**v FIJI**

**LOST 26-51**
Fiji: 5G 2PG 2T
Scotland: 2G 4PG
Suva, 26 May 1998

D.J. Lee **2C 4PG**

† H.R. Gilmour **1T**
C.A. Murray
I.C. Jardine [a]
S.L. Longstaff

G.P.J. Townsend
B.W. Redpath

† G.R. McIlwham
G.C. Bulloch **1T**
† M.C. Proudfoot [1]
S. Murray [2]
S.B. Grimes
* R.I. Wainwright
E.W. Peters
A.J. Roxburgh

a Rep by R.J.S. Shepherd
1 Rep by M.J. Stewart
2 Rep by S.J. Campbell

**1st v AUSTRALIA**

**LOST 3-45**
Australia: 4G 4PG 1T
Scotland: 1PG
Sydney, 13 June 1998

† G.H. Metcalfe

D.J. Lee **1PG**
C.A. Murray
R.J.S. Shepherd
S.L. Longstaff

G.P.J. Townsend
B.W. Redpath

D.I.W. Hilton
G.C. Bulloch [1]
M.C. Proudfoot
S.B. Grimes
S. Murray
* R.I. Wainwright
E.W. Peters
† G.L. Simpson [2]

1 Rep by K.D. McKenzie
2 Rep by A.J. Roxburgh

**2nd v AUSTRALIA**

**LOST 11-33**
Australia: 2G 3PG 2T
Scotland: 2PG 1T
Brisbane, 20 June 1998

G.H. Metcalfe [3]

D.J. Lee **2PG**
C.A. Murray [1]
R.J.S. Shepherd
S.L. Longstaff

G.P.J. Townsend
B.W. Redpath

D.I.W. Hilton [2]
K.D. McKenzie
M.C. Proudfoot
S.B. Grimes [4]
S. Murray
* R.I. Wainwright
E.W. Peters
G.L. Simpson [5]

1 Rep by C.A. Joiner
2 Rep by G.R. McIlwham
3 Rep by D.W. Hodge **1T**
4 Rep by S.J. Campbell
5 Rep by A.J. Roxburgh

### FACT FILE

- The hiding at Murrayfield by the Springboks is Scotland's record losing margin in Tests and most points conceded in a home Test.
- Scotland conceded 50 points in a championship match for the first time when beaten 51-16 at Murrayfield by France.
- The summer tour saw new record defeats by Fiji and Australia. Fiji became the first team outside the eight senior IB nations to score 50 points against Scotland.

### FINAL TABLE

| | P | W | D | L | F | A | Pts |
|---|---|---|---|---|---|---|---|
| France | 4 | 4 | 0 | 0 | 144 | 49 | 8 |
| England | 4 | 3 | 0 | 1 | 146 | 87 | 6 |
| Wales | 4 | 2 | 0 | 2 | 75 | 145 | 4 |
| **Scotland** | **4** | **1** | **0** | **3** | **66** | **120** | **2** |
| Ireland | 4 | 0 | 0 | 4 | 70 | 100 | 0 |

## 1998-99

### Tour Match

**v SOUTH AFRICA**

**LOST 10-35**
Scotland: 1G 1PG
SA: 2G 2PG 3T
Murrayfield, 21 Nov 1998

D.J. Lee [1]

A.V. Tait [4]
† M.J.M. Mayer
† J.A. Leslie
C.A. Murray

D.W. Hodge 1PG 1C 1T
* B.W. Redpath [5]

T.J. Smith
G.C. Bulloch
A.P. Burnell [3]
S. Murray
G.W. Weir
P. Walton [2]
E.W. Peters
† A.C. Pountney

1 Rep by G.P.J. Townsend
2 Rep by † M.D. Leslie
3 Rep by D.I.W. Hilton
4 Rep by K.M. Logan
5 Rep by G. Armstrong

### Five Nations Championship

**v WALES**

**WON 33-20**
Scotland: 2G 3PG 2T
Wales: 2G 2PG
Murrayfield, 6 Feb 1999

G.H. Metcalfe

C.A. Murray
G.P.J. Townsend 1T
J.A. Leslie 1T
K.M. Logan 2C 2PG

D.W. Hodge [2] 1PG
* G. Armstrong

T.J. Smith
G.C. Bulloch
A.P. Burnell [4]
S. Murray 1T
G.W. Weir [1]
P. Walton [3]
E.W. Peters
M.D. Leslie [a]

1 Rep by S.B. Grimes
2 Rep by A.V. Tait 1T
a/3 Rep by A.C. Pountney
4 Rep by D.I.W. Hilton

**v ENGLAND**

**LOST 21-24**
England: 3G 1PG
Scotland: 3G
Twickenham, 20 Feb 1999

G.H. Metcalfe

C.A. Murray
A.V. Tait 2T
J.A. Leslie
K.M. Logan 3C

G.P.J. Townsend 1T
* G. Armstrong

T.J. Smith
G.C. Bulloch
A.P. Burnell [2]
S. Murray
S.B. Grimes
P. Walton [1]
E.W. Peters
M.D. Leslie

1 Rep by A.C. Pountney
2 Rep by D.I.W. Hilton

### Friendly

**v ITALY**

**LOST 30-12**
Scotland: 3G 3PG
Italy: 1G 1T
Murrayfield, 6 Mar 1999

G.H. Metcalfe

C.A. Murray 1T
A.V. Tait [3]
J.A. Leslie
K.M. Logan 3PG 3C 1T

G.P.J. Townsend 1T
† I.T. Fairley [1]

T.J. Smith [5]
G.C. Bulloch
A.P. Burnell
S. Murray
S.B. Grimes [4]
P. Walton
* E.W. Peters [2]
M.D. Leslie [a]

1 Rep by † G.G. Burns
a/2 Rep by A.C. Pountney
3 Rep by S.L. Longstaff
4 Rep by A.I. Reed
5 Rep by D.I.W. Hilton

### Five Nations Championship

**v IRELAND**

**WON 30-13**
Scotland: 2G 2PG 2T
Ireland: 1G‡ 2PG
Murrayfield, 20 Mar 1999

G.H. Metcalfe

C.A. Murray [3] 2T
A.V. Tait
J.A. Leslie
K.M. Logan 2PG 2C

G.P.J. Townsend 1T
* G. Armstrong [5]

T.J. Smith [1]
G.C. Bulloch [4]
A.P. Burnell
S. Murray
S.B. Grimes 1T
P. Walton [2]
E.W. Peters
M.D. Leslie

‡includes penalty try
1 Rep by D.I.W. Hilton
2 Rep by A.C. Pountney
3 Rep by S.L. Longstaff
4 Rep by † S.J. Brotherstone
5 Rep by I.T. Fairley

**v FRANCE**

**WON 36-22**
France: 2G 1PG 1T
Scotland: 4G 1PG 1T
Stade de France, 10 Apr 1999

G.H. Metcalfe

C.A. Murray
A.V. Tait 2T
J.A. Leslie
K.M. Logan 1PG 4C

G.P.J. Townsend 1T
* G. Armstrong

D.I.W. Hilton [1]
G.C. Bulloch
A.P. Burnell
S. Murray [3]
S.B. Grimes
A.C. Pountney [2]
S.J. Reid
M.D. Leslie 2T

1 Rep by G. Graham
2 Rep by P. Walton
3 Rep by A.I. Reed

## 1998-99 continued

### World Cup Warm-up Matches

**FACT FILE**

- Scotland were winners of the last-ever Five Nations Championship, on points difference.
- It was the first time that they collected the championship trophy (introduced in 1993). The side scored 120 points in the four matches, a new Scotland championship record. John Leslie scored the quickest try in Test history, crossing nine seconds after the kick-off against Wales.

**FINAL TABLE**

| | P | W | D | L | F | A | Pts |
|---|---|---|---|---|---|---|---|
| **Scotland** | **4** | **3** | **0** | **1** | **120** | **79** | **6** |
| England | 4 | 3 | 0 | 1 | 103 | 78 | 6 |
| Wales | 4 | 2 | 0 | 2 | 109 | 126 | 4 |
| Ireland | 4 | 1 | 0 | 3 | 66 | 90 | 2 |
| France | 4 | 1 | 0 | 3 | 75 | 100 | 2 |

**v ARGENTINA**

**LOST 22-31**
Scotland: 2G 1PG 1T
Argentina: 2G 3PG 1DG 1T
Murrayfield, 21 Aug 1999

G.H.Metcalfe 1T

C.A.Murray 2
A.V.Tait 1T
† J.G.McLaren 5
K.M.Logan 1PG 2C

D.W.Hodge
* G.Armstrong

T.J.Smith
G.C.Bulloch
A.P.Burnell 1
S.Murray
S.B.Grimes 4
P.Walton 3 1T
S.J.Reid
A.C.Pountney

1 Rep by G.Graham
2 Rep by S.L.Longstaff
3 Rep by G.L.Simpson
4 Rep by G.W.Weir
5 Rep by C.M.Chalmers

**v ROMANIA**

**WON 60-19**
Scotland: 7G‡ 2PG 1T
Romania: 1G 4PG
Hampden Park, 28 Aug 1999

G.H.Metcalfe

S.L.Longstaff
A.V.Tait 1T
J.G.McLaren 1T
K.M.Logan 2PG 5C 2T

D.W.Hodge 2C
* G.Armstrong 1

T.J.Smith 1T
† R.R.Russell
G.Graham 3
S.Murray
S.B.Grimes 1T
P.Walton 2
G.L.Simpson 4
M.D.Leslie 1T

‡includes a penalty try
1 Rep by B.W.Redpath
2 Rep by † C.G.Mather
3 Rep by D.I.W.Hilton
4 Rep by G.W.Weir

*Cameron Murray touches down for Scotland's first try against Ireland at Murrayfield in 1999.*

## 1999 Fourth Rugby World Cup

### Group Matches

**v SOUTH AFRICA**

**LOST 29-46**
Scotland: 2G 4PG 1DG
SA: 5G 2PG 1T
Murrayfield, 3 Oct 1999

G.H. Metcalfe

C.A. Murray
A.V. Tait 1T
J.A. Leslie [1]
K.M. Logan 4PG 2C

G.P.J. Townsend 1DG
* G. Armstrong

T.J. Smith
G.C. Bulloch
G. Graham [4]
S. Murray [3]
S.B. Grimes
M.D. Leslie 1T
G.L. Simpson [2]
A.C. Pountney

1 Rep by M.J.M. Mayer
2 Rep by P. Walton
3 Rep by G.W. Weir
4 Rep by D.I.W. Hilton

**v URUGUAY**

**WON 43-12**
Scotland: 5G 1PG 1T
Uruguay: 4PG
Murrayfield, 8 Oct 1999

G.H. Metcalfe 1T

C.A. Murray [5]
A.V. Tait
M.J.M. Mayer
K.M. Logan 1PG 5C

G.P.J. Townsend 1T
* G. Armstrong [1] 1T

T.J. Smith
G.C. Bulloch [3]
G. Graham [2]
S. Murray
S.B. Grimes
M.D. Leslie [4] 1T
G.L. Simpson 1T
A.C. Pountney

1 Rep by B.W. Redpath
2 Rep by D.I.W. Hilton
3 Rep by R.R. Russell 1T
4 Rep by P. Walton
5 Rep by S.L. Longstaff

**v SPAIN**

**WON 48-0**
Scotland: 5G‡ 1PG 2T
Spain: Nil
Murrayfield, 16 Oct 1999

C.D. Paterson

C.A. Murray 1T
M.J.M. Mayer
J.G. McLaren [1] 1T
S.L. Longstaff 1T

D.W. Hodge 1PG 5C 1T
* B.W. Redpath [2]

D.I.W. Hilton
R.R. Russell
A.P. Burnell
G.W. Weir
A.I. Reed
P. Walton
S.J. Reid
C.G. Mather 2T

‡includes penalty try
1 Rep by G.P.J. Townsend
2 Rep by I.T. Fairley

### Quarter-final

**v SAMOA**

**WON 35-20**
Scotland: 1G‡ 5PG 1DG 2T
Samoa: 2G 2PG
Murrayfield, 20 Oct 1999

G.H. Metcalfe

C.A. Murray 1T
M.J.M. Mayer
J.G. McLaren
K.M. Logan 5PG 1C

G.P.J. Townsend [3] 1DG
* G. Armstrong

T.J. Smith
G.C. Bulloch
G. Graham [4]
S. Murray [2]
G.W. Weir
M.D. Leslie [5] 1T
G.L. Simpson
A.C. Pountney [1]

‡includes penalty try
1 Rep by C.G. Mather
2 Rep by S.B. Grimes
3 Rep by D.W. Hodge
4 Rep by A.P. Burnell
5 Rep by R.R. Russell

**v NEW ZEALAND**

**LOST 18-30**
Scotland: 1G 1PG 1DG 1T
NZ: 2G 2PG 2T
Murrayfield, 24 Oct 1999

G.H. Metcalfe

C.A. Murray 1T
A.V. Tait
M.J.M. Mayer
K.M. Logan 1PG 1C

G.P.J. Townsend 1DG
* G. Armstrong

T.J. Smith
G.C. Bulloch [3]
A.P. Burnell [2]
S. Murray
G.W. Weir [1]
M.D. Leslie
G.L. Simpson
A.C. Pountney 1T

1 Rep by S.B. Grimes
2 Rep by G. Graham
3 Rep by R.R. Russell

**FACT FILE**

- Scotland reached the quarter-finals and for the fourth time in four tournaments played their last match of a World Cup campaign against the All Blacks.

## 1999-2000

### Six Nations Championship

**v ITALY**

**LOST 20-34**
Italy: 1G 6PG 3DG
Scotland: 2G 1PG 1DG
Rome, 5 Feb 2000

G.H. Metcalfe

S.L. Longstaff
M.J.M. Mayer
* J.A. Leslie [1]
K.M. Logan 1C

G.P.J. Townsend 1PG 1DG 1C
B.W. Redpath

T.J. Smith
G.C. Bulloch 1T
M.J. Stewart [2]
S. Murray [3]
S.B. Grimes
M.D. Leslie 1T
G.L. Simpson [a]
A.C. Pountney

1 Rep by J.G. McLaren
2 Rep by D.I.W. Hilton [4]
3 Rep by G.W. Weir
4 Rep by (M.J. Stewart)
a Rep by S.J. Reid

**v IRELAND**

**LOST 22-44**
Ireland: 5G 3PG
Scotland: 2G 1PG 1T
Lansdowne Road, 19 Feb 2000

G.H. Metcalfe 1T

S.L. Longstaff
M.J.M. Mayer
A.G. Shiel
K.M. Logan 1PG 2C 1T

G.P.J. Townsend
* B.W. Redpath [3]

T.J. Smith
G.C. Bulloch [4]
M.J. Stewart [2]
S. Murray [1]
S.B. Grimes
M.D. Leslie
G.L. Simpson
A.C. Pountney

1 Rep by G.W. Weir
2 Rep by G. Graham [5] 1T
3 Rep by A.D. Nicol
4 Rep by R.R. Russell
5 Rep by (M.J. Stewart)

**v FRANCE**

**LOST 16-28**
Scotland: 1G 3PG
France: 2G 3PG 1T
Murrayfield, 4 Mar 2000

C.D. Paterson 2PG 1C

G.H. Metcalfe
J.G. McLaren [3]
* J.A. Leslie
K.M. Logan 1PG

G.P.J. Townsend
A.D. Nicol 1T

T.J. Smith
S.J. Brotherstone
M.J. Stewart [1]
S. Murray
G.W. Weir [2]
M.D. Leslie
S.J. Reid [a]
A.C. Pountney

1 Rep by D.I.W. Hilton
2 Rep by S.B. Grimes
3 Rep by D.W. Hodge
a Rep by C.G. Mather

**v WALES**

**LOST 18-26**
Wales: 2G 4PG
Scotland: 1G 2PG 1T
Cardiff Arms Park, 18 Mar 2000

C.D. Paterson

† C.C. Moir
G.P.J. Townsend 1T
* J.A. Leslie
G.H. Metcalfe

D.W. Hodge 2PG 1C
A.D. Nicol

T.J. Smith
S.J. Brotherstone [1]
M.J. Stewart [2]
S. Murray
S.B. Grimes
M.D. Leslie 1T
S.J. Reid
A.C. Pountney

1 Rep by G.C. Bulloch
2 Rep by D.I.W. Hilton

**v ENGLAND**

**WON 19-13**
Scotland: 1G 4PG
England: 1G 2PG
Murrayfield, 2 Apr 2000

C.D. Paterson

C.C. Moir
G.P.J. Townsend
J.G. McLaren
G.H. Metcalfe

D.W. Hodge 4PG 1C 1T
* A.D. Nicol

T.J. Smith
S.J. Brotherstone
M.J. Stewart [1]
S. Murray
† R. Metcalfe
† J.P.R. White
M.D. Leslie [a]
A.C. Pountney

1 Rep by G.R. McIlwham
a Rep by S.J. Reid

**FACT FILE**

- The new Six Nations tournament opened with Scotland losing in Italy.
- Scotland beat England at Murrayfield for the first time in 10 years and ended their longest run of defeats (10 including a Rugby World Cup game in 1991) against the English.

**FINAL TABLE**

| | P | W | D | L | F | A | Pts |
|---|---|---|---|---|---|---|---|
| England | 5 | 4 | 0 | 1 | 183 | 70 | 8 |
| France | 5 | 3 | 0 | 2 | 140 | 92 | 6 |
| Ireland | 5 | 3 | 0 | 2 | 168 | 133 | 6 |
| Wales | 5 | 3 | 0 | 2 | 111 | 135 | 6 |
| **Scotland** | **5** | **1** | **0** | **4** | **95** | **145** | **2** |
| Italy | 5 | 1 | 0 | 4 | 106 | 228 | 2 |

## 1999-2000 continued

### Tour Matches

**1st v NEW ZEALAND**

**LOST 20-69**
NZ: 7G 4T
Scotland: 2G 2PG
Dunedin, 24 Jun 2000

C.D. Paterson

C.C. Moir
G.P.J. Townsend 2
J.G. McLaren 4
S.L. Longstaff

D.W. Hodge 2PG 2C
* A.D. Nicol

T.J. Smith
G.C. Bulloch
B.D. Stewart 5
S. Murray 1
R. Metcalfe 1T
J.P.R. White
† R.S. Beattie
M.D. Leslie 3

1 Rep by † I.A. Fullarton
2 Rep by A.G. Shiel
3 Rep by G.L. Simpson 1T
4 Rep by C.A. Joiner
5 Rep by M.J. Stewart

**2nd v NEW ZEALAND**

**LOST 14-48**
NZ: 4G 4T
Scotland: 2G
Auckland, 1 Jul 2000

C.D. Paterson 1T

C.A. Murray 1T
G.P.J. Townsend
A.G. Shiel
C.A. Joiner

D.W. Hodge 2C
* A.D. Nicol 4

T.J. Smith
G.C. Bulloch 5
B.D. Stewart 1
I.A. Fullarton
R. Metcalfe 2
J.P.R. White
† J.M. Petrie 3
M.D. Leslie

1 Rep by G.R. McIlwham
2 Rep by † N.J. Hines
3 Rep by R.S. Beattie
4 Rep by † G. Beveridge
5 Rep by † S. Scott

**FACT FILE**

- New Zealand's 69-20 win in Dunedin is the highest score conceded by Scotland in a Test.

## 2000-01

### Tour Matches

**v UNITED STATES**

**WON 53-6**
Scotland: 4G 5PG 2T
US: 2PG
Murrayfield, 4 Nov 2000

C.D. Paterson 1T

C.A. Murray 3
† A.J. Bulloch
J.A. Leslie 2T
† J.F. Steel

G.P.J. Townsend 6 5PG 4C 2T
B.W. Redpath 7

T.J. Smith
S.J. Brotherstone a/5
G. Graham 1
S. Murray 4
S.B. Grimes
J.M. Petrie 2
† S.M. Taylor
* A.C. Pountney 1T

1 Rep by G.R. McIlwham
2 Rep by J.P.R. White
3 Rep by C.A. Joiner
4 Rep by R. Metcalfe
a/5 Rep by S. Scott
6 Rep by D.W. Hodge
7 Rep by G. Beveridge

**v AUSTRALIA**

**LOST 9-30**
Scotland: 3PG
Australia: 3G 3PG
Murrayfield, 11 Nov 2000

C.D. Paterson

C.A. Murray
A.J. Bulloch
J.A. Leslie
J.F. Steel

G.P.J. Townsend 3PG
B.W. Redpath

T.J. Smith
S.J. Brotherstone 1
G. Graham 2
S. Murray
S.B. Grimes 3
J.M. Petrie 4
S.M. Taylor
* A.C. Pountney

1 Rep by G.C. Bulloch
2 Rep by G.R. McIlwham
3 Rep by R. Metcalfe
4 Rep by J.P.R. White 5
5 Rep by (G. Graham)

**v SAMOA**

**WON 31-8**
Scotland: 1G 3PG 3T
Samoa: 1PG 1T
Murrayfield, 18 Nov 2000

C.D. Paterson

C.A. Murray
A.J. Bulloch 5 1T
J.A. Leslie
K.M. Logan 1T

G.P.J. Townsend 3PG 1C
B.W. Redpath 4

T.J. Smith 1T
S.J. Brotherstone 3
G. Graham 1
S. Murray
R.Metcalfe 2
J.P.R. White a/6
J.M. Petrie 1T
* A.C. Pountney

1 Rep by G.R. McIlwham
2 Rep by S.B. Grimes
3 Rep by G.C. Bulloch
4 Rep by G. Beveridge
5 Rep by D.W. Hodge
a/6 Rep by R.S. Beattie

## 2000-01 continued

## Six Nations Championship

### v FRANCE

**LOST 6-16**
France: 1G 3PG
Scotland: 2PG
Stade de France, 4 Feb 2001

C.D. Paterson

C.A. Murray
J.G. McLaren [6]
J.A. Leslie [a]
K.M. Logan 2PG

G.P.J. Townsend [1]
* A.D. Nicol [4]

T.J. Smith
G.C. Bulloch [5]
M.J. Stewart [3]
S. Murray
R.Metcalfe [2]
M.D. Leslie
J.M. Petrie [7]
A.C. Pountney

1 Rep by D.W. Hodge
2 Rep by S.B. Grimes
3 Rep by G.R. McIlwham
4 Rep by B.W. Redpath
5 Rep by R.R. Russell
a/6 Rep by A.J. Bulloch
7 Rep by J.P.R. White

### v WALES

**DRAWN 28-28**
Scotland: 2G 3PG 1T
Wales: 1G 4PG 3DG
Murrayfield, 17 Feb 2001

C.D. Paterson 1T

C.A. Murray [3]
J.G. McLaren 1T
J.A. Leslie
K.M. Logan 3PG 1C

D.W. Hodge 1C
* A.D. Nicol

T.J. Smith 1T
G.C. Bulloch
M.J. Stewart [1]
S. Murray
R.Metcalfe [2]
M.D. Leslie
J.M. Petrie
A.C. Pountney

1 Rep by G.R. McIlwham
2 Rep by S.B. Grimes
3 Rep by J.M. Craig

### v ENGLAND

**LOST 3-43**
England: 5G 1PG 1T
Scotland: 1PG
Twickenham, 3 Mar 2001

C.D. Paterson

C.A. Murray [4]
A.J. Bulloch [5]
J.A. Leslie
K.M. Logan

D.W. Hodge 1PG
* A.D. Nicol [3]

T.J. Smith
G.C. Bulloch
M.J. Stewart [1]
S. Murray
R.Metcalfe [2]
M.D. Leslie
S.M. Taylor
A.C. Pountney

1 Rep by G.R. McIlwham
2 Rep by S.B. Grimes
3 Rep by B.W. Redpath
4 Rep by J.M. Craig
5 Rep by J.G. McLaren

### v ITALY

**WON 23-19**
Scotland: 5PG 1DG 1T
Italy: 1G 4PG
Murrayfield, 17 Mar 2001

C.D. Paterson

J.M. Craig [2]
G.P.J. Townsend
J.A. Leslie
K.M. Logan

D.W. Hodge 5PG 1DG
B.W. Redpath

T.J. Smith 1T
G.C. Bulloch [4]
M.J. Stewart [1]
S. Murray
S.B. Grimes
M.D. Leslie
S.M. Taylor [3]
* A.C. Pountney

1 Rep by G.R. McIlwham
2 Rep by C.A. Murray
3 Rep by J.M. Petrie
4 Rep by S. Scott

### v IRELAND

**WON 32-10**
Scotland: 3G 2PG 1T
Ireland: 1G 1PG
Murrayfield, 22 Sep 2001

G.H. Metcalfe

J.F. Steel
J.G. McLaren
J.A. Leslie [2] 1T
C.D. Paterson 2PG 2C

G.P.J. Townsend [6] 1C
B.W. Redpath [7]

T.J. Smith 1T
G.C. Bulloch [5]
M.J. Stewart [1]
J.P.R. White [3]
S. Murray
G.L. Simpson [4]
S.M. Taylor
* A.C. Pountney 1T

1 Rep by G. Graham
2 Rep by † A.R. Henderson 1T
3 Rep by S.B. Grimes
4 Rep by J.M. Petrie
5 Rep by S. Scott
6 Rep by D.W. Hodge
7 Rep by A.D. Nicol

### FACT FILE

- The draw with Wales at Murrayfield was the first between the sides since 1922, the first of the series at Murrayfield and the highest score-draw in Test history.
- For the first time Scotland had to play a championship game out of season, the outbreak of foot-and-mouth disease causing the postponement of the Irish match from April until September.

### FINAL TABLE

| | P | W | D | L | F | A | Pts |
|---|---|---|---|---|---|---|---|
| England | 5 | 4 | 0 | 1 | 229 | 80 | 8 |
| Ireland | 5 | 4 | 0 | 1 | 129 | 89 | 8 |
| **Scotland** | **5** | **2** | **1** | **2** | **92** | **116** | **5** |
| Wales | 5 | 2 | 1 | 2 | 125 | 166 | 5 |
| France | 5 | 2 | 0 | 3 | 115 | 138 | 4 |
| Italy | 5 | 0 | 0 | 5 | 106 | 207 | 0 |

## 2001-02

### Tour Matches

**v TONGA**

**WON 43-20**
Scotland: 4G 5PG
Tonga: 5PG 1T
Murrayfield, 10 Nov 2001

G.H. Metcalfe **1T**

J.F. Steel
J.G. McLaren [4] **1T**
J.A. Leslie
C.A. Murray [3]

† G. Ross **5PG 4C**
A.D Nicol [5]

* T.J. Smith
G.C. Bulloch [6]
M.J. Stewart [2]
S. Murray
S.B. Grimes
J.P.R. White
J.M. Petrie
† A.L. Mower [1]

1 Rep by G.L. Simpson **1T**
2 Rep by G. Graham
3 Rep by † R.E. Reid **1T**
4 Rep by A.R. Henderson
5 Rep by G.G. Burns
6 Rep by S. Scott

**v ARGENTINA**

**LOST 16-25**
Scotland: 2PG 2T
Argentina: 1G 6PG
Murrayfield, 18 Nov 2001

D.J. Lee **1T**

C.A. Murray
J.G. McLaren
J.A. Leslie
R.E. Reid

G.P.J. Townsend **2PG 1T**
A.D Nicol

* T.J. Smith
G.C. Bulloch
M.J. Stewart [2]
S. Murray
S.B. Grimes
J.P.R. White
J.M. Petrie [1]
A.L. Mower

1 Rep by G.L. Simpson
2 Rep by G. Graham

**v NEW ZEALAND**

**LOST 6-37**
Scotland: 2PG
NZ: 2G 6PG 1T
Murrayfield, 24 Nov 2001

† B.J. Laney

J.F. Steel
J.G. McLaren
J.A. Leslie [4]
C.D. Paterson **2PG**

G.P.J. Townsend
A.D Nicol [3]

* T.J. Smith
G.C. Bulloch [5]
M.J. Stewart [1]
S. Murray [6]
S.B. Grimes
J.P.R. White
G.L. Simpson [2]
A.L. Mower

1 Rep by G. Graham
2 Rep by S.M. Taylor
3 Rep by G.G. Burns
4 Rep by A.R. Henderson
5 Rep by S. Scott
6 Rep by I.A. Fullarton

*Martin Johnson attempts to tackle as Tom Smith runs at the England defence.*

## 2001-02 continued

## Six Nations Championship

### v ENGLAND

**LOST 3-29**
Scotland: 1PG
England: 3G 1PG 1T
Murrayfield, 2 Feb 2002

G.H. Metcalfe

B.J. Laney
J.G. McLaren
G.P.J. Townsend
C.D. Paterson

D.W. Hodge 1PG
B.W. Redpath

T.J. Smith [1]
G.C. Bulloch
M.J. Stewart
S. Murray
S.B. Grimes
J.P.R. White
S.M. Taylor
* A.C. Pountney

1 Rep by G. Graham

### v ITALY

**WON 29-12**
Italy: 4PG
Scotland: 2G 5PG
Rome, 16 Feb 2002

B.J. Laney 5PG 2C 1T

G.H. Metcalfe
J.G. McLaren
A.R. Henderson
C.D. Paterson

G.P.J. Townsend 1T
* B.W. Redpath

T.J. Smith
G.C. Bulloch
M.J. Stewart [1]
S. Murray
S.B. Grimes
J.P.R. White
S.M. Taylor
A.L. Mower [2]

1 Rep by G. Graham
2 Rep by M.D. Leslie

### v IRELAND

**LOST 22-43**
Ireland: 3G 4PG 2T
Scotland: 1G 5PG
Lansdowne Road, 2 Mar 2002

B.J. Laney 5PG 1C

G.H. Metcalfe [3]
J.G. McLaren
A.R. Henderson
C.D. Paterson

G.P.J. Townsend
* B.W. Redpath

T.J. Smith
G.C. Bulloch
M.J. Stewart [2]
S. Murray
S.B. Grimes
J.P.R. White [1]
S.M. Taylor
A.C. Pountney

1 Rep by M.D. Leslie 1T
2 Rep by G. Graham
3 Rep by K.M. Logan

### v FRANCE

**LOST 10-22**
Scotland: 1G 1PG
France: 2G 1PG 1T
Murrayfield, 23 Mar 2002

B.J. Laney 1PG 1C

G.H. Metcalfe
J.G. McLaren [4]
J.A. Leslie
C.D. Paterson

G.P.J. Townsend
* B.W. Redpath 1T

T.J. Smith
G.C. Bulloch [3]
M.J. Stewart [1]
S. Murray [2]
J.P.R. White
M.D. Leslie [a]
S.M. Taylor
A.C. Pountney

1 Rep by G. Graham
2 Rep by S.B. Grimes
3 Rep by R.R. Russell
4 Rep by K.M. Logan
a Rep by J.M. Petrie

### v WALES

**WON 27-22**
Wales: 1G 5PG
Scotland: 1G 5PG 1T
Cardiff Arms Park, 6 Apr 2002

B.J. Laney [6] 4PG 1C

K.M. Logan [3]
J.G. McLaren
J.A. Leslie
C.D. Paterson

G.P.J. Townsend
* B.W. Redpath

T.J. Smith
G.C. Bulloch [5] 2T
M.J. Stewart [1]
S. Murray
J.P.R. White [2]
M.D. Leslie [4]
S.M. Taylor
A.C. Pountney

1 Rep by G. Graham
2 Rep by S.B. Grimes
3 Rep by G.H. Metcalfe
4 Rep by J.M. Petrie
5 Rep by R.R. Russell
6 Rep by D.W. Hodge 1PG

### FACT FILE

- Gordon Ross' 23 points against Tonga at Murrayfield set a new record for most points by a Scotland player on a Test debut.
- Bill McLaren, the voice of rugby for 50 years, made his last Test commentary in the Wales v Scotland match.
- Against Wales, Gregor Townsend became Scotland's most-capped player.

### FINAL TABLE

| | P | W | D | L | F | A | Pts |
|---|---|---|---|---|---|---|---|
| France | 5 | 5 | 0 | 0 | 156 | 75 | 10 |
| England | 5 | 4 | 0 | 1 | 184 | 53 | 8 |
| Ireland | 5 | 3 | 0 | 2 | 145 | 138 | 6 |
| **Scotland** | **5** | **2** | **0** | **3** | **91** | **128** | **4** |
| Wales | 5 | 1 | 0 | 4 | 119 | 188 | 2 |
| Italy | 5 | 0 | 0 | 5 | 70 | 183 | 0 |

## 2001-02 continued

### Tour Matches

**v CANADA**

**LOST 23-26**
Canada: 2G 4PG
Scotland: 1G 2PG 2T
Vancouver, 15 Jun 2002

G.H. Metcalfe 4

† R.C. Kerr
† A. Craig
B.J. Laney 2PG 1C
C.D. Paterson 1T

D.W. Hodge
† M.R.L. Blair 1T

M.J. Stewart 2
G.C. Bulloch 3
† C.J. Smith
N.J. Hines
* S.B. Grimes
J.P.R. White
J.M. Petrie 1
S.M. Taylor 1T

1 Rep by † D.J.H. Macfadyen
2 Rep by † A.F. Jacobsen
3 Rep by S.J. Brotherstone
4 Rep by † B.G. Hinshelwood

**v UNITED STATES**

**WON 65-23**
US: 2G 3PG
Scotland: 6G 1PG 4T
San Francisco, 22 Jun 2002

G.H. Metcalfe 1

R.C. Kerr 4 1T
A. Craig 1T
B.J. Laney 1PG 6C 1T
C.D. Paterson 2T

D.W. Hodge 2T
M.R.L. Blair 5

A.F. Jacobsen 2
G.C. Bulloch 6
M.J. Stewart 3
N.J. Hines 1T
* S.B. Grimes
J.P.R. White 7 1T
S.M. Taylor
D.J.H. Macfadyen

1 Rep by A.R. Henderson 1T
2 Rep by C.J. Smith
3 Rep by (A.F. Jacobsen)
4 Rep by † M.P. di Rollo
5 Rep by G.G. Burns
6 Rep by S. Scott
7 Rep by † A.J.A. Hall

*Andy Craig powers over the line to score one of his hat-trick of tries against Fiji at Murrayfield in November, 2002.*

## 2002-03

### Tour Matches

**v ROMANIA**

**WON 37-10**
Scotland: 3G 2PG 2T
Romania: 1G 1PG
Murrayfield, 9 Nov 2002

† J.S.D. Moffat **1T**

† N. Walker
A. Craig 5
B.J. Laney **2PG 3C**
C.D. Paterson **1T**

G. Ross 4
* B.W. Redpath

T.J. Smith 1
G.C. Bulloch
† B.A.F. Douglas
S. Murray 2
S.B. Grimes **1T**
M.D. Leslie 7 **1T**
S.M. Taylor 3
A.C. Pountney **1T**

1 Rep by M.J. Stewart 6
2 Rep by N.J. Hines
3 Rep by J.M. Petrie
4 Rep by G.P.J. Townsend
5 Rep by B.G. Hinshelwood
6 Rep by (T.J. Smith)
7 Rep by S. Scott

**v SOUTH AFRICA**

**WON 21-6**
Scotland: 1G 3PG 1T
SA: 2PG
Murrayfield, 16 Nov 2002

J.S.D. Moffat

N. Walker 3 **1T**
A. Craig
B.J. Laney **3PG 1C**
C.D. Paterson

G. Ross 1
* B.W. Redpath

T.J. Smith 4
G.C. Bulloch
B.A.F. Douglas
S. Murray 5
S.B. Grimes 2
M.D. Leslie
S.M. Taylor
A.C. Pountney **1T**

1 Rep by G.P.J. Townsend
2 Rep by J.P.R. White
3 Rep by B.G. Hinshelwood
4 Rep by D.I.W. Hilton
5 Rep by N.J. Hines

**v FIJI**

**WON 36-22**
Scotland: 1G 3PG 4T
Fiji: 4PG 2T
Murrayfield, 24 Nov 2002

B.G. Hinshelwood

N. Walker
A. Craig **3T**
B.J. Laney **3PG 1C 1T**
C.D. Paterson 2

G.P.J. Townsend 5
* B.W. Redpath 6

T.J. Smith
G.C. Bulloch 4
B.A.F. Douglas
J.P.R. White 1
S.B. Grimes **1T**
S.M. Taylor
J.M. Petrie 3
A.C. Pountney

1 Rep by N.J. Hines
2 Rep by J.S.D. Moffat
3 Rep by M.D. Leslie
4 Rep by S. Scott
5 Rep by G. Ross
6 Rep by G. Beveridge

### Six Nations Championship

**v IRELAND**

**LOST 6-36**
Scotland: 2PG
Ireland: 3G 5PG
Murrayfield, 16 Feb 2003

G.H. Metcalfe

K.M. Logan
A. Craig
B.J. Laney
C.D. Paterson

G. Ross 2 **2PG**
* B.W. Redpath

T.J. Smith
G.C. Bulloch
B.A.F. Douglas 1
S. Murray
S.B. Grimes
M.D. Leslie
S.M. Taylor
A.L. Mower

1 Rep by † G.Kerr
2 Rep by G.P.J. Townsend

**v FRANCE**

**LOST 3-38**
France: 3G 4PG 1T
Scotland: 1PG
Stade de France, 23 Feb 2003

G.H. Metcalfe

C.D. Paterson **1PG**
G.P.J. Townsend
† K.N. Utterson
K.M. Logan

B.J. Laney 2
* B.W. Redpath a/4

T.J. Smith
G.C. Bulloch
B.A.F. Douglas 5
S. Murray 1
S.B. Grimes
M.D. Leslie
S.M. Taylor
A.L. Mower b/3

1 Rep by J.P.R. White
2 Rep by A. Craig
b/3 Rep by J.M Petrie
a/4 Rep by M.R.L. Blair
5 Rep by G. Kerr 6
6 Rep by [B.A.F. Douglas]

**v WALES**

**WON 30-22**
Scotland: 3G 3PG
Wales: 2G 1PG 1T
Murrayfield, 8 Mar 2003

G.H. Metcalfe

C.D. Paterson **1T 3C 3PG**
J.G. McLaren
K.N. Utterson 1
K.M. Logan

G.P.J. Townsend 7
* B.W. Redpath 3

T.J. Smith
G.C. Bulloch 5
B.A.F. Douglas 2 **1T**
S.B. Grimes 4
S.Murray
J.P.R. White 6
S.M. Taylor **1T**
A.L. Mower

1 Rep by A. Craig
2 Rep by G. Kerr
3 Rep by M.R.L. Blair
4 Rep by N.J. Hines
5 Rep by R.R Russell
6 Rep by J.M. Petrie
7 Rep by G. Ross

## 2002-03

## Six Nations Championship

**v ENGLAND**

**LOST 9-40**
England: 4G 4PG
Scotland: 3PG
Twickenham, 22 Mar 2003

G.H. Metcalfe

C.D. Paterson **3PG**
J.G McLaren [2]
A. Craig
K.M. Logan

G.P.J. Townsend
* B.W Redpath

T.J. Smith
G.C. Bulloch
B.A.F. Douglas [4]
S. Murray [1]
N.J. Hines
J.P.R White
S.M. Taylor
A.L. Mower [3]

1 Rep by S.B. Grimes
2 Rep by K.N. Utterson
3 Rep by R.S Beattie
4 Rep by G. Kerr

**v ITALY**

**WON 33-25**
Scotland: 2G 3PG 2T
Italy: 2G 2PG 1T
Murrayfield, 29 Mar 2003

G.H. Metcalfe

C.D. Paterson **1T 2C 3PG**
J.G McLaren **1T**
A. Craig
K.M. Logan **1T**

G.P.J. Townsend
* B.W. Redpath

T.J. Smith
G.C. Bulloch [3]
B.A.F. Douglas
S. Murray [2]
N.J Hines
J.P.R White [1] **1T**
S.M. Taylor
A.L. Mower

1 Rep by R.S. Beattie
2 Rep by S.B. Grimes
3 Rep by R.R. Russell

### FACT FILE

- Captain Bryan Redpath became Scotland's most-capped scrum-half when he appeared against England, overtaking the record previously held by Gary Armstrong.
- Gordon Bulloch became Scotland's second hooker to appear in 50 Tests when he took the field in Durban.

### FINAL TABLE

| | P | W | D | L | F | A | Pts |
|---|---|---|---|---|---|---|---|
| England | 5 | 5 | 0 | 0 | 173 | 46 | 10 |
| Ireland | 5 | 4 | 0 | 1 | 119 | 97 | 8 |
| France | 5 | 3 | 0 | 2 | 153 | 75 | 6 |
| **Scotland** | **5** | **2** | **0** | **3** | **81** | **161** | **4** |
| Italy | 5 | 1 | 0 | 4 | 100 | 185 | 2 |
| Wales | 5 | 0 | 0 | 5 | 82 | 144 | 0 |

## Tour Matches

**1st v SOUTH AFRICA**

**LOST 25-29**
South Africa: 2G 5PG
Scotland: 2G 2PG 1T
Durban, 7 June 2003

G.H. Metcalfe

C.D. Paterson **1T 2C 2PG**
A. Craig **1T**
A.R. Henderson [4]
K.M. Logan

G.P.J. Townsend
* B.W Redpath

G. Kerr
G.C. Bulloch [2]
B.A.F. Douglas
S. Murray
N.J. Hines
J.P.R White [1] **1T**
S.M. Taylor
A.L. Mower [3]

1 Rep by M.D. Leslie
2 Rep by R.R. Russell
3 Rep by J.M. Petrie
4 Rep by J.G. McLaren

**2nd v SOUTH AFRICA**

**LOST 19-28**
South Africa: 1G 6PG 1DG
Scotland: 1G 4PG
Johannesburg, 14 June 2003

G.H. Metcalfe

C.D. Paterson **1C 4PG**
A. Craig **1T**
A.R. Henderson [7]
K.M. Logan

G.P.J. Townsend [4]
* B.W Redpath [6]

G. Kerr [2]
G.C. Bulloch [3]
B.A.F. Douglas
S. Murray
N.J. Hines [1]
J.P.R White
S.M. Taylor
A.L. Mower [5]

1 Rep by M.D. Leslie
2 Rep by G.R. McIlwham
3 Rep by R.R. Russell
4 Rep by G. Ross
5 Rep by J.M. Petrie
6 Rep by M.R.L. Blair
7 Rep by B.J. Laney

# International Appearances (up to 31 July 2003)

Note: Years given for International Championship matches are for second half of season; e.g. 1932 means season 1931-32. Years for all other matches refer to the actual year of the match. Abbreviations used are as follows: A – Australia; Arg – Argentina; Bb – Barbarians; C – Canada; E – England; F – France; Fj – Fiji; I – Ireland; It – Italy; Iv – Ivory Coast; J – Japan; M – Maoris; Nm – Namibia; NZ – New Zealand; P – President's XV; Pt – Portugal; R – Romania; SA – South Africa; Sm – Samoa; Sp – Spain; Tg – Tonga; U – Uruguay; US – United States; W – Wales; WS – Western Samoa; Z – Zimbabwe. (R) – Replacement or substitute; (t) – temporary replacement; [ ] – Rugby World Cup appearances. When a series has taken place, figures are used to denote the particular matches in which players have featured. Thus NZ 1, 3 would indicate that a player has appeared in the First and Third Tests of the relevant series against New Zealand.

## A

**Abercrombie, C.H.** (United Services) 1910 *I, E*, 1911 *F, W*, 1913 *F, W*

**Abercrombie, J.G.** (Edinburgh U) 1949 *F, W, I*, 1950 *F, W, I, E*

**Agnew, W.C.C.** (Stewart's Coll FP) 1930 *W, I*

**Ainslie, R.** (Edinburgh Inst FP) 1879 *I, E*, 1880 *I, E*, 1881 *E*, 1882 *I, E*

**Ainslie, T.** (Edinburgh Inst FP) 1881 *E*, 1882 *I, E*, 1883 *W, I, E*, 1884 *W, I, E*, 1885 *W, I* 1,2

**Aitchison, G.R.** (Edinburgh Wands) 1883 *I*

**Aitchison, T.G.** (Gala) 1929 *W, I, E*

**Aitken, A.I.** (Edinburgh Inst FP) 1889 *I*

**Aitken, G.G.** (Oxford U) 1924 *W, I, E*, 1925 *F, W, I, E*, 1929 *F*

**Aitken, J.** (Gala) 1977 *E, I, F*, 1981 *F, W, E, I, NZ* 1,2, *R, A*, 1982 *E, I, F, W*, 1983 *F, W, E, NZ*, 1984 *W, E, I, F, R*

**Aitken, R.** (London Scottish) 1947 *W*

**Allan, B.** (Glasgow Acad) 1881 *I*

**Allan, J.** (Edinburgh Acad) 1990 *NZ* 1, 1991, *W, I, R*, [*J, I, WS, E, NZ*]

**Allan, J.L.** (Melrose) 1952 *F, W, I*, 1953 *W*

**Allan, J.L.F.** (Cambridge U) 1957 *I, E*

**Allan, J.W.** (Melrose) 1927 *F*, 1928 *I*, 1929 *F, W, I, E*, 1930 *F, E*, 1931 *F, W, I, E*, 1932 *SA, W, I*, 1934 *I, E*

**Allan, R.C.** (Hutchesons' GSFP) 1969 *I*

**Allardice, W.D.** (Aberdeen GSFP) 1947 *A*, 1948 *F, W, I*, 1949 *F, W, I, E*

**Allen, H.W.** (Glasgow Acad) 1873 *E*

**Anderson, A.H.** (Glasgow Acad) 1894 *I*

**Anderson, D.G.** (London Scottish) 1889 *I*, 1890 *W, I, E*, 1891 *W, E*, 1892 *W, E*

**Anderson, E.** (Stewart's Coll FP) 1947 *I, E*

**Anderson, J.W.** (W of Scotland) 1872 *E*

**Anderson, T.** (Merchiston) 1882 *I*

**Angus, A.W.** (Watsonians) 1909 *W*, 1910 *F, W, E*, 1911 *W, I*, 1912 *F, W, I, E, SA*, 1913 *F, W*, 1914 *E*, 1920 *F, W, I, E*

**Anton, P.A.** (St Andrew's U) 1873 *E*

**Armstrong, G.** (Jedforest, Newcastle) 1988 *A*, 1989 *W, E, I, F, Fj, R*, 1990 *I, F, W, E, NZ* 1,2, *Arg*, 1991 *F, W, E, I, R*, [*J, I, WS, E, NZ*], 1993 *I, F, W, E*, 1994 *E, I*, 1996 *NZ*, 1,2, *A*, 1997 *W, SA (R)*, *1998 It, I, F, W, E, SA (R)*, 1999 *W, E, I, F, Arg, R*, [*SA, U, Sm, NZ*]

**Arneil, R.J.** (Edinburgh Acads, Leicester and Northampton) 1968 *I, E, A*, 1969 *F, W, I, E, SA*, 1970 *F, W, I, E, A*, 1971 *F, W, I, E (2[1C])*, *1972 F, W, E, NZ*

**Arthur, A.** (Glasgow Acad) 1875 *E*, 1876 *E*

**Arthur, J.W.** (Glasgow Acad) 1871 *E*, 1872 *E*

**Asher, A.G.G.** (Oxford U) 1882 *I*, 1884 *W, I, E*, 1885 *W*, 1886 *I, E*

**Auld, W.** (W of Scotland) 1889 *W*, 1890 *W*

**Auldjo, L.J.** (Abertay) 1878 *E*

## B

**Bain, D. McL.** (Oxford U) 1911 *E*, 1912 *F, W, E, SA*, 1913 *F, W, I, E*, 1914 *W, I*

**Baird, G.R.T.** (Kelso) 1981 *A*, 1982 *E, I, F, W, A* 1,2, 1983 *I, F, W, E, NZ*, 1984 *W, E, I, F, A*, 1985 *I, W, E*, 1986 *F, W, E, I, R*, 1987 *E*, 1988 *I*

**Balfour, A.** (Watsonians) 1896 *W, I, E*, 1897 *E*

**Balfour, L.M.** (Edinburgh Acads) 1872 *E*

**Bannerman, E.M.** (Edinburgh Acads) 1872 *E*, 1873 *E*

**Bannerman, J.M.** (Glasgow HSFP) 1921 *F, W, I, E*, 1922 *F, W, I, E*, 1923 *F, W, I, E*, 1924 *F, W, I, E*, 1925 *F, W, I, E*, 1926 *F, W, I, E*, 1927 *F, W, I, E, A*, 1928 *F, W, I, E*, 1929 *F, W, I, E*

**Barnes, I.A.** (Hawick) 1972 *W*, 1974 *F (R)*, *1975 E (R), NZ*, 1977 *I, F, W*

**Barrie, R.W.** (Hawick) 1936 *E*

**Bearne, K.R.F.** (Cambridge U, London Scottish) 1960 *F, W*

**Beattie, J.A.** (Hawick) 1929 *F, W*, 1930 *W*, 1931 *F, W, I, E*, 1932 *SA, W, I, E*, 1933 *W, E, I*, 1934 *I, E*, 1935 *W, I, E, NZ*, 1936 *W, I, E*

**Beattie, J.R.** (Glasgow Acad) 1980 *I, F, W, E*, 1981 *F, W, E, I*, 1983 *F, W, E, NZ*, 1984 *E (R), R, A*, 1985 *I*, 1986 *F, W, E, I, R*, 1987 *I, F, W, E*

**Beattie, R.S.** (Newcastle, Bristol) 2000 *NZ* 1,2*(R)*, *Sm (R)*, 2003 *E(R), It(R)*

**Bedell-Sivright, D.R.** (Cambridge U, Edinburgh U) 1900 *W*, 1901 *W, I, E*, 1902 *W, I, E*, 1903 *W, I*, 1904 *W, I, E*, 1905 *NZ*, 1906 *W, I, E, SA*, 1907 *W, I, E*, 1908 *W, I*

**Bedell-Sivright, J.V.** (Cambridge U) 1902 *W*

**Begbie, T.A.** (Edinburgh Wands) 1881 *I, E*

**Bell, D.L.** (Watsonians) 1975 *I, F, W, E*

**Bell, J.A.** (Clydesdale) 1901 *W, I, E*, 1902 *W, I, E*

**Bell, L.H.I.** (Edinburgh Acads) 1900 *E*, 1904 *W, I*

**Berkeley, W.V.** (Oxford U) 1926 *F*, 1929 *F, W, I*

**Berry, C.W.** (Fettesian-Lorettonians) 1884 *I, E*, 1885 *W, I* 1, 1887 *I, W, E*, 1888 *W, I*

**Bertram, D.M.** (Watsonians) 1922 *F, W, I, E*, 1923 *F, W, I, E*, 1924 *W, I, E*

**Beveridge, G.** (Glasgow) 2000 *NZ* 2*(R)*, *US (R)*, *Sm (R)*, 2002 *Fj(R)*

**Biggar, A.G.** (London Scottish) 1969 *SA*, 1970 *F, I, E, A*, 1971 *F, W, I, E (2[1C])*, *1972 F, W*

**Biggar, M.A.** (London Scottish) 1975 *I, F, W, E*, 1976 *W, E, I*, 1977 *I, F, W*, 1978 *I, F, W, E, NZ*, 1979 *W, E, I, F, NZ*, 1980 *I, F, W, E*

**Birkett, G.A.** (Harlequins, London Scottish) 1975 *NZ*

**Bishop, J.M.** (Glasgow Acad) 1893 *I*

**Bisset, A.A.** (RIE Coll) 1904 *W*

**Black, A.W.** (Edinburgh U) 1947 *F, W*, 1948 *E*, 1950 *W, I, E*

**Black, W.P.** (Glasgow HSFP) 1948 *F, W, I, E*, 1951 *E*

**Blackadder, W.F.** (W of Scotland) 1938 *E*

**Blaikie, C.F.** (Heriot's FP) 1963 *I, E*, 1966 *E*, 1968 *A*, 1969 *F, W, I, E*

**Blair, M.R.L.** (Edinburgh) 2002 *C, US*, 2003 *F(t+R), W* 1*(R), SA* 2 *(R)*

**Blair, P.C.B.** (Cambridge U) 1912 *SA*, 1913 *F, W, I, E*

**Bolton, W.H.** (W of Scotland) 1876 *E*

**Borthwick, J.B.** (Stewart's Coll FP) 1938 *W, I*

**Bos, F.H. ten** (Oxford U, London Scottish) 1959 *E*, 1960 *F, W, SA*, 1961 *F, SA, W, I, E*, 1962 *F, W, I, E*, 1963 *F, W, I, E*

**Boswell, J.D.** (W of Scotland) 1889 *W, I*, 1890 *W, I, E*, 1891 *W, I, E*, 1892 *W, I, E*, 1893 *I, E*, 1894 *I, E*

**Bowie, T.C.** (Watsonians) 1913 *I, E*, 1914 *I, E*

**Boyd, G.M.** (Glasgow HSFP) 1926 *E*

**Boyd, J.L.** (United Services) 1912 *E, SA*

**Boyle, A.C.W.** (London Scottish) 1963 *F, W, I*

**Boyle, A.H.W.** (St Thomas's Hospital, London Scottish) 1966 *A*, 1967 *F, NZ*, 1968 *F, W, I*

**Brash, J.C.** (Cambridge U) 1961 *E*

**Breakey, R.W.** (Gosforth) 1978 *E*

**Brewis, N.T.** (Edinburgh Inst FP) 1876 *E*, 1878 *E*, 1879 *I, E*, 1880 *I, E*

**Brewster, A.K.** (Stewart's-Melville FP) 1977 *E*, 1980 *I, F*, 1986 *E, I, R*

**Brotherstone, S.J.** (Melrose, Brive, Newcastle) 1999 *I (R)*, 2000 *F, W, E, US, A, Sm*, 2002 *C (R)*

**Brown, A.H.** (Heriot's FP) 1928 *E*, 1929 *F, W*

**Brown, A.R.** (Gala) 1971 *E (2[1C]), 1972 F, W, E*

**Brown, C.H.C.** (Dunfermline) 1929 *E*

**Brown, D.I.** (Cambridge U) 1933 *W, E, I*

**Brown, G.L.** (W of Scotland) 1969 *SA*, 1970 *F, W (R), I, E, A*, 1971 *F, W, I, E (2[1C]), 1972 F, W, E, NZ*, 1973 *E (R), P*, 1974 *W, E, I, F*, 1975 *I, F, W, E, A*, 1976 *F, W, E, I*

**Brown, J.A.** (Glasgow Acad) 1908 *W, I*

**Brown, J.B.** (Glasgow Acad) 1879 *I, E*, 1880 *I, E*, 1881 *I, E*, 1882 *I, E*, 1883 *W, I, E*, 1884 *W, I, E*, 1885 *I* 1,2, 1886 *W, I, E*

**Brown, P.C.** (W of Scotland, Gala) 1964 *F, NZ, W, I, E*, 1965 *I, E, SA*, 1966 *A*, 1969 *I, E*, 1970 *W, E*, 1971 *F, W, I, E (2[1C]), 1972 F, W, E, NZ*, 1973 *F, W, I, E, P*

**Brown, T.G.** (Heriot's FP) 1929 *W*

**Brown, W.D.** (Glasgow Acad) 1871 *E*, 1872 *E*, 1873 *E*, 1874 *E*, 1875 *E*

**Brown, W.S.** (Edinburgh Inst FP) 1880 *I, E*, 1882 *I, E*, 1883 *W, E*

**Browning, A.** (Glasgow HSFP) 1920 *I*, 1922 *F, W, I*, 1923 *W, I, E*

**Bruce, C.R.** (Glasgow Acad) 1947 *F, W, I, E*, 1949 *F, W, I, E*

**Bruce, N.S.** (Blackheath, Army and London Scottish) 1958 *F, A, I, E*, 1959 *F, W, I, E*, 1960 *F, W, I, E, SA*, 1961 *F, SA, W, I, E*, 1962 *F, W, I, E*, 1963 *F, W, I, E*, 1964 *F, NZ, W, I, E*

**Bruce, R.M.** (Gordonians) 1947 *A*, 1948 *F, W, I*

**Bruce-Lockhart, J.H.** (London Scottish) 1913 *W*, 1920 *E*

**Bruce-Lockhart, L.** (London Scottish) 1948 *E*, 1950 *F, W*, 1953 *I, E*

**Bruce-Lockhart, R.B.** (Cambridge U and London Scottish) 1937 *I*, 1939 *I, E*

**Bryce, C.C.** (Glasgow Acad) 1873 *E*, 1874 *E*

**Bryce, R.D.H.** (W of Scotland) 1973 *I (R)*

**Bryce, W.E.** (Selkirk) 1922 *W, I, E*, 1923 *F, W, I, E*, 1924 *F, W, I, E*

**Brydon, W.R.C.** (Heriot's FP) 1939 *W*

**Buchanan, A.** (Royal HSFP) 1871 *E*

**Buchanan, F.G.** (Kelvinside Acads and Oxford U) 1910 *F*, 1911 *F, W*

**Buchanan, J.C.R.** (Stewart's Coll FP) 1921 *W, I, E*, 1922 *W, I, E*, 1923 *F, W, I, E*, 1924 *F, W, I, E*, 1925 *F, I*

**Buchanan-Smith, G.A.E.** (London Scottish, Heriot's FP) 1989 *Fj (R), 1990 Arg*

**Bucher, A.M.** (Edinburgh Acads) 1897 *E*

**Budge, G.M.** (Edinburgh Wands) 1950 *F, W, I, E*

**Bullmore, H.H.** (Edinburgh U) 1902 *I*

**Bulloch, A.J.** (Glasgow) 2000 *US, A, Sm*, 2001 *F (t+R), E*

**Bulloch, G.C.** (West of Scotland, Glasgow) 1997 *SA*, 1998 *It, I, F, W, E, Fj, A* 1, *SA*, 1999 *W, E, It, I, F, Arg, [SA, U, Sm, NZ]*, 2000 *It, I, W (R), NZ* 1,2, *A (R), Sm (R), 2001 F, W, E, It, I, Tg, Arg, NZ*, 2002 *E, It, I, F, W, C, US, R, SA, Fj*, 2003 *I* 1, *F, W* 1, *E, It* 1, *SA* 1,2

**Burnell, A.P.** (London Scottish, Montferrand) 1989 *E, I, F, Fj, R*, 1990 *I, F, W, E, Arg*, 1991 *F, W, E, I, R, [J, Z, I, WS, E, NZ]*, 1992 *E, I, F, W*, 1993 *I, F, W, E, NZ*, 1994 *W, E, I, F, Arg* 1,2, *SA*, 1995 *[Iv, Tg (R), F (R)], WS*, 1998 *E, SA*, 1999 *W, E, It, I, F, Arg, [Sp, Sm (R), NZ]*

**Burnet, P.J.** (London Scottish and Edinburgh Acads) 1960 *SA*

**Burnet, W.** (Hawick) 1912 *E*

**Burnet, W.A.** (W of Scotland) 1934 *W*, 1935 *W, I, E, NZ*, 1936 *W, I, E*

**Burnett, J.N.** (Heriot's FP) 1980 *I, F, W, E*

**Burns, G.G.** (Watsonians, Edinburgh) 1999 *It (R), 2001 Tg (R), NZ (R), 2002 US (R)*

**Burrell, G.** (Gala) 1950 *F, W, I*, 1951 *SA*

# C

**Cairns, A.G.** (Watsonians) 1903 *W, I, E*, 1904 *W, I, E*, 1905 *W, I, E*, 1906 *W, I, E*

**Calder, F.** (Stewart's-Melville FP) 1986 *F, W, E, I, R*, 1987 *I, F, W, E, [F, Z, R, NZ]*, 1988 *I, F, W, E*, 1989 *W, E, I, F, R*, 1990 *I, F, W, E, NZ* 1,2, 1991 *R, [J, I, WS, E, NZ]*

**Calder, J.H.** (Stewart's-Melville FP) 1981 *F, W, E, I, NZ* 1,2, *R, A*, 1982 *E, I, F, W, A* 1,2, 1983 *I, F, W, E, NZ*, 1984 *W, E, I, F, A*, 1985 *I, F, W*

**Callander, G.J.** (Kelso) 1984 *R*, 1988 *I, F, W, E, A*

**Cameron, A.** (Glasgow HSFP) 1948 *W*, 1950 *I, E*, 1951 *F, W, I, E, SA*, 1953 *I, E*, 1955 *F, W, I, E*, 1956 *F, W, I*

**Cameron, A.D.** (Hillhead HSFP) 1951 *F*, 1954 *F, W*

**Cameron, A.W.** (Watsonians) 1887 *W*, 1893 *W*, 1894 *I*

**Cameron, D.** (Glasgow HSFP) 1953 *I, E*, 1954 *F, NZ, I, E*

**Cameron, N.W.** (Glasgow U) 1952 *E*, 1953 *F, W*

**Campbell, A.J.** (Hawick) 1984 *I, F, R*, 1985 *I, F, W, E*, 1986 *F, W, E, I, R*, 1988 *F, W, A*

**Campbell, G.T.** (London Scottish) 1892 *W, I, E*, 1893 *I, E*, 1894 *W, I, E*, 1895 *W, I, E*, 1896 *W, I, E*, 1897 *I*, 1899 *I*, 1900 *E*

**Campbell, H.H.** (Cambridge U, London Scottish) 1947 *I, E*, 1948 *I, E*

**Campbell, J.A.** (W of Scotland) 1878 *E*, 1879 *I, E*, 1881 *I, E*

**Campbell, J.A.** (Cambridge U) 1900 *I*

**Campbell, N.M.** (London Scottish) 1956 *F, W*

**Campbell, S.J.** (Dundee HSFP) 1995 *C, I, F, W, E, R, [Iv, NZ (R)], WS (t), 1996 I, F, W, E*, 1997 *A, SA*, 1998 *Fj (R), A 2(R)*

**Campbell-Lamerton, J.R.E.** (London Scottish) 1986 *F*, 1987 *[Z, R(R)]*

**Campbell-Lamerton, M.J.** (Halifax, Army, London Scottish) 1961 *F, SA, W, I*, 1962 *F, W, I, E*, 1963 *F, W, I, E*, 1964 *I, E*, 1965 *F, W, I, E, SA*, 1966 *F, W, I, E*

**Carmichael, A.B.** (W of Scotland) 1967 *I, NZ*, 1968 *F, W, I, E, A*, 1969 *F, W, I, E, SA*, 1970 *F, W, I, E, A*, 1971 *F, W, I, E (2[1C]), 1972 F, W, E, NZ*, 1973 *F, W, I, E, P*, 1974 *W, E, I, F*, 1975 *I, F, W, E, NZ, A*, 1976 *F, W, E, I*, 1977 *E, I (R), F, W*, 1978 *I*

**Carmichael, J.H.** (Watsonians) 1921 *F, W, I*

**Carrick, J.S.** (Glasgow Acad) 1876 *E*, 1877 *E*

**Cassels, D.Y.** (W of Scotland) 1880 *E*, 1881 *I*, 1882 *I, E*, 1883 *W, I, E*

**Cathcart, C.W.** (Edinburgh U) 1872 *E*, 1873 *E*, 1876 *E*

**Cawkwell, G.L.** (Oxford U) 1947 *F*

**Chalmers, C.M.** (Melrose) 1989 *W, E, I, F, Fj*, 1990 *I, F, W, E, NZ* 1,2, *Arg*, 1991 *F, W, E, I, R*, [*J, Z (R), I, WS, E, NZ*], 1992 *E, I, F, W, A* 1,2, 1993 *I, F, W, E, NZ*, 1994 *W, SA*, 1995 *C, I, F, W, E, R*, [*Iv, Tg, F, NZ*], *WS*, 1996 *A, It*, 1997 *W, I, F, A (R), SA*, 1998 *It, I, F, W, E*, 1999 *Arg (R)*

**Chalmers, T.** (Glasgow Acad) 1871 *E*, 1872 *E*, 1873 *E*, 1874 *E*, 1875 *E*, 1876 *E*

**Chambers, H.F.T.** (Edinburgh U) 1888 *W, I*, 1889 *W, I*

**Charters, R.G.** (Hawick) 1955 *W, I, E*

**Chisholm, D.H.** (Melrose) 1964 *I, E*, 1965 *E, SA*, 1966 *F, I, E, A*, 1967 *F, W, NZ*, 1968 *F, W, I*

**Chisholm, R.W.T.** (Melrose) 1955 *I, E*, 1956 *F, W, I, E*, 1958 *F, W, A, I*, 1960 *SA*

**Church, W.C.** (Glasgow Acad) 1906 *W*

**Clark, R.L.** (Edinburgh Wands, Royal Navy) 1972 *F, W, E, NZ*, 1973 *F, W, I, E, P*

**Clauss, P.R.A.** (Oxford U) 1891 *W, I, E*, 1892 *W, E*, 1895 *I*

**Clay, A.T.** (Edinburgh Acads) 1886 *W, I, E*, 1887 *I, W, E*, 1888 *W*

**Clunies-Ross, A.** (St Andrew's U) 1871 *E*

**Coltman, S.** (Hawick) 1948 *I*, 1949 *F, W, I, E*

**Colville, A.G.** (Merchistonians, Blackheath) 1871 *E*, 1872 *E*

**Connell, G.C.** (Trinity Acads and London Scottish) 1968 *E, A*, 1969 *F, E*, 1970 *F*

**Cooper, M. McG.** (Oxford U) 1936 *W, I*

**Corcoran, I.** (Gala) 1992 *A* 1*(R)*

**Cordial, I.F.** (Edinburgh Wands) 1952 *F, W, I, E*

**Cotter, J.L.** (Hillhead HSFP) 1934 *I, E*

**Cottington, G.S.** (Kelso) 1934 *I, E*, 1935 *W, I*, 1936 *E*

**Coughtrie, S.** (Edinburgh Acads) 1959 *F, W, I, E*, 1962 *W, I, E*, 1963 *F, W, I, E*

**Couper, J.H.** (W of Scotland) 1896 *W, I*, 1899 *I*

**Coutts, F.H.** (Melrose, Army) 1947 *W, I, E*

**Coutts, I.D.F.** (Old Alleynians) 1951 *F*, 1952 *E*

**Cowan, R.C.** (Selkirk) 1961 *F*, 1962 *F, W, I, E*

**Cowie, W.L.K.** (Edinburgh Wands) 1953 *E*

**Cownie, W.B.** (Watsonians) 1893 *W, I, E*, 1894 *W, I, E*, 1895 *W, I, E*

**Crabbie, G.E.** (Edinburgh Acads) 1904 *W*

**Crabbie, J.E.** (Edinburgh Acads, Oxford U) 1900 *W*, 1902 *I*, 1903 *W, I*, 1904 *E*, 1905 *W*

**Craig, A.** (Orrell) 2002 *C, US, R, SA, Fj*, 2003 *I* 1, *F(R), W* 1*(R), E, It* 1, *SA* 1,2

**Craig, J.B.** (Heriot's FP) 1939 *W*

**Craig, J.M.** (W of Scotland, Glasgow) 1997 *A*, 2001 *W (R), E (R), It*

**Cramb, R.I.** (Harlequins) 1987 [*R(R)*], *1988 I, F, A*

**Cranston, A.G.** (Hawick) 1976 *W, E, I*, 1977 *E, W*, 1978 *F (R), W, E, NZ*, 1981 *NZ* 1,2

**Crawford, J.A.** (Army, London Scottish) 1934 *I*

**Crawford, W.H.** (United Services, RN) 1938 *W, I, E*, 1939 *W, E*

**Crichton-Miller, D.** (Gloucester) 1931 *W, I, E*

**Crole, G.B.** (Oxford U) 1920 *F, W, I, E*

**Cronin, D.F.** (Bath, London Scottish, Bourges, Wasps) 1988 *I, F, W, E, A*, 1989 *W, E, I, F, Fj, R*, 1990 *I, F, W, E, NZ* 1,2, 1991 *F, W, E, I, R*, [*Z*], 1992 *A* 2, 1993 *I, F, W; E, NZ*, 1995 *C, I, F, [Tg, F, NZ]*, *WS*, 1996 *NZ* 1,2, *A, It*, 1997 *F (R)*, *1998 I, F, W, E*

**Cross, M.** (Merchistonians) 1875 *E*, 1876 *E*, 1877 *I, E*, 1878 *E*, 1879 *I, E*, 1880 *I, E*

**Cross, W.** (Merchistonians) 1871 *E*, 1872 *E*

**Cumming, R.S.** (Aberdeen U) 1921 *F, W*

**Cunningham, G.** (Oxford U) 1908 *W, I*, 1909 *W, E*, 1910 *F, I, E*, 1911 *E*

**Cunningham, R.F.** (Gala) 1978 *NZ*, 1979 *W, E*

**Currie, L.R.** (Dunfermline) 1947 *A*, 1948 *F, W, I*, 1949 *F, W, I, E*

**Cuthbertson, W.** (Kilmarnock, Harlequins) 1980 *I*, 1981 *W, E, I; NZ* 1,2, *R, A*, 1982 *E, I, F, W, A* 1,2, 1983 *I, F, W, NZ*, 1984 *W, E, A*

# D

**Dalgleish, A.** (Gala) 1890 *W, E*, 1891 *W, I*, 1892 *W*, 1893 *W*, 1894 *W, I*

**Dalgleish, K.J.** (Edinburgh Wands, Cambridge U) 1951 *I, E*, 1953 *F, W*

**Dallas, J.D.** (Watsonians) 1903 *E*

**Davidson, J.A.** (London Scottish, Edinburgh Wands) 1959 *E*, 1960 *I, E*

**Davidson, J.N.G.** (Edinburgh U) 1952 *F, W, I, E*, 1953 *F, W*, 1954 *F*

**Davidson, J.P.** (RIE Coll) 1873 *E*, 1874 *E*

**Davidson, R.S.** (Royal HSFP) 1893 *E*

**Davies, D.S.** (Hawick) 1922 *F, W, I, E*, 1923 *F, W, I, E*, 1924 *F, E*, 1925 *W, I, E*, 1926 *F, W, I, E*, 1927 *F, W, I*

**Dawson, J.C.** (Glasgow Acad) 1947 *A*, 1948 *F, W*, 1949 *F, W, I*, 1950 *F, W, I, E*, 1951 *F, W, I, E, SA*, 1952 *F, W, I, E*, 1953 *E*

**Deans, C.T.** (Hawick) 1978 *F, W, E, NZ*, 1979 *W, E, I, F, NZ*, 1980 *I, F*, 1981 *F, W, E, I, NZ* 1,2, *R, A*, 1982 *E, I, F, W, A* 1,2, 1983 *I, F, W, E, NZ*, 1984 *W, E, I, F, A*, 1985 *I, F, W, E*, 1986 *F, W, E, I, R*, 1987 *I, F, W, E*, [*F, Z, R, NZ*]

**Deans, D.T.** (Hawick) 1968 *E*

**Deas, D.W.** (Heriot's FP) 1947 *F, W*

**Dick, L.G.** (Loughborough Colls, Jordanhill, Swansea) 1972 *W (R), E*, 1974 *W, E, I, F*, 1975 *I, F, W, E, NZ, A*, 1976 *F*, 1977 *E*

**Dick, R.C.S.** (Cambridge U, Guy's Hospital) 1934 *W, I, E*, 1935 *W, I, E, NZ*, 1936 *W, I, E*, 1937 *W*, 1938 *W, I, E*

**Dickson, G.** (Gala) 1978 *NZ*, 1979 *W, E, I, F, NZ*, 1980 *W*, 1981 *F*, 1982 *W (R)*

**Dickson, M.R.** (Edinburgh U) 1905 *I*

**Dickson, W.M.** (Blackheath, Oxford U) 1912 *F, W, E, SA*, 1913 *F, W, I*

**Di Rollo, M.P.** (Edinburgh) 2002 *US (R)*

**Dobson, J.** (Glasgow Acad) 1911 *E*, 1912 *F, W, I, E, SA*

**Dobson, J.D.** (Glasgow Acad) 1910 *I*

**Dobson, W.G.** (Heriot's FP) 1922 *W, I, E*

**Docherty, J.T.** (Glasgow HSFP) 1955 *F, W*, 1956 *E*, 1958 *F, W, A, I, E*

**Dods, F.P.** (Edinburgh Acads) 1901 *I*

**Dods, J.H.** (Edinburgh Acads) 1895 *W, I, E*, 1896 *W, I, E*, 1897 *I, E*

**Dods, M.** (Gala, Northampton) 1994 *I (t), Arg* 1,2, 1995 *WS*, 1996 *I, F, W, E*

**Dods, P.W.** (Gala) 1983 *I, F, W, E, NZ*, 1984 *W, E, I, F, R, A*, 1985 *I, F, W, E*, 1989 *W, E, I, F*, 1991 *I (R), R*, [*Z, NZ (R)*]

**Donald, D.G.** (Oxford U) 1914 *W, I*

**Donald, R.L.H.** (Glasgow HSFP) 1921 *W, I, E*

**Donaldson, W.P.** (Oxford U, W of Scotland) 1893 *I*, 1894 *I*, 1895 *E*, 1896 *I*, *E*, 1899 *I*
**Don Wauchope, A.R.** (Fettesian-Lorettonians) 1881 *E*, 1882 *E*, 1883 *W*, 1884 *W*, *I*, *E*, 1885 *W*, *I* 1,2, 1886 *W*, *I*, *E*, 1888 *I*
**Don Wauchope, P.H.** (Fettesian-Lorettonians) 1885 *I* 1,2, 1886 *W*, 1887 *I*, *W*, *E*
**Dorward, A.F.** (Cambridge U, Gala) 1950 *F*, 1951 *SA*, 1952 *W*, *I*, *E*, 1953 *F*, *W*, *E*, 1955 *F*, 1956 *I*, *E*, 1957 *F*, *W*, *I*, *E*
**Dorward, T.F.** (Gala) 1938 *W*, *I*, *E*, 1939 *I*, *E*
**Douglas, B.A.F.** (Borders) 2002 *R*, *SA*, *Fj*, 2003 *I* 1, *F*, *W* 1, *E*, *It* 1, *SA* 1,2
**Douglas, G.** (Jedforest) 1921 *W*
**Douglas, J.** (Stewart's Coll FP) 1961 *F*, *SA*, *W*, *I*, *E*, 1962 *F*, *W*, *I*, *E*, 1963 *F*, *W*, *I*
**Douty, P.S.** (London Scottish) 1927 *A*, 1928 *F*, *W*
**Drew, D.** (Glasgow Acad) 1871 *E*, 1876 *E*
**Druitt, W.A.H.** (London Scottish) 1936 *W*, *I*, *E*
**Drummond, A.H.** (Kelvinside Acads) 1938 *W*, *I*
**Drummond, C.W.** (Melrose) 1947 *F*, *W*, *I*, *E*, 1948 *F*, *I*, *E*, 1950 *F*, *W*, *I*, *E*
**Drybrough, A.S.** (Edinburgh Wands, Merchistonians) 1902 *I*, 1903 *I*
**Dryden, R.H.** (Watsonians) 1937 *E*
**Drysdale, D.** (Heriot's FP) 1923 *F*, *W*, *I*, *E*, 1924 *F*, *W*, *I*, *E*, 1925 *F*, *W*, *I*, *E*, 1926 *F*, *W*, *I*, *E*, 1927 *F*, *W*, *I*, *E*, *A*, 1928 *F*, *W*, *I*, *E*, 1929 *F*
**Duff, P.L.** (Glasgow Acad) 1936 *W*, *I*, 1938 *W*, *I*, *E*, 1939 *W*
**Duffy, H.** (Jedforest) 1955 *F*
**Duke, A.** (Royal HSFP) 1888 *W*, *I*, 1889 *W*, *I*, 1890 *W*, *I*
**Duncan, A.W.** (Edinburgh U) 1901 *W*, *I*, *E*, 1902 *W*, *I*, *E*
**Duncan, D.D.** (Oxford U) 1920 *F*, *W*, *I*, *E*
**Duncan, M.D.F.** (W of Scotland) 1986 *F*, *W*, *E*, *R*, 1987 *I*, *F*, *W*, *E*, *[F, Z, R, NZ]*, 1988 *I*, *F*, *W*, *E*, *A*, 1989 *W*
**Duncan, M.M.** (Fettesian-Lorettonians) 1888 *W*
**Dunlop, J.W.** (W of Scotland) 1875 *E*
**Dunlop, Q.** (W of Scotland) 1971 *E (2[1C])*
**Dykes, A.S.** (Glasgow Acad) 1932 *E*
**Dykes, J.C.** (Glasgow Acad) 1922 *F*, *E*, 1924 *I*, 1925 *F*, *W*, *I*, 1926 *F*, *W*, *I*, *E*, 1927 *F*, *W*, *I*, *E*, *A*, 1928 *F*, *I*, 1929 *F*, *W*, *I*
**Dykes, J.M.** (Clydesdale, Glasgow HSFP) 1898 *I*, *E*, 1899 *W*, *E*, 1900 *W*, *I*, 1901 *W*, *I*, *E*, 1902 *E*

# E

**Edwards, D.B.** (Heriot's FP) 1960 *I*, *E*, *SA*
**Edwards, N.G.B.** (Harlequins, Northampton) 1992 *E*, *I*, *F*, *W*, *A* 1, 1994 *W*
**Elgie, M.K.** (London Scottish) 1954 *NZ*, *I*, *E*, *W*, 1955 *F*, *W*, *I*, *E*
**Elliot, C.** (Langholm) 1958 *E*, 1959 *F*, 1960 *F*, 1963 *E*, 1964 *F*, *NZ*, *W*, *I*, *E*, 1965 *F*, *W*, *I*
**Elliot, M.** (Hawick) 1895 *W*, 1896 *E*, 1897 *I*, *E*, 1898 *I*, *E*
**Elliot, T.** (Gala) 1905 *E*
**Elliot, T.** (Gala) 1955 *W*, *I*, *E*, 1956 *F*, *W*, *I*, *E*, 1957 *F*, *W*, *I*, *E*, 1958 *W*, *A*, *I*
**Elliot, T.G.** (Langholm) 1968 *W*, *A*, 1969 *F*, *W*, 1970 *E*
**Elliot, W.I.D.** (Edinburgh Acads) 1947 *F*, *W*, *E*, *A*, 1948 *F*, *W*, *I*, *E*, 1949 *F*, *W*, *I*, *E*, 1950 *F*, *W*, *I*, *E*, 1951 *F*, *W*, *I*, *E*, *SA*, 1952 *F*, *W*, *I*, *E*, 1954 *NZ*, *I*, *E*, *W*
**Ellis, D.G.** (Currie) 1997 *W*, *E*, *I*, *F*
**Emslie, W.D.** (Royal HSFP) 1930 *F*, 1932 *I*
**Eriksson, B.R.S.** (London Scottish) 1996 *NZ* 1, *A*, 1997 *E*
**Evans, H.L.** (Edinburgh U) 1885 *I* 1,2
**Ewart, E.N.** (Glasgow Acad) 1879 *E*, 1880 *I*, *E*

# F

**Fahmy, Dr E.C.** (Abertillery) 1920 *F*, *W*, *I*, *E*
**Fairley, I.T.** (Kelso, Edinburgh) 1999 *It*, *I (R)*, *[Sp (R)]*
**Fasson, F.H.** (London Scottish, Edinburgh Wands) 1900 *W*, 1901 *W*, *I*, 1902 *W*, *E*
**Fell, A.N.** (Edinburgh U) 1901 *W*, *I*, *E*, 1902 *W*, *E*, 1903 *W*, *E*
**Ferguson, J.H.** (Gala) 1928 *W*
**Ferguson, W.G.** (Royal HSFP) 1927 *A*, 1928 *F*, *W*, *I*, *E*
**Fergusson, E.A.J.** (Oxford U) 1954 *F*, *NZ*, *I*, *E*, *W*
**Finlay, A.B.** (Edinburgh Acads) 1875 *E*
**Finlay, J.F.** (Edinburgh Acads) 1871 *E*, 1872 *E*, 1874 *E*, 1875 *E*
**Finlay, N.J.** (Edinburgh Acads) 1875 *E*, 1876 *E*, 1878 *E*, 1879 *I*, *E*, 1880 *I*, *E*, 1881 *I*, *E*
**Finlay, R.** (Watsonians) 1948 *E*
**Fisher, A.T.** (Waterloo, Watsonians) 1947 *I*, *E*
**Fisher, C.D.** (Waterloo) 1975 *NZ*, *A*, 1976 *W*, *E*, *I*
**Fisher, D.** (W of Scotland) 1893 *I*
**Fisher, J.P.** (Royal HSFP, London Scottish) 1963 *E*, 1964 *F*, *NZ*, *W*, *I*, *E*, 1965 *F*, *W*, *I*, *E*, *SA*, 1966 *F*, *W*, *I*, *E*, *A*, 1967 *F*, *W*, *I*, *E*, *NZ*, 1968 *F*, *W*, *I*, *E*
**Fleming, C.J.N.** (Edinburgh Wands) 1896 *I*, *E*, 1897 *I*
**Fleming, G.R.** (Glasgow Acad) 1875 *E*, 1876 *E*
**Fletcher, H.N.** (Edinburgh U) 1904 *E*, 1905 *W*
**Flett, A.B.** (Edinburgh U) 1901 *W*, *I*, *E*, 1902 *W*, *I*
**Forbes, J.L.** (Watsonians) 1905 *W*, 1906 *I*, *E*
**Ford, D.St.C.** (United Services, RN) 1930 *I*, *E*, 1931 *E*, 1932 *W*, *I*
**Ford, J.R.** (Gala) 1893 *I*
**Forrest, J.E.** (Glasgow Acad) 1932 *SA*, 1935 *E*, *NZ*
**Forrest, J.G.S.** (Cambridge U) 1938 *W*, *I*, *E*
**Forrest, W.T.** (Hawick) 1903 *W*, *I*, *E*, 1904 *W*, *I*, *E*, 1905 *W*, *I*
**Forsayth, H.H.** (Oxford U) 1921 *F*, *W*, *I*, *E*, 1922 *W*, *I*, *E*
**Forsyth, I.W.** (Stewart's Coll FP) 1972 *NZ*, 1973 *F*, *W*, *I*, *E*, *P*
**Forsyth, J.** (Edinburgh U) 1871 *E*
**Foster, R.A.** (Hawick) 1930 *W*, 1932 *SA*, *I*, *E*
**Fox, J.** (Gala) 1952 *F*, *W*, *I*, *E*
**Frame, J.N.M.** (Edinburgh U, Gala) 1967 *NZ*, 1968 *F*, *W*, *I*, *E*, 1969 *W*, *I*, *E*, *SA*, 1970 *F*, *W*, *I*, *E*, *A*, 1971 *F*, *W*, *I*, *E* *(2[1C])*, 1972 *F*, *W*, *E*, 1973 *P (R)*
**France, C.** (Kelvinside Acads) 1903 *I*
**Fraser, C.F.P.** (Glasgow U) 1888 *W*, 1889 *W*
**Fraser, J.W.** (Edinburgh Inst FP) 1881 *E*
**Fraser, R.** (Cambridge U) 1911 *F*, *W*, *I*, *E*
**French, J.** (Glasgow Acad) 1886 *W*, 1887 *I*, *W*, *E*
**Frew, A.** (Edinburgh U) 1901 *W*, *I*, *E*
**Frew, G.M.** (Glasgow HSFP) 1906 *SA*, 1907 *W*, *I*, *E*, 1908 *W*, *I*, *E*, 1909 *W*, *I*, *E*, 1910 *F*, *W*, *I*, 1911 *I*, *E*
**Friebe, J.P.** (Glasgow HSFP) 1952 *E*
**Fullarton, I.A.** (Edinburgh) 2000 *NZ* 1*(R)*,2, 2001 *NZ (R)*
**Fulton, A.K.** (Edinburgh U, Dollar Acads) 1952 *F*, 1954 *F*
**Fyfe, K.C.** (Cambridge U, Sale, London Scottish) 1933 *W*, *E*, 1934 *E*, 1935 *W*, *I*, *E*, *NZ*, 1936 *W*, *E*, 1939 *I*

# G

**Gallie, G.H.** (Edinburgh Acads) 1939 *W*
**Gallie, R.A.** (Glasgow Acad) 1920 *F*, *W*, *I*, *E*, 1921 *F*, *W*, *I*, *E*
**Gammell, W.B.B.** (Edinburgh Wands) 1977 *I*, *F*, *W*, 1978 *W*, *E*

**Geddes, I.C.** (London Scottish) 1906 *SA*, 1907 *W, I, E*, 1908 *W, E*

**Geddes, K.I.** (London Scottish) 1947 *F, W, I, E*

**Gedge, H.T.S.** (Oxford U, London Scottish, Edinburgh Wands) 1894 *W, I, E*, 1896 *E*, 1899 *W, E*

**Gedge, P.M.S.** (Edinburgh Wands) 1933 *I*

**Gemmill, R.** (Glasgow HSFP) 1950 *F, W, I, E*, 1951 *F, W, I*

**Gibson, W.R.** (Royal HSFP) 1891 *I, E*, 1892 *W, I, E*, 1893 *W, I, E*, 1894 *W, I, E*, 1895 *W, I, E*

**Gilbert-Smith, D.S.** (London Scottish) 1952 *E*

**Gilchrist, J.** (Glasgow Acad) 1925 *F*

**Gill, A.D.** (Gala) 1973 *P*, 1974 *W, E, I, F*

**Gillespie, J.I.** (Edinburgh Acads) 1899 *E*, 1900 *W, E*, 1901 *W, I, E*, 1902 *W, I*, 1904 *I, E*

**Gillies, A.C.** (Watsonians) 1924 *W, I, E*, 1925 *F, W, E*, 1926 *F, W*, 1927 *F, W, I, E*

**Gilmour, H.R.** (Heriot's FP) 1998 *Fj*

**Gilray, C.M.** (Oxford U, London Scottish) 1908 *E*, 1909 *W, E*, 1912 *I*

**Glasgow, I.C.** (Heriot's FP) 1997 *F (R)*

**Glasgow, R.J.C.** (Dunfermline) 1962 *F, W, I, E*, 1963 *I, E*, 1964 *I, E*, 1965 *W, I*

**Glen, W.S.** (Edinburgh Wands) 1955 *W*

**Gloag, L.G.** (Cambridge U) 1949 *F, W, I, E*

**Goodfellow, J.** (Langholm) 1928 *W, I, E*

**Goodhue, F.W.J.** (London Scottish) 1890 *W, I, E*, 1891 *W, I, E*, 1892 *W, I, E*

**Gordon, R.** (Edinburgh Wands) 1951 *W*, 1952 *F, W, I, E*, 1953 *W*

**Gordon, R.E.** (Royal Artillery) 1913 *F, W, I*

**Gordon, R.J.** (London Scottish) 1982 *A* 1,2

**Gore, A.C.** (London Scottish) 1882 *I*

**Gossman, B.M.** (W of Scotland) 1980 *W*, 1983 *F, W*

**Gossman, J.S.** (W of Scotland) 1980 *E (R)*

**Gowans, J.J.** (Cambridge U, London Scottish) 1893 *W*, 1894 *W, E*, 1895 *W, I, E*, 1896 *I, E*

**Gowland, G.C.** (London Scottish) 1908 *W*, 1909 *W, E*, 1910 *F, W, I, E*

**Gracie, A.L.** (Harlequins) 1921 *F, W, I, E*, 1922 *F, W, I, E*, 1923 *F, W, I, E*, 1924 *F*

**Graham, G.** (Newcastle) 1997 *A (R), SA (R), 1998 I, F (R), W (R), 1999 F (R), Arg (R), R, [SA, U, Sm, NZ (R)], 2000 I (R), US, A, Sm*, 2001 *I (R), Tg (R), Arg (R), NZ (R)*, 2002 *E (R), It (R), I (R), F (R), W (R)*

**Graham, I.N.** (Edinburgh Acads) 1939 *I, E*

**Graham, J.** (Kelso) 1926 *I, E*, 1927 *F, W, I, E, A*, 1928 *F, W, I, E*, 1930 *I, E*, 1932 *SA, W*

**Graham, J.H.S.** (Edinburgh Acads) 1876 *E*, 1877 *I, E*, 1878 *E*, 1879 *I, E*, 1880 *I, E*, 1881 *I, E*

**Grant, D.** (Hawick) 1965 *F, E, SA*, 1966 *F, W, I, E, A*, 1967 *F, W, I, E, NZ*, 1968 *F*

**Grant, D.M.** (East Midlands) 1911 *W, I*

**Grant, M.L.** (Harlequins) 1955 *F*, 1956 *F, W*, 1957 *F*

**Grant, T.O.** (Hawick) 1960 *I, E, SA*, 1964 *F, NZ, W*

**Grant, W.St.C.** (Craigmount) 1873 *E*, 1874 *E*

**Gray, C.A.** (Nottingham) 1989 *W, E, I, F, Fj, R*, 1990 *I, F, W, E, NZ* 1,2, *Arg*, 1991 *F, W, E, I, [J, I, WS, E, NZ]*

**Gray, D.** (W of Scotland) 1978 *E*, 1979 *I, F, NZ*, 1980 *I, F, W, E*, 1981 *F*

**Gray, G.L.** (Gala) 1935 *NZ*, 1937 *W, I, E*

**Gray, T.** (Northampton, Heriot's FP) 1950 *E*, 1951 *F, E*

**Greenlees, H.D.** (Leicester) 1927 *A*, 1928 *F, W*, 1929 *I, E*, 1930 *E*

**Greenlees, J.R.C.** (Cambridge U, Kelvinside Acads) 1900 *I*, 1902 *W, I, E*, 1903 *W, I, E*

**Greenwood, J.T.** (Dunfermline and Perthshire Acads) 1952 *F*, 1955 *F, W, I, E*, 1956 *F, W, I, E*, 1957 *F, W, E*, 1958 *F, W, A, I, E*, 1959 *F, W, I*

**Greig, A.** (Glasgow HSFP) 1911 *I*

**Greig, L.L.** (Glasgow Acad, United Services) 1905 *NZ*, 1906 *SA*, 1907 *W*, 1908 *W, I*

**Greig, R.C.** (Glasgow Acad) 1893 *W*, 1897 *I*

**Grieve, C.F.** (Oxford U) 1935 *W*, 1936 *E*

**Grieve, R.M.** (Kelso) 1935 *W, I, E, NZ*, 1936 *W, I, E*

**Grimes, S.B.** (Watsonians, Newcastle) 1997 *A (t+R), 1998 I (R), F (R), W (R), E (R), Fj, A* 1, 2, 1999 *W (R), E, It, I, F, Arg, R, [SA, U, Sm (R), NZ (R)], 2000 It, I, F (R), W, US, A, Sm (R), 2001 F (R), W (R), E (R), It, I (R), Tg, Arg, NZ*, 2002 *E, It, I, F (R), W (R), C, US, R, SA, Fj*, 2003 *I* 1, *F, W* 1, *E(R), It* 1*(R)*

**Gunn, A.W.** (Royal HSFP) 1912 *F, W, I, SA*, 1913 *F*

# H

**Hall, A.J.A.** (Glasgow) 2002 *US (R)*

**Hamilton, A.S.** (Headingley) 1914 *W*, 1920 *F*

**Hamilton, H.M.** (W of Scotland) 1874 *E*, 1875 *E*

**Hannah, R.S.M.** (W of Scotland) 1971 *I*

**Harrower, P.R.** (London Scottish) 1885 *W*

**Hart, J.G.M.** (London Scottish) 1951 *SA*

**Hart, T.M.** (Glasgow U) 1930 *W, I*

**Hart, W.** (Melrose) 1960 *SA*

**Harvey, L.** (Greenock Wands) 1899 *I*

**Hastie, A.J.** (Melrose) 1961 *W, I, E*, 1964 *I, E*, 1965 *E, SA*, 1966 *F, W, I, E, A*, 1967 *F, W, I, NZ*, 1968 *F, W*

**Hastie, I.R.** (Kelso) 1955 *F*, 1958 *F, E*, 1959 *F, W, I*

**Hastie, J.D.H.** (Melrose) 1938 *W, I, E*

**Hastings, A.G.** (Cambridge U, Watsonians, London Scottish) 1986 *F, W, E, I, R*, 1987 *I, F, W, E, [F, Z, R, NZ]*, 1988 *I, F, W, E, A*, 1989 *Fj, R*, 1990 *I, F, W, E, NZ* 1,2, *Arg*, 1991 *F, W, E, I, [J, I, WS, E, NZ]*, 1992 *E, I, F, W, A* 1, 1993 *I, F, W, E, NZ*, 1994 *W, E, I, F, SA*, 1995 *C, I, F, W, E, R, [Iv, Tg, F, NZ]*

**Hastings, S.** (Watsonians) 1986 *F, W, E, I, R*, 1987 *I, F, W, [R]*, 1988 *I, F, W, A*, 1989 *W, E, I, F, Fj, R*, 1990 *I, F, W, E, NZ* 1,2, *Arg*, 1991 *F, W, E, I, [J, Z, I, WS, E, NZ]*, 1992 *E, I, F, W, A* 1,2, 1993 *I, F, W, E, NZ*, 1994 *E, I, F, SA*, 1995 *W, E, R (R), [Tg, F, NZ]*, 1996 *I, F, W, E, NZ* 2, *It*, 1997 *W, E (R)*

**Hay, B.H.** (Boroughmuir) 1975 *NZ, A*, 1976 *F*, 1978 *I, F, W, E, NZ*, 1979 *W, E, I, F, NZ*, 1980 *I, F, W, E*, 1981 *F, W, E, I, NZ* 1,2

**Hay, J.A.** (Hawick) 1995 *WS*

**Hay-Gordon, J.R.** (Edinburgh Acads) 1875 *E*, 1877 *I, E*

**Hegarty, C.B.** (Hawick) 1978 *I, F, W, E*

**Hegarty, J.J.** (Hawick) 1951 *F*, 1953 *F, W, I, E*, 1955 *F*

**Henderson, A.R.** (Glasgow) 2001 *I (R), Tg (R), NZ (R), 2002 It, I, US (R)*, 2003 *SA* 1,2

**Henderson, B.C.** (Edinburgh Wands) 1963 *E*, 1964 *F, I, E*, 1965 *F, W, I, E*, 1966 *F, W, I, E*

**Henderson, F.W.** (London Scottish) 1900 *W, I*

**Henderson, I.C.** (Edinburgh Acads) 1939 *I, E*, 1947 *F, W, E, A*, 1948 *I, E*

**Henderson, J.H.** (Oxford U, Richmond) 1953 *F, W, I, E*, 1954 *F, NZ, I, E, W*

**Henderson, J.M.** (Edinburgh Acads) 1933 *W, E, I*

**Henderson, J.Y.M.** (Watsonians) 1911 *E*

**Henderson, M.M.** (Dunfermline) 1937 *W, I, E*

**Henderson, N.F.** (London Scottish) 1892 *I*

**Henderson, R.G.** (Newcastle Northern) 1924 *I, E*

**Hendrie, K.G.P.** (Heriot's FP) 1924 *F, W, I*

**Hendry, T.L.** (Clydesdale) 1893 *W, I, E*, 1895 *I*

**Henriksen, E.H.** (Royal HSFP) 1953 *I*

**Hepburn, D.P.** (Woodford) 1947 *A*, 1948 *F, W, I, E*, 1949 *F, W, I, E*

**Heron, G.** (Glasgow Acad) 1874 *E*, 1875 *E*

**Hill, C.C.P.** (St Andrew's U) 1912 *F, I*

**Hilton, D.I.W.** (Bath, Glasgow) 1995 *C, I, F, W, E, R*, [*Tg, F, NZ*], *WS*, 1996 *I, F, W, E, NZ* 1,2, *A, It*, 1997 *W, A, SA*, 1998 *It, I (R), F, W, E, A* 1,2, *SA (R)*, *1999 W (R), E (R), It (R), I (R), F, R (R)*, *[SA (R), U (R), Sp*], 2000 *It (R), F (R), W (R)*, 2002 *SA(R)*

**Hines, N.J.** (Edinburgh) 2000 *NZ* 2*(R)*, 2002 *C, US, R(R), SA(R), Fj(R)*, 2003 *W* 1*(R), E, It* 1, *SA* 1,2

**Hinshelwood, A.J.W.** (London Scottish) 1966 *F, W, I, E, A*, 1967 *F, W, I, E, NZ*, 1968 *F, W, I, E, A*, 1969 *F, W, I, SA*, 1970 *F, W*

**Hinshelwood, B.G.** (Worcester) 2002 *C (R), R(R), SA(R), Fj*

**Hodge D.W.** (Watsonians, Edinburgh) 1997 *F (R), A, SA (t+R)*, *1998 A 2(R), SA*, 1999 *W, Arg, R*, [*Sp, Sm (R)*], *2000 F (R), W, E, NZ* 1,2, *US (R), Sm (R)*, *2001 F (R), W, E, It, I (R)*, *2002 E, W (R), C, US*

**Hodgson, C.G.** (London Scottish) 1968 *I, E*

**Hogg, C.D.** (Melrose) 1992 *A* 1,2, 1993 *NZ (R)*, *1994 Arg* 1,2

**Hogg, C.G.** (Boroughmuir) 1978 *F (R), W (R)*

**Holmes, S.D.** (London Scottish) 1998 *It, I, F*

**Holms, W.F.** (RIE Coll) 1886 *W, E*, 1887 *I, E*, 1889 *W, I*

**Horsburgh, G.B.** (London Scottish) 1937 *W, I, E*, 1938 *W, I, E*, 1939 *W, I, E*

**Howie, D.D.** (Kirkcaldy) 1912 *F, W, I, E, SA*, 1913 *F, W*

**Howie, R.A.** (Kirkcaldy) 1924 *F, W, I, E*, 1925 *W, I, E*

**Hoyer-Millar, G.C.** (Oxford U) 1953 *I*

**Huggan, J.L.** (London Scottish) 1914 *E*

**Hume, J.** (Royal HSFP) 1912 *F*, 1920 *F*, 1921 *F, W, I, E*, 1922 *F*

**Hume, J.W.G.** (Oxford U, Edinburgh Wands) 1928 *I*, 1930 *F*

**Hunter, F.** (Edinburgh U) 1882 *I*

**Hunter, I.G.** (Selkirk) 1984 *I (R)*, *1985 F (R), W, E*

**Hunter, J.M.** (Cambridge U) 1947 *F*

**Hunter, M.D.** (Glasgow High) 1974 *F*

**Hunter, W.J.** (Hawick) 1964 *F, NZ, W*, 1967 *F, W, I, E*

**Hutchison, W.R.** (Glasgow HSFP) 1911 *E*

**Hutton, A.H.M.** (Dunfermline) 1932 *I*

**Hutton, J.E.** (Harlequins) 1930 *E*, 1931 *F*

# I

**Inglis, H.M.** (Edinburgh Acads) 1951 *F, W, I, E, SA*, 1952 *W, I*

**Inglis, J.M.** (Selkirk) 1952 *E*

**Inglis, W.M.** (Cambridge U, Royal Engineers) 1937 *W, I, E*, 1938 *W, I, E*

**Innes, J.R.S.** (Aberdeen GSFP) 1939 *W, I, E*, 1947 *A*, 1948 *F, W, I, E*

**Ireland, J.C.H.** (Glasgow HSFP) 1925 *W, I, E*, 1926 *F, W, I, E*, 1927 *F, W, I, E*

**Irvine, A.R.** (Heriot's FP) 1972 *NZ*, 1973 *F, W, I, E, P*, 1974 *W, E, I, F*, 1975 *I, F, W, E, NZ, A*, 1976 *F, W, E, I*, 1977 *E, I, F, W*, 1978 *I, F, E, NZ*, 1979 *W, E, I, F, NZ*, 1980 *I, F, W, E*, 1981 *F, W, E, I, NZ* 1,2, *R, A*, 1982 *E, I, F, W, A* 1,2

**Irvine, D.R.** (Edinburgh Acads) 1878 *E*, 1879 *I, E*

**Irvine, R.W.** (Edinburgh Acads) 1871 *E*, 1872 *E*, 1873 *E*, 1874 *E*, 1875 *E*, 1876 *E*, 1877 *I, E*, 1878 *E*, 1879 *I, E*, 1880 *I, E*

**Irvine T.W.** (Edinburgh Acads) 1885 *I* 1,2, 1886 *W, I, E*, 1887 *I, W, E*, 1888 *W, I*, 1889 *I*

# J

**Jackson, K.L.T.** (Oxford U) 1933 *W, E, I*, 1934 *W*

**Jackson, T.G.H.** (Army) 1947 *F, W, E, A*, 1948 *F, W, I, E*, 1949 *F, W, I, E*

**Jackson, W.D.** (Hawick) 1964 *I*, 1965 *E, SA*, 1968 *A*, 1969 *F, W, I, E*

**Jacobsen, A.F.** (Edinburgh) 2002 *C (R), US*

**Jamieson, J.** (W of Scotland) 1883 *W, I, E*, 1884 *W, I, E*, 1885 *W, I* 1,2

**Jardine, I.C.** (Stirling County) 1993 *NZ*, 1994 *W, E (R), Arg* 1,2, 1995 *C, I, F*, [*Tg, F (t & R), NZ (R)*], 1996 *I, F, W, E, NZ* 1,2, 1998 *Fj*

**Jeffrey, J.** (Kelso) 1984 *A*, 1985 *I, E*, 1986 *F, W, E, I, R*, 1987 *I, F, W, E*, [*F, Z, R*], 1988 *I, W, A*, 1989 *W, E, I, F, Fj, R*, 1990 *I, F, W, E, NZ* 1,2, *Arg*, 1991 *F, W, E, I*, [*J, I, WS, E, NZ*]

**Johnston, D.I.** (Watsonians) 1979 *NZ*, 1980 *I, F, W, E*, 1981 *R, A*, 1982 *E, I, F, W, A* 1,2, 1983 *I, F, W, NZ*, 1984 *W, E, I, F, R*, 1986 *F, W, E, I, R*

**Johnston, H.H.** (Edinburgh Collegian FP) 1877 *I, E*

**Johnston, J.** (Melrose) 1951 *SA*, 1952 *F, W, I, E*

**Johnston, W.C.** (Glasgow HSFP) 1922 *F*

**Johnston, W.G.S.** (Cambridge U) 1935 *W, I*, 1937 *W, I, E*

**Joiner, C.A.** (Melrose, Leicester) 1994 *Arg* 1,2, 1995 *C, I, F, W, E, R*, [*Iv, Tg, F, NZ*], 1996 *I, F, W, E, NZ* 1, 1997 *SA*, 1998 *It, I, A* 2*(R)*, 2000 *NZ* 1*(R)*,2, *US (R)*

**Jones, P.M.** (Gloucester) 1992 *W (R)*

**Junor, J.E.** (Glasgow Acad) 1876 *E*, 1877 *I, E*, 1878 *E*, 1879 *E*, 1881 *I*

# K

**Keddie, R.R.** (Watsonians) 1967 *NZ*

**Keith, G.J.** (Wasps) 1968 *F, W*

**Keller, D.H.** (London Scottish) 1949 *F, W, I, E*, 1950 *F, W, I*

**Kelly, R.F.** (Watsonians) 1927 *A*, 1928 *F, W, E*

**Kemp, J.W.Y.** (Glasgow HSFP) 1954 *W*, 1955 *F, W, I, E*, 1956 *F, W, I, E*, 1957 *F, W, I, E*, 1958 *F, W, A, I, E*, 1959 *F, W, I, E*, 1960 *F, W, I, E, SA*

**Kennedy, A.E.** (Watsonians) 1983 *NZ*, 1984 *W, E, A*

**Kennedy, F.** (Stewart's Coll FP) 1920 *F, W, I, E*, 1921 *E*

**Kennedy, N.** (W of Scotland) 1903 *W, I, E*

**Ker, A.B.M.** (Kelso) 1988 *W, E*

**Ker, H.T.** (Glasgow Acad) 1887 *I, W, E*, 1888 *I*, 1889 *W*, 1890 *I, E*

**Kerr, D.S.** (Heriot's FP) 1923 *F, W*, 1924 *F*, 1926 *I, E*, 1927 *W, I, E*, 1928 *I, E*

**Kerr, G.** (Leeds) 2003 *I* 1*(R), F(R), W* 1*(R), E(R), SA* 1,2

**Kerr, G.C.** (Old Dunelmians, Edinburgh Wands) 1898 *I, E*, 1899 *I, W, E*, 1900 *W, I, E*

**Kerr, J.M.** (Heriot's FP) 1935 *NZ*, 1936 *I, E*, 1937 *W, I*

**Kerr, R.C.** (Glasgow) 2002 *C, US*

**Kerr, W.** (London Scottish) 1953 *E*

**Kidston, D.W.** (Glasgow Acad) 1883 *W, E*

**Kidston, W.H.** (W of Scotland) 1874 *E*

**Kilgour, I.J.** (RMC Sandhurst) 1921 *F*

**King, J.H.F.** (Selkirk) 1953 *F, W, E*, 1954 *E*

**Kininmonth, P.W.** (Oxford U, Richmond) 1949 *F, W, I, E*, 1950 *F, W, I, E*, 1951 *F, W, I, E, SA*, 1952 *F, W, I*, 1954 *F, NZ, I, E, W*

**Kinnear, R.M.** (Heriot's FP) 1926 *F, W, I*

**Knox, J.** (Kelvinside Acads) 1903 *W, I, E*

**Kyle, W.E.** (Hawick) 1902 *W, I, E*, 1903 *W, I, E*, 1904 *W, I, E*, 1905 *W, I, E, NZ*, 1906 *W, I, E*, 1908 *E*, 1909 *W, I, E*, 1910 *W*

# L

**Laidlaw, A.S.** (Hawick) 1897 *I*

**Laidlaw, F.A.L.** (Melrose) 1965 *F, W, I, E, SA*, 1966 *F, W, I, E, A*, 1967 *F, W, I, E, NZ*, 1968 *F, W, I, A*, 1969 *F, W, I, E, SA*, 1970 *F, W, I, E, A*, 1971 *F, W, I*

**Laidlaw, R.J.** (Jedforest) 1980 *I, F, W, E*, 1981 *F, W, E, I, NZ* 1,2, *R, A*, 1982 *E, I, F, W, A* 1,2, 1983 *I, F, W, E, NZ*, 1984 *W, E, I, F, R, A*, 1985 *I, F*, 1986 *F, W, E, I, R*, 1987 *I, F, W, E*, [*F, R, NZ*], 1988 *I, F, W, E*

**Laing, A.D.** (Royal HSFP) 1914 *W, I, E*, 1920 *F, W, I*, 1921 *F*

**Lambie, I.K.** (Watsonians) 1978 *NZ (R), 1979 W, E, NZ*

**Lambie, L.B.** (Glasgow HSFP) 1934 *W, I, E*, 1935 *W, I, E, NZ*

**Lamond, G.A.W.** (Kelvinside Acads) 1899 *W, E*, 1905 *E*

**Laney, B.J.** (Edinburgh) 2001 *NZ*, 2002 *E, It, I, F, W, C, US, R, SA, Fj*, 2003 *I* 1, *F, SA* 2 *(R)*

**Lang, D.** (Paisley) 1876 *E*, 1877 *I*

**Langrish, R.W.** (London Scottish) 1930 *F*, 1931 *F, W, I*

**Lauder, W.** (Neath) 1969 *I, E, SA*, 1970 *F, W, I, A*, 1973 *F*, 1974 *W, E, I, F*, 1975 *I, F, NZ, A*, 1976 *F*, 1977 *E*

**Laughland, I.H.P.** (London Scottish) 1959 *F*, 1960 *F, W, I, E*, 1961 *SA, W, I, E*, 1962 *F, W, I, E*, 1963 *F, W, I*, 1964 *F, NZ, W, I, E*, 1965 *F, W, I, E, SA*, 1966 *F, W, I, E*, 1967 *E*

**Lawrie, J.R.** (Melrose) 1922 *F, W, I, E*, 1923 *F, W, I, E*, 1924 *W, I, E*

**Lawrie, K.G.** (Gala) 1980 *F (R), W, E*

**Lawson, A.J.M.** (Edinburgh Wands, London Scottish) 1972 *F (R), E*, 1973 *F*, 1974 *W, E*, 1976 *E, I*, 1977 *E*, 1978 *NZ*, 1979 *W, E, I, F, NZ*, 1980 *W (R)*

**Lawther, T.H.B.** (Old Millhillians) 1932 *SA, W*

**Ledingham, G.A.** (Aberdeen GSFP) 1913 *F*

**Lee, D.J.** (London Scottish, Edinburgh) 1998 *I (R), F, W, E, Fj, A* 1,2, *SA*, 2001 *Arg*

**Lees, J.B.** (Gala) 1947 *I, A*, 1948 *F, W, E*

**Leggatt, H.T.O.** (Watsonians) 1891 *W, I, E*, 1892 *W, I*, 1893 *W, E*, 1894 *I, E*

**Lely, W.G.** (Cambridge U, London Scottish) 1909 *I*

**Leslie, D.G.** (Dundee HSFP, W of Scotland, Gala) 1975 *I, F, W, E, NZ, A*, 1976 *F, W, E, I*, 1978 *NZ*, 1980 *E*, 1981 *W, E, I, NZ* 1,2, *R, A*, 1982 *E*, 1983 *I, F, W, E*, 1984 *W, E, I, F, R*, 1985 *F, W, E*

**Leslie, J.A.** (Glasgow, Northampton) 1998 *SA*, 1999 *W, E, It, I, F*, [*SA*], 2000 *It, F, W, US, A, Sm*, 2001 *F, W, E, It, I, Tg, Arg, NZ*, 2002 *F, W*

**Leslie, M.D.** (Edinburgh) 1998 *SA (R)*, *1999 W, E, It, I, F, R*, [*SA, U, Sm, NZ*], 2000 *It, I, F, W, E, NZ* 1,2, 2001 *F, W, E, It*, 2002 *It (R), I (R), F, W, R, SA, Fj(R)*, 2003 *I* 1, *F, SA* 1 *(R)*, 2 *(R)*

**Liddell, E.H.** (Edinburgh U) 1922 *F, W, I*, 1923 *F, W, I, E*

**Lind, H.** (Dunfermline) 1928 *I*, 1931 *F, W, I, E*, 1932 *SA, W, E*, 1933 *W, E, I*, 1934 *W, I, E*, 1935 *I*, 1936 *E*

**Lindsay, A.B.** (London Hospital) 1910 *I*, 1911 *I*

**Lindsay, G.C.** (London Scottish) 1884 *W*, 1885 *I* 1, 1887 *W, E*

**Lindsay-Watson, R.H.** (Hawick) 1909 *I*

**Lineen, S.R.P.** (Boroughmuir) 1989 *W, E, I, F, Fj, R*, 1990 *I, F, W, E, NZ* 1,2, *Arg*, 1991 *F, W, E, I, R*, [*J, Z, I, E, NZ*], 1992 *E, I, F, W, A* 1,2

**Little, A.W.** (Hawick) 1905 *W*

**Logan, K.M.** (Stirling County, Wasps) 1992 *A* 2, 1993 *E (R), NZ (t), 1994 W, E, I, F, Arg* 1,2, *SA*, 1995 *C, I, F, W, E, R*, [*Iv, Tg, F, NZ*], *WS*, 1996 *W (R), NZ* 1,2, *A, It*, 1997 *W, E, I, F, A*, 1998 *I, F, SA (R), 1999 W, E, It, I, F, Arg, R*, [*SA, U, Sm, NZ*], 2000 *It, I, F, Sm*, 2001 *F, W, E, It*, 2002 *I (R), F (R), W*, 2003 *I* 1, *F, W* 1, *E, It* 1, *SA* 1,2

**Logan, W.R.** (Edinburgh U, Edinburgh Wands) 1931 *E*, 1932 *SA, W, I*, 1933 *W, E, I*, 1934 *W, I, E*, 1935 *W, I, E, NZ*, 1936 *W, I, E*, 1937 *W, I, E*

**Longstaff, S.L.** (Dundee HSFP, Glasgow) 1998 *F (R), W, E, Fj, A* 1,2 1999 *It (R), I (R), Arg (R), R*, [*U (R), Sp*], 2000 *It, I, NZ* 1

**Lorraine, H.D.B.** (Oxford U) 1933 *W, E, I*

**Loudoun-Shand, E.G.** (Oxford U) 1913 *E*

**Lowe, J.D.** (Heriot's FP) 1934 *W*

**Lumsden, I.J.M.** (Bath, Watsonians) 1947 *F, W, A*, 1949 *F, W, I, E*

**Lyall, G.G.** (Gala) 1947 *A*, 1948 *F, W, I, E*

**Lyall, W.J.C.** (Edinburgh Acads) 1871 *E*

# M

**Mabon, J.T.** (Jedforest) 1898 *I, E*, 1899 *I*, 1900 *I*

**Macarthur, J.P.** (Waterloo) 1932 *E*

**MacCallum, J.C.** (Watsonians) 1905 *E, NZ*, 1906 *W, I, E, SA*, 1907 *W, I, E*, 1908 *W, I, E*, 1909 *W, I, E*, 1910 *F, W, I, E*, 1911 *F, I, E*, 1912 *F, W, I, E*

**McClung, T.** (Edinburgh Acads) 1956 *I, E*, 1957 *W, I, E*, 1959 *F, W, I*, 1960 *W*

**McClure, G.B.** (W of Scotland) 1873 *E*

**McClure, J.H.** (W of Scotland) 1872 *E*

**McCowan, D.** (W of Scotland) 1880 *I, E*, 1881 *I, E*, 1882 *I, E*, 1883 *I, E*, 1884 *I, E*

**McCowat, R.H.** (Glasgow Acad) 1905 *I*

**McCrae, I.G.** (Gordonians) 1967 *E*, 1968 *I*, 1969 *F (R), W*, 1972 *F, NZ*

**McCrow, J.W.S.** (Edinburgh Acads) 1921 *I*

**Macdonald, A.E.D.** (Heriot's FP) 1993 *NZ*

**McDonald, C.** (Jedforest) 1947 *A*

**Macdonald, D.C.** (Edinburgh U) 1953 *F, W*, 1958 *I, E*

**Macdonald, D.S.M.** (Oxford U, London Scottish, W of Scotland) 1977 *E, I, F, W*, 1978 *I, W, E*

**Macdonald, J.D.** (London Scottish, Army) 1966 *F, W, I, E*, 1967 *F, W, I, E*

**Macdonald, J.M.** (Edinburgh Wands) 1911 *W*

**Macdonald, J.S.** (Edinburgh U) 1903 *E*, 1904 *W, I, E*, 1905 *W*

**Macdonald, K.R.** (Stewart's Coll FP) 1956 *F, W, I*, 1957 *W, I, E*

**Macdonald, R.** (Edinburgh U) 1950 *F, W, I, E*

**McDonald, W.A.** (Glasgow U) 1889 *W*, 1892 *I, E*

**Macdonald, W.G.** (London Scottish) 1969 *I (R)*

**Macdougall, J.B.** (Greenock Wands, Wakefield) 1913 *F*, 1914 *I*, 1921 *F, I, E*

**McEwan, M.C.** (Edinburgh Acads) 1886 *E*, 1887 *I, W, E*, 1888 *W, I*, 1889 *W, I*, 1890 *W, I, E*, 1891 *W, I, E*, 1892 *E*

**MacEwan, N.A.** (Gala, Highland) 1971 *F, W, I, E (2[1C]), 1972 F, W, E, NZ*, 1973 *F, W, I, E, P*, 1974 *W, E, I, F*, 1975 *W, E*

**McEwan, W.M.C.** (Edinburgh Acads) 1894 *W, E*, 1895 *W, E*, 1896 *W, I, E*, 1897 *I, E*, 1898 *I, E*, 1899 *I, W, E*, 1900 *W, E*

**MacEwen, R.K.G.** (Cambridge U, London Scottish) 1954 *F, NZ, I, W*, 1956 *F, W, I, E*, 1957 *F, W, I, E*, 1958 *W*

**Macfadyen, D.J.H.** (Glasgow) 2002 *C (R), US*

**Macfarlan, D.J.** (London Scottish) 1883 *W*, 1884 *W, I, E*, 1886 *W, I*, 1887 *I*, 1888 *I*

**McFarlane, J.L.H.** (Edinburgh U) 1871 *E*, 1872 *E*, 1873 *E*

**McGaughey, S.K.** (Hawick) 1984 *R*

**McGeechan, I.R.** (Headingley) 1972 *NZ*, 1973 *F, W, I, E, P*, 1974 *W, E, I, F*, 1975 *I, F, W, E, NZ, A*, 1976 *F, W, E, I*, 1977 *E, I, F, W*, 1978 *I, F, W, NZ*, 1979 *W, E, I, F*

**McGlashan, T.P.L.** (Royal HSFP) 1947 *F, I, E*, 1954 *F, NZ, I, E, W*

**MacGregor, D.G.** (Watsonians, Pontypridd) 1907 *W, I, E*

**MacGregor, G.** (Cambridge U) 1890 *W, I, E*, 1891 *W, I, E*, 1893 *W, I, E*, 1894 *W, I, E*, 1896 *E*

**MacGregor, I.A.A.** (Hillhead HSFP, Llanelli) 1955 *I, E*, 1956 *F, W, I, E*, 1957 *F, W, I*

**MacGregor, J.R.** (Edinburgh U) 1909 *I*

**McGuinness, G.M.** (W of Scotland) 1982 *A* 1,2, 1983 *I*, 1985 *I, F, W, E*

**McHarg, A.F.** (W of Scotland, London Scottish) 1968 *I, E, A*, 1969 *F, W, I, E*, 1971 *F, W, I, E (2[1C])*, 1972 *F, E, NZ*, 1973 *F, W, I, E, P*, 1974 *W, E, I, F*, 1975 *I, F, W, E, NZ, A*, 1976 *F, W, E, I*, 1977 *E, I, F, W*, 1978 *I, F, W, NZ*, 1979 *W, E*

**McIlwham, G.R.** (Glasgow Hawks, Glasgow) 1998 *Fj, A* 2*(R)*, 2000 *E (R), NZ* 2*(R), US (R), A (R), Sm (R)*, 2001 *F (R), W (R), E (R), It (R)*, 2003 *SA* 2 *(R)*

**McIndoe, F.** (Glasgow Acad) 1886 *W, I*

**MacIntyre, I.** (Edinburgh Wands) 1890 *W, I, E*, 1891 *W, I, E*

**McIvor, D.J.** (Edinburgh Acads) 1992 *E, I, F, W*, 1993 *NZ*, 1994 *SA*

**Mackay, E.B.** (Glasgow Acad) 1920 *W*, 1922 *E*

**McKeating, E.** (Heriot's FP) 1957 *F, W*, 1961 *SA, W, I, E*

**McKelvey, G.** (Watsonians) 1997 *A*

**McKendrick, J.G.** (W of Scotland) 1889 *I*

**Mackenzie, A.D.G.** (Selkirk) 1984 *A*

**Mackenzie, C.J.G.** (United Services) 1921 *E*

**Mackenzie, D.D.** (Edinburgh U) 1947 *W, I, E*, 1948 *F, W, I*

**Mackenzie, D.K.A.** (Edinburgh Wands) 1939 *I, E*

**Mackenzie, J.M.** (Edinburgh U) 1905 *NZ*, 1909 *W, I, E*, 1910 *W, I, E*, 1911 *W, I*

**McKenzie, K.D.** (Stirling County) 1994 *Arg* 1,2, 1995 *R*, [*Iv*], 1996 *I, F, W, E, NZ* 1,2, *A, It*, 1998 *A* 1*(R)*, 2

**Mackenzie, R.C.** (Glasgow Acad) 1877 *I, E*, 1881 *I, E*

**Mackie, G.Y.** (Highland) 1975 *A*, 1976 *F, W*, 1978 *F*

**MacKinnon, A.** (London Scottish) 1898 *I, E*, 1899 *I, W, E*, 1900 *E*

**Mackintosh, C.E.W.C.** (London Scottish) 1924 *F*

**Mackintosh, H.S.** (Glasgow U, W of Scotland) 1929 *F, W, I, E*, 1930 *F, W, I, E*, 1931 *F, W, I, E*, 1932 *SA, W, I, E*

**MacLachlan, L.P.** (Oxford U, London Scottish) 1954 *NZ, I, E, W*

**Maclagan, W.E.** (Edinburgh Acads) 1878 *E*, 1879 *I, E*, 1880 *I, E*, 1881 *I, E*, 1882 *I, E*, 1883 *W, I, E*, 1884 *W, I, E*, 1885 *W, I* 1,2, 1887 *I, W, E*, 1888 *W, I*, 1890 *W, I, E*

**McLaren, A.** (Durham County) 1931 *F*

**McLaren, E.** (London Scottish, Royal HSFP) 1923 *F, W, I, E*, 1924 *F*

**McLaren, J.G.** (Bourgoin, Glasgow, Bordeaux-Bègles) 1999 *Arg, R*, [*Sp, Sm*], 2000 *It (R), F, E, NZ* 1, 2001 *F, W, E (R), I, Tg, Arg, NZ*, 2002 *E, It, I, F, W*, 2003 *W* 1, *E, It* 1, *SA* 1 *(R)*

**McLauchlan, J.** (Jordanhill) 1969 *E, SA*, 1970 *F, W*, 1971 *F, W, I, E (2[1C])*, 1972 *F, W, E, NZ*, 1973 *F, W, I, E, P*, 1974 *W, E, I, F*, 1975 *I, F, W, E, NZ, A*, 1976 *F, W, E, I*, 1977 *W*, 1978 *I, F, W, E, NZ*, 1979 *W, E, I, F, NZ*

**McLean, D.I.** (Royal HSFP) 1947 *I, E*

**Maclennan, W.D.** (Watsonians) 1947 *F, I*

**MacLeod, D.A.** (Glasgow U) 1886 *I, E*

**MacLeod, G.** (Edinburgh Acads) 1878 *E*, 1882 *I*

**McLeod, H.F.** (Hawick) 1954 *F, NZ, I, E, W*, 1955 *F, W, I, E*, 1956 *F, W, I, E*, 1957 *F, W, I, E*, 1958 *F, W, A, I, E*, 1959 *F, W, I, E*, 1960 *F, W, I, E, SA*, 1961 *F, SA, W, I, E*, 1962 *F, W, I, E*

**MacLeod, K.G.** (Cambridge U) 1905 *NZ*, 1906 *W, I, E, SA*,1907 *W, I, E*, 1908 *I, E*

**MacLeod, L.M.** (Cambridge U) 1904 *W, I, E*, 1905 *W, I, NZ*

**Macleod, W.M.** (Fettesian-Lorettonians, Edinburgh Wands) 1886 *W, I*

**McMillan, K.H.D.** (Sale) 1953 *F, W, I, E*

**MacMillan, R.G.** (London Scottish) 1887 *W, I, E*, 1890 *W, I, E*, 1891 *W, E*, 1892 *W, I, E*, 1893 *W, E*, 1894 *W, I, E*, 1895 *W, I, E*, 1897 *I, E*

**MacMyn, D.J.** (Cambridge U, London Scottish) 1925 *F, W, I, E*, 1926 *F, W, I, E*, 1927 *E, A*, 1928 *F*

**McNeil, A.S.B.** (Watsonians) 1935 *I*

**McPartlin, J.J.** (Harlequins, Oxford U) 1960 *F, W*, 1962 *F, W, I, E*

**Macphail, J.A.R.** (Edinburgh Acads) 1949 *E*, 1951 *SA*

**Macpherson, D.G.** (London Hospital) 1910 *I, E*

**Macpherson, G.P.S.** (Oxford U, Edinburgh Acads) 1922 *F, W, I, E*, 1924 *W, E*, 1925 *F, W, E*, 1927 *F, W, I, E*, 1928 *F, W, E*, 1929 *I, E*, 1930 *F, W, I, E*, 1931 *W, E*, 1932 *SA, E*

**Macpherson, N.C.** (Newport) 1920 *W, I, E*, 1921 *F, E*, 1923 *I, E*

**McQueen, S.B.** (Waterloo) 1923 *F, W, I, E*

**Macrae, D.J.** (St Andrew's U) 1937 *W, I, E*, 1938 *W, I, E*, 1939 *W, I, E*

**Madsen, D.F.** (Gosforth) 1974 *W, E, I, F*, 1975 *I, F, W, E*, 1976 *F*, 1977 *E, I, F, W*, 1978 *I*

**Mair, N.G.R.** (Edinburgh U) 1951 *F, W, I, E*

**Maitland, G.** (Edinburgh Inst FP) 1885 *W, I* 2

**Maitland, R.** (Edinburgh Inst FP) 1881 *E*, 1882 *I, E*, 1884 *W*, 1885 *W*

**Maitland, R.P.** (Royal Artillery) 1872 *E*

**Malcolm, A.G.** (Glasgow U) 1888 *I*

**Manson, J.J.** (Dundee HSFP) 1995 *E (R)*

**Marsh, J.** (Edinburgh Inst FP) 1889 *W, I*

**Marshall, A.** (Edinburgh Acads) 1875 *E*

**Marshall, G.R.** (Selkirk) 1988 *A (R)*, 1989 *Fj*, 1990 *Arg*, 1991 [*Z*]

**Marshall, J.C.** (London Scottish) 1954 *F, NZ, I, E, W*

**Marshall, K.W.** (Edinburgh Acads) 1934 *W, I, E*, 1935 *W, I, E*, 1936 *W*, 1937 *E*

**Marshall, T.R.** (Edinburgh Acads) 1871 *E*, 1872 *E*, 1873 *E*, 1874 *E*

**Marshall, W.** (Edinburgh Acads) 1872 *E*

**Martin, H.** (Edinburgh Acads, Oxford U) 1908 *W, I, E*, 1909 *W, E*

**Masters, W.H.** (Edinburgh Inst FP) 1879 *I*, 1880 *I, E*

**Mather, C.G.** (Edinburgh) 1999 *R (R)*, [*Sp, Sm (R)*], 2000 *F (t)*

**Maxwell, F.T.** (Royal Engineers) 1872 *E*

**Maxwell, G.H.H.P.** (Edinburgh Acads, RAF, London Scottish) 1913 *I, E*, 1914 *W, I, E*, 1920 *W, E*, 1921 *F, W, I, E*, 1922 *F, E*

**Maxwell, J.M.** (Langholm) 1957 *I*

**Mayer, M.J.M.** (Watsonians, Edinburgh) 1998 *SA*, 1999 [*SA (R), U, Sp, Sm, NZ*], 2000 *It, I*

**Mein, J.** (Edinburgh Acads) 1871 *E*, 1872 *E*, 1873 *E*, 1874 *E*, 1875 *E*

**Melville, C.L.** (Army) 1937 *W, I, E*

**Menzies, H.F.** (W of Scotland) 1893 *W, I*, 1894 *W, E*

**Metcalfe, G.H.** (Glasgow Hawks, Glasgow) 1998 *A* 1,2, 1999 *W, E, It, I, F, Arg, R, [SA, U, Sm, NZ]*, 2000 *It, I, F, W, E*, 2001 *I, Tg*, 2002 *E, It, I, F, W (R), C, US*, 2003 *I* 1, *F, W* 1, *E, It* 1, *SA* 1,2

**Metcalfe, R.** (Northampton, Edinburgh) 2000 *E, NZ* 1,2, *US (R), A (R), Sm*, 2001 *F, W, E*

**Methuen, A.** (London Scottish) 1889 *W, I*

**Michie, E.J.S.** (Aberdeen U, Aberdeen GSFP) 1954 *F, NZ, I, E*, 1955 *W, I, E*, 1956 *F, W, I, E*, 1957 *F, W, I, E*

**Millar, J.N.** (W of Scotland) 1892 *W, I, E*, 1893 *W*, 1895 *I, E*

**Millar, R.K.** (London Scottish) 1924 *I*

**Millican, J.G.** (Edinburgh U) 1973 *W, I, E*

**Milne, C.J.B.** (Fettesian-Lorettonians, W of Scotland) 1886 *W, I, E*

**Milne, D.F.** (Heriot's FP) 1991 [J(R)]

**Milne, I.G.** (Heriot's FP, Harlequins) 1979 *I, F, NZ*, 1980 *I, F*, 1981 *NZ* 1,2, *R, A*, 1982 *E, I, F, W, A* 1,2, 1983 *I, F, W, E, NZ*, 1984 *W, E, I, F, A*, 1985 *F, W, E*, 1986 *F, W, E, I, R*, 1987 *I, F, W, E, [F, Z, NZ]*, 1988 *A*, 1989 *W*, 1990 *NZ* 1,2

**Milne, K.S.** (Heriot's FP) 1989 *W, E, I, F, Fj, R*, 1990 *I, F, W, E, NZ* 2, *Arg*, 1991 *F, W (R), E, [Z]*, 1992 *E, I, F, W, A* 1, 1993 *I, F, W, E, NZ*, 1994 *W, E, I, F, SA*, 1995 *C, I, F, W, E, [Tg, F, NZ]*

**Milne, W.M.** (Glasgow Acad) 1904 *I, E*, 1905 *W, I*

**Milroy, E.** (Watsonians) 1910 *W*, 1911 *E*, 1912 *W, I, E, SA*, 1913 *F, W, I, E*, 1914 *I, E*

**Mitchell, G.W.E.** (Edinburgh Wands) 1967 *NZ*, 1968 *F, W*

**Mitchell, J.G.** (W of Scotland) 1885 *W, I* 1,2

**Moffat, J.S.D.** (Edinburgh) 2002 *R, SA, Fj(R)*

**Moir, C.C.** (Northampton) 2000 *W, E, NZ* 1

**Moncreiff, F.J.** (Edinburgh Acads) 1871 *E*, 1872 *E*, 1873 *E*

**Monteith, H.G.** (Cambridge U, London Scottish) 1905 *E*, 1906 *W, I, E, SA*, 1907 *W, I*, 1908 *E*

**Monypenny, D.B.** (London Scottish) 1899 *I, W, E*

**Moodie, A.R.** (St Andrew's U) 1909 *E*, 1910 *F*, 1911 *F*

**Moore, A.** (Edinburgh Acads) 1990 *NZ* 2, *Arg*, 1991 *F, W, E*

**Morgan, D.W.** (Stewart's-Melville FP) 1973 *W, I, E, P*, 1974 *I, F*, 1975 *I, F, W, E, NZ, A*, 1976 *F, W*, 1977 *I, F, W*, 1978 *I, F, W, E*

**Morrison, I.R.** (London Scottish) 1993 *I, F, W, E*, 1994 *W, SA*, 1995 *C, I, F, W, E, R, [Tg, F, NZ]*

**Morrison, M.C.** (Royal HSFP) 1896 *W, I, E*, 1897 *I, E*, 1898 *I, E*, 1899 *I, W, E*, 1900 *W, E*, 1901 *W, I, E*, 1902 *W, I, E*, 1903 *W, I*, 1904 *W, I, E*

**Morrison, R.H.** (Edinburgh U) 1886 *W, I, E*

**Morrison, W.H.** (Edinburgh Acads) 1900 *W*

**Morton, D.S.** (W of Scotland) 1887 *I, W, E*, 1888 *W, I*, 1889 *W, I*, 1890 *I, E*

**Mowat, J.G.** (Glasgow Acad) 1883 *W, E*

**Mower, A.L.** (Newcastle) 2001 *Tg, Arg, NZ*, 2002 *It*, 2003 *I* 1, *F, W* 1, *E, It* 1, *SA* 1,2

**Muir, D.E.** (Heriot's FP) 1950 *F, W, I, E*, 1952 *W, I, E*

**Munnoch, N.M.** (Watsonians) 1952 *F, W, I*

**Munro, D.S.** (Glasgow High Kelvinside) 1994 *W, E, I, F, Arg* 1,2, 1997 *W (R)*

**Munro, P.** (Oxford U, London Scottish) 1905 *W, I, E, NZ*, 1906 *W, I, E, SA*, 1907 *I, E*, 1911 *F, W, I*

**Munro, R.** (St Andrew's U) 1871 *E*

**Munro, S.** (Ayr, W of Scotland) 1980 *I, F*, 1981 *F, W, E, I, NZ* 1,2, *R*, 1984 *W*

**Munro, W.H.** (Glasgow HSFP) 1947 *I, E*

**Murdoch, W.C.W.** (Hillhead HSFP) 1935 *E, NZ*, 1936 *W, I*, 1939 *E*, 1948 *F, W, I, E*

**Murray, C.A.** (Hawick, Edinburgh) 1998 *E (R), Fj, A* 1,2, *SA*, 1999 *W, E, It, I, F, Arg, [SA, U, Sp, Sm, NZ]*, 2000 *NZ* 2, *US, A, Sm*, 2001 *F, W, E, It (R), Tg, Arg*

**Murray, G.M.** (Glasgow Acad) 1921 *I*, 1926 *W*

**Murray, H.M.** (Glasgow U) 1936 *W, I*

**Murray, K.T.** (Hawick) 1985 *I, F, W*

**Murray, R.O.** (Cambridge U) 1935 *W, E*

**Murray, S.** (Bedford, Saracens, Edinburgh) 1997 *A, SA*, 1998 *It, Fj, A* 1,2, *SA*, 1999 *W, E, It, I, F, Arg, R, [SA, U, Sm, NZ]*, 2000 *It, I, F, W, E, NZ* 1, *US, A, Sm*, 2001 *F, W, E, It, I, Tg, Arg, NZ*, 2002 *E, It, I, F, W, R, SA*, 2003 *I* 1, *F, W* 1, *E, It* 1, *SA* 1,2

**Murray, W.A.K.** (London Scottish) 1920 *F, I*, 1921 *F*

# N

**Napier, H.M.** (W of Scotland) 1877 *I, E*, 1878 *E*, 1879 *I, E*

**Neill, J.B.** (Edinburgh Acads) 1963 *E*, 1964 *F, NZ, W, I, E*, 1965 *F*

**Neill, R.M.** (Edinburgh Acads) 1901 *E*, 1902 *I*

**Neilson, G.T.** (W of Scotland) 1891 *W, I, E*, 1892 *W, E*, 1893 *W*, 1894 *W, I*, 1895 *W, I, E*, 1896 *W, I, E*

**Neilson, J.A.** (Glasgow Acad) 1878 *E*, 1879 *E*

**Neilson, R.T.** (W of Scotland) 1898 *I, E*, 1899 *I, W*, 1900 *I, E*

**Neilson, T.** (W of Scotland) 1874 *E*

**Neilson, W.** (Merchiston, Cambridge U, London Scottish) 1891 *W, E*, 1892 *W, I, E*, 1893 *I, E*, 1894 *E*, 1895 *W, I, E*, 1896 *I*, 1897 *I, E*

**Neilson, W.G.** (Merchistonians) 1894 *E*

**Nelson, J.B.** (Glasgow Acad) 1925 *F, W, I, E*, 1926 *F, W, I, E*, 1927 *F, W, I, E*, 1928 *I, E*, 1929 *F, W, I, E*, 1930 *F, W, I, E*, 1931 *F, W, I*

**Nelson, T.A.** (Oxford U) 1898 *E*

**Nichol, J.A.** (Royal HSFP) 1955 *W, I, E*

**Nichol, S.A.** (Selkirk) 1994 *Arg* 2*(R)*

**Nicol, A.D.** (Dundee HSFP, Bath, Glasgow) 1992 *E, I, F, W, A* 1,2, 1993 *NZ*, 1994 *W*, 1997 *A, SA*, 2000 *I (R), F, W, E, NZ* 1,2, 2001 *F, W, E, I (R), Tg, Arg, NZ*

**Nimmo, C.S.** (Watsonians) 1920 *E*

# O

**Ogilvy, C.** (Hawick) 1911 *I, E*, 1912 *I*

**Oliver, G.H.** (Hawick) 1987 [Z], 1990 *NZ* 2*(R)*, 1991 [Z]

**Oliver, G.K.** (Gala) 1970 *A*

**Orr, C.E.** (W of Scotland) 1887 *I, E, W*, 1888 *W, I*, 1889 *W, I*, 1890 *W, I, E*, 1891 *W, I, E*, 1892 *W, I, E*

**Orr, H.J.** (London Scottish) 1903 *W, I, E*, 1904 *W, I*

**Orr, J.E.** (W of Scotland) 1889 *I*, 1890 *W, I, E*, 1891 *W, I, E*, 1892 *W, I, E*, 1893 *I, E*

**Orr, J.H.** (Edinburgh City Police) 1947 *F, W*

**Osler, F.L.** (Edinburgh U) 1911 *F, W*

# P

**Park, J.** (Royal HSFP) 1934 *W*

**Paterson, C.D.** (Edinburgh) 1999 *[Sp]*, 2000 *F, W, E, NZ* 1,2, *US, A, Sm*, 2001 *F, W, E, It, I, NZ*, 2002 *E, It, I, F, W, C, US, R, SA, Fj*, 2003 *I* 1, *F, W* 1, *E, It* 1, *SA* 1,2

**Paterson, D.S.** (Gala) 1969 *SA*, 1970 *I, E, A*, 1971 *F, W, I, E (2[1C])*, 1972 *W*

**Paterson, G.Q.** (Edinburgh Acads) 1876 *E*

**Paterson, J.R.** (Birkenhead Park) 1925 *F, W, I, E*, 1926 *F, W, I, E*, 1927 *F, W, I, E, A*, 1928 *F, W, I, E*, 1929 *F, W, I, E*

**Patterson, D.** (Hawick) 1896 *W*

**Patterson, D.W.** (West Hartlepool) 1994 *SA*, 1995 *[Tg]*

**Pattullo, G.L.** (Panmure) 1920 *F, W, I, E*

**Paxton, I.A.M.** (Selkirk) 1981 *NZ* 1,2, *R, A*, 1982 *E, I, F, W, A* 1,2, 1983 *I, E, NZ*, 1984 *W, E, I, F*, 1985 *I (R), F, W, E*, 1986 *W, E, I, R*, 1987 *I, F, W, E*, *[F, Z, R, NZ]*, 1988 *I, E, A*

**Paxton, R.E.** (Kelso) 1982 *I, A* 2*(R)*

**Pearson, J.** (Watsonians) 1909 *I, E*, 1910 *F, W, I, E*, 1911 *F*, 1912 *F, W, SA*, 1913 *I, E*

**Pender, I.M.** (London Scottish) 1914 *E*

**Pender, N.E.K.** (Hawick) 1977 *I*, 1978 *F, W, E*

**Penman, W.M.** (RAF) 1939 *I*

**Peterkin, W.A.** (Edinburgh U) 1881 *E*, 1883 *I*, 1884 *W, I, E*, 1885 *W, I* 1,2

**Peters, E.W.** (Bath) 1995 *C, I, F, W, E, R*, *[Tg, F, NZ]*, 1996 *I, F, W, E, NZ* 1,2, *A, It*, 1997 *A, SA*, 1998 *W, E, Fj, A* 1,2, *SA*, 1999 *W, E, It, I*

**Petrie, A.G.** (Royal HSFP) 1873 *E*, 1874 *E*, 1875 *E*, 1876 *E*, 1877 *I, E*, 1878 *E*, 1879 *I, E*, 1880 *I, E*

**Petrie, J.M.** (Glasgow) 2000 *NZ* 2, *US, A, Sm*, 2001 *F, W, It (R), I (R), Tg, Arg*, 2002 *F (t), W (R), C, R(R), Fj*, 2003 *F(t+R), W* 1*(R), SA* 1 *(R)*, 2 *(R)*

**Philp, A.** (Edinburgh Inst FP) 1882 *E*

**Pocock, E.I.** (Edinburgh Wands) 1877 *I, E*

**Pollock, J.A.** (Gosforth) 1982 *W*, 1983 *E, NZ*, 1984 *E (R), I, F, R*, 1985 *F*

**Polson, A.H.** (Gala) 1930 *E*

**Pountney, A.C.** (Northhampton) 1998 *SA*, 1999 *W (t+R), E (R), It (t+R), I (R), F, Arg*, *[SA, U, Sm, NZ]*, 2000 *It, I, F, W, E, US,A, Sm*, 2001 *F, W, E, It, I*, 2002 *E, I, F, W, R, SA, Fj*

**Proudfoot, M.C.** (Melrose) 1998 *Fj, A* 1,2

**Purdie, W.** (Jedforest) 1939 *W, I, E*

**Purves, A.B.H.L.** (London Scottish) 1906 *W, I, E, SA*, 1907 *W, I, E*, 1908 *W, I, E*

**Purves, W.D.C.L.** (London Scottish) 1912 *F, W, I, SA*, 1913 *I, E*

# R

**Rea, C.W.W.** (W of Scotland, Headingley) 1968 *A*, 1969 *F, W, I, SA*, 1970 *F, W, I, A*, 1971 *F, W, E (2[1C])*

**Redpath, B.W.** (Melrose, Narbonne, Sale) 1993 *NZ (t)*, 1994 *E (t), F, Arg* 1,2, 1995 *C, I, F, W, E, R*, *[Iv, F, NZ]*, *WS*, 1996 *I, F, W, E. A (R), It*, 1997 *E, I, F*, 1998 *Fj, A* 1,2, *SA*, 1999 *R (R)*, *[U (R), Sp]*, 2000 *It, I, US, A, Sm*, 2001 *F (R), E (R), It, I*, 2002 *E, It, I, F, W, R, SA, Fj*, 2003 *I* 1, *F, W* 1, *E, It* 1, *SA* 1,2

**Reed, A.I.** (Bath, Wasps) 1993 *I, F, W, E*, 1994 *E, I, F, Arg* 1,2, *SA*, 1996 *It*, 1997 *W, E, I, F*, 1999 *It (R), F (R)*, *[Sp]*

**Reid, C.** (Edinburgh Acads) 1881 *I, E*, 1882 *I, E*, 1883 *W, I, E*, 1884 *W, I, E*, 1885 *W, I* 1,2, 1886 *W, I, E*, 1887 *I, W, E*, 1888 *W, I*

**Reid, J.** (Edinburgh Wands) 1874 *E*, 1875 *E*, 1876 *E*, 1877 *I, E*

**Reid, J.M.** (Edinburgh Acads) 1898 *I, E*, 1899 *I*

**Reid, M.F.** (Loretto) 1883 *I, E*

**Reid, R.E.** (Glasgow) 2001 *Tg (R), Arg*

**Reid, S.J.** (Boroughmuir, Leeds, Narbonne) 1995 *WS*, 1999 *F, Arg*, *[Sp]*, 2000 *It (t), F, W, E (t)*

**Reid-Kerr, J.** (Greenock Wand) 1909 *E*

**Relph, W.K.L.** (Stewart's Coll FP) 1955 *F, W, I, E*

**Renny-Tailyour, H.W.** (Royal Engineers) 1872 *E*

**Renwick, J.M.** (Hawick) 1972 *F, W, E, NZ*, 1973 *F*, 1974 *W, E, I, F*, 1975 *I, F, W, E, NZ, A*, 1976 *F, W, E (R)*, 1977 *I, F, W*, 1978 *I, F, W, E, NZ*, 1979 *W, E, I, F, NZ*, 1980 *I, F, W, E*, 1981 *F, W, E, I, NZ* 1,2, *R, A*, 1982 *E, I, F, W*, 1983 *I, F, W, E*, 1984 *R*

**Renwick, W.L.** (London Scottish) 1989 *R*

**Renwick, W.N.** (London Scottish, Edinburgh Wands) 1938 *E*, 1939 *W*

**Richardson, J.F.** (Edinburgh Acads) 1994 *SA*

**Ritchie, G.** (Merchistonians) 1871 *E*

**Ritchie, G.F.** (Dundee HSFP) 1932 *E*

**Ritchie, J.M.** (Watsonians) 1933 *W, E, I*, 1934 *W, I, E*

**Ritchie, W.T.** (Cambridge U) 1905 *I, E*

**Robb, G.H.** (Glasgow U) 1881 *I*, 1885 *W*

**Roberts, G.** (Watsonians) 1938 *W, I, E*, 1939 *W, E*

**Robertson, A.H.** (W of Scotland) 1871 *E*

**Robertson, A.W.** (Edinburgh Acads) 1897 *E*

**Robertson, D.** (Edinburgh Acads) 1875 *E*

**Robertson, D.D.** (Cambridge U) 1893 *W*

**Robertson, I.** (London Scottish, Watsonians) 1968 *E*, 1969 *E, SA*, 1970 *F, W, I, E, A*

**Robertson, I.P.M.** (Watsonians) 1910 *F*

**Robertson, J.** (Clydesdale) 1908 *E*

**Robertson, K.W.** (Melrose) 1978 *NZ*, 1979 *W, E, I, F, NZ*, 1980 *W, E*, 1981 *F, W, E, I, R, A*, 1982 *E, I, F, A* 1,2, 1983 *I, F, W, E*, 1984 *E, I, F, R, A*, 1985 *I, F, W, E*, 1986 *I*, 1987 *F (R), W, E*, *[F, Z, NZ]*, 1988 *E, A*, 1989 *E, I, F*

**Robertson, L.** (London Scottish United Services) 1908 *E*, 1911 *W*, 1912 *W, I, E, SA*, 1913 *W, I, E*

**Robertson, M.A.** (Gala) 1958 *F*

**Robertson, R.D.** (London Scottish) 1912 *F*

**Robson, A.** (Hawick) 1954 *F*, 1955 *F, W, I, E*, 1956 *F, W, I, E*, 1957 *F, W, I, E*, 1958 *W, A, I, E*, 1959 *F, W, I, E*, 1960 *F*

**Rodd, J.A.T.** (United Services, RN, London Scottish) 1958 *F, W, A, I, E*, 1960 *F, W*, 1962 *F*, 1964 *F, NZ, W*, 1965 *F, W, I*

**Rogerson, J.** (Kelvinside Acads) 1894 *W*

**Roland, E.T.** (Edinburgh Acads) 1884 *I, E*

**Rollo, D.M.D.** (Howe of Fife) 1959 *E*, 1960 *F, W, I, E, SA*, 1961 *F, SA, W, I, E*, 1962 *F, W, E*, 1963 *F, W, I, E*, 1964 *F, NZ, W, I, E*, 1965 *F, W, I, E, SA*, 1966 *F, W, I, E, A*, 1967 *F, W, E, NZ*, 1968 *F, W, I*

**Rose, D.M.** (Jedforest) 1951 *F, W, I, E, SA*, 1953 *F, W*

**Ross, A.** (Kilmarnock) 1924 *F, W*

**Ross, A.** (Royal HSFP) 1905 *W, I, E*, 1909 *W, I*

**Ross, A.R.** (Edinburgh U) 1911 *W*, 1914 *W, I, E*

**Ross, E.J.** (London Scottish) 1904 *W*

**Ross, G.** (Edinburgh, Leeds) 2001 *Tg*, 2002 *R, SA, Fj(R)*, 2003 *I* 1, *W* 1*(R), SA* 2 *(R)*

**Ross, G.T.** (Watsonians) 1954 *NZ, I, E, W*

**Ross, I.A.** (Hillhead HSFP) 1951 *F, W, I, E*

**Ross, J.** (London Scottish) 1901 *W, I, E*, 1902 *W*, 1903 *E*

**Ross, K.I.** (Boroughmuir FP) 1961 *SA, W, I, E*, 1962 *F, W, I, E*, 1963 *F, W, E*

**Ross, W.A.** (Hillhead HSFP) 1937 *W, E*

**Rottenburg, H.** (Cambridge U, London Scottish) 1899 *W, E*, 1900 *W, I, E*

**Roughead, W.N.** (Edinburgh Acads, London Scottish) 1927 *A*, 1928 *F, W, I, E*, 1930 *I, E*, 1931 *F, W, I, E*, 1932 *W*

**Rowan, N.A.** (Boroughmuir) 1980 *W, E*, 1981 *F, W, E, I*, 1984 *R*, 1985 *I*, 1987 *[R]*, 1988 *I, F, W, E*

**Rowand, R.** (Glasgow HSFP) 1930 *F, W*, 1932 *E*, 1933 *W, E, I*, 1934 *W*

**Roxburgh, A.J.** (Kelso) 1997 *A*, 1998 *It, F (R), W, E, Fj, A* 1*(R)*,2*(R)*

**Roy, A.** (Waterloo) 1938 *W, I, E*, 1939 *W, I, E*

**Russell, R.R.** (Saracens) 1999 *R*, [*U (R), Sp, Sm (R), NZ (R)], 2000 I (R), 2001 F (R), 2002 F (R), W (R)*, 2003 *W* 1*(R), It* 1*(R), SA* 1 *(R)*, 2 *(R)*

**Russell, W.L.** (Glasgow Acad) 1905 *NZ*, 1906 *W, I, E*

**Rutherford, J.Y.** (Selkirk) 1979 *W, E, I, F, NZ*, 1980 *I, F, E*, 1981 *F, W, E, I, NZ* 1,2, *A*, 1982 *E, I, F, W, A* 1,2, 1983 *E, NZ*, 1984 *W, E, I, F, R*, 1985 *I, F, W, E*, 1986 *F, W, E, I, R*, 1987 *I, F, W, E*, [*F*]

# S

**Sampson, R.W.F.** (London Scottish) 1939 *W*, 1947 *W*

**Sanderson, G.A.** (Royal HSFP) 1907 *W, I, E*, 1908 *I*

**Sanderson, J.L.P.** (Edinburgh Acads) 1873 *E*

**Schulze, D.G.** (London Scottish) 1905 *E*, 1907 *I, E*, 1908 *W, I, E*, 1909 *W, I, E*, 1910 *W, I, E*, 1911 *W*

**Scobie, R.M.** (Royal Military Coll) 1914 *W, I, E*

**Scotland, K.J.F.** (Heriot's FP, Cambridge U, Leicester) 1957 *F, W, I, E*, 1958 *E*, 1959 *F, W, I, E*, 1960 *F, W, I, E*, 1961 *F, SA, W, I, E*, 1962 *F, W, I, E*, 1963 *F, W, I, E*, 1965 *F*

**Scott, D.M.** (Langholm, Watsonians) 1950 *I, E*, 1951 *W, I, E, SA*, 1952 *F, W, I*, 1953 *F*

**Scott, J.M.B.** (Edinburgh Acads) 1907 *E*, 1908 *W, I, E*, 1909 *W, I, E*, 1910 *F, W, I, E*, 1911 *F, W, I*, 1912 *W, I, E, SA*, 1913 *W, I, E*

**Scott, J.S.** (St Andrew's U) 1950 *E*

**Scott, J.W.** (Stewart's Coll FP) 1925 *F, W, I, E*, 1926 *F, W, I, E*, 1927 *F, W, I, E, A*, 1928 *F, W, E*, 1929 *E*, 1930 *F*

**Scott, M.** (Dunfermline) 1992 *A* 2

**Scott, R.** (Hawick) 1898 *I*, 1900 *I, E*

**Scott, S.** (Edinburgh, Borders) 2000 *NZ* 2 *(R), US (t+R), 2001 It (R), I (R), Tg (R), NZ (R), 2002 US (R), R(R), Fj(R),*

**Scott, T.** (Langholm, Hawick) 1896 *W*, 1897 *I, E*, 1898 *I, E*, 1899 *I, W, E*, 1900 *W, I, E*

**Scott, T.M.** (Hawick) 1893 *E*, 1895 *W, I, E*, 1896 *W, E*, 1897 *I, E*, 1898 *I, E*, 1900 *W, I*

**Scott, W.P.** (W of Scotland) 1900 *I, E*, 1902 *I, E*, 1903 *W, I, E*, 1904 *W, I, E*, 1905 *W, I, E, NZ*, 1906 *W, I, E, SA*, 1907 *W, I, E*

**Scoular, J.G.** (Cambridge U) 1905 *NZ*, 1906 *W, I, E, SA*

**Selby, J.A.R.** (Watsonians) 1920 *W, I*

**Shackleton, J.A.P.** (London Scottish) 1959 *E*, 1963 *F, W*, 1964 *NZ, W*, 1965 *I, SA*

**Sharp, A.V.** (Bristol) 1994 *E, I, F, Arg* 1,2 *SA*

**Sharp, G.** (Stewart's FP, Army) 1960 *F*, 1964 *F, NZ, W*

**Shaw, G.D.** (Sale) 1935 *NZ*, 1936 *W*, 1937 *W, I, E*, 1939 *I*

**Shaw, I.** (Glasgow HSFP) 1937 *I*

**Shaw, J.N.** (Edinburgh Acads) 1921 *W, I*

**Shaw, R.W.** (Glasgow HSFP) 1934 *W, I, E*, 1935 *W, I, E, NZ*, 1936 *W, I, E*, 1937 *W, I, E*, 1938 *W, I, E*, 1939 *W, I, E*

**Shedden, D.** (W of Scotland) 1972 *NZ*, 1973 *F, W, I, E, P*, 1976 *W, E, I*, 1977 *I, F, W*, 1978 *I, F, W*

**Shepherd, R.J.S.** (Melrose) 1995 *WS*, 1996 *I, F, W, E, NZ* 1,2, *A, It*, 1997 *W, E, I, F, SA*, 1998 *It, I, W (R), Fj (t), A* 1,2

**Shiel, A.G.** (Melrose, Edinburgh) 1991 [*I (R), WS*], 1993 *I, F, W, E, NZ*, 1994 *Arg* 1,2, *SA*, 1995 *R*, [*Iv, F, NZ*], *WS*, 2000 *I, NZ* 1*(R)*,2

**Shillinglaw, R.B.** (Gala, Army) 1960 *I, E, SA*, 1961 *F, SA*

**Simmers, B.M.** (Glasgow Acad) 1965 *F, W*, 1966 *A*, 1967 *F, W, I*, 1971 *F (R)*

**Simmers, W.M.** (Glasgow Acad) 1926 *W, I, E*, 1927 *F, W, I, E, A*, 1928 *F, W, I, E*, 1929 *F, W, I, E*, 1930 *F, W, I, E*, 1931 *F, W, I, E*, 1932 *SA, W, I, E*

**Simpson, G.L.** (Kirkcaldy, Glasgow) 1998 *A* 1,2, 1999 *Arg (R), R*, [*SA, U, Sm, NZ*], 2000 *It, I, NZ* 1*(R)*, 2001 *I, Tg (R), Arg (R), NZ*

**Simpson, J.W.** (Royal HSFP) 1893 *I, E*, 1894 *W, I, E*, 1895 *W, I, E*, 1896 *W, I*, 1897 *E*, 1899 *W, E*

**Simpson, R.S.** (Glasgow Acad) 1923 *I*

**Simson, E.D.** (Edinburgh U, London Scottish) 1902 *E*, 1903 *W, I, E*, 1904 *W, I, E*, 1905 *W, I, E, NZ*, 1906 *W, I, E*, 1907 *W, I, E*

**Simson, J.T.** (Watsonians) 1905 *NZ*, 1909 *W, I, E*, 1910 *F, W*, 1911 *I*

**Simson, R.F.** (London Scottish) 1911 *E*

**Sloan, A.T.** (Edinburgh Acads) 1914 *W*, 1920 *F, W, I, E*, 1921 *F, W, I, E*

**Sloan, D.A.** (Edinburgh Acads, London Scottish) 1950 *F, W, E*, 1951 *W, I, E*, 1953 *F*

**Sloan, T.** (Glasgow Acad, Oxford U) 1905 *NZ*, 1906 *W, SA*, 1907 *W, E*, 1908 *W*, 1909 *I*

**Smeaton, P.W.** (Edinburgh Acads) 1881 *I*, 1883 *I, E*

**Smith, A.R.** (Oxford U) 1895 *W, I, E*, 1896 *W, I*, 1897 *I, E*, 1898 *I, E*, 1900 *I, E*

**Smith, A.R.** (Cambridge U, Gosforth, Ebbw Vale, Edinburgh Wands) 1955 *W, I, E*, 1956 *F, W, I, E*, 1957 *F, W, I, E*, 1958 *F, W, A, I*, 1959 *F, W, I, E*, 1960 *F, W, I, E, SA*, 1961 *F, SA, W, I, E*, 1962 *F, W, I, E*

**Smith, C.J.** (Edinburgh) 2002 *C, US (R)*

**Smith, D.W.C.** (London Scottish) 1949 *F, W, I, E*, 1950 *F, W, I*, 1953 *I*

**Smith, E.R.** (Edinburgh Acads) 1879 *I*

**Smith, G.K.** (Kelso) 1957 *I, E*, 1958 *F, W, A*, 1959 *F, W, I, E*, 1960 *F, W, I, E*, 1961 *F, SA, W, I, E*

**Smith, H.O.** (Watsonians) 1895 *W*, 1896 *W, I, E*, 1898 *I, E*, 1899 *W, I, E*, 1900 *E*, 1902 *E*

**Smith, I.R.** (Gloucester, Moseley) 1992 *E, I, W, A* 1,2, 1994 *E (R), I, F, Arg* 1,2, 1995 [*Iv*], *WS*, 1996 *I, F, W, E, NZ* 1,2, *A, It*, 1997 *E, I, F, A, SA*

**Smith, I.S.** (Oxford U, Edinburgh U) 1924 *W, I, E*, 1925 *F, W, I, E*, 1926 *F, W, I, E*, 1927 *F, I, E*, 1929 *F, W, I, E*, 1930 *F, W, I*, 1931 *F, W, I, E*, 1932 *SA, W, I, E*, 1933 *W, E, I*

**Smith I.S.G.** (London Scottish) 1969 *SA*, 1970 *F, W, I, E*, 1971 *F, W, I*

**Smith, M.A.** (London Scottish) 1970 *W, I, E, A*

**Smith, R.T.** (Kelso) 1929 *F, W, I, E*, 1930 *F, W, I*

**Smith, S.H.** (Glasgow Acad) 1877 *I*, 1878 *E*

**Smith, T.J.** (Gala) 1983 *E, NZ*, 1985 *I, F*

**Smith T.J.** (Watsonians, Dundee HSFP, Glasgow, Brive, Northampton) 1997 *E, I, F*, 1998 *SA*, 1999 *W, E, It, I, Arg, R*, [*SA, U, Sm, NZ*], 2000 *It, I, F, W, E, NZ* 1,2, *US, A, Sm*, 2001 *F, W, E, It, I, Tg, Arg, NZ*, 2002 *E, It, I, F, W, R, SA, Fj*, 2003 *I* 1, *F, W* 1, *E, It* 1

**Sole, D.M.B.** (Bath, Edinburgh Acads) 1986 *F, W*, 1987 *I, F, W, E*, [*F, Z, R, NZ*], 1988 *I, F, W, E, A*, 1989 *W, E, I, F, Fj, R*, 1990 *I, F, W, E, NZ* 1,2, *Arg*, 1991 *F, W, E, I, R*, [*J, I, WS, E, NZ*], 1992 *E, I, F, W, A* 1,2

**Somerville, D.** (Edinburgh Inst FP) 1879 *I*, 1882 *I*, 1883 *W, I, E*, 1884 *W*

**Speirs, L.M.** (Watsonians) 1906 *SA*, 1907 *W, I, E*, 1908 *W, I, E*, 1910 *F, W, E*

**Spence, K.M.** (Oxford U) 1953 *I*

**Spencer, E.** (Clydesdale) 1898 *I*

**Stagg, P.K.** (Sale) 1965 *F, W, E, SA*, 1966 *F, W, I, E, A*, 1967 *F, W, I, E, NZ*, 1968 *F, W, I, E, A*, 1969 *F, W, I (R), SA*, 1970 *F, W, I, E, A*

**Stanger, A.G.** (Hawick) 1989 *Fj, R*, 1990 *I, F, W, E, NZ* 1,2, *Arg*, 1991 *F, W, E, I, R*, [*J, Z, I, WS, E, NZ*], 1992 *E, I, F, W, A* 1,2, 1993 *I, F, W, E, NZ*, 1994 *W, E, I, F, SA*, 1995 *R*, [*Iv*], 1996 *NZ* 2, *A, It*, 1997 *W, E, I, F, A, SA*, 1998 *It, I (R), F, W, E*

**Stark, D.A.** (Boroughmuir, Melrose, Glasgow Hawks) 1993 *I, F, W, E,* 1996 *NZ 2(R), It (R),* 1997 *W (R), E, SA*

**Steel, J.F.** (Glasgow) 2000 *US, A,* 2001 *I, Tg, NZ*

**Steele, W.C.C.** (Langholm, Bedford, RAF, London Scottish) 1969 *E,* 1971 *F, W, I, E (2[1C]),* 1972 *F, W, E, NZ,* 1973 *F, W, I, E,* 1975 *I, F, W, E, NZ (R),* 1976 *W, E, I,* 1977 *E*

**Stephen, A.E.** (W of Scotland) 1885 *W,* 1886 *I*

**Steven, P.D.** (Heriot's FP) 1984 *A,* 1985 *F, W, E*

**Steven, R.** (Edinburgh Wands) 1962 *I*

**Stevenson, A.K.** (Glasgow Acad) 1922 *F,* 1923 *F, W, E*

**Stevenson, A.M.** (Glasgow U) 1911 *F*

**Stevenson, G.D.** (Hawick) 1956 *E,* 1957 *F,* 1958 *F, W, A, I, E,* 1959 *W, I, E,* 1960 *W, I, E, SA,* 1961 *F, SA, W, I, E,* 1963 *F, W, I,* 1964 *E,* 1965 *F*

**Stevenson, H.J.** (Edinburgh Acads) 1888 *W, I,* 1889 *W, I,* 1890 *W, I, E,* 1891 *W, I, E,* 1892 *W, I, E,* 1893 *I, E*

**Stevenson, L.E.** (Edinburgh U) 1888 *W*

**Stevenson, R.C.** (London Scottish) 1897 *I, E,* 1898 *E,* 1899 *I, W, E*

**Stevenson, R.C.** (St Andrew's U) 1910 *F, I, E,* 1911 *F, W, I*

**Stevenson, W.H.** (Glasgow Acad) 1925 *F*

**Stewart, A.K.** (Edinburgh U) 1874 *E,* 1876 *E*

**Stewart, A.M.** (Edinburgh Acads) 1914 *W*

**Stewart, B.D.** (Edinburgh Acads, Edinburgh) 1996 *NZ 2, A,* 2000 *NZ 1,2*

**Stewart, C.A.R.** (W of Scotland) 1880 *I, E*

**Stewart, C.E.B.** (Kelso) 1960 *W,* 1961 *F*

**Stewart, J.** (Glasgow HSFP) 1930 *F*

**Stewart, J.L.** (Edinburgh Acads) 1921 *I*

**Stewart M.J.** (Northampton) 1996 *It,* 1997 *W, E, I, F, A, SA,* 1998 *It, I, F, W, Fj (R),* 2000 *It, I, F, W, E, NZ 1(R),* 2001 *F, W, E, It, I, Tg, Arg, NZ,* 2002 *E, It, I, F, W, C, US, R(R)*

**Stewart, M.S.** (Stewart's Coll FP) 1932 *SA, W, I,* 1933 *W, E, I,* 1934 *W, I, E*

**Stewart, W.A.** (London Hospital) 1913 *F, W, I,* 1914 *W*

**Steyn, S.S.L.** (Oxford U) 1911 *E,* 1912 *I*

**Strachan, G.M.** (Jordanhill) 1971 *E (C) (R),* 1973 *W, I, E, P*

**Stronach, R.S.** (Glasgow Acad) 1901 *W, E,* 1905 *W, I, E*

**Stuart, C.D.** (W of Scotland) 1909 *I,* 1910 *F, W, I, E,* 1911 *I, E*

**Stuart, L.M.** (Glasgow HSFP) 1923 *F, W, I, E,* 1924 *F,* 1928 *E,* 1930 *I, E*

**Suddon, N.** (Hawick) 1965 *W, I, E, SA,* 1966 *A,* 1968 *E, A,* 1969 *F, W, I,* 1970 *I, E, A*

**Sutherland, W.R.** (Hawick) 1910 *W, E,* 1911 *F, E,* 1912 *F, W, E, SA,* 1913 *F, W, I, E,* 1914 *W*

**Swan, J.S.** (Army, London Scottish, Leicester) 1953 *E,* 1954 *F, NZ, I, E, W,* 1955 *F, W, I, E,* 1956 *F, W, I, E,* 1957 *F, W,* 1958 *F*

**Swan, M.W.** (Oxford U, London Scottish) 1958 *F, W, A, I, E,* 1959 *F, W, I*

**Sweet, J.B.** (Glasgow HSFP) 1913 *E,* 1914 *I*

**Symington, A.W.** (Cambridge U) 1914 *W, E*

# T

**Tait, A.V.** (Kelso, Newcastle, Edinburgh) 1987 *[F(R), Z, R, NZ],* 1988 *I, F, W, E,* 1997 *I, F, A,* 1998 *It, I, F, W, E, SA,* 1999 *W (R), E, It, I, F, Arg, R, [A, U, NZ]*

**Tait, J.G.** (Edinburgh Acads) 1880 *I,* 1885 *I 2*

**Tait, P.W.** (Royal HSFP) 1935 *E*

**Taylor, E.G.** (Oxford U) 1927 *W, A*

**Taylor, R.C.** (Kelvinside-West) 1951 *W, I, E, SA*

**Taylor, S.M.** (Edinburgh) 2000 *US, A,* 2001 *E, It, I, NZ (R),* 2002 *E, It, I, F, W, C, US, R, SA, Fj,* 2003 *I 1, F, W 1, E, It 1, SA 1,2*

**Telfer, C.M.** (Hawick) 1968 *A,* 1969 *F, W, I, E,* 1972 *F, W, E,* 1973 *W, I, E, P,* 1974 *W, E, I,* 1975 *A,* 1976 *F*

**Telfer, J.W.** (Melrose) 1964 *F, NZ, W, I, E,* 1965 *F, W, I,* 1966 *F, W, I, E,* 1967 *W, I, E,* 1968 *E, A,* 1969 *F, W, I, E, SA,* 1970 *F, W, I*

**Tennent, J.M.** (W of Scotland) 1909 *W, I, E,* 1910 *F, W, E*

**Thom, D.A.** (London Scottish) 1934 *W,* 1935 *W, I, E, NZ*

**Thom, G.** (Kirkcaldy) 1920 *F, W, I, E*

**Thom, J.R.** (Watsonians) 1933 *W, E, I*

**Thomson, A.E.** (United Services) 1921 *F, W, E*

**Thomson, A.M.** (St Andrew's U) 1949 *I*

**Thomson, B.E.** (Oxford U) 1953 *F, W, I*

**Thomson, I.H.M.** (Heriot's FP, Army) 1951 *W, I,* 1952 *F, W, I,* 1953 *I, E*

**Thomson, J.S.** (Glasgow Acad) 1871 *E*

**Thomson, R.H.** (London Scottish, PUC) 1960 *I, E, SA,* 1961 *F, SA, W, I, E,* 1963 *F, W, I, E,* 1964 *F, NZ, W*

**Thomson, W.H.** (W of Scotland) 1906 *SA*

**Thomson, W.J.** (W of Scotland) 1899 *W, E,* 1900 *W*

**Timms, A.B.** (Edinburgh U, Edinburgh Wands) 1896 *W,* 1900 *W, I,* 1901 *W, I, E,* 1902 *W, E,* 1903 *W, E,* 1904 *I, E,* 1905 *I, E*

**Tod, H.B.** (Gala) 1911 *F*

**Tod, J.** (Watsonians) 1884 *W, I, E,* 1885 *W, I 1,2,* 1886 *W, I, E*

**Todd, J.K.** (Glasgow Acad) 1874 *E,* 1875 *E*

**Tolmie, J.M.** (Glasgow HSFP) 1922 *E*

**Tomes, A.J.** (Hawick) 1976 *E, I,* 1977 *E,* 1978 *I, F, W, E, NZ,* 1979 *W, E, I, F, NZ,* 1980 *F, W, E,* 1981 *F, W, E, I, NZ 1,2, R, A,* 1982 *E, I, F, W, A 1,2,* 1983 *I, F, W,* 1984 *W, E, I, F, R, A,* 1985 *W, E,* 1987 *I, F, E (R), [F, Z, R, NZ]*

**Torrie, T.J.** (Edinburgh Acads) 1877 *E*

**Townsend, G.P.J.** (Gala, Northampton, Brive, Castres, Borders) 1993 *E (R),* 1994 *W, E, I, F, Arg 1,2,* 1995 *C, I, F, W, E, WS,* 1996 *I, F, W, E, NZ 1,2, A, It,* 1997 *W, E, I, F, A, SA,* 1998 *It, I, F, W, E, Fj, A 1,2, SA (R),* 1999 *W, E, It, I, F, [SA, U, Sp (R), Sm, NZ],* 2000 *It, I, F, W, E, NZ 1,2, US, A, Sm,* 2001 *F, It, I, Arg, NZ,* 2002 *E, It, I, F, W, R(R), SA(R), Fj,* 2003 *I 1(R), F, W 1, E, It 1, SA 1,2*

**Tukalo, I.** (Selkirk) 1985 *I,* 1987 *I, F, W, E, [F, Z, R, NZ],* 1988 *F, W, E, A,* 1989 *W, E, I, F, Fj,* 1990 *I, F, W, E, NZ 1,* 1991 *I, R, [J, Z, I, WS, E, NZ],* 1992 *E, I, F, W, A 1,2*

**Turk, A.S.** (Langholm) 1971 *E (R)*

**Turnbull, D.J.** (Hawick) 1987 *[NZ],* 1988 *F, E,* 1990 *E (R),* 1991 *F, W, E, I, R, [Z],* 1993 *I, F, W, E,* 1994 *W*

**Turnbull, F.O.** (Kelso) 1951 *F, SA*

**Turnbull, G.O.** (W of Scotland) 1896 *I, E,* 1897 *I, E,* 1904 *W*

**Turnbull, P.** (Edinburgh Acads) 1901 *W, I, E,* 1902 *W, I, E*

**Turner, F.H.** (Oxford U, Liverpool) 1911 *F, W, I, E,* 1912 *F, W, I, E, SA,* 1913 *F, W, I, E,* 1914 *I, E*

**Turner, J.W.C.** (Gala) 1966 *W, A,* 1967 *F, W, I, E, NZ,* 1968 *F, W, I, E, A,* 1969 *F,* 1970 *E, A,* 1971 *F, W, I, E (2[1C])*

# U

**Usher, C.M.** (United Services, Edinburgh Wands) 1912 *E,* 1913 *F, W, I, E,* 1914 *E,* 1920 *F, W, I, E,* 1921 *W, E,* 1922 *F, W, I, E*

**Utterson, K.N.** (Borders) 2003 *F, W 1, E(R)*

# V

**Valentine, A.R.** (RNAS, Anthorn) 1953 *F, W, I*

**Valentine, D.D.** (Hawick) 1947 *I, E*

**Veitch, J.P.** (Royal HSFP) 1882 *E*, 1883 *I*, 1884 *W, I, E*, 1885 *I* 1,2, 1886 *E*

**Villar, C.** (Edinburgh Wands) 1876 *E*, 1877 *I, E*

# W

**Waddell, G.H.** (London Scottish, Cambridge U) 1957 *E*, 1958 *F, W, A, I, E*, 1959 *F, W, I, E*, 1960 *I, E, SA*, 1961 *F*, 1962 *F, W, I, E*

**Waddell, H.** (Glasgow Acad) 1924 *F, W, I, E*, 1925 *I, E*, 1926 *F, W, I, E*, 1927 *F, W, I, E*, 1930 *W*

**Wade, A.L.** (London Scottish) 1908 *E*

**Wainwright, R.I.** (Edinburgh Acads, West Hartlepool, Watsonians, Army, Dundee HSFP) 1992 *I (R), F, A* 1,2, 1993 *NZ*, 1994 *W, E*, 1995 *C, I, F, W, E, R*, [*Iv, Tg, F, NZ*], *WS*, 1996 *I, F, W, E, NZ* 1,2, 1997 *W, E, I, F, SA*, 1998 *It, I, F, W, E, Fj, A* 1,2

**Walker, A.** (W of Scotland) 1881 *I*, 1882 *E*, 1883 *W, I, E*

**Walker, A.W.** (Cambridge U, Birkenhead Park) 1931 *F, W, I, E*, 1932 *I*

**Walker, J.G.** (W of Scotland) 1882 *E*, 1883 *W*

**Walker, M.** (Oxford U) 1952 *F*

**Walker, N.** (Borders) 2002 *R, SA, Fj*

**Wallace, A.C.** (Oxford U) 1923 *F*, 1924 *F, W, E*, 1925 *F, W, I, E*, 1926 *F*

**Wallace, W.M.** (Cambridge U) 1913 *E*, 1914 *W, I, E*

**Wallace, M.I.** (Glasgow High Kelvinside) 1996 *A, It*, 1997 *W*

**Walls, W.A.** (Glasgow Acad) 1882 *E*, 1883 *W, I, E*, 1884 *W, I, E*, 1886 *W, I, E*

**Walter, M.W.** (London Scottish) 1906 *I, E, SA*, 1907 *W, I*, 1908 *W, I*, 1910 *I*

**Walton, P.** (Northampton, Newcastle) 1994 *E, I, F, Arg* 1,2, 1995 [*Iv*], 1997 *W, E, I, F, SA (R), 1998 I, F, SA*, 1999 *W, E, It, I, F (R), Arg, R*, [*SA (R), U (R), Sp*]

**Warren, J.R.** (Glasgow Acad) 1914 *I*

**Warren, R.C.** (Glasgow Acad) 1922 *W, I*, 1930 *W, I, E*

**Waters, F.H.** (Cambridge U, London Scottish) 1930 *F, W, I, E*, 1932 *SA, W, I*

**Waters, J.A.** (Selkirk) 1933 *W, E, I*, 1934 *W, I, E*, 1935 *W, I, E, NZ*, 1936 *W, I, E*, 1937 *W, I, E*

**Waters, J.B.** (Cambridge U) 1904 *I, E*

**Watherston, J.G.** (Edinburgh Wands) 1934 *I, E*

**Watherston, W.R.A.** (London Scottish) 1963 *F, W, I*

**Watson, D.H.** (Glasgow Acad) 1876 *E*, 1877 *I, E*

**Watson, W.S.** (Boroughmuir) 1974 *W, E, I, F*, 1975 *NZ*, 1977 *I, F, W*, 1979 *I, F*

**Watt, A.G.J.** (Glasgow High Kelvinside) 1991 [*Z*], 1993 *I, NZ*, 1994 *Arg* 2(t & R)

**Watt, A.G.M.** (Edinburgh Acads) 1947 *F, W, I, A*, 1948 *F, W*

**Weatherstone, T.G.** (Stewart's Coll FP) 1952 *E*, 1953 *I, E*, 1954 *F, NZ, I, E, W*, 1955 *F*, 1958 *W, A, I, E*, 1959 *W, I, E*

**Weir, G.W.** (Melrose, Newcastle) 1990 *Arg*, 1991 *R*, [*J, Z, I, WS, E, NZ*], 1992 *E, I, F, W, A* 1,2, 1993 *I, F, W, E, NZ*, 1994 *W (R), E, I, F, SA*, 1995 *F (R), W, E, R*, [*Iv, Tg, F, NZ*], *WS*, 1996 *I, F, W, E, NZ* 1,2, *A, It (R), 1997 W, E, I, F*, 1998 *It, I, F, W, E, SA*, 1999 *W, Arg (R), R (R)*, [*SA (R), Sp, Sm, NZ*], 2000 *It (R), I (R), F*

**Welsh, R.** (Watsonians) 1895 *W, I, E*, 1896 *W*

**Welsh, R.B.** (Hawick) 1967 *I, E*

**Welsh, W.B.** (Hawick) 1927 *A*, 1928 *F, W, I*, 1929 *I, E*, 1930 *F, W, I, E*, 1931 *F, W, I, E*, 1932 *SA, W, I, E*, 1933 *W, E, I*

**Welsh, W.H.** (Edinburgh U) 1900 *I, E*, 1901 *W, I, E*, 1902 *W, I, E*

**Wemyss, A.** (Gala, Edinburgh Wands) 1914 *W, I*, 1920 *F, E*, 1922 *F, W, I*

**West, L.** (Edinburgh U, West Hartlepool) 1903 *W, I, E*, 1905 *I, E, NZ*, 1906 *W, I, E*

**Weston, V.G.** (Kelvinside Acads) 1936 *I, E*

**White, D.B.** (Gala, London Scottish) 1982 *F, W, A* 1,2, 1987 *W, E*, [*F, R, NZ*], 1988 *I, F, W, E, A*, 1989 *W, E, I, F, Fj, R*, 1990 *I, F, W, E, NZ* 1,2, 1991 *F, W, E, I, R*, [*J, Z, I, WS, E, NZ*], 1992 *E, I, F, W*

**White, D.M.** (Kelvinside Acads) 1963 *F, W, I, E*

**White, J.P.R.** (Glasgow) 2000 *E, NZ* 1,2, *US (R), A (R), Sm*, 2001 *F (R), I, Tg, Arg, NZ*, 2002 *E, It, I, F, W, C, US, SA(R), Fj*, 2003 *F(R), W* 1, *E, It* 1, *SA* 1,2

**White, T.B.** (Edinburgh Acads) 1888 *W, I*, 1889 *W*

**Whittington, T.P.** (Merchistonians) 1873 *E*

**Whitworth, R.J.E.** (London Scottish) 1936 *I*

**Whyte, D.J.** (Edinburgh Wands) 1965 *W, I, E, SA*, 1966 *F, W, I, E, A*, 1967 *F, W, I, E*

**Will, J.G.** (Cambridge U) 1912 *F, W, I, E*, 1914 *W, I, E*

**Wilson, A.W.** (Dunfermline) 1931 *F, I, E*

**Wilson, G.A.** (Oxford U) 1949 *F, W, E*

**Wilson, G.R.** (Royal HSFP) 1886 *E*, 1890 *W, I, E*, 1891 *I*

**Wilson, J.H.** (Watsonians) 1953 *I*

**Wilson, J.S.** (St Andrew's U) 1931 *F, W, I, E*, 1932 *E*

**Wilson, J.S.** (United Services, London Scottish) 1908 *I*, 1909 *W*

**Wilson, R.** (London Scottish) 1976 *E, I*, 1977 *E, I, F*, 1978 *I, F*, 1981 *R*, 1983 *I*

**Wilson, R.L.** (Gala) 1951 *F, W, I, E, SA*, 1953 *F, W, E*

**Wilson, R.W.** (W of Scotland) 1873 *E*, 1874 *E*

**Wilson, S.** (Oxford U, London Scottish) 1964 *F, NZ, W, I, E*, 1965 *W, I, E, SA*, 1966 *F, W, I, A*, 1967 *F, W, I, E, NZ*, 1968 *F, W, I, E*

**Wood, A.** (Royal HSFP) 1873 *E*, 1874 *E*, 1875 *E*

**Wood, G.** (Gala) 1931 *W, I*, 1932 *W, I, E*

**Woodburn, J.C.** (Kelvinside Acads) 1892 *I*

**Woodrow, A.N.** (Glasgow Acad) 1887 *I, W, E*

**Wotherspoon, W.** (W of Scotland) 1891 *I*, 1892 *I*, 1893 *W, E*, 1894 *W, I, E*

**Wright, F.A.** (Edinburgh Acads) 1932 *E*

**Wright, H.B.** (Watsonians) 1894 *W*

**Wright, K.M.** (London Scottish) 1929 *F, W, I, E*

**Wright, P.H.** (Boroughmuir) 1992 *A* 1,2, 1993 *F, W, E*, 1994 *W*, 1995 *C, I, F, W, E, R*, [*Iv, Tg, F, NZ*], 1996 *W, E, NZ* 1

**Wright, R.W.J.** (Edinburgh Wands) 1973 *F*

**Wright, S.T.H.** (Stewart's Coll FP) 1949 *E*

**Wright, T.** (Hawick) 1947 *A*

**Wyllie, D.S.** (Stewart's-Melville FP) 1984 *A*, 1985 *W (R), E*, 1987 *I, F*, [*F, Z, R, NZ*], 1989 *R*, 1991 *R*, [*J (R), Z*], 1993 *NZ (R), 1994 W (R), E, I, F*

# Y

**Young, A.H.** (Edinburgh Acads) 1874 *E*

**Young, E.T.** (Glasgow Acad) 1914 *E*

**Young, R.G.** (Watsonians) 1970 *W*

**Young, T.E.B.** (Durham) 1911 *F*

**Young, W.B.** (Cambridge U, London Scottish) 1937 *W, I, E*, 1938 *W, I, E*, 1939 *W, I, E*, 1948 *E*